Social Dynamics
of the
Life Course

THE LIFE COURSE AND AGING
An Aldine de Gruyter Series of Texts and Monographs

SERIES EDITORS

Vern L. Bengtson, *University of Southern California*
Victor W. Marshall, *University of North Carolina, Chapel Hill*

Gerald Handel
Making a Life in Yorkville
*Experience and Meaning in the
Life Course Narrative of an Urban Working-Class Man*

Vern L. Bengtson and Ariela Lowenstein (eds.)
Global Aging and Challenges to Families

Walter R. Heinz and Victor W. Marshall (eds.)
Social Dynamics of the Life Course
Transitions, Institutions, and Interrelations

Social Dynamics of the Life Course

Transitions, Institutions, and Interrelations

editors

Walter R. Heinz
Victor W. Marshall

ALDINE DE GRUYTER
NEW YORK

About the Editors

Walter R. Heinz Professor of Sociology and Social Psychology; Director, Graduate School of Social Sciences, University of Bremen

Victor W. Marshall Professor of Sociology, and Director of the Institute on Aging, University of North Carolina at Chapel Hill, Carolina

Copyright © 2003 Walter de Gruyter, Inc., New York

ALDINE DE GRUYTER
A division of Walter de Gruyter, Inc.
200 Saw Mill River Road
Hawthorne, New York 10532

This publication is printed on acid free paper

Library of Congress Cataloging-in-Publication Data

Social dynamics of the life course : transitions, institutions, and interrelations / Walter R. Heinz and Victor W. Marshall (eds.).
    p. cm. — (The life course and aging)
"Based on presentations given at the closing symposium of the special research program "Status Passages and Risks in the Life Course" at the University of Bremen"—Pref.
Includes bibliographical references and index.
    ISBN 0-202-30694-1 (alk. paper) — ISBN 0-202-30695-X (pbk. : alk. paper)
    1. Life cycle, Human. 2. Life change events. 3. Social institutions.
 4. Social change. I. Heinz, Walter R. II. Marshall, Victor W. III. Series.

HQ799.95.S58 2003
305.2—dc21

                                        2003010564

Manufactured in the United States of America
10 9 8 7 6 5 4 3 2 1

CONTENTS

Preface

In this book you will find selected contributions to life-course theory and research that are based on presentations given at the closing symposium of the Special Research Program "Status Passages and Risks in the Life Course" at the University of Bremen. This meeting attracted more than 150 participants from all over the world. We invited leading life-course scholars to present, discuss, and comment on the progress of life-course studies in the context of the Bremen research program. We asked participants to reflect upon the new concepts and methods and to discuss the future possibilities of comparative life-course studies.

The research program conducted by the Life-Course Center at the University of Bremen was generously funded by the German Research Foundation (DFG) and the University of Bremen for a period of fourteen years. In this institutional context it was possible to set up a series of longitudinal (retrospective and prospective) studies in Germany focused on transitions and linked lives, and to elaborate a set of core concepts and integrated methods for analyzing the modern life course.

The symposium was held two weeks after the September 11, 2002, terror attacks against the World Trade Center and the Pentagon. We are extremely grateful that most of the invited scholars from the United States decided to come to Bremen though these attacks were tragic interventions into many lives. At the conference there was a feeling of solidarity with those who decided not to attend and the conviction that terrorism should not prevent international gatherings.

We express our gratitude to our authors who revised their papers, to Ben Veghte for revising and improving the manuscripts of non-English-speaking authors and last not least Lisa Bäuml, who spent many weeks editing and proofreading manuscripts and checking references. Special appreciation is due to Werner Dressel, who was responsible for the organization and successful implementation of our symposium.

The symposium was made possible by support from the German Research Foundation and the University of Bremen, whose president and provost supported and promoted the research center since its very beginning. The symposium was cosponsored by the Cornell Careers Institute of Cornell University, by the Life-Course Center of the University of Minnesota, and by the Institute on Aging, University of North Carolina at Chapel Hill.

Walter R. Heinz and Victor W. Marshall

Contributors

Claudia Born
Senior Lecturer, Family and Gender Studies; International Coordinator, Faculty of Human and Health Sciences, University of Bremen, Germany

Marlis Buchmann
Professor of Sociology, University of Zürich, and the Swiss Federal Institute of Technology; Fellow, Center for Advanced Study in the Behavioral Sciences, Stanford, California

Sonja Drobnič
Professor of Sociology/Empirical Social Research, University of Erfurt, Germany

Glen H. Elder, Jr.
Howard W. Odum Distinguished Professor of Sociology and Research Professor of Psychology, University of North Carolina at Chapel Hill, Carolina

Susanne Falk
Sociologist, and Research Collaborator, Bavarian State Institute for Higher Education at Munich, Germany

Frank F. Furstenberg
Zellerbach Family Professor of Sociology, University of Pennsylvania

Walter R. Heinz
Professor of Sociology and Social Psychology; Director, Graduate School of Social Sciences, University of Bremen

Irene Kriesi
Research Collaborator, Department of Sociology, University of Zürich, and the Swiss Federal Institute of Technology

Helga Krüger
Professor of Sociology, University of Bremen, Germany

Lutz Leisering
Professor of Social Policy, Department of Sociology, and the Institute for Global Society Studies, University of Bielefeld, Germany

Victor W. Marshall
Professor of Sociology, and Director of the Institute on Aging, University of North Carolina at Chapel Hill, Carolina

Phyllis Moen
Ferris Family Professor of Life-Course Studies, Cornell University

Margaret Mueller
Postdoctoral fellow, Carolina Population Center and the Center for Developmental Science, University of North Carolina at Chapel Hill

Andrea Pfeifer
Sociologist, and Research Collaborator, Statistical Office of Canton City of Basel

Stefan Sacchi
Sociologist, and Senior Research Collaborator, Department of Sociology, Swiss Federal Institute of Technology

Reinhold Sackmann
Senior Lecturer, Department of Sociology, University of Bremen, Germany

Hildegard Schaeper
Sociologist, and Senior Researcher, Higher Education Information System, Hanover, Germany

Karl F. Schumann
Professor of Criminology, Law Faculty, University of Bremen, Germany

Ansgar Weymann
Professor of Sociology, Graduate School of Social Sciences, University of Bremen; Chair, Institute for Empirical and Applied Sociology (EMPAS)

Matthias Wingens
Senior Lecturer, Department of Sociology, University of Bremen, Germany

Introduction

Walter R. Heinz

Few areas of social science document the consequences of social change at the end of the twentieth century better than life-course research. It focuses on the relationship between institutions and individuals across the life span and illuminates the impact of modernization on the shaping of biographies. Industrial service societies are characterized by historically new contingencies of living arrangements and biographies. These contingencies differ according to the extent to which life-course patterns are regulated by social institutions. In the continental European context, life-course institutions still define the timing and sequencing of transitions across the life course. In less regulated societies, like the United States and Great Britain, biographies and living arrangements are shaped more by the interaction of markets, social networks, and individual decisions. In active welfare states, institutional resources and rules continue to mediate the effects of social change on the life course. In the age of globalization, it is likely that individual biographies will become more flexible and have to be shaped with less institutional guidance and support.

Research conducted at the Special Research Center "Status Passages and Risks in the Life Course" over a period of almost fifteen years, was based on the concept of a dynamic interaction between institutions and individual actors in order to illuminate changes in the societal organization of life courses and to analyze emerging patterns of individual coordination of life spheres, transitions, and sequences. The relationship between institutional control and guidance on the one hand and individual biographies on the other hand is a critical feature of processes of societal and cultural modernization, which have led to less continuity in the life course and increasing demands for individuals to become responsible for a proper sequencing of biographical transitions. Processes of deregulation of the labor market, flexibility of employment patterns, and discontinuities of family life require a self-organized and self-reflexive shaping of biographies. Structural and cultural transformations have not only extended the shape of life-course options, but have also socially differentiated the opportunities to negotiate passages and sequences in the social systems of education, employment, family, social assistance, and retirement. The spread of individualized life courses and the flexibility of living arrangements, however, are not independent of social origin, level of education, occupation, and, last but not least, gender; they are linked to the structural trends of the economy, labor markets, and the welfare state.

In contrast to demographic conceptions, which see the life cycle as a succession of statuses that individuals occupy as a result of aging, in the Bremen approach the life course is defined neither as age-grading nor as life cycle, but as a sequence of status configurations, a sequence of transitions related to the participation of individuals in different life spheres, mainly education, work, family, and welfare. This institution- and agency-centered approach characterizes the life-course research program in Bremen, which on the one hand differs from biographical, case-oriented perspectives, and on the other hand takes into account individual agency as part of the interaction between institutions and life courses. Individuals participate in various life spheres and institutional fields in a biographical sequence, and sometimes simultaneously. North American and European societies differ in the extent that these sequences of transitions are controlled, regulated, or guided by the state and its institutional fabric. Based on longitudinal research, life-course dynamics have been illuminated that are structured by relationships between welfare state, institutions, gender relations, and occupational labor markets. Such an approach highlights the frames of specific life-course regimes: Transitions, sequences, and interrelations constitute the modern life course, which is shaped through exchanges between institutional guidance and resources and individual decisions and learning processes. To the extent to which these social dynamics are institutionalized as life-course policy, there is a certain degree of security and predictability of life for individuals and social groups as well as for society. Life-course policy, however, also tends to reproduce structures of social inequality and contributes to social divisions in society. This is especially marked in regard to gender relations, occupational opportunities, labor-market segmentation, the division of labor in the family, and the eligibility for social security benefits.

At this time in history it is relatively easy to answer the question why the life course has become a prominent topic of interdisciplinary social theory and empirical research. It coincides with the accelerated social change in the last quarter of the twentieth century. The economy has put international interdependencies on the agenda; globalization also has its impact on labor markets, income distributions, and welfare spending. National political decision-making occurs in a context of transnational frameworks, for instance, in the context of evolving European integration. These processes also affect national life-course policies, for instance, concerning unemployment and social benefits, labor mobility, and lifelong learning. There is agreement among life-course researchers that waves of cultural and institutional destandardization and re-regulation have been contributing to precarious sequences and extended pathways through the education and employment systems.

The life course has become the arena in which structural changes are being transformed into new interfaces between institutional resources and gatekeeping as well as individual actions concerning well-being, social involvement, participation in education, employment, and family-making. Today, the life course has become a flexible, time-dependent social configuration that is co-constructed by individuals and institutions, a configuration that evolves in a loosely coupled relationship between social structure and the outcomes of individual decisions. At the same time, life courses are still path dependent because they are related to a society's institutional fabric. Careers, social networks, and interpersonal relationships are embedded in macrosocial structures that provide directives and versions of personal futures that can be promoted or constrained by institutions. A change in life-course regimes, therefore, will result from the decline of institutional control and resources as well as the discontinuity of interpersonal relationships in various life spheres.

Life-course research is a field of social studies that calls for explanations of continuity and change by conducting relational instead of purely individual analysis.

The contributions to this volume are organized around four themes:

First, tradition and innovation in life-course research with a comparative perspective on North American and European approaches. The respective strength of the evolving research perspectives and steps toward a convergence concerning core concepts and methodology are discussed. This concerns the effects of social transformations on the life course, the impact of different institutional rationalities on the shaping of interrelated biographies, and a proposal to conduct life-course research in an integrated panel design.

Second, transitions and sequences with a focus on conceptual developments and on labor-market structures, gender relations, and employment histories. A model for analyzing sequence types is presented that is related to institutional frameworks of transitions. Results of longitudinal studies from Switzerland and West and East Germany about the relationship between labor-market segmentation, work histories, and employment opportunities are discussed in the context of institutionalized gender relations.

Third, a core theme of the Bremen life-course approach is institutional gatekeeping in regard to rules and resources for life-course sequences and linked lives. Again, conceptual and empirically grounded discussions are presented that look at the interface of structural change and the extent to which institutions are shaping the life course.

Fourth, strong impulses for a nonindividualistic, relational perspective on the life course comes from the concepts of "linked lives" or "interrelated life courses." This theme is represented by discussions of dual career arrangements, the interdependence of life and work histories of couples, and the effects of long-term social and cultural changes on gender relations.

A short review of the contributions follows in order to show conceptual/theoretical developments as well as empirical/grounded trends of convergence in life-course studies. Ideal types of life-course approaches and their mutual influences are presented by Marshall and Mueller with a focus on North American and European perspectives. While life-course research has started with a concentration on age structure and socialization across the life course with reference to social mobility, the concept has become more refined regarding four basic time-dependent categories: timing of transition; sequencing of transitions; duration of state/episode, and pacing of multiple transitions. In addition to conceptual differentiations, the North American approach has mainly followed Glen Elder's life-course principles, which focus on the social mechanisms through which cohort characteristics are operating in the shaping of lives in the context of historical circumstances. The Bremen approach has emphasized biographies as embedded in structures of the welfare state, labor markets, occupational ranks, and family relations. It represents a constructionist-biographical and institutional-life-course policy approach. While individual transitions over the life course are the central topic of North American research, European perspectives pay more attention to social-structural circumstances and social institutions that regulate turning points in biographies. Sequences in the life course are shaped by social timetables that are shared in a culture and that are implied in the institutional regulations concerning transitions in different life spheres. The issues of life chances and social inequality are also implied in the life-course policy of the welfare state, which guarantees and distributes resources for coping with transition risks (illness, unemployment, retirement). There is convergence in respect to the concepts for analyzing the arrangements between family and employment that highlight the notion of interrelated life courses that are resulting from negotiations in the context of conflicting institutional rules and resources.

This theme is taken up by Krüger, who introduces a conceptual framework for analyzing gender regimes and the processes of individualization of the life course. From an institution/actor perspective she argues that life-course conceptions and theories of individualization must be supplemented by a systematic analysis of interrelated life courses. As the case of Germany exemplifies, there are path-dependent arrangements that build on gender inequality in the division of labor in regard to employment and family obligations. This refers to the ways in which institutional linkages between different life spheres penetrate the arrangements and biographies of couples. Krüger distinguishes three institutional logics that impact on individual life courses: the "attainment rationality," which defines the preparation and performance in labor markets and careers. The "tandem logic" of life refers to the linkages between the life area institutions of family and labor market. In contrast to more conventional approaches, Krüger argues that both women's and men's life courses imply the tandem logic of the labor market and the family. Finally, there is the "back-up logic," which refers to institutions that are adjacent to the life courses of family members, for example, nursing institutions and the school, which takes it for granted that the family is in charge of children at the intersection of public and private accountability. Thus, gender inequality in the life course is generated and reproduced by the different rationalities of institutions.

Historical time and place in which birth cohorts are placed have a long-lasting effect on life-course transitions as Elder emphasizes. Based on his seminal California birth cohort studies, he proposes an imaginary study: How would the German "Children of the Great Depression" have fared, what would their life courses have been like in contrast to North American cohorts who experienced the Great Depression in the 1930s? Deprivation and social disadvantages caused by economic hardship affected most families, but life-course effects varied according to the life stage and gender of the children. Elder introduces observations from the Soviet Union, China, and East Germany, societies that experienced dramatic structural changes that created new institutional systems and social pathways after system change. According to Elder, a main challenge for life-course research is the assessment of contextual changes across the life course and their effects by comparative longitudinal studies: How do people select themselves into situations in changing times and places that continue to shape their lives?

Such a challenge requires the combination of quantitative and qualitative research methods in longitudinal studies. To the extent to which social change has made life courses less standardized, such a research design can improve our understanding of the consequences of restructuring and institutional transformation for the timing and duration of transitions and entire life sequences. A flexible pooling of evidence from population and case study material, however, requires a careful cross-reference of standardized and narratively produced data sets. As Heinz suggests, there is the possibility of combining multicase narratives with comparative case analysis across life-course transitions by an integrative panel design that permits alternating between macropanels (surveys) and micropanels (case interviews).

In respect to core terms of life-course research like transitions and trajectories, Sackmann and Wingens argue that there is a need to specify the linkages between transitions, status passages, sequences, and trajectories. They present a typology of sequence types as a tool for analyzing life courses, a model that focuses on the link between any two transitions: rupture, interruption, change, and the combined states of bridge, return, and fusion. This typology assumes that life-course policy provides standards for dealing with structurally ambivalent status transitions by giving them institutional recognition and/or resources. The meaning and timing of a combined state are then constructed by individuals in the context of these institutionalized forms. The typology is illustrated by reference to several transition patterns: school-to-work, work-to-family, separation/divorce, and deviance. The notion of sequence types is a candidate for substituting the theoretically vague concept of trajectory.

A telling example of sequence types is Buchmann et al.'s empirical analysis of the effects of labor-market segmentation and organizational strategies on the duration of women's employment interruptions with retrospective life-course data from Switzerland. They ask whether the rate of employment exits is linked to occupational status and intraorganizational rank. Event-history analysis documents that, net of individual characteristics, occupation, type and size of firm, and organizational rank are related to women's labor-force attachment. Occupation-specific segments offer different options for continuous employment and higher positions in the company greatly reduce the likelihood that women exit the labor force. Thus, both organizational and labor-market segmentation theories contribute to an explanation of exit and reentry transitions in the labor market.

In addition to company strategies and gendered labor markets, there are important effects of the gender culture (role models) and gender regimes (structure relations) on the discontinuity of women's employment. As Schaeper and Falk argue, the introduction of the West German gender regime in the former German Democratic Republic (GDR) could have led to a convergence of life-course patterns. However, they show, with a focus on the duration of women's domestic role after childbirth, that a different pattern is still observable in the former GDR. The West-German gender order concerning work and family life has become part of the East German life-course policy, but women continue to consider the role configuration of motherhood and gainful employment as essential for their life courses. Thus, there is limited convergence (extending the duration of parental leave) and persisting difference (preference for full-time employment) concerning gender culture.

These results turn our attention to the overall relevance of the life-course policy for the structuring of work and family biographies. Individuals' control over transitions and sequences as well as the duration of family, employment, or social assistance episodes can be facilitated or constrained by life-course policies that operate through institutional rules and resources. Institutions provide, reproduce, and sometimes modify the scope of legitimate decisions in regard to the timing and pacing of transitions and careers. They may reduce transaction costs for individual and collective actors by transforming uncertainty into calculable risks across the life course. As Weymann demonstrates by referring to the former German Democratic Republic, social transformations have led to a less controlling policy, to a decline of institutional guidance, and to a more individualized opportunity structure for which the population was not prepared. Another example for the bearing of life-course policies on the pathways and turning points in individual lives is the emergence of supranational sets of rules that have to be adapted by the respective national institutions. This is the case in the process of European integration, where new governance principles tend to promote a more market-driven education system and a deregulation of the labor market.

Leisering and Schumann discuss the issue of institutionalized life-course regulations from the perspective of normative patterns for biographical decision-making across the life course. In their view, which is exemplified by reference to the trend toward a more active welfare policy in Germany, institutions and individuals negotiate life-course sequences by using resources, credits, social assistance, and protective rights or claims. Leisering and Schumann introduce a typology of institutional competence, which refers to the institutions' responsibility for specific transitions in the form of gatekeeping, their guidelines, their criteria of coordination, and finally, the exchanges between institutions and individuals in respect to options and regulations. The latter dimension is of special interest in regard to a relational approach in life-course analysis because it highlights that biographical decisions concerning educational, employment, social assistance, family, and retirement pathways result from negotiations between institutional gatekeepers, structures of opportunities, and individual goals and expectations. Leisering and Schumann agree with Weymann that the main characteristics of the German life-course policy are a high degree of regulation, a curb on wage labor (late labor-market entry and early exit), and inequality structured by social origin and gender. These regulative principles are embedded in a corporatist framework, where institutions tend to contribute to the coordination of problematic sequences across the life course according to universalist criteria.

Institutions, however, can also be selective in respect to their contribution to the individual's shaping of the life course. Frank Furstenberg argues that institutions in the United States have a class bias, which he documents in regard to the shaping of the early life course. Institutions tend to support affluent families, while working-class and poor families are more or less directed toward self-help and kinship support. In the United States, life-course policy puts a premium on families: Parents are expected to manage their children's opportunities for the transition toward adulthood. In contrast to European welfare states, government and welfare programs are regarded as undermining the family's responsibility for accumulating resources for their offspring's future. Affluent and privileged families use institutions for paving their children's pathway into an elite education. They prepare them for acceptance in an elite college; this preparation begins early by selecting private schools, and culminates in the rite-of-passage of leaving home for a four-year residential college. Children and young persons who grew up in middle-class families are also strongly influenced by family values that claim autonomy and a responsibility to promote the biographies of the family's members without public assistance. In contrast to upper- and middle-class families, families at the bottom of society suffer from marital instability and raise children under economic circumstances that are much worse today than in the 1970s. These families lack access to childcare facilities and need to be supported by extended kin. In addition, high rates of involuntary social and residential mobility combine with a lack of social and cultural capital and result in a widening education gap until graduation from public high schools.

In regard to structural contingencies of the life course, there are different models of dual-career arrangements within and between social classes in times of volatile labor markets and institutional deregulation. As Moen argues, in the United States the lockstep process from education, to continuous employment, with promotion until retirement, which was embedded in institutional fabrics, used to standardize the (male) life course, which had been connected to the "breadwinner/homemaker template," which tended to separate family tasks from labor-market participation. Today, interrelationships between partners' occupational careers evolve on a "moving platform," which is characterized by an institutional lag. This lag arises from the cultural ideal of continuous lifelong employment, and a workforce that has the family as a backup institution. However, men and women in the U.S. labor market are increasingly without any backup and without institutional support that would provide resources for coordinating family and employment on the basis of gender equality. Grounded in empirical data about middle-class couples, Moen shows that there are different models for career development, with the dominance of a neotraditionalist arrangement among most dual-earner couples.

The interdependence of life-work histories is analyzed by Drobnič in the conceptual framework proposed by Elder, in order to examine the connections between social change and the individual life course as mediated by the household. With data from the German Socio-Economic Panel, the family determinants of employment careers of women and the effects of the work and family history of wives on husbands' retirement are analyzed.

The combination of children and fully employed husbands drives women out of the labor market. This contrasts to the predictions from the economic theory of the family, which assumes that housework and employment will be divided according to the principle of comparative advantage. The data analyzed by Drobnič document that employment transitions are structured by the gender regime. More specifically, when the husband has a higher occupational position than his wife, a strict division of paid and domestic work is found. These effects must not be generalized; they depend on the institutional regulations and social policy provisions that impact on individual life-course decisions via linked lives. These results are similar to the analysis of longitudinal data presented by Buchmann et al. and Schaeper and Falk. This kind of research is important because it refers to the consequences of institutional lag for gendered life-work arrangements. From a biographical perspective, we should know more about the ways individuals themselves perceive and negotiate transitions that are embedded in the different models of coordinating interdependent life courses.

This question is taken up by Born in her qualitative study of three West-German family formation generations with the intent to find out whether there is a move toward gender equality. She argues that at the intersection of socially structured gender relations and institutional spheres a diversity of arrangements has evolved in the second half of the twentieth century. For Germany she presents evidence from interviews with couples from two generations and young adults who anticipate their future family life. She discovers that there is a synchronization of gender roles on the intellectual level but neotraditionalism concerning factual arrangements. Men seem to have caught up with egalitarian concepts, and women seem to take equality in the partnership for granted. Born suggests that there is a change from complementarity (in the 1950s) to demanding equality (in the 1970s) to a neotraditional division of labor (in the 1990s), which she explains as a rational consequence of the conflicting demands of institutional rules and resources concerning the life areas of family and employment. Thus, we see a change on the cultural level toward more equality, which supports young women's expectations concerning an egalitarian relationship. This expectation is not taken for granted from the point of view of the male partner, but has to be negotiated in decision-making processes as an issue that concerns the couple as a unit of interrelationships.

The contributions in this volume provide a new look at the social dynamics of the modern life course and invite us to think in a cross-national perspective. They document a research strategy that was advocated recently by Neil Smelser at the 2002 World Congress of the International Sociological Association in Brisbane, Australia, systematizing contexts, working across disciplinary boundaries and forming a collaborative enterprise among scholars across cultural barriers.

I

Tradition and Innovation in Life-Course Research

| 1 |

Theoretical Roots of the Life-Course Perspective

Victor W. Marshall and Margaret M. Mueller

INTRODUCTION

The life-course perspective has attained a remarkable degree of institutionalization in contemporary social theory and research. Those who use the life-course perspective seek to understand it and, following its core principles, this leads them to seek its intellectual origins. These are found in many theoretical niches of several academic disciplines. The rapid growth, the eagerness to legitimize the perspective as an outgrowth of many intellectual currents, and its multidisciplinary nature have contributed a diversity of meaning as to just what this "life-course perspective" might be.

We first sketch some early theoretical approaches, such as status attainment theory and socialization theory, that have been considered to contribute to what became the life-course perspective. Second, we describe the formalization of the perspective in North America, by Riley, Neugarten, and others, leading to its systematic description by Elder. Third, we review further developments that have led to differentiation in the perspective. This section includes a discussion of some European contributions to life-course theorizing. The fourth section turns to a specific theme in life-course research and theory in both North America and Europe, the extent to which the life course is orderly or standardized. This theme is explored with a focus on work and the life course. This provides a reference point for a discussion in the concluding section, of the mutual influences between the North American and Bremen approaches.

We begin with some caveats. While an admirable feature of the life-course perspective is its multidisciplinarity, our approach is sociologically centered. Much life-course research is strongly influenced by developmental psychology, but this is not our emphasis here. Second, while the latter half of the life course has not been a focus of life-course research in the Bremen tradition, we will have something of a later-life or aging focus in our examples. While a major contribution of the Bremen perspective has been to further the understanding of the transition to adulthood, a complementary contribution of North American scholarship has been to bring aging and later life into the life-course picture [Elder (1992) makes the same point]. Third, we recognize that to cover so much ground in so few words requires a high degree of abstraction, with the consequent danger that we ignore important differentiation within "ideal types" describing a North American and a Bremen perspective. Fourth, many European and North American contributions to the life-course perspective could not be included in this overview. Fifth, we focus on conceptual and theoretical issues and ignore important methodological developments.

EARLY ORIGINS OF THE LIFE-COURSE PERSPECTIVE

It is arbitrary as to who shall be considered a life-course theorist or what should be considered a life-course concept because it is always possible to go back further in tracing intellectual influences. Like Elder (1992, 1998), we find it useful to identify some early contributions, dating before the life-course perspective would be agreed to have crystallized during the 1960s. Our account draws on but in some ways goes beyond his own discussions.

Leonard Cain as Paradigm Builder

C. Wright Mills (1959) provided a powerful imagery for life-course studies in the first two pages of his classic, *The Sociological Imagination.* He saw this imagination as seeking the connections between personal troubles and public issues and between biography and history.[1]

However, we recognize Leonard D. Cain, Jr., for pulling a lot of material together and actually using the rubric, "life course." He did so in an important essay, "Life Course and Social Structure" (1964), in which he aimed "to identify, isolate, and systematize a life course, or age status, frame of reference," as well as to "contribute to the advancement of a sociology of age status" (ibid.:273). He noted that neither aging nor the life course were represented as categories in *Sociological Abstracts,* yet he summarized, in this as well as in an earlier publication (Cain 1959), a wealth of information from sociology, anthropology, demography, history, developmental psychology, and even biology in terms of a life-course framework. In doing so he provided a rudimentary paradigm for life-course theorizing.

In his 1964 essay he clearly articulated the concept of age structure as a system of statuses, and one dimension of social structure. He noted that other terms such as "life cycle," "life span," and "career" as well as "stages of life" and "aging" itself, are approximate synonyms for the concept "life course" (Cain 1964:277).[2] Cain defined "life course" as a term used "to refer primarily to those successive statuses individuals are called upon to occupy in various cultures and walks of life as a result of aging," and "age status" refers to "the system developed by a culture to give order and predictability to the course followed by individuals" (ibid.:278).

Cain himself cites Linton (1940, 1942) and Eisenstadt (1956) as antecedent concerning age structure, but to emphasize process he drew on Anselm Strauss's critique of the static nature of work at that time.[3] In what may be an early invocation of Elder's principle of "agency" (Elder 1994, 1998), he cites Strauss as arguing that institutions do not wholly shape individual identity and perspective: "Also important is 'the open-ended, tentative, exploratory, hypothetical, problematical, devious, changeable, and only partly-unified character of human course of action'" (Cain 1964:286, citing Strauss 1959:91). Moreover, Cain notes, Strauss emphasized that socialization is a lifelong process, that age structure is socially created, and that the unfolding of human lives is shaped by history. With these and many other earlier foundations, Cain lays out the foundation of a sociology of the life course: "Every member of a society is called upon to move through a succession of age statuses. Every society, therefore, has the tasks of preparing individual members for subsequent age statuses, of absorbing them into the successive statuses along with removing them from formerly occupied status, and of proclaiming to, or providing other means of communicating to, the society that the transfers have been accomplished" (Cain 1964:287). The key concepts of Cain's approach are therefore (1) differentiation of statuses on the basis of age, thus, an *age status system*, (2) *socialization* for passage into and out of age statuses, (3) formalized means to affect such changes in status, *rites of passage*, (4) *age grading* of people of similar ages into age statuses, and (5) establishment of interaction patterns among those of different age sets,[4] or *generational phenomena* (Cain, 1964:287).

A Related Intellectual Tradition: Status-Attainment Models of the Life Course

The first related development came from studies of social mobility. Glen Elder (1992) has provided a concise historical account of the status-attainment research tradition, which he characterizes as one of the major intellectual streams flowing into the life-course perspective. Blau and Duncan published *The American Occupational Structure* in 1967 and it had a profound influence on the field of sociology, both conceptually and methodologically, for it popularized path analysis. It applied path analysis to time-ordered variables, for example, linking father's education and occupation to child's education, to child's first job, and to child's subsequent occupation. This and subsequent work in status attainment, notably the sequel, *Socioeconomic Background and Achievement,* by Duncan, Featherman, and Duncan (1972), did not fully adopt all elements of the life-course perspective because the studies were male-centric (failing to recognize gender differentiation) and also neglected the historical context (Elder 1992). Nevertheless, they contributed to life-course understanding of career contingencies, diversity, and stratification in the life course. We can frame these issues to some extent in terms of the principle of heterogeneity or differentiation over time (cumulative advantage) as it is now discussed among life-course researchers such as O'Rand (1995, 2001; O'Rand and Henretta 1999).

Elder also places Hogan's (1980, 1981) research on early-life transitions in the status attainment and occupational mobility approach. A student of Featherman, Hogan had read Elder's 1975 paper, "Age Differentiation and the Life Course." He explicitly says he uses a life-course perspective and he emphasizes the importance of historical conditions as these differentially affect life-course transitions to adulthood. Moreover, he investigates the temporal ordering of life-course events and their duration in different life-course configuration states, thus making advances over the ahistorical status attainment model (Hogan 1978).

Another Related Development: Adult Socialization

Perspectives arise, and are articulated and sustained in informal social networks and "invisible colleges" as well as in visible organizational contexts such as departments, research institutes, and funding programs. In the United States, among the formal organizations contributing to development of the life-course perspective was the Social Science Research Council (SSRC). The council and its committees were and continue to be formally multidisciplinary. As early as 1940 the SSRC was alerted (by Ernest W. Burgess, a member of the Committee on Social Adjustment) to the need for more information about the behavior and adjustment of the aged (Maddox and Wiley 1976). Burgess invoked an individual-society distinction by suggesting that any problems of adjustment could be rectified either by individual adaptation or societal adaptation to the changing needs of individuals (noted in Calhoun 1978:105). By midcentury, the interests and research support of the council had led to support for research at Michigan and Chicago. In an era when the baby-boom generation were children, and interest in youth was keen, aging also made it onto the agenda. In 1963, another committee of the council, the Committee on Socialization, held a conference on "socialization and social structure," which played a major role in extending the notion of socialization throughout the life course. For example: Orville Brim, who organized the conference, published his contribution to it under the title, "Socialization through the Life Cycle" (Brim 1966); Howard S. Becker's contribution became the classic paper, "Personal Change in Adult Life" (1964) and committee chairman John Clausen's edited book that also traces back to the conference makes the case for socialization as a life-long concept (Clausen 1968).[5] In 1977, SSRC established two new committees, one on the middle years (chaired by Orville Brim) and one on the theme of life-course perspectives on human development (chaired by Matilda White Riley) (Elder 1994).

THE NORTH AMERICAN FORMALIZATION OF THE LIFE-COURSE PERSPECTIVE

Matilda White Riley and Institutionalization of the General Paradigm

Fifteen years after Cain brought together previous work as a foundation for a North American paradigm of the life course, another sociologist, Matilda White Riley, crystallized what she called the "emerging" life-course perspective in four "central premises," each of which can be seen as a reaction to perceived limitations of earlier theoretical perspectives or research practice:

> 1. Aging is a life-long process of growing up and growing old. It starts with birth (or with conception) and ends in death . . .
> 2. Aging consists of three sets of processes—biological, psychological, and social; and these three processes are all systematically interactive with one another over the life course . . .
> 3. The life-course pattern of any particular person (or cohort of persons all born at the same time) is affected by social and environmental change (or history) . . .
> 4. New patterns of aging can cause social change. That is, social change not only molds the course of individual lives but, when many persons in the same cohort are affected in similar ways, the change in their collective lives can in turn also produce social change. (Riley 1979:4)

The first two premises are perhaps unremarkable or at least hard to argue against. The third premise is important because it has not been as well observed in North American life-course research as it has in European research, or so we believe. This premise emphasizes that biographies are profoundly influenced by the social, political, and economic contexts, as Mills (1959) had observed, and thus the aging experience is different for different birth cohorts, as Mannheim ([1928] 1952) had argued. It also implies that the experiences of one cohort in a given age category cannot be reliably generalized to other cohorts, whose encounter with history will have been distinct. The fourth premise reacts against strict social or demographic determinists, to argue that individuals or cohort members can act to change social structure (again, consistent with Mannheim's position).

As Riley has noted, it is the intersection of individual and cohort aging (cohort flow) with age structure that defines the territory of the life course. Conceptualization of age structure was contributed by not only Riley, but also Neugarten.

Neugarten, the Life Course, and the Importance of Time

Bernice Neugarten contributed a very "strong" view of age structure:

> Every society has a system of social expectations regarding age-appropriate behavior. The individual passes through a socially-regulated cycle from birth to death . . . a succession of socially-delineated age-status, each with its recognized rights, duties, and obligations. . . . This normative pattern is adhered to, more or less consistently, by most persons. (Neugarten 1970)

Her imagery was highly deterministic: "For any social group it can be demonstrated that norms and age expectations act as a system of social controls, as prods and brakes upon behavior, in some instances hastening an event, in others, delaying it" (ibid.). Riley's view, although rooted in structural functionalism, was less deterministic. Riley made it clear that "aging" is a verb and not a noun, as it is so often used in North American gerontology. This implies a principle that she advocated in a later book (Riley, Abeles, and Teitelbaum 1982), namely, that history is important and aging occurs as a dynamic process of change in changing social contexts.

Neugarten's chapter with Hagestad (1976) in the "Handbook of Aging and the Social Sciences" was titled, "Age and the Life Course," and it had an important role in codifying a great deal of aging research in life-course terms. In addition, Neugarten and Hagestad emphasized the importance of time and timing issues, the awareness of age norms about the expected timing of life-course transitions, cohort differences in the timing of role transitions, and multiple timetables in different institutions of society. These issues are further explored in a chapter by Hagestad and Neugarten (1985) with the same title, in the next edition of the *Handbook*. Building on this, Settersten and Mayer distinguish the following temporal concepts:

Timing refers to the age at which given transitions occur in the life course. *Sequencing* refers to the order in which transitions are experienced over the life course. *Duration* refers to the length of time spent in any given state. *Spacing* refers to the amount of time between two or more transitions, the pace at which multiple transitions are experienced. (1997:252)

Neugarten saw the life-course perspective as evolving from earlier work on age stratification, including her own, and from life-span developmental psychology, as developed by Schaie and others (e.g., Baltes and Schaie 1973).[6] However, there were other strands of theorizing, trying to sort out the duality of the structure of the life course, that is, the biographical experiencing of, and sometimes shaping of, that social structure (see Marshall 1981).

Elder's Elaboration of the North American Life-Course Approach

It is now time to introduce Elder's further articulation of the North American life-course paradigm.[7] He has provided the most systematic formulation of the principles and concepts of the life course, and his five "principles of the life course" have been widely published (Elder 1994, 1998; Elder and Johnson 2003).[8] In addition to the five principles, a number of other more specific concepts are frequently evoked by North American life-course scholars. Let us first briefly review the five principles.

1. Human Development and Aging Are Lifelong Processes. Recognition that lives are lived the long way and that aging happens across the life span has resulted in a notable shift from "age-specific" studies to research that reaches across the life course. The life-course perspective developed in tandem with the evolution of longitudinal data resources, which enabled analyses suited to the study of lives over time. We know that earlier experience and the meanings attached to them are carried into new situations [and that] the impact of an event or transition in life is thus shaped by this context of personal biography (Elder and Johnson 2003). Research following children into adolescence, adulthood, and through later life allows linkages to be made between earlier and later life-course experiences.

2. Historical Time and Place: The life course of individuals is embedded in and shaped by the historical times and places they experience over their lifetime. Historical change often differentiates the lives of men and women in successive birth cohorts. History is said to take the form of a "period effect" when the impact of a major social event such as a war, or a social policy change like welfare reform, is relatively uniform across the population. For example, the years immediately following World War II were characterized by deprivation throughout much of Europe, unlike the prosperity experienced in North America (Elder and Johnson 2003). But cohorts are not affected uniformly by social phenomena. Mayer (1988) and his colleagues have found that the cohort of German men born between 1915 and 1925 lost as many as nine years of their occupational careers because of the war, and many were unable to find employment afterward. This cohort of men suffered high rates of imprisonment and at least one quarter did not survive the war. Cohort effects are determined by the *timing* of social events, to which we now turn.

3. Timing: The antecedents and consequences of life transitions and events vary according to their timing in a person's life. Elder's work, *Children of the Great Depression* ([1974] 1999) is one of the best illustrations of why social phenomena do not have uniform effects across members of a population, namely, *timing*. Both the timing (*when* they occur) and sequencing patterns (in what *order* they occur) of life events condition the effects they have on the subsequent life course.

There also exist clear generalized expectations for when certain events *should* occur, and normative sanctions for not following the socially prescribed timetable. Events such as job loss or widowhood are especially difficult and potentially disruptive when they happen "off-time," particularly when they occur too early in a person's life (Neugarten, Moore, and Lowe 1965).

4. Linked Lives: Lives are lived interdependently and social-historical influences are expressed through this network of relationships. The principle of linked lives is the core principle for a large group of North American life-course researchers. The principle focuses on the fact that lives are not lived in isolation, but are experienced interdependently. Our actions are determined by and in turn influence the actions of those to whom we are closely linked. Oftentimes, events in the life of one person set the course of another person on a trajectory that may not have been anticipated. For example, when a woman has a child, her mother is suddenly placed into the role of "grandmother"—an event over which the mother herself had little control. Hagestad (1981) calls these "ripple effects," while Riley refers to them as "counter transitions" (in Burton and Bengtson 1985).

Urie Bronfenbrenner's *Ecology of Human Development* (1979) brought the multiple contexts of lives to the fore of developmental life-span psychology. Adult lives simultaneously take place within at least two, if not more, contexts: work and home. Tamara Hareven has contributed to the understanding of the relationship between timing and linked lives in her work on the intersection of family, industrial, and individual time, noting that they are not always well synchronized (Hareven 1982). Both Angela O'Rand (O'Rand, Henretta, and Krecker 1992) and Phyllis Moen (Han and

Moen 1999; Moen and Han 2001) have drawn attention to "coupled careers" and the way in which couples synchronize their work and retirement plans. While family is the most obvious example of linked lives, colleagues, friends, neighbors, and numerous others comprise the network of ties within which individuals are embedded, giving each experience a distinct orienting context. Toni Antonucci (1990) has illustrated how kith and kin ties supplement and complement each other at various stages of life and in different contexts, creating a "convoy" of social support over the life course.

5. Human Agency: Individuals construct their own life course through the choices and actions they take within the opportunities and constraints of history and social circumstances. This principle, which is consistent with Riley's premise that new patterns of aging can cause social change, has been used in many different ways in the life-course literature, but it is most useful simply as a reminder that human lives are not fully shaped or determined by social circumstances (or for that matter by biology) (Marshall 2000). The principle also directs attention to planful change both at the individual and collective levels, such as at the political level. Finally, this principle also acts against a strict determinism that, for example, is found in rational choice and other utilitarian models. People may try to act rationally but they cannot act in a purely rational manner because they lack complete information or the capacity to make complex calculations of the costs and benefits of different life pathways from which they choose. This complex construct of agency at times reduces to the sense that people "just do things" that seem "rational enough" to them as they seek to overcome barriers or to take advantage of opportunities.

ADDITIONAL CONCEPTUAL AND THEORETICAL DEVELOPMENTS

In a very schematic way, we have presented the historical development of the life-course perspective in North America. However, we have neglected several issues that we now develop topically. Considering these allows us to draw on several other life-course theorists and to introduce some additional concepts that take us further than those already considered.

Cohorts and Generations: Fuzzy Concepts

Among the key concepts of the life-course perspective in North America, the concept of cohort has been critical (Uhlenberg and Miner 1995). Yet equally, the concept has been confusing in its use and in relation to the concept of generation. Ryder's (1965) paper "The Cohort as a Concept in the Study of Social Change" continues to have an influence, including its recommendation to restrict the term "generation" to the kinship realm. This advice has been repeated frequently in North America (e.g., Glenn 1977; Kertzer 1983; Uhlenberg and Miner 1995). Kertzer's (1983) assertion that the term "generation," used to refer to historically defined cohorts, is a "liability to science" may strike European social scientists as somewhat extreme; and counterarguments to this view suggest that to restrict the term "generation" to the kinship domain broadens the conceptual demands on the term "cohort." Although the term "cohort" is most frequently used as a methodological device to array data in relation to year of birth or some other event (Maddox and Wiley 1976; Marshall 1983) it is also used in the literature to refer to social realities along the lines articulated by Mannheim ([1928] 1952) in his classical treatment of generation or, for that matter, along the lines of its use in popular culture, as referring to the "baby-boom generation," the "beat generation," or "generation x." At Bremen, the term "generation" has been used in the Mannheimian sense, and without apology (Sackmann and Weymann 1991; Weymann 1996). In North America, Marshall (1983) has argued that the term "generation" should continue to be employed in aging and life-course research in order to preserve an ability to link biography to historical reality; and Bengtson, Cutler, Mangen, and Marshall (1985) suggest that the term "generational cohort" be used with this intent, so as to distinguish the concept from kinship generations and also from cohort used in the methodological sense.

Whatever the terminology employed, from a theoretical standpoint it is critical to differentiate cohort as Riley used the concept from generation in Mannheim's sense. Hardy and Waite capture the way in which the concept of cohort was "loaded" by Ryder with meaning beyond the statistical or methodological array of data: "Ryder argued that structural transformations of society could be linked to population processes through the mechanisms of cohort succession and cohort replacement. Rather than emphasize the development of shared consciousness, Ryder spoke of equality in person-years of exposure; rather than attempt to untangle the mechanisms whereby the 'fresh contact' of new members is translated into actions that ultimately transform social structure, Ryder argued that a comparison of different cohorts is a powerful strategy for studying social change. Ryder argued that it was rare for a cohort to act as a unit, but held that cohorts 'could be implicated in the process of social change without presuming the self-conscious development of a shared sense of purpose'" (Hardy and Waite 1997:5).

But this approach leaves unanswered the question, Where are the social processes through which cohort characteristics operate so as to shape the lives of cohort members, or through which a group of like-situated cohort members may develop a consciousness of shared interests and purpose so as to bring about social change?

Connections between Cohorts

North American life-course scholars have made important contributions to an additional dimension of life course, the linkages between cohorts. According to Uhlenberg and Miner (1995), this has been approached in two areas: linkages among the generations in families, and linkages among cohorts in terms of interdependency and resource flows. The linkages among kinship generations have been codified by Bengtson and colleagues in terms of the "intergenerational solidarity framework" (Bengtson and Schrader 1982), which describes six dimensions of these relationships and also provides measurement approaches that have been widely used (e.g., Rossi and Rossi 1990; Roberts, Richards, and Bengtson 1991). The dimensions are *normative* (concerning norms specific to filial piety or kinship obligations among the generations), *affectual, associational* (contact), *functional* (exchange of help), *consensual* (agreement as to beliefs and values), and *structural* (size and geographic dispersion); and these have been shown to be discrete dimensions rather than simply aspects of a metaconstruct of generational solidarity (Atkinson, Kivett, and Campbell 1986; Roberts and Bengtson 1990). The focus of research using these dimensions has been in the field of gerontology but as the issues are intergenerational, they could easily be applied over the entire life course (Bengtson and Allen 1993). Despite its obvious success in guiding empirical research, the formulation has been criticized by Marshall, Matthews, and Rosenthal (1993) for reflecting too consensual (structural-functionalist) a view of family life, and these authors also point out that the very success and widespread use of the model has had the effect of narrowing the vision of family life to these dimensions while ignoring many other important and interesting aspects.

A related conceptual development by Bengtson and colleagues concerns the psychological connections between the generations. As this work evolved, the terminology changed from "developmental stake" (Bengtson and Kuypers 1971) to "generational stake" (Bengtson 1979) to "intergenerational stake" (Marshall 1995). The theoretical interpretation of the concept has changed as well, but it refers in general to an empirical finding in generational research—that the parental generation reports feeling closer to or more heavily invested in its children than the children report about their own relationship to their parents. The "developmental" aspect refers to psychological needs of growing children to gain independence from their parents, coupled with a putative psychological stance on the part of the parents to see their own success in terms of return on years of investment in their children. Hagestad (1982) has extended the reach of the concept to raise a number of research questions about parent-child relationships over the life course.

The second kind of linkage described by Uhlenberg and Miner (1995) is between cohorts (or generational cohorts) in terms of resources, and here much of the work has focused on generational equity issues (Bengtson and Achenbaum 1993; Bengtson and Harootyan 1994). As the so-called generational equity debate has been framed by conservative thinkers and policy advocates largely in terms of formal transfers (taxes, pension, health care, etc.), the major contribution of life-course theorists (and this has been as much addressed in Europe as in North America)[9] has been to document the very large volume of informal exchanges, most of which occur through intergenerational relationships. However, in addition, Bengtson in particular has stressed the theoretically important point that the bonds linking generations go well beyond informal exchange relationships, for instance in a "generational contract" in welfare state policy.

Biographical Experience of the Life Course

But what of the individual, or the cohort member, experiencing the life course as structure? Neugarten's view, as noted above, was highly deterministic. However, largely from the symbolic interactionist and phenomenological traditions, less deterministic views were set forth, based on an imagery of the individual as having some form of agency (Elder 1994, 1998). There is a line of conceptual refinement that encompasses the concepts of "career," "status passage," and "trajectory," leading from Everett C. Hughes through Anselm Strauss to Glen Elder and others who have largely followed Elder in this.

Hughes distinguishes between objective and subjective careers in a manner that recognizes a distinction between biography and social structure:

> In a highly and rigidly structured society, a career consists, objectively, of a series of status and clearly defined offices. In a freer one, the individual has more latitude for creating his own position or choosing from a number of existing ones . . . but unless complete disorder reigns, there will be typical sequences of position, achievement, responsibility, and even of adventure. . . . Subjectively, a career is the moving perspective in which the person sees his life as whole and interprets the meaning of his various attributes, actions, and the things which happen to him. (Hughes 1971:137)

The term *career* has a long history in American sociology (Becker and Strauss 1956; Hughes 1971). While the term was first used in the work and occupations literature, such as by Wilensky (1961, and see below), it has become a metaphor for histories and patterns embracing not only work but education, family, health, and other transitions (Moen and Han 2001; Moen 1998).

The term "status passage" was coined by Glaser and Strauss (1971) and has been adopted by the Bremen life-course group (Heinz 1997) and by others (e.g., Levy 1997). However, it is less prominently used in North America than the "transitions and trajectories" formulation of Elder. A number of dimensions of careers or status passages are outlined in the works of Becker (e.g., 1964; Becker and Strauss 1956), Glaser and Strauss (1971), Hughes (1937, 1971), and Marshall (1980). The biography has been a focus of European life-course research (Bertaux and Kohli 1984; Kohli 1986).

DISORDER IN THE LIFE COURSE: THE CASE OF WORK

Elder describes two general traditions of life-course study: kin and age based. He places status attainment research in the kinship tradition, with key concepts including "generation, intergenerational transmission, and the life cycle—a reproductive process in human populations" (Elder 1992:633). Elder's focus on kinship is American-centered, and does not identify a third tradition, one admittedly more central to European life-course studies, the area of work. Nevertheless, his own research pays considerable attention to work (Elder [1974] 1999:Ch. 7; Elder and Pavalko 1993; Elder, Pavalko, and Hastings 1991). We now explore one specific area, orderliness in the life course, that has been investigated in this specific context.

Leonard Cain, in the 1964 article mentioned earlier, articulated the life course as having three major stages:

> In a sense, during the life course an individual experiences his personal division of labor, including minimally a "preparation for work" stage, a "breadwinner" stage, and a "retirement" stage. The breadwinner stage frequently involves a periodic modification or reassignment of work; this, strictly speaking, encompasses a career. (Cain 1964:298)

This preceded by twenty-two years the appearance in English of Kohli's similar tripartite conceptualization of the life course in terms of work as "periods of preparation, 'activity,' and retirement" (Kohli 1986:72; see also Kohli and Rein 1991).[10] This tripartite division of the life course has been much criticized as failing to recognize the complexity of work even at the time that it was formulated, but it is important for two reasons. First, much of public policy concerning the life course is predicated on the assumption that this simple life course is normatively experienced. Thus, departures from it are a cause of concern. Second, the tripartite framework serves as a reference point to better see the complexity and variability of the working life course (Marshall, Heinz, Krüger, and Verma 2001).

A much neglected early work and life-course scholar is Harold Wilensky (1960, 1961), who published papers on occupational careers in the early 1960s, drawing theoretical inspiration from Durkheim and Mannheim. He decried the paucity of studies of work history, suggesting that career mobility may be more "fateful" than intergenerational mobility for the understanding of modern society. The studies he did locate "leave no doubt that modern adult life imposes frequent shifts between jobs, occupations, employers, and workplaces; but they tell us little of the consequences for person and social structure" (Wilensky 1961:523). Wilensky defined career "in structural terms" as "a succession of related jobs, arranged in a hierarchy of prestige, through which persons move in an ordered (more-or-less predictable) sequence. Corollaries are that the job pattern is instituted (socially recognized and sanctioned within some social unit) and persists (the system is maintained over more than one generation of recruits)" (ibid.:523). This very structural definition of career is narrowly confined to the occupational realm. Nevertheless, Wilensky's articulation of four dimensions of objective careers (number of roles played, frequency of contact and time in each, role integration or coherence, and stability or duration of relationships) can be generalized to any form of career.

Given the recent attention to demonstrating a decline in the orderliness or stability of careers and to investigating the causes and consequences of career instability (Marshall and Clarke 1998; Marshall, Clarke, and Ballantyne 2001; Marshall et al. 2001)[11] it is perhaps proper to acknowledge Wilensky's innovation in explicitly introducing "orderliness" as an important sociological dimension of occupational careers and in demonstrating its relationship to a number of specific indicators of social integration. By 1987, Rindfuss, Swicegood, and Rosenfeld had demonstrated with national-level, longitudinal American data that there is indeed considerable disorder in the life course, or at least in the school-to-work transition and the transition to parenthood. It is also interesting to note that forty years ago Wilensky concluded, based on his data, that "most men . . . never experience the joy of a life plan because most work situations do not afford the necessary stable progression over the worklife. There is a good deal of chaos in modern labor markets, chaos intrinsic to urban-industrial society" (Wilensky 1961:523–24).

One area of considerable concern in both Bremen and North American research is the reciprocal relationship between health and work over the life course. However, North American researchers have paid more attention to selection and causation processes throughout the life course than is evident in Bremen. The finding that older adults who work are healthier can be interpreted in one of two ways (Verbrugge 1985). Employment in later life may foster better health through ties to institutions, integration, social cohesion, and access to information, but perhaps it is the healthier older individuals who are still able to work, the more sickly and frail people withdrawing from the labor force early.

Americans are additionally concerned that older adults who are unhealthy often need to continue working in order to receive health insurance benefits to cover medical costs. Some evidence suggests that disorderly working careers are *caused* by health problems (Iwatsubo, Derriennic, and Cassou 1991; Mutchler, Burr, Pienta, and Massagli 1997; Pavalko and Smith 1999) but there is also evidence that disorderly careers *lead* to health problems (Marshall and Clarke 1998; Marshall et al. 2001; Pavalko, Elder, and Clipp 1993). This relationship, which is no doubt reciprocal, can only be understood if selection is taken into account, and it is most directly resolved through longitudinal research strategies.

MUTUAL INFLUENCES IN NORTH AMERICAN AND EUROPEAN LIFE-COURSE THEORIZING

We have described, both historically and topically, the key concepts of the life-course perspective. Some of these concepts are key components of the life-course perspective as found in the Bremen research and elsewhere in Europe, while others are more uniquely North American. While Glen Elder has explicitly outlined the contemporary North American model, a European model is harder to define. Mayer and Schoepflin (1989) have described a model of the life-course perspective that draws on both European and North American sources. Their main focus is on the role of the welfare state (see below). This contrasts with the Bremen approach, which focuses on both macrolevel and social psychological aspects of the life course. Walter Heinz has done the most to delineate the Bremen model, identifying three approaches to life-course research, and we take this Bremen model as a point of contrast to North American approaches.

The first element in the Bremen model is the *cohort approach,* with a focus on social change, timing, duration, and sequences of life-course transitions from generation to generation. Next is the *constructionist* approach to agency, which focuses on personal narratives about individual action and social contexts as they interact in the construction of biographies over time. Last, an *institutional* approach emphasizes the interplay of policy and individuals in the regulation, timing, and sequencing of life-course transitions in states. While North America and European researchers pay equal attention to cohort approaches, Bremen researchers have made more contributions to the way of understanding constructionist and institutional dimensions of the life course, and these constitute the strongest contrasts between the two approaches.

DIFFERENCES, MUTUAL INFLUENCES, AND SIMILARITIES

We compare the North American and European approaches under specific headings.

Transitions, Trajectories, Status Passages, and Careers

These four concepts are used differentially by scholars to refer to transition phenomena. In Elder's terminology, the life course is comprised of a series of transitions, which are embedded in trajectories that give them distinct form and meaning (Elder 1995). This terminology is used by most North American researchers although some in the symbolic interactionist and phenomenological tradition use the term "career" or "status passage," and these terms have been borrowed by European scholars. The Bremen group uses the concept of *sequencing* to transform the notion of status passage into a concept of transitions and trajectories over complete life courses (see Sackmann and Wingens, Chapter 5 in this volume).

Social Time

Life-course theorists across the globe have used the concept of social time to refer to "the ordering of life-course events, and the taking on of social roles, in accordance with age-linked expectations, sanctions and options" (Gee 1987:266, drawing on Elder 1978). There are culturally shared "social timetables," with expectations for the age one should be at leaving school, marrying, having children, retiring, and even becoming a widow (Gee 1987; Martin Matthews 1987; Neugarten 1977). Neugarten, Moore, and Lowe (1965) were the first to explicitly refer to social time in this way as "social clocks." Expectations for timing give a degree of regularity to the life course. Individuals can reference these shared expectations as to timing in order to assess if they are early, on time, or late in these transitions. Age norms appear to be more elusive in North America (Settersten and Hagestad 1996) than in Germany, where age-graded transitions are more fully institutionalized, particularly in terms of education and work. Therefore, social time has been conceptualized with reference to institutional regulation of life-course transitions (Heinz 1992).

Cumulative Advantage and Disadvantage (The Matthew Effect)

The concepts of cumulative advantage and disadvantage in the life-course perspective refer to the "Matthew Effect," a term coined by Robert Merton and drawn from the Gospel of St. Matthew. The verse states: "For unto every one that hath shall be given and he shall have abundance: but from him that hath not shall be taken away even that which he hath" (quoted in Merton 1968). The Matthew Effect describes how individuals who are already healthy, educated, and have a stable income are able to accrue health benefits, more education, better jobs, and even more income over the course of their lives. Conversely, those without any social or cultural capital have no way to garner any of these benefits. Bremen life-course research has tended to focus on adolescence and young adulthood based on the belief that these formative periods are crucial determinants of the subsequent adult life one leads (Heinz 1996; Becker 1991). However, in German sociology (e.g., Berger and Sopp 1995), there is also found the notion of *temporalized social inequality,* which indicates that periods of disadvantage over the life course are creating intracohort differences in the quality of life.

While there is generally more variability within cohorts than between, differences are far greater at the end of life than at the beginning. By the end of their lives, initially disadvantaged cohort members are doing far worse relative to their advantaged counterparts than they were at the beginning of life. As the upper strata and lower strata move even further apart and differentials in various indicators of well-being increase over time, we see a process of *cohort differentiation* with age. This view has been extensively explored in North American life-course research (O'Rand and Henretta 1999).

Linked Lives

We have already noted and so will just briefly restate here the prominence of linked lives in North American research, which has now also become a primary focus in work done at Bremen. A major example is in the study of work careers and the notable contributions by Peter Blossfeld to understanding of coupled careers (Blossfeld 1995; Blossfeld, Drobnič, and Rohwer, no date). Born and Krüger have been developing the notion of interrelated life courses (see Krüger, Chapter 2 in this volume), which build on inter- and intragenerational relationships. For other examples of linked lives research, see Part IV of this volume.

The focus on individual transitions over the life course differs between North America and Bremen

It should be apparent that North American life-course theorists pay more attention to individual transitions over the life course, and less attention to social institutions and social structures, than their European colleagues. This is shown by a focus on transitions or life stages considered by the investigators to be crucial or critical for the subsequent life-course experience, and also by a focus on disentangling the processes that select one into a transition from the net impact of that transition on the life course.

While transitions are the fundamental building blocks of trajectories, North American researchers have noted that some transitional events are particularly crucial, at times significantly altering the current trajectory. These critical transitions are identified as *turning points* (Abbott 1997). *Timing* of the occurrence of turning points is important. Additionally, social phenomena may result in turning points for certain subgroups of the population only. For example, Elder's (1974) work, *Children of the Great Depression*, shows how military service during World War II was often a turning point for all men (Elder, Shanahan, and Clipp 1994), but particularly for the most disadvantaged youth because it provided them with an opportunity to develop skills and further education through the G.I. Bill that they might not have otherwise had.

The Bremen approach focuses more on institutionalized transitions that may become turning points, for instance, when a passage from vocational training leads into unemployment instead of a career. This occurred to many young men and women after the collapse of the German Democratic Republic (Sackmann and Wingens 2001).

Biography

While Elder's principle of agency focuses on how individuals construct their own life courses through the choices and actions they take within the opportunities and constraints of history and social circumstances, this notion of "construction of the life-course biography" takes very different forms in North America and Bremen. Work in the Bremen tradition centers on the construction of *meaning* and making sense of one's life course, rather than how the choices one makes early in life influence and construct the subsequent life course he or she lives. Bremen scholars pay more attention to processes such as "subjective appraisal" of the life course, making meaning, and negotiating the social structure. As a result of its larger emphasis on both biographical self-organization and institutional regulation in the pursuit of life-course options and negotiating risks, Bremen research requires a greater use of qualitative research and integration of quantitative and qualitative approaches to understanding life-course processes (Kluge and Kelle 2001).

Regina Becker-Schmidt's (1997) work on continuity and discontinuity in women's lives, and Geissler and Krüger's (1992) work on biographical continuity, life planning, and life review are prime examples. Attention is paid to issues of narratives, subjective appraisal, and biography construction in North America (Handel 2003), but primarily by scholars of human development or psychology (Cohler 1988). A major American constructionist approach to the individual life course is that of Holstein and Gubrium (2000). Their project is to try to understand how it is that people "assemble, give form to, and *use* images of the life course to make sense of their lives and experiences through time" (ibid.:ix).Their approach is rooted in phenomenology but sympathetic to symbolic interactionist theory.

Bremen and European Researchers Have Been More Successful in Conceptualizing Social Structure

While North Americans have stressed the importance of paying attention to age structure as an aspect of social structure, they have neither conceptualized age structure as broadly, nor paid as much attention to other aspects of social structure, as have Bremen and other European scholars. This may reflect the structural-functionalist approach to social structure (as defined by status positions and roles) that is so common in North America. This is the concept of social structure that is found in Cain, Wilensky, Riley and Riley (1994), and Elder.[12] In contrast, Levy (1997:90) calls for a less abstract notion of social structure, seeing it as "made up of various, interrelated subsystems that have specific structural and cultural properties," including not only vertical hierarchies of social differentiation but horizontally differentiated institutions with their own histories.

Martin Kohli (1986) argued that the life course itself has become a social institution, supplanting age as a basis of social organization but nevertheless remaining tied to age. He linked this to a decline in the importance of status, locality, and family and to the rise of individualization. Kohli explicitly argued that it is the "system of labour" that organizes the life course (ibid.:272). On the other hand, Karl Ulrich Mayer emphasizes the role of the state, "because the modern state defines the interrelationship between institutional realms in which distinct aspects of the life course are played out. The state defines, for instance, rules for entry into retirement, the transition between full-time schooling and full-time work, and entry into and exit from marriage" (Mayer 1988:229). Mayer also mentions the state's control over military service. In brief, Kohli argued that the life course was socially constructed around work, while Mayer emphasizes the role of the state in terms of work and other domains of social life.[13] North American scholars have rarely paid attention to the role of the state in shaping the life course. For example, there is no parallel in North American research to Mayer's (1997) or Leisering and Leibfried's (1999) life-course analysis of the German welfare state.

Risk and Individualization

The Bremen life-course group emphasizes the importance of risk in their research on the life course, to help address the social causes of change and instability in institutionalized life courses and the consequences for individuals. Germany is a society in which work has had a more powerful regulating influence on the life course than in many other countries; yet economic and political change, including the unification of Germany, has reduced this regulation. Heinz captures this trend as follows:

> In recent years the balance of social options and risks in the life course has been tied together by the formula of "individualization." . . . It seems premature to interpret these changes as a radically new pattern of social relations between institutions and individuals who have been set free from class relations and cultural traditions. But as life courses have become more dependent on developments in the labor market, individuals are experiencing rather new conflicts and risks that may lead to a variety of innovative, compensatory or irregular status passages that combine traditional norms, self-centered values and extended options. (1997:13)

In view of this development, decision dilemmas and biographical strain increase when options for qualification and training, employment, and family relations have to be considered simultaneously and when decisions intersect with the rise of becoming dependent on the welfare system. Others from the same Bremen group stress that individualization does not mean freedom:

> Rather, "individualisation" means the rise of "secondary" institutions which control individual behaviour less directly than did the older, collectivist institutions. . . . "Individualisation" in this sense offers individuals chances to pursue their goals, but at the same time puts more pressure on them to take personal control over their lives under the given circumstances. (Leisering and Leibfried 1999:20)

The trend toward individualization has tremendous policy implications in terms of social security, the social welfare safety net, and social cohesion and it is a major concept used by Bremen researchers in their studies of the German welfare state and employment, family, social assistance, and retirement careers.

CONCLUSION

As Elder has previously noted, something important seemed to be happening in the United States in the 1960s that brought together in a more systematic way some of the ideas that had been articulated by others (Elder 1992, 1998). We have described a rich history of North American life-course theorizing prior to and since the 1960s but we have also noted a great deal of similarity in some respects between European and North American conceptualization. We cannot help but notice some striking differences as well.

It is clear that Bremen and other European life-course researchers have paid more attention than North American researchers to macrolevel social structure, and especially concerning the role of the state. We traced the refinement of the conceptualization of age structure per se by a succession of North American life-course theorists, but these same theorists have not attended well to other aspects of social structure. On the other hand, North American scholars have much more systematically investigated a number of contextual influences on the life course. With the tremendous advances made in hierarchical linear modeling, they have investigated the relative influences of school, neighborhood, family, peer groups, and so forth. While theorizing has not kept up with statistical modeling in this area, North American life-course researchers have at least stressed the importance of theory development in this area.

At the microlevel, North American and European life-course scholars have both paid attention to biography and life-course transitions. However, they have done so in different ways. North Americans have contributed in a detailed or fine-grained way to the discussion of orderliness and disorderliness in the life course, whereas European scholarship in this area has painted a portrait of life-course complexity with a broader brush. North Americans have been more inductive in developing an appreciation for disorder, inferring its existence from large-scale empirical studies of patterns and sequences of life events. Europeans, on the other hand, appear to be more deductive in their approach, discussing macrolevel changes leading to the "risk society." North American scholars have developed complex concepts to describe orderliness, such as timing, duration, and spacing of events, and have modeled trajectories in these terms. On the other hand, European scholars have provided a greater wealth of qualitative data to describe the *meaning* of biography, transitions, and trajectories under conditions of societal change.

We have also called attention to some substantive differences of emphasis between North American and European research, again taking Bremen as our reference point for Europe. A major contribution of North American scholars to life-course research has been to extend the substantive concern in the life course to later life. Much North American life-course research in aging has focused on the family, and a related conceptual contribution has been the delineation of different forms of social relationship linking generations in the family. North American researchers have not addressed the domain of work as extensively in an explicit life-course context as has been the case in Europe.

Some of the differences between North American and European life-course research reflect long-recognized contrasts between North American and European sociology, such as the greater emphasis in Europe on realist and political economy theoretical approaches. Some differences reflect institutionalization of research efforts in specific research centers. Settersten and Mayer (1997) call for moving away from fragmentation of life-course studies into different areas such as aging, work and occupations, demography and family studies, psychology, biology, and sociology. One of the important general contributions that North American scholars have made to research in the life course has been through their efforts at codification and the systematic explication of the life-course perspective. That work is far from complete. Cross-fertilization will lead to greater conceptual cohesion of the life-course perspective.

ACKNOWLEDGMENTS

We would like to acknowledge both Glen Elder and Walter Heinz for their general support of our efforts, as well as critical reviews of earlier drafts.

NOTES

1. Note the many issues, including emphasis on history and linked lives, in the following excerpts: "The facts of contemporary history are also facts about the success and failure of individual men and women. When a society is industrialized, a peasant becomes a worker; a feudal lord is liquidated or becomes a businessman. When classes rise or fall, a man is employed or unemployed; when the rate of investment goes up or down a man takes new heart or goes broke. When wars happen, an insurance salesman becomes a rocket launcher; a store clerk, a radar man; a wife lives alone; a child grows up without a father. Neither the life of an individual nor the history of a society can be understood without understanding both" (Mills 1959:3).

2. Also noted: concepts by the anthropologists Margaret Mead (1939) and Ruth Benedict (1946), respectively "life plot" and "arc of life."

3. The Bremen life-course approach also builds on Strauss's microsociology and methodology.

4. Cain's choice of "age set" is unfortunate here because he means a more generic age status category, whereas the term "age set" in anthropology has a more specific meaning as a social category into which one is born and remains throughout life (Foner and Kertzer 1978; Radcliffe-Brown 1929).

5. Others at the 1963 conference included Henry Maas, Reuben Hill, and Irving Rosow, who made important contributions to the sociology of aging, and Hill especially to life-course and family studies. The account draws on Calhoun (1978), Brim

and Wheeler's (1966) preface to their book, for membership lists published in Clausen (1968:377) and the SSHRC newsletter, *Items,* especially vol. 34 (1):20.

6. A review of psychological strands in the life-course perspective is beyond our scope. For overviews of the role of life-span developmental psychology and its relationship to the life-course perspective, see Elder 1998; Havighurst 1973, and several chapters in Baltes and Schaie 1973 and Baltes and Brim 1980).

7. Elder describes the emergence of the life-course perspective in the context of his now-classic study, *Children of the Great Depression* (Elder [1974] 1999), which he sees as drawing together several of the strands we mention (ibid.:Ch. 11).

8. For an earlier systematic treatment, with just three principles, see Elder (1975).

9. See, for example, Arber and Attias-Donfut (2000) and Walker (1996).

10. Based on an article in German published a few years earlier.

11. The interval since Wilensky's work saw important contributions in this area by Elder and his colleagues (Elder and Pavalko 1993; Elder, Shanahan and Clipp 1994; Pavalko, Elder and Clipp 1993) and by Hogan (1981).

12. An exception is John Meyer (1988), who emphasizes the socially constructed nature of age grading of the life course, a more general rationalization of social life in which the institutionalized life course provides meaning for the development of any individual life, pervasive but "loose" in its effects. See Marshall (1995) for a critical discussion.

13. Another major figure from Europe, Anne-Marie Guillemard, had also been arguing that the life course is socially constructed, focusing on work and retirement issues and also, like Mayer, on the role of the state. See Guillemard (1986, 2000; Guillemard and Rein 1993).

REFERENCES

Abbott, Andrew. 1997. "On the Concept of Turning Point." *Comparative Social Research* 16:85–105.

Antonucci, Toni C. 1990. "Social Supports and Social Relationships." Pp. 205–27 in *Handbook of Aging and the Social Sciences,* 3rd ed., edited by R. H. Binstock and L. K. George. New York: Academic Press.

Arber, Sara and Claudine Attias-Donfut (Eds.). 2000. *The Myth of Generational Conflict: The Family and State in Aging Societies.* London/New York: Routledge.

Atkinson, M. P., V. R. Kivett, and R. T. Campbell. 1986. "Intergenerational Solidarity: An Examination of a Theoretical Model." *Journal of Gerontology* 41:408–16.

Baltes, Paul B. and Orville G. Brim, Jr. (Eds.). 1980. *Life-Span Development and Behavior,* Vol. 3. New York: Academic Press.

Baltes, Paul L. and Warner K. Schaie. 1973. *Life-Span Developmental Psychology: Personality and Socialization.* New York: Academic Press.

Becker, Henk (Ed.). 1991. *Life Histories and Generations.* Utrecht: Isor.

Becker, Howard S. 1964. "Personal Change in Adult Life." *Sociometry* 27(1):40–52.

Becker, Howard S. and Anselm Strauss. 1956. "Careers, Personality and Adult Socialization." *American Journal of Sociology* 62:253–63.

Becker-Schmidt, Regina. 1997. "Continuity and Discontinuity in Women's Life Courses." Pp. 138–45 in *Theoretical Advances in Life-Course Research*, Vol. I of *Status Passages and Risks in the Life Course*, 2nd ed., edited by W. R. Heinz. Weinheim: Deutscher Studien Verlag.

Benedict, Ruth. 1946. *The Chrysanthemum and the Sword*. Boston: Houghton.

Bengtson, Vern L. 1979. "Research Perspectives on Intergenerational Interaction." Pp. 37–57 in *Aging Parents*, edited by P. Ragan. Los Angeles: University of Southern California Press.

Bengtson, Vern L. and Andrew Achenbaum (Eds.). 1993. *The Changing Contract across Generations*. Hawthorne, NY: Aldine de Gruyter.

Bengtson, Vern L. and K. R. Allen. 1993. "The Life-Course Perspective Applied to Families Over Time." Pp. 469–98 in *Source Book of Family Theories and Methods: A Contextual Approach*, edited by P. Boss, W. Doherty, R. LaRossa, W. Schuum, and S. Steinmetz. New York: Plenum.

Bengtson, Vern L., Neal E. Cutler, David J. Mangen, and Victor W. Marshall. 1985. "Generations, Cohorts, and Relations between Age Groups." Pp. 304–38 in *Handbook of Aging and the Social Sciences*, 2nd ed., edited by R. H. Binstock and E. Shanas. New York: Van Nostrand Reinhold.

Bengtson, Vern L. and Robert A. Harootyan (Eds.). 1994. *Intergenerational Linkages: Hidden Connections in American Society*. New York: Springer.

Bengtson, Vern L. and Joseph A. Kuypers. 1971. "Generational Difference and the 'Developmental Stake.'" *Aging and Human Development* 2:249–60.

Bengtson, Vern L. and Sandi Schrader. 1982. "Parent-Child Relations." Pp. 115–86 in *Research Instruments in Social Gerontology*, Vol. 2, edited by D. L. Mangen and W. A. Peterson. Minneapolis: University of Minnesota Press.

Berger, Peter and Peter Sopp (Eds.). 1995. *Sozialstruktur und Lebenslauf*. Opladen: Leske and Budrich.

Bertaux, Daniel and Martin Kohli. 1984. "The Life Story Approach: A Continental View." *Annual Review of Sociology* 10:215–17.

Blau, Peter M. and Otis Dudley Duncan. 1967. *The American Occupational Structure*. New York: The Free Press.

Blossfeld, Hans-Peter. 1995. "Changes in the Process of Family Formation and Women's Growing Economic Independence: A Comparison of Nine Countries." In *The New Role of Women. Family Formation in Modern Societies*, edited by H.-P. Blossfeld. Boulder, CO: Westview.

Blossfeld, Hans-Peter, Sonja Drobnič, and Götz Rohwer (no date). "Employment Patterns: A Crossroad between Class and Gender." Arbeitspapier no. 33, SFB 186, Bremen.

Brim, Orville G., Jr. 1966. "Socialization Through the Life Cycle." In *Socialization after Childhood: Two Essays*, edited by O. G. Brim, Jr., and S. Wheeler: Two Essays. New York: Wiley.

Brim, Orville G., Jr., and S. Wheeler (Eds.). 1966. *Socialization after Childhood: Two Essays*. New York: Wiley.

Bronfenbrenner, Urie. 1979. *The Ecology of Human Development: Experiments by Nature and Design*. Cambridge, MA: Harvard University Press.

Burton, Linda M. and Vern L. Bengtson. 1985. "Black Grandmothers: Issues of Timing and Continuity of Roles." Pp. 61–77 in *Grandparenthood*, edited by V. L. Bengtson and J. F. Roberston. Beverly Hills, CA: Sage.

Cain, Leonard D., Jr. 1959. "The Sociology of Aging: A Trend Report and Bibliography." *Current Sociology* 8:57–133.

Cain, Leonard D., Jr. 1964. "Life Course and Social Structure." Pp. 272–309 in *Handbook of Modern Sociology*, edited by R. E. L. Faris. Chicago: Rand McNally.

Calhoun, Richard B. 1978. *In Search of the New Old: Redefining Old Age in America, 1945–1970*. New York/Oxford: Elsevier.

Clausen, John A. (Ed.). 1968. *Socialization and Society*. Boston: Little, Brown.

Cohler, Bertram J. 1988. "The Human Studies and the Life History: The Social Service Review Lecture." *Social Service Review* 62(December):555–75.

Duncan, Otis Dudley, David L. Featherman, and Beverly Duncan. 1972. *Socioeconomic Background and Achievement*. New York: Seminar.

Eisenstadt, S. N. 1956. *From Generation to Generation: Age Groups and Social Structure*. Glencoe, IL: Free Press.

Elder, Glen H., Jr. 1974. *Children of the Great Depression: Social Change in Life Experience*. Chicago: University of Chicago Press.

Elder, Glen H., Jr. 1975. "Age Differentiation in the Life Course." *Annual Review of Sociology* 1:165–90.

Elder, Glen H., Jr. 1978. "Approaches to Social Change and the Family." Pp. 1–38 in *Turning Points: Historical and Sociological Essays on the Family*, edited by J. Demos and S. S. Boocock. Chicago: University of Chicago Press. (Supplement to *American Journal of Sociology* 84).

Elder, Glen H., Jr. 1992. "Models of the Life Course." *Contemporary Sociology: A Journal of Reviews* 21(5):632–35.

Elder, Glen H., Jr. 1994. "Time, Human Agency, and Social Change: Perspectives on the Life Course." *Social Psychology Quarterly* 57(1):4–15.

Elder, Glen H., Jr. 1995. "The Life Course Paradigm: Social Change and Individual Development." Pp. 101–36 in *Examining Lives in Context: Perspectives on the Ecology of Human Development*, edited by P. Moen, G. H. Elder, Jr., and K. Lüscher. Washington, DC: American Psychological Association.

Elder, Glen H., Jr. 1998. "The Life Course and Human Development." Pp. 939–91 in *Handbook of Child Psychology*, Vol. 1, edited by R. M. Lerner. New York: Wiley.

Elder, Glen H., Jr. [1974] 1999. *Children of the Great Depression: Social Change in Life Experience*, 25th anniversary edition. Chicago: University of Chicago Press.

Elder, Glen H., Jr., and Monica Kirkpatrick Johnson. 2003. "The Life Course and Aging: Challenges, Lessons and New Directions." Pp. 49–81 in *Invitation to the Life Course: Toward a New Understanding of Later Life*, edited by Richard Settersten. New York: Baywood.

Elder, Glen H., Jr., and Eliza K. Pavalko. 1993. "Work Careers in Men's Later Years: Transitions, Trajectories, and Historical Change." *Journal of Gerontology: Social Sciences* 48(4):S180–S91.

Elder, Glen H., Jr., Eliza K. Pavalko, and Thomas J. Hastings. 1991. "Talent, History, and the Fulfillment of Promise." *Psychiatry* 54(August):251–67.

Elder, Glen H., Jr., Michael J. Shanahan, and Elizabeth C. Clipp. 1994. "When War Comes to Men's Lives: Life-Course Patterns in Family, Work, and Health." *Psychology and Aging* 9:5–16.

Foner, Anne and David Kertzer. 1978. "Transitions over the Life Course: Lessons from Age-Set Societies." *American Sociological Review* 39(April):187–96.

Gee, Ellen M. 1987. "Historical Change in the Family Life Course of Canadian Men and Women." Pp. 265–87 in *Aging in Canada: Social Perspectives*, 2nd ed., edited by V. W. Marshall. Markham, Ontario: Fitzhenry and Whiteside.

Geissler, Birgit and Helga Krüger. 1992. "Balancing the Life Course in Response to Institutional Requirements." Pp. 151–67 in *Institutions and Gatekeeping in the Life Course*. Vol. III of *Status Passages and the Life Course*, edited by W. R. Heinz. Weinheim: Deutscher Studien Verlag.

Glaser, Barney G. and Anselm Strauss. 1971. *Status Passage*. Chicago: Aldine, Atherton.

Glenn, Noval D. 1977. *Cohort Analysis*. Beverly Hills, CA/London: Sage.

Guillemard, Anne-Marie. 1986. *Le Déclin du Social: Formation et Crise des Politiques de la Vieillesse*. Paris: Presses Universitaires de France.

Guillemard, Anne-Marie. 2000. *Aging and the Welfare-State Crisis*. Newark: University of Delaware Press, and London: Associated University Press.

Guillemard, Anne-Marie and Martin Rein. 1993. "Comparative Patterns of Retirement: Recent Trends in Developed Societies." *Annual Review of Sociology* 19:469–503.

Hagestad, Gunhild O. 1981. "Problems and Promises in the Social Psychology of Intergenerational Relations." Pp. 11–46 in *Aging: Stability and Change in the Family*, edited by R. Fogel. New York: Academic Press.

Hagestad, Gunhild O. 1982. "Parent and Child: Generations in the Family." Pp. 485–99 in *Review of Human Development*, edited by T. M. Field, A. Huston, H. C. Quay, L. Troll, and G. E. Finley. New York: Wiley.

Hagestad, Gunhild O. and Bernice L. Neugarten. 1985. "Age and the Life Course." Pp. 35–61 in *Handbook of Aging and the Social Sciences*, 2nd ed., edited by R. H. Binstock, Ethel Shanas, and Associates. New York: Van Nostrand Reinhold.

Han, Shin-Kap and Phyllis Moen. 1999. "Clocking Out: Temporal Patterning of Retirement." *American Journal of Sociology* 105(1):191–236.

Handel, G. 2003. *Making a Life in Yorkville: Experience and Meaning in the Life-Course Narrative of an Urban Working-Class Man*. New York: Aldine de Gruyter.

Hardy, Melissa A. and Linda Waite. 1997. "Doing Time: Reconciling Biography with History in the Study of Social Change." Pp. 1–21 in *Studying Aging and Social Change: Conceptual and Methodological Issues*, edited by M. A. Hardy. Thousand Oaks, CA: Sage.

Hareven, Tamara K. 1982. *Family Time and Industrial Time: The Relationship between the Family and Work in a New England Industrial Community*. Cambridge: Cambridge University Press.

Havighurst, Robert J. 1973. "History of Developmental Psychology: Socialization and Personality Development through the Life Span." Pp. 4–25 in *Life-Span Developmental Psychology: Personality and Socialization*, edited by P. Baltes and K. Warner Schaie. New York: Academic Press.

Heinz, Walter R. 1992. "Institutional Gatekeeping and Biographical Agency." Pp. 9–27 in *Institutions and Gatekeeping in the Life Course*. Vol. III of *Status Passages and the Life Course*, edited by W. R. Heinz. Weinheim: Deutscher Studien Verlag.

Heinz, Walter R. 1996. "Status Passages as Micro-Macro Linkages in Life-Course Research." Pp. 51–66 in *Society and Biography: Interrelationships between Social Structure, Institutions and the Life Course*. Vol. IX of *Status Passages and the Life*

Course, edited by A. Weymann and W. R. Heinz. Weinheim: Deutscher Studien Verlag.

Heinz, Walter R. 1997. "Status Passages, Social Risks and the Life Course: A Conceptual Framework." Pp. 9–21 in *Theoretical Advances in Life-Course Research.* Vol. I of *Status Passages and the Life Course,* 2nd ed., edited by W. R. Heinz. Weinheim: Deutscher Studien Verlag.

Hogan, Dennis P. 1978. "The Variable Order of Events in the Life Course." *American Sociological Review* 43:573–86.

Hogan, Dennis P. 1980. "The Transition to Adulthood as a Career Contingency." *American Sociological Review* 45:261–76.

Hogan, Dennis P. 1981. *Transitions and Social Change: The Early Lives of American Men.* New York: Academic Press.

Holstein, James A. and Jaber F. Gubrium. 2000. *Constructing the Life Course,* 2nd ed. Dix Hills, NY: General Hall.

Hughes, Everett C. 1937. "Institutional Office and the Person." *American Journal of Sociology* 43(November):404–13.

Hughes, Everett C. 1971. *The Sociological Eye: Selected Papers.* Chicago: Aldine, Atherton.

Iwatsubo, Y., F. Derriennic and B. Cassou. 1991. "Relationship Between Job-Loss Mobility During Working Life and Health Status After Retirement: A Cross-Sectional Study of 627 Subjects Living in the Paris Area." *British Journal of Industrial Medicine* 48:721-28.

Kertzer, David L. 1983. "Generation as a Sociological Problem." *Annual Review of Sociology* 9:125–49.

Kluge, Susann and Udo Kelle (Eds.). 2001. *Methodeninnovation in der Lebenslaufforschung.* Weinheim/Munich: Juventa.

Kohli, Martin. 1986. "The World We Forgot: A Historical Review of the Life Course." Pp. 271–303 in *Later Life: The Social Psychology of Aging,* edited by V. W. Marshall. Beverly Hills, CA: Sage.

Kohli, Martin and Martin Rein. 1991. "The Changing Balance of Work and Retirement." Pp. 1–35 in *Time for Retirement: Comparative Studies of Early Exit from the Labor Force,* edited by M. Kohli, M. Rein, A.-M. Guillemard, and H. van Gunsteren. Cambridge: Cambridge University Press.

Leisering, Lutz and S. Leibfried. 1999. *Time and Poverty in Western Welfare States.* Cambridge: Cambridge University Press.

Levy, René. 1997. "Status Passages as Critical Life-Course Transitions. A Theoretical Sketch." Pp. 74–96 in *Theoretical Advances in Life-Course Research.* Vol. I of *Status Passages and the Life Course,* 2nd ed., edited by W. R. Heinz. Weinheim: Deutscher Studien Verlag.

Linton, Ralph. 1940. "A Neglected Aspect of Social Organization." *American Journal of Sociology* 45:870–86.

Linton, Ralph. 1942. "Age and Sex Categories." *American Sociological Review* 7:589–603.

Maddox, George L. and James Wiley. 1976. "Scope, Concepts and Methods in the Study of Aging." Pp. 3–34 in *Handbook of Aging and the Social Sciences,* edited by R. H. Binstock and E. Shanas. New York: Van Nostrand Reinhold.

Mannheim, Karl. [1928] 1952. "The Problem of Generations." Pp. 276–322 in *Essays on the Sociology of Knowledge*, edited by D. Kecskemeti. London: Routledge and Kegan Paul.

Marshall, Victor W. 1980. "No Exit: An Interpretive Perspective on Aging." Pp. 51–60 in *Aging in Canada: Social Perspectives*, edited by V. W. Marshall. Markham, Canada: Fitzhenry and Whiteside; adapted from V. W. Marshall 1979. "No Exit: A Symbolic Interactionist Perspective on Aging." *International Journal of Aging and Human Development* 9(4):345–58.

Marshall, Victor W. 1981. "State of the Art Lecture: The Sociology of Aging." Pp. 76–144 in *Canadian Gerontological Collection*, Vol. III, edited by J. Crawford. Winnipeg: Canadian Association on Gerontology.

Marshall, Victor W. 1983. "Generations, Age Groups and Cohorts: Conceptual Distinctions." *Canadian Journal on Aging* 2(2):51–61.

Marshall, Victor W. 1995. "Social Models of Aging." *Canadian Journal on Aging* 14(1):12–34.

Marshall, Victor W. 2000. "Agency, Structure, and the Life Course in the Era of Reflexive Modernization." Paper presented in symposium "The Life Course in the 21st Century," American Sociological Association meetings, Washington D.C., August. http://www.aging.unc.edu/infocenter/resources/2000/marshallv.pdf.

Marshall, Victor W. and Philippa J. Clarke. 1998. "Facilitating the Transition from Employment to Retirement." Pp. 171–207 in *Determinants of Health. Adults and Seniors. Canada Health Action: Building the Legacy*. Papers commissioned by the National Forum on Health, Vol. 2. Ste Foy, Quebec: Editions MultiMondes.

Marshall, Victor W., Philippa J. Clarke, and Peri J. Ballantyne. 2001. "Instability in the Retirement Transition: Effects on Health and Well-Being in a Canadian Study." *Research on Aging* 23(4):379–409.

Marshall, Victor W., Walter R. Heinz, Helga Krüger, and Anil Verma (Eds.). 2001. *Restructuring Work and the Life Course*. Toronto: University of Toronto Press.

Marshall, Victor W., Sarah H. Matthews, and Carolyn J. Rosenthal. 1993. "Elusiveness of Family Life: A Challenge for the Sociology of Aging." *Annual Review of Gerontology and Geriatrics* 13:39–71.

Martin Matthews, Anne. 1987. "Widowhood as an Expectable Life Event." Pp. 343–66 in *Aging in Canada: Social Perspectives*, edited by V. W. Marshall. Markham, Ontario: Fitzhenry and Whiteside.

Mayer, Karl Ulrich. 1988. "German Survivors of World War II. The Impact on the Life Course of the Collective Experience of Birth Cohorts." Pp. 229–46 in *Social Structures and Human Lives*, Vol. 1 of *Social Change and the Life Course*, edited by M. W. Riley in association with B. J. Huber and B. B. Hess. Newbury Park, CA: Sage.

Mayer, Karl Ulrich. 1997. "Life Courses in the Welfare State." Pp. 146–58 in *Theoretical Advances in Life-Course Research. Status Passages and Risks in the Life Course*, Vol. I, 2nd ed., edited by W. R. Heinz. Weinheim: Deutscher Studien Verlag.

Mayer, Karl Ulrich and Urs Schoepflin. 1989. "The State and the Life Course." *Annual Review of Sociology* 15:187–209.

Mead, Margaret. 1939. "On the Concept of Plot in Culture." *Transactions of the New York Academy of Science* II, 2(1):24–28.

Merton, Robert K. 1968. "The Matthew Effect in Science: Theoretical and Empirical Investigations." *Science* 199:55–63.

Meyer, J. W. 1988. "The Life Course as a Cultural Construction." Pp. 49–62 in *Social Structures and Human Lives*. Vol. I of *Social Change and the Life Course*, edited by M. W. Riley in association with B. J. Huber and B. B. Hess. Newbury Park, CA: Sage.

Mills, C. Wright. 1959. *The Sociological Imagination*. New York: Grove.

Moen, Phyllis. 1998. "Recasting Careers: Changing Reference Groups, Risks, and Realities." *Generations* 42(Spring):40–45.

Moen, Phyllis and Shin-Kap Han. 2001. "Reframing Careers: Work, Family and Gender." Pp. 424–45 in *Restructuring Work and the Life Course*, edited by V. W. Marshall, W. R. Heinz, H. Krüger, and A. Verma. Toronto: University of Toronto Press.

Mutchler, J. E., J. A. Burr, A. M. Pienta, and M. P. Massagli. 1997. "Pathways to Labor-Force Exit: Work Transitions and Work Instability." *Journal of Gerontology: Social Sciences* 52B(1):13–26.

Neugarten, Bernice L. 1970. "Dynamics of Transition of Middle Age to Old Age." *Journal of Geriatric Psychiatry* 4(1):71–87.

Neugarten, Bernice L. 1977. "Personality and Aging." Pp. 626–48 in *Handbook of the Psychology of Aging*, edited by J. E. Birren and K. Warner Schaie. New York: Van Nostrand Reinhold.

Neugarten, Bernice L. and Gunhild O. Hagestad. 1976. "Age and the Life Course." Pp. 35–55 in *Handbook of Aging and the Social Sciences*, edited by R. H. Binstock, E. Shanas, and Associates. New York: Van Nostrand Reinhold.

Neugarten, Bernice L., Joan W. Moore, and John C. Lowe. 1965. "Age Norms, Age Constraints, and Adult Socialization." *American Journal of Sociology* 70(6): 710–17.

O'Rand, Angela M. 1995. "The Cumulative Stratification of the Life Course." Pp. 188–207 in *Handbook of Aging and the Social Sciences*, 4th ed., edited by R. H. Binstock, L. K. George, and Associates. San Diego: Academic Press.

O'Rand, Angela M. 2001. "Stratification and the Life Course: The Forms of Life-Course Capital and Their Interrelationships." Pp. 197–213 in *Handbook of Aging and the Social Sciences*, 5th ed., edited by R. H. Binstock, L. K. George, and Associates. San Diego: Academic Press.

O'Rand, Angela M. and John C. Henretta. 1999. *Age and Inequality: Diverse Pathways through Later Life*. Boulder, CO: Westview.

O'Rand, Angela M., John C. Henretta, and M. L. Krecker. 1992. "Family Pathways to Retirement." Pp. 81–98 in *Families and Retirement*, edited by M. Szinovacz, D. J. Ekerdt, and B. H. Vinick. Newbury Park, CA: Sage.

Pavalko, Eliza K., Glen H. Elder, Jr., and Elizabeth C. Clipp. 1993. "Worklives and Longevity: Insights from a Life-Course Perspective." *Journal of Health and Social Behavior* 34:363–80.

Pavalko, Eliza K., and B. Smith. 1999. "The Rhythm of Work: Health Effects on Women's Health Dynamics." *Social Forces* 77:1141-62.

Radcliffe-Brown, A. R. 1929. "Age Organization—Terminology." Letter. *Man* (January), p. 21.

Riley, Matilda White. 1979. "Introduction: Life-Course Perspectives." Pp. 3–13 in *Aging from Birth to Death*, edited by M. W. Riley. Boulder, CO: Westview (for the American Association for the Advancement of Science.

Riley, Matilda White, Ronald P. Abeles, and Michael S. Teitelbaum (Eds.). 1982.

Aging from Birth to Death. Boulder, CO: Westview for the American Academy for the Advancement of Science.

Riley, Matilda White and John W. Riley, Jr. 1994. "Structural Lag: Past and Future." Pp. 15–36 in *Age and Structural Lag. Society's Failure to Provide Meaningful Opportunities in Work, Family and Leisure,* edited by M. W. Riley, R. L. Kahn, and A. Foner. New York: Wiley.

Rindfuss, R. R., C. G. Swicegood, and R. A. Rosenfeld. 1987. "Disorder in the Life Course: How Common and Does It Matter?" *American Sociological Review* 52(6):785–801.

Roberts, R. E. L. and V. L. Bengtson. 1990. "Is Intergenerational Solidarity a Unidimensional Construct? A Second Test of a Formal Model." *Journal of Gerontology* 45:S12–S20.

Roberts, R. E. L., Leslie N. Richards, and Vern L. Bengtson. 1991. "Intergenerational Solidarity in Families: Untangling the Ties That Bind." Pp. 11–46 in *Families: Intergenerational and Generational Connections,* edited by S. P. Pfeifer and M. Sussman. New York: Haworth.

Rossi, Alice S. and Peter H. Rossi. 1990. *Of Human Bonding: Parent-Child Relationships across the Life Course.* Hawthorne, NY: Aldine de Gruyter.

Ryder, Norman B. 1965. "The Cohort as a Concept in the Study of Social Change." *American Sociological Review* 30(6):843–61.

Sackmann, Reinhold and Ansgar Weymann. 1991. "Generations, Social Time and 'Conjunctive' Experience." Pp. 247–74 in *Life Histories and Generations,* edited by H. A. Becker. Utrecht: ISOR.

Sackmann, Reinhold and Matthias Wingens. 2001. *Strukturen des Lebenslaufs.* Weinheim/Munich: Juventa.

Settersten, Richard A., Jr., and Gunhild Hagestad. 1996. "What's the Latest? II. Cultural Age Deadlines for Educational and Work Transitions." *Gerontologist* 36(5):602–13.

Settersten, Richard A., Jr., and Karl Ulrich Mayer. 1997. "The Measurement of Age, Age Structuring, and the Life Course." *Annual Review of Sociology* 23:233–61.

Strauss, Anselm. 1959. *Mirrors and Masks.* Glencoe, IL: Free Press.

Uhlenberg, Peter and Sonia Miner. 1995. "Life Course and Aging: A Cohort Perspective." Pp. 208–28 in *Handbook of Aging and the Social Sciences,* 4th ed., edited by R. H. Binstock, L. K. George, and Associates. San Diego: Academic Press.

Verbrugge, Louis M. 1985. "Gender and Health: An Update on Hypotheses and Evidence." *Journal of Health and Social Behavior* 26:156–82.

Walker, Alan (Ed.). 1996. *The New Generational Contract. Intergenerational Relations, Old Age and Welfare.* London: UCL.

Weymann, Ansgar. 1996. "Modernization, Generational Relations and the Economy of Life Time." *International Journal of Sociology and Social Policy* 16(4): 37–57.

Wilensky, Harold L. 1960. "Work, Careers, and Social Integration." *International Social Science Journal* 12(Fall):543–60.

Wilensky, Harold L. 1961. "Orderly Careers and Social Participation: The Impact of Work History on Social Integration in the Middle Mass." *American Sociological Review* 26(4):521–39.

| 2 |

The Life-Course Regime

Ambiguities Between Interrelatedness and Individualization

Helga Krüger

INTRODUCTION

Life-course research and the individualization paradigm share a focus on the issue of agency and social structure, and both consider life courses as units of individual progression over biographical time. Both highlight the role of institutional contexts in the framing of biographies, but they differ in the extent to which they accentuate the standardization of modern life-course patterns (Heinz 1999; Blossfeld 1986) or their deregulation (Sackmann and Wingens 2001b; Beck 1992; Bertram and Dannenbeck 1990). Although life-course arrangements are becoming more dynamic, more self-directed, and negotiated, it is no coincidence that the concept of individualization as an indicator of deregulation processes originated in Germany. Cross-national studies show Germany still at the forefront of the postindustrialized countries with strong life-course regimes, due to structural linkages between social background and educational attainment, between educational credentials and labor-market entry placements, and between employment careers and retirement benefits. For countries with a more open framing of individual options and opportunities, the individualization paradigm plays a lesser role.

Life-course research and the individualization paradigm also share the issue of gender. Whereas in Anglo-American life-course approaches, which tend to neglect the individualization paradigm, the category "gender" has generated important inputs into life-course theory (McDaniel

33

2001; McMullin 1995; Hagestad 1992), in countries with a strong life-course regime, like Germany, gender is embedded in a notion of the life course that is centered around education, employment, and retirement (Mayer, Allmendinger, and Huinink 1991). Thus, gender is considered as an individual status variable and tends to be connected to individualization and its effects on female's employment commitment. Both life-course theory and the individualization paradigm have for a long time avoided the analysis of *interrelationships between* life courses, and research on household and career arrangements of couples has only recently been adopted from Anglo-America in Europe (Blossfeld and Drobnič 2001a). Thus, in German feminist studies on structure and agency, both the individualization paradigm and life-course research are blamed for being gender biased with respect to the social construction of interdependencies between life settings (Knapp and Wetterer 2001; Klammer et al. 2000; Becker-Schmidt 1987, 1998).

Gender-specific notions and nation-specific awareness of life-course standardization raise questions about the units of analysis and their conceptualization. Empirical findings from the Bremen Life-Course Center lead to the thesis developed below, that the relevance of both gender as an analytical category of life-course structuring, and individualization as an analytical category of social change, correlate with the selection of institutions under scrutiny as well as the biographical time frame selected from an entire life trajectory. We assume that the ensemble of institutions causes conflicting solutions within and between both life stages and interrelated lives. The outcomes may reinforce individualization *and* interdependencies simultaneously, but the interaction of both also redefines male and female life courses as differently framed. If so, old realities are reproduced and challenge the scope of life-course theory and its assumptions about structure and personal choices on the one hand, and the interrelatedness of lives and linking institutions, on the other.

In the following I will start by questioning the referential system between institutions that are of relevance to life-course theory. The analysis highlights institutional conjunctions that relate to different aspects of life, such as continuity patterns *within* the life span, the gendering *within* and *between* the life paths of both sexes, and the social ordering of linkages *between* them and those of dependent others. The interlacing of these logics of life-course structuring reveals that the life-course regime does not exclusively center around the regulation of *life stages* in their biographical succession, but more on the regulation of *life areas*. From the perspective of interrelatedness and linking institutions I will argue that changes in gender norms and orientations of couples who are seeking new work-life arrangements are blocked by the persistence of institutional linking mechanisms that penetrate their lives, regardless of whether individuals enter into private relationships with each other or whether they plan and pursue their lives as "singles." The conclusions about the extent to which the life-course regime might foster conflicting participation patterns in male and female life courses will emphasize that life-course theory and research have to redefine their frame of reference with respect to the impact of a profoundly gendered social order on the direction of social change.

INDIVIDUALIZATION, INTERDEPENDENCIES, AND THE LIFE COURSE: WHAT TYPE OF INSTITUTION MATTERS TO WHAT EXTENT?

Basic Assumptions

A comparison of different approaches in life-course theory illustrates the extent to which issues and findings are linked to implicit or explicit assumptions about the markers of life-course dynamics (Sørensen 1990). Most of the studies depict historical or personal events in biographical time and their effects in accordance with aging. Others concentrate on transitions between specific life stages, on the duration of life phases, or on changes in participation patterns and status configurations over the life span (Marshall and Mueller, Chapter 1 in this volume; Heinz and Krüger 2001; Sackmann and Wingens 2001b). The latter approaches can easily be connected to the concept of a specific life-course regime that includes a multiple logic of institutionalized normalcy assumptions. These claim to provide the temporal and social context for individuals' attempts to shape their own biographies and encompass biographical decision-making, planning, and stock-taking (Krüger 2001; Heinz 1997; Kohli 1986, 1994; Mayer 1991).

Although the institutional approach corresponds more or less loosely to age stages, its empirical conceptualization accentuates a labor-market-centered sequential view of the life course. As Sørensen (1990) pointed out, this constitutes a frame of reference with little space for gendered realities and gender relations. Furthermore, this concept has to be questioned because it refers mainly to institutions that are related to the labor market.

In the following section I will therefore try to capture and identify the range of institutions involved. I will start with the dominant frame of reference, which refers to the succession of life stages, and consider the empirical potential of the selected institutions for life-course analysis. I then will stepwise widen this view.

Life-Sequencing Institutions or the Attainment Logic of Life

The education system, the labor market, and the pension system, which certainly are the institutions most systematically discussed in life-course

Table 2.1   Structural Positioning between Educational Certificates and the Labor Market

Entry Qualification Required	Occupational Positions
University degree (Diplom, Magister, Staatsexamen, Doktorgrad): full academic level	Teacher, doctor, professional scientist, top manager, lawyer, pharmacist, etc.; senior civil servant, etc.
Polytechnic degree (Diplom FH): polytechnic academic level	Engineer, social worker, middle management, top secretary, etc.; upper intermediate civil service, etc.
Technical college graduate (Meisterbrief; Fachschulabschluss): master craftsman level	Master artisan (master painter, master motor mechanic, etc.), secretary, technician, nurse, etc.; intermediate civil servant, etc.
Vocational training certificate (Facharbeiter-/Fachangestellterbrief; Berufsfachschulabschluss): skilled-worker level	Electrician, hairdresser, sales personnel, typist, qualified office worker, child care worker, medical/dental assistant, etc.; lower civil service, etc.
No vocational education/training: unskilled/semiskilled level	Office and administrative assistant, assembly line worker, road worker, cleaner, etc.

research worldwide, function in ways that can channel individuals to varying extents from participation in one to participation in the next institution according to a country's specific institutional regime. These institutions are assumed to organize the life course around the employment system and divide modern life into three stages: one of preparation for work, one of economic activity, and one of retirement (Kohli 1986, 1994). In Germany, these institutions refer extensively to each other by means of operating rules both within and between them. Since an individual's social location in subsequent institutional participation largely depends on their achievement in the preceding ones, the junctions between the stages provide biographical succession with a specific rationale of orientations and personal guidelines in pursuing long-term goals over the life span. The result is a virtually inevitable *attainment logic of life,* even if delays or mismatches between status passages from one institutional sphere to the next occur (Krüger 2001; Heinz 1997; Weymann and Heinz 1996; Kohli 1986). The personal "journey" from one institutional domain to the next is itself institutionally regulated by certificates.[1] Due to historical political regulation, the presumed correspondences between educational levels and labor-market entrance positions display a certain order in Germany (see Table 2.1)[2] (Krüger 1990:120)

Chances for upgrading from one level of entrance qualification required for labor-market positioning to the next are rich within the educational system and its multifold educational pathways, but scarce within the labor market itself. In distinction to internal labor markets, which dominate in the Anglo-American societies and in which career patterns depend more on access to firms' informal training for specific job assignments than on educational level at entry, in occupationally structured markets hierarchical entry allocation combines with horizontal segmentation between occupations (Heinz 1996). This practice facilitates workers' mobility between companies because they acknowledge externally certified skill profiles, but it links upward mobility to specific occupational career structures and to starting position within a specific hierarchical level. In consequence, German career patterns rely on nationwide recognized certificates, and foster the importance of attained educational credentials within the life span of *preparation* for paid work. In a life-course perspective, institutionally regulated rules of positioning will pass on the level attained in general education to occupational education (Heinz 1999), to the attained equivalence of entrance chances for occupational careers, and to benefits when retired (Allmendinger 1994).

Within these institutional conjunctions we nowadays witness the extension of biographical time between exit and entry phases, along with increasing numbers of people in upgrading processes within the educational system, and a corresponding deregulation of age norms—including age norms with respect to retirement. But we also observe the weakening of the German-specific path dependencies themselves under globalization and international recruitment practices, which to a certain extent ignore occupation-specific credentials (Mayer 2001). Together with indicators for a growing rejection of work orientation among youth themselves, the debate on individualization and deregulation in the life course has been intensified (Sackmann and Wingens 2001a).

Studies on segmentation *within* each level of allocation, however, unveil another story, which refers to a second mechanism of social positioning, neither affected nor weakened by individualization so far (Born and Krüger 2001; Klement 2001; Rabe-Kleberg 1987). This positioning order overlaps with labor-market hierarchies and demonstrates the existence of another referential system between institutions. This system of linkages does not pertain to *status attainment* but rather to *gender* in relation to *types of work*. The longitudinal axis of biographical progression over time seems to be afflicted by a horizontal one, which combines gender and positioning with the notion of male/female employment and family work.

Although the mainstream debate refers to the family as an appendix, of relevance only to female life courses (Mayer et al., 1991; Tölke 1987), it is worthwhile scrutinizing the logic of articulation between the labor market and the family for both sexes, and to question the extent to which the family itself is affected by the labor market's radiation. In widening the perspective on institutional sequencing and the status attainment logic, I will therefore incorporate the *simultaneous* grasp of institutions and concentrate on effects of status enhancement (see also Moen 2001; McDaniel 2001; Levy 1996; Moen and Erickson 1995; Marshall 1995; McMullin 1995). For Germany we will consider the interweaving of the labor market and the family in adult lives and their structural linkages to each other, which, in line with the attainment logic of institutions, may also encompass both men and women.

Life-Area Institutions or the Tandem Logic of Life

The labor market and the family can be described as life-area institutions that shape adult lives during the same span of biographical time. We can analyze their effects as issues of personal behavior in linked lives, but more exciting for life-course theory may be the fact that Germany and the Anglo-American world still follow considerably contrasting models of linked life arrangements. While studies on coupled careers in the United States (see Moen, Chapter 11 in this volume) show the growing importance of a two-earner model, in Germany in spite of similarly changing gender roles the interweaving of the labor market with the family incorporates specific conjunctions that favor the one-earner/one-homemaker model and reveal a deeply rooted *structure of relatedness* embedded in our social order. The articulation between both areas, again, derives from the German life-course regime, which implements a structural *tandem logic of life*. The linking rules basically hinder individualization, and have nothing in common with love. Love will cushion the effects on individuals, but will not affect the social order itself.

The mutually reinforcing main constituents of this social order are the income policy, the gendered segmentation of the labor market, and the daily work timetables.

In Germany the legacy from the late nineteenth and the early twentieth century, including the increasingly powerful trade unions' fight for family wages, means that the family itself constitutes an integral part of official *incomes policy*. Earnings are protected by a wage system that is presumed to support a whole family by means of one earner's income—and that avoids public expenditure for full-time daycare or all-day schooling by means of one person at home. These days, 59 percent of households with one or more children correspond to the one-earner/one-homemaker model (in the United States this is the case in just 9.4 percent of households; see Han and Moen 2001), and regardless of their educational level the percentage of fathers working overtime considerably outnumbers nonfathers, while part-time employment is nearly twice as common among nonfathers as among fathers (BMFSFJ 2003: 247, 248; see also Daly 2000; Kulawik 1999).

The *gendered segmentation of the labor market*, which constitutes the second ingredient of relational life-course policy, sustains the same features of the one-breadwinner/one-homemaker model. The family wage system was only put into practice in male-dominated labor-market segments, which were and are mainly industry, manufacturing, and the senior and upper intermediate service sectors. In the female-dominated consumer and personal services, as well as in large parts of the intermediate and the lower civil service sector, earnings are hardly sufficient for one person to live on, let alone a whole family (Pfau-Effinger 1999). Female stereotyped occupations below the academic level (and that is a two-thirds majority) also lack promotion opportunities (Gottschall 2000), as employees located here are mainly burdened with the expectation of a limited stay (Klement 2001).

The third constituent of the steering of life-course relations, which results from *daily work timetables*, also clearly exhibits the tandem logic of life. The synchronization of daily working schedules (Mückenberger 1989) follows the same notion of an earner's day out and a corresponding homemaker's day in. Repair services, chimney sweeps, delivery of goods and parcels, etc., count on a person being at home, as they provide their services only during the same time frame of daily work timetables, while the opening hours of early childcare and kindergartens do not cover transportation times between home, kindergarten, and location of employment. German half-day schooling with its varying starting and finishing times does not even correspond to the hours of regular part-time work.

The income (and taxation) system, gender-structured career paths, and daily work timetables establish a specific tandem logic that contradicts gender equality. The tandem conjunctions places women in the labor market at a disadvantage. In the case of raising a family, the same conjunctions enhance pressure on the male partner's earning commitment, and on the female partner's time commitment to family engagement. As a result, the demands of both life areas are constantly present in married women's consciousness, but not in men's. In answer to the question, What organizes your day? the mothers we interviewed often replied like this one: "Well, I am employed, I've got my child—and the housework, the garden, my husband and the washing" (Krüger et al. 1987:5). In answering the same question fathers spoke of their job obligations, overtime, promotion—the family is "forgotten." Mary Douglas (1987) would call this blindness an "institutionally organized social forgetting."

This type of "forgetting" about the role of the family also facilitates some blindness in life-course approaches themselves: in research on female life courses we emphasize their family status, and attribute their employment patterns to their family commitment (Blossfeld and Drobnič 2001b; Huinink 2000; Tölke 1987). In men's life-course analysis we generally ignore fatherhood and eclipse any family status (see critically Tölke 1996).

The lack of information not only makes it hard to discover social change in male life orientations that might be related to young men's growing commitment to family life (Witzel and Kühn 2001; see also Born, Chapter 13 in this volume), but also we might be seduced into overestimating the family as a female life-course marker. Hakim's preference theory (Hakim 1998; Blossfeld and Hakim 1997) for instance refers to female labor-market participation as the result of individual choices between three types of orientation: (a) to full-time employment, also during motherhood; (b) to part-time employment in order to reconcile family and paid work; (c) to leaving paid work when starting a family or raising children. But what about the effects of women's labor-market position, with its low income and lack of career prospects?

Findings from our own research on occupationally specific opportunities to benefit from acquired educational skills in female occupations show remarkable differences in line with the type of occupation trained for, but nearly independent of marital status. The results come from a cohort analysis of the life-course patterns of 2130 women who completed their vocational training in 1960, 1970, or 1980 in one of the ten most common occupations practiced by women in Western Germany.[3] We discovered that, independent of cohort effects, the total number of years in paid labor varied according to the occupations under study. Occupations determine the proportions of years spent in skilled work, and those in nonskilled employment and those in employment exempt from social insurance.[4] Regardless of time-outs or breaks, within the comparable time span, in all three cohorts nurses spent between 65 and 75 percent of their maximum potential working years as nurses, whereas hairdressers spent only between 35 and 40 percent of their time working as hairdressers, and the corresponding proportion of years hotel receptionists accumulated in their occupation only added up to 20 percent—with reciprocal variations in years of nonpaid work or of the other two types of employment (the results for all three cohorts are summarized in Figure 2.1). In childless couples (about 22 percent over the cohorts) the occupationally specific patterns of participation in employment commensurate with acquired educational skills, crossovers into nonskilled work, or in low-income and reduced-hour jobs that are insurance exempt were nearly the same. In contrast to common explications of female employment patterns, the occupationally specific utility rates of educationally acquired skills in the labor market cannot be linked to full-time or part-time opportunities, as the proportion of women in full-time or part-time employment were *quite equally* distributed among both employees in their occupations trained for and those in nonskilled work (Figures 2.2 and 2.3).

The findings illustrate the role of the labor market by means of the specific example of different degrees of occupational utility that unfold over time. As these act out their effects on employment trajectories indepen-

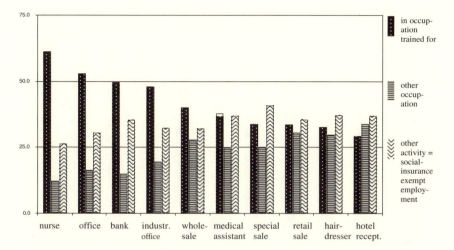

Figure 2.1   Women's Activities in the Occupations Trained For, in Other Occupations, and Other Activities (Percentage of Years), All Cohorts By Initial Qualification.

dently of family status, partner's income, or the presence or number of children we have to clearly distinguish between the input of the labor market and family-induced risks of employment continuity or reduction of paid work (Born 2000).

Different degrees of occupationally typical downgrading call into question the importance of mere preferences for one or the other area in female life-course patterns. Thus, due to generalized assumptions on family effects, push or pull effects of the labor market itself on married women's employment participation are often ignored (see critically also Procter 2001; Crompton and Harris 1998). Conversely, we lack nearly any information about profit rates of family support in male career patterns (for an exception see Tölke 1996). In correspondence to a deeply rooted gender bias in life-course analysis, we risk underestimating that both institutions—the labor market and the family—impose their rationale on both male and female life courses and we tend to ignore the fact that both female and male life courses are governed by both life-area institutions.

Adjacent Life-Course Institutions or the Backup Logic of Life

A third referential system between institutions that acts out its effects on biographies refers to the sharing of costs between the family and the state with respect to intergenerational obligations in interrelated lives. Its rules relate to institutions adjacent to the family and employment tandem.

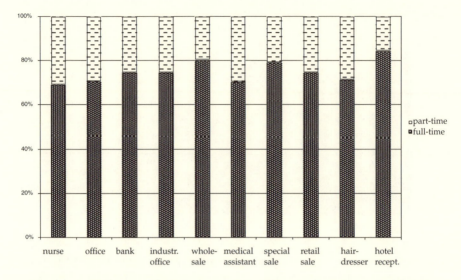

Figure 2.2 Proportion of Full-Time and Part-Time Work in Occupation Trained For, By Initial Qualification.

Arlie Hochschild (1997) vividly described the demands of modern family management in the United States in terms of a "third shift," in addition to paid employment and housework. The situation for those starting families in Germany is even further complicated by the operating hours of consumer-relevant services such as car inspection, physician's consulting times, opening hours for shopping and hairdressing (Geissler and Oechsle 2001), but even more so by institutions that share the care of dependent family members. These are the various kindergartens for different age groups; half-day school sessions with irregular starting and finishing times, which barely correspond to the opening hours of kindergartens; and institutions for the care of the ill and elderly, which discharge patients without first notifying the family of the need for full- or part-time family care. All together, such institutional factors interrupt any regular timetables of employment and require the flexible availability of a home-based carer. In other words, these institutions take for granted or presuppose tandem arrangements that are based on the breadwinner/homemaker model, and they actively help to partially or completely exclude caregiving partners from employment for varying durations in their life courses, and set free the earning partner from time-consuming intergenerational obligations (Bird 2001).

   The adjacent institutions force parents' life courses into their program of a mutually referential arrangement of life, and reflect family members' participation in society according to gender, age, and institutional

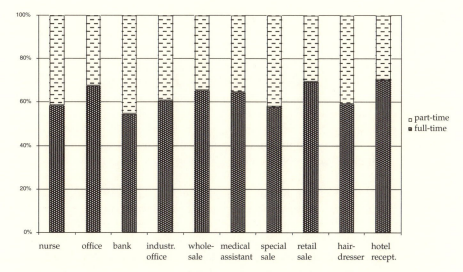

Figure 2.3 Proportion of Full-Time and Part-Time, Qualified Women Working in Occupations Not Trained For, By Initial Qualification.

demands. The policies of these institutions are fundamentally bound up with the German welfare state and its preference for the model of one-breadwinner/one-homemaker families (Kulawik 1999). The regulatory practice turns the role of the family into a flexible backup resource to complement the state's budget and substantially facilitates the state's policy to win public support for bringing women back into the labor market in times of labor scarcity, or to reduce women's employment opportunities by pushing public education and caring needs back onto the family (Heinze, Schmidt, and Strünck 1997; Offe 1984). In line with economic swings in Germany it is not just a moral imperative that fosters private intergenerational obligations, but also the state's organization of support for reproductive work. Its functioning creates and imposes a gendered *backup logic* of life for both the breadwinner and the homemaker (Daly 2000; Kulawik 1999; Pfau-Effinger 1999).

First Conclusions: Redefining the Units of Relevance in Life-Course Analysis

In recapitulating and evaluating the entire institutional conjunctions with life-course relevance uncovered so far, we may state the coexistence of three quite distinct units of life-course structure. The referential system between institutions highlights the rules of

1. the *attainment logic,* which rests on the serial program of successfully progressing through education, labor-market positioning, and corresponding retirement benefits, and which emphasizes status attainment;

2. the *tandem logic* of the labor market and the family in the period of adulthood, which not only requires personal arrangements for work sharing, but favors unequal accentuation with respect to employment career and family care between the sexes;

3. the *backup logic* of private and public costs and benefits in intergenerational life-course settings, which results from the rules of sharing care and reproductive work between the state and the family.

The institutions claim to guide biographical decision-making through preparation for and continuation in paid work, as well as through the balance between life areas and life settings of dependent others. They are all parts that together form the German life-course regime. The resulting perspectives on behavior, however, do not fit together easily, as in the examples of the homemaker being removed from the attainment logic in the market and of the breadwinner who is eclipsed from the backup logic of intergenerational management obligations.

In German approaches, mismatches between institutional demands have been deciphered in male life courses with respect to life-sequencing institutions and individualization, and in female life courses with respect to family work and employment participation. But we can say that all three logics encompass the life course of both sexes, and provide the temporal and social context for biographical planning and stock-taking for men and women. Individualization processes only result from the declining frequency of successful transitions within the attainment logic of life, but do not affect the grid of interdependencies within the tandem and the backup logic of life. The inherited solutions foster specific relations between gendered life courses and they presuppose gender inequality irrespective of social change.

However, the question remains whether relationality between the sexes forms a structural category for deciphering *the* life course, or just the specific life span of linked lives. We therefore should consider the extent to which relationality also matters in single lives, or whether at least those without children can shake off the contradictions of the life-course regime extended above.

SINGLE LIVES OR THE INDIVIDUALIZATION PARADIGM TURNED UPSIDE DOWN

German men and women seem to be aware of the fact that—mainly due to the backup logic of life—interrelated lives do not form an easygoing nexus with respect to gender equality. For many years Germany has been the country with the lowest birth rate in Europe, and with the highest rate of childless couples (BMFSFJ 2003:88). Married or not, within the last fifty years the number of couples without children has come to outnumber those with children, even if we include single parents among the latter (Klammer et al. 2000). The proportion of people who have children is shrinking dramatically, while the desire to have children has not actually decreased. Empirical findings show that the failure to realize planned parenthood mainly relates to personal reactions to the contradictory effects of children on status attainment in the market (Huinink and Brähler 2000; Nave-Herz 1988). Thus childlessness might be considered an effect of individualization.

However, in our search for indicators in life-sequencing institutions, which might *postulate* individuals' life courses as if they were linked even though people might follow the notion of individualization, we discover traces of presumed relationality in each of the institutions of life-course relevance. These traces, which are evidence of path dependencies reaching back to the early stages of the last century, are to be found in:

1. The occupational system. In male-dominated labor-market segments and positions we find the provision of a family wage regardless of de facto partnerships, whether married or single, whether father or not. In contrast, only female graduates from higher education—a qualification level that was unknown for women at Bismarck's time—gain from this system. Women with qualifications below this level (and that is a two-thirds majority), whether married or single, are mainly located in female stereotyped occupations lacking career ladders or promotion prospects (Klement 2001; Gottschall 2000; Krüger 1999). In addition, gatekeepers within the companies deciding on promotions for graduates from higher education expect that even unmarried women will in the future be burdened with familial obligations—and prefer to promote men instead (Gottschall 2000). The gender connotations attributed to different areas of work are reflected in an employment arrangement that *assumes* the linking of the male and the female life course—and, with or without a family, endow the male with income and employment privileges, but discriminate against a female person.

2. The education system. Below the tertiary level, which about only one-third of German youth enter, the discovery of occupational training as a pivot for gendered allocations to different types of work still dominates today (Kleinau and Mayer 1996; Brinker-Gabler 1979). Its effects of producing *gendered life-course differences,* in the structural sense of the cultural concept of *doing gender* (West and Zimmerman 1987),[5] result from the channeling of youth into two types of occupational pathways to adulthood that dramatically differ. On the one hand, there is the well-known dual system of education and training, the apprenticeship, in which male youths predominate, and which is presumed to lead to "existence-securing" occupations; on the other hand, we have the school-based vocational educational system for female youths, which leads to streaming into "natural vocations," to use the nomenclature of Bismarck's time (Mayer 1992). Their curricula prepare for reproductive work and short-term employment in families or in the personal service sector in order to keep alive female youth's orientation toward seeking to raise a family on their own and to fully concentrate on the homemaking role (Schlüter 1987).

In comparing the pathways from school to work in eleven countries, Shavit and Müller identified systemic variables that determine the extent to which the transition system enhances or inhibits the career chances of its students. These are "the extent to which the national educational system is standardized; the extent to which vocational secondary education teaches specific rather than general skills, and, finally, the extent to which there is a linkage between schools and firms, which facilitates the job placement of graduates" (2000:449). The authors used data on the relationship between educational qualifications and occupational attainment in the careers of men. We are grateful for this clarifying remark, because their country-differentiating findings about the advantages/disadvantages of specific national pathways to work precisely mirror the gendered differences in the two educational pathways for the gendered world of work in Germany itself.

In assessing the education system up to the end of the secondary level in Germany, the authors only took into consideration the apprenticeship system. But due to social change in the labor market and the growth of the service sector, the proportion of pathways that follow the route of school-based vocational education to employment is rising, and today covers 127 different occupations (Stooß 1997). The market value of these qualifications is not guaranteed by skill protection, nor are the occupational skills recognized in standardized wage rates for the same type of work. There are no formal bridges between school and firms, as is the case in the dual system (apprenticeship). This lack of sustainability of returns on prior investments in human capital facilitates labor-force adjustment is in line with market fluctuations and social assistance policies (Pfau-Effinger 1999), but diminishes the chances for employment careers.

In short, in anticipation of the tandem logic in later life, the gendered pathways to employment provide occupational certificates with clearly gendered chances for labor-market payoffs, whether their holders opt for marriage or not. And while youth (like most of our life-course researchers, see Blossfeld and Drobnič 2001b; Shavit and Müller 2000; Mayer 1990; Allmendinger 1989; Tölke 1987) concentrate on educational *levels*, they miss the point of educationally induced *work-typification* effects, and its gendered outcomes in the long run of life, whether pursued as a single or a married person (Krüger 1999).

3. The *system of social control*. From the point of view of the German welfare state the structuring of gendered pathways through work is reflected in old-age pensions (Allmendinger 1994). But the system of social control also antedates the preferred relatedness of life areas in regulations with respect to deviant behavior among youth. Girls considered deviant are usually delivered into the hands of female behavior-improving welfare institutions, while boys considered deviant are encouraged to attain better educational and occupational qualifications via special training programs delivered by schooling experts (Seus 1998).

The interplay of gendered attributions within the labor market, the education system, and the state's intervention practices undermine, to a certain extent, cultural change. Our studies on changes in gender norms for modes of participation in the family and the labor market[6] clearly show the extent to which early structural course-setting within the education system combined with dead-end jobs and gatekeepers' selection practices in the labor market creep in to what others may call choices (Blossfeld and Hakim 1997). Whereas in the immediate postwar period the breadwinner/homemaker model seemed to have been a self-evident cultural certainty, and husbands often argued quite simply, saying: "Well, a wife is a housewife. Once married she has to stay at home" (Born, Krüger, and Lorenz-Meyer 1996:117), norms have changed for their sons and daughters, who favor the ideal of equal participation with respect to family roles. But the results of bargaining between the younger couples showed virtually the same results as in their parents' lives (Krüger 2001). In referring to these bargaining processes, the sons whom we interviewed replied in similar ways to this one: "Well, and then we want to marry and have a child, and then we'll have to see, . . . I mean, she works in a kindergarten, is highly qualified—and doesn't earn much, and won't in the future. But for me it looks really good at the office, even if it is a bit uncertain" (Krüger 2001:417). The number of daughters who very reluctantly gave in or who rejected motherhood and/or marriage rose remarkably.[7] In fact, in rational calculations of family costs and career patterns, the gender differences in income prospects imported in terms of labor-market resources acquired within their earlier life span as singles hardly allow for anything other than an arrangement within the classical gendered family solution.

In summary, the dominating logic of life areas not only runs through the linked lives, but also implements its linkage hooks into the lives of singles very early on. These hooks foster the difference in male and female employment patterns over the life span, as singles or as couples, and penetrate all types of life arrangements. In consequence, whichever way we

look at it, the compounds that form the German life-course regime add up
to a contradictory but powerful framework that insinuates interrelations
and affects people regardless of whether individuals enter into formally or
informally secured personal relationships with each other, or whether they
plan to enter into generational or gender interrelations, or whether they
decide to avoid them.

INTERPRETATION: LIFE-COURSE REGIME AND
SOCIAL STRUCTURE

In institution-actor approaches, as outlined first by Anthony Giddens
(1984) and within which I want to locate my arguments, it is assumed that
the life course is structured by the relationship between, on the one hand,
individuals as actors who shape their own biographies and, on the other
hand, institutions that frame subjective action and orientations. But this
wide-ranging assumption is imprecise with respect to systems of reference
between the institutions themselves. The resulting logics for biographies
might be only very conditionally attuned to each other, and people might
not be willing or able to follow such normalcy assumptions. However, life-
course research that questions institutional influences on individuals'
biographies leads into the depths of the social system of a given society. In
Germany, the embeddedness of life courses in frames of reference between
institutions combines life areas and life-sequencing institutions, and the
interlacing of both relates to the production and reproduction of its social
order.

The attempt to balance institutions' different demands means to act
within a threefold rationale of inequality:

- within social stratification arising from the hierarchically segmented
  education and occupational systems, which nevertheless stress the
  logic of status attainment;
- between men and women because of horizontal segmentation in the
  preparation for types of work and their gendered positioning in the
  labor market, which display the logic of unequal tandem arrangements;
- between the family and the time-framing power of external adjacent
  institutions for reproductive work, which bind social dependencies
  in gender relations and foster intergenerational obligations.

From the perspective of life-course theory we have to state that the
empirical findings imply a necessary expansion of the dominant notion of
the German life-course regime as exclusively centered around the prepa-

ration for work, employment activity, and retirement. Instead, the life-course regime includes not one but a threefold system of reference between institutions, which acts out its inputs on life sequencing, life-area coordination, and the management of dependent lives. The institutional rationales are not attuned to each other and they challenge individual behavior in the search for reconciling competing solutions. These tend to elevate gender to a pivotal mechanism of resilience in dealing with con-tradictions between institutional demands of status attainment and inter-dependencies between life courses. The resulting arrangements display disproportionate subordination between the sexes.

In establishing this gender order, however, it is important to distinguish between institutions that *generate* gender inequality in the life course—these are the life-sequencing institutions (education—labor market—retirement); those that *work with* gender difference as a basic principle—these are the tan-dem institutions (the occupational and the family system); and, finally, those that *require* the existence of gender differences—these are the institutions adjacent to reproductive work. And whether we choose an approach incor-porating discourse theory, theories of gender and power, of interactionism or structuralism, without an analysis of the historically deeply rooted sources of the sociostructural production of the interrelatedness of lives, our conclusions might be incomplete or even inadequate.

In countries with a loose life-course regime, such as the United States, the investigation of linked lives and coordinational challenges in dual-career families has been an issue of central interest since the start of life-course research. Countries with a strong institutional framing of the life course, like Germany, distinguish themselves from these countries by a clear and very distinct differentiation between male and female life-course parameters that is also evident in the lives of single people. The combina-tion of gendered parameters and individualization instead leads to the identification of a contradictory relationship with individualization, result-ing in a life-course paradox per se. The more the institutional connections within the attainment logic are weakened, the stronger the need to fulfill the behavioral imperatives of the tandem, and the backup logic becomes: from the children's point of view, with respect to the early development of basic resources for the demands of the education phase; from the point of view of the elderly, with respect to the increasing dependence on others associated with the prolonged duration of care-dependent life stages; from the point of view of middle-aged adults, with respect to the safety nets for increasing employment risks. The life-course regime of interrelations has not diminished, but it has certainly become more uncomfortable, and its coordination more difficult.

Mainstream research has largely missed this point and is still failing to produce a life-course theory that is equally valid for both men and women.

In view of the opposing outcomes for men and women of the German interdependency paradigm, the "institutionally organized social forgetting" (Douglas 1987) of the tandem logic in men's lives could make it easier for male researchers to adopt the Anglo-American perspective on "linked lives." In doing so the focus is on personal arrangements of just a specific *life span*, but the fact that presumed or de facto relationality between the sexes penetrates the entire life course and its embeddedness in "linking institutions" is ignored. Thus, from a sociological perspective, we have to state that in a life-course regime with a strong life-sequencing program there is a need for enlargement and modification in order to overcome the neglect of empirical research on the importance of life-area regulations and adjacent institutional demands. We cannot deny the importance of bringing in the issue of gendered realities, and of revealing the power of the structural constraints that for a long time have determined the ceiling for both individualization and interdependencies in interwoven and in single lives.

NOTES

1. These regulations vary enormously between countries. They are one of the main ingredients of a specific society's institutional life-course regime. There are countries with highly institutionalized definitions of equivalence between educational certificates and ranges of occupational positions, like Germany, Austria, and—to a somewhat lesser extent—Switzerland. Other countries operate with firm-specific recruiting systems, by selective linking arrangements between certain educational institutions and firms, or other kinds of regulation. For recent comparisons, see Culpepper and Finegold (1999), Shavit and Müller (1998), and Kerckhoff (1995).

2. The stratification of linked levels results from two historically separate systems of regulation, each of which controlled access to particular occupations and occupational hierarchies. These were/are, on the one hand, incorporated protection processes for skills developed through the artisan and craft guilds, which formed a bottom-up stratification: the casual laborer (*Tagelöhner*), the journeyman (*Geselle*), and the master craftsman (*Meister*); nowadays the unskilled/semiskilled worker, skilled worker, and those possessing intermediate-level specialist qualifications. On the other hand, Germany developed a top-down hierarchy within the civil service that included four levels: the senior, the upper intermediate, the intermediate, and the lower civil servant, each of which is today still contingent on the level of educational qualification at entry. The structuring of educational/vocational and job correspondence from the level of the unskilled worker up to the academic spread into the private sector, and only here, under pressure from globalization processes, have the strongly regulated boundaries of recruitment practices started to show some deregulation. Nevertheless, even in company internal training and promotion systems, entrance qualifications play a role with respect to access to or exclusion from such careers, and again, only recently have the inclusion/exclusion practices begun to change (cf. Krüger 1990).

3. The study, conducted by Claudia Born and the author in the Bremen Life-Course Center, was financed by the German Research Foundation (DFG), carried out between 1997 and 1999 via standardized postal questionnaires, and sent out to 6000 women. The sample was selected randomly from the archives of the chambers of commerce, which supervised and certified the women's vocational training. Despite a high mobility rate and name changes due to marriage, addresses were successfully updated with the help of the national network of residents' registration offices (*Einwohnermeldeämter*).

4. The occupations included were nurse, qualified office employee, qualified office worker in industry, qualified bank employee, doctor's clerical and medical assistant, wholesale and export employee, hairdresser, specialist sales assistant (butcher/baker), retail sales assistant (other branches), and qualified hotel personnel. The occupations included do not differ from each other with respect to the level of labor-market entrance status and covered about 70 percent of all women who had undergone official vocational training in their respective cohort. The total potential time in employment was calculated as the time between completing vocational training and data collection in 1997 and was set at 100 percent, which permitted a comparison of the different time spans for which each cohort could be observed. The analysis focused on the proportion of time the women trained in different occupations spent in different employment activities: working in the field trained for, in other fields, mostly with a loss of qualification and income, and in employment exempt from social insurance (less than 20 hours a week or up to a certain maximum monthly income, which in 2002 was 325 Euro).

5. West and Zimmermann use the term to describe the gendering effects of everyday interaction that cannot occur without the interactants attributing and deciphering behavior in accordance with the sex of the actors and consequently stabilizing gendered frames of action.

6. The three projects, conducted by Claudia Born and the author within the Bremen Life-Course Center between 1988 and 1996, combined quantitative life-course data and qualitative in-depth interviews. The first sample consisted of 248 married women who were in their sixties when interviewed. Again, addresses were taken randomly from the final examination lists of the relevant chambers of commerce, industry, and trade/crafts for the five occupations of interest (first project). We then investigated the life courses and personal interpretations of their still living, not-divorced husbands who consented (n = 128; second project). The third project concentrated on their (adult) sons and daughters (n = 326).

7. In the mid-Seventies in Germany, the birth rate dramatically shrank within a period of five years. For the first time, births could replace only 60 percent of the parents' generation (Höhn 1980).

REFERENCES

Allmendinger, Jutta. 1989. *Career Mobility Dynamics. A Comparative Analysis of the United States, Norway, and West Germany*. Studien und Berichte 49. Berlin: Max-Planck-Institut für Bildungsforschung.

Allmendinger, Jutta. 1994. *Lebensverlauf und Sozialpolitik. Die Ungleichheit von Mann und Frau und ihr öffentlicher Ertrag.* Frankfurt a.M.: Campus.

Beck, Ulrich. 1992. *Risk Society.* Newbury Park: Sage.

Becker-Schmidt, Regina. 1987. "Die doppelte Vergesellschaftung: Die doppelte Unterdrückung: Besonderheiten der Frauenforschung in den Sozialwissenschaften." Pp. 10–25 in *Die andere Hälfte der Gesellschaft,* edited by L. Unterkircher and I. Wagner. Wien: ÖGB-Verlag.

Becker-Schmidt, Regina. 1998. "Relationalität zwischen den Geschlechtern, Konnexionen im Geschlechterverhältnis." *Zeitschrift für Frauenforschung* 16(3): 5–21. Hanover: Forschungsinstitut Frau und Gesellschaft.

Bertram, Hans and Clemens Dannenbeck. 1990. "Pluralisierung von Lebenslagen und Individualisierung von Lebensführungen." Pp. 207–29 in *Lebenslagen, Lebensläufe, Lebensstile. Soziale Welt, Sonderband,* edited by P. A. Berger and S. Hradil. Göttingen: Verlag Otto Schwartz & Co.

Bird, Kate. 2001. "Parental Leave in Germany: An Institution with Two Faces?" Pp. 55–90 in *Institutionen und Lebenslauf im Wandel,* edited by L. Leisering, R. Müller, and K. Schumann. München: Juventa.

Blossfeld, Hans-Peter. 1986. "Career Opportunities in the Federal Republic of Germany: A Dynamic Approach to the Study of Life Course, Cohort, and Period Effects." *European Sociological Review* 3(2):208–25.

Blossfeld, Hans-Peter and Sonja Drobnič (Eds.). 2001a. *Careers of Couples in Contemporary Society: From Male Breadwinner to Dual-Earner Families.* Oxford: Oxford University Press.

Blossfeld, Hans-Peter and Sonja Drobnič. 2001b. "A Cross-National Comparative Approach to Couples' Careers." Pp. 1–15 in *Careers of Couples in Contemporary Society. From Male Breadwinner to Dual-Earner Families,* edited by H.-P. Blossfeld and S. Drobnič. Oxford: Oxford University Press.

Blossfeld, Hans-Peter and Catherine Hakim (Eds.). 1997. *Between Equalization and Marginalization: Women Working Part-Time in Europe and the United States of America.* Oxford: Oxford University Press.

Born, Claudia. 2000. "Erstausbildung und weiblicher Lebenslauf. Was (nicht nur) junge Frauen bezüglich der Berufswahl wissen sollten." Pp. 50–65 in *Übergänge. Individualisierung, Flexibilisierung und Institutionalisierung des Lebensverlaufs,* edited by W. R. Heinz. Special edition, *Zeitschrift für Soziologie der Erziehung und Sozialisation.* Weinheim: Juventa.

Born, Claudia and Helga Krüger (Eds.). 2001. *Individualisierung und Verflechtung. Geschlecht und Generation im Lebenslaufregime.* Weinheim/München: Juventa.

Born, Claudia, Helga Krüger, and Dagmar Lorenz-Meyer. 1996. *Der unentdeckte Wandel. Annäherung an das Verhältnis von Struktur und Norm im weiblichen Lebenslauf.* Berlin: Sigma.

Brinker-Gabler, Gisela (Ed.). 1979. *Frauenarbeit und Beruf. Die Frau in der Gesellschaft. Frühe Texte.* Frankfurt a.M.: Fischer Taschenbuch Verlag.

Bundesministerium für Familie, Senioren, Frauen und Jugend (BMFSFJ). 2003. *Die Familie im Spiegel der amtlichen Statistik.* Bonn: Kohlhammer.

Crompton, Rosemary and Fiona Harris. 1998. "Explaining Women's Employment Patterns: 'Orientations to Work' Revisited." *British Journal of Sociology* 49(1): 118–36.

Culpepper, Pepper D. and David Finegold (Eds.). 1999. *The German Skills Machine: Sustaining Comparative Advantage in a Global Economy.* New York/Oxford: Berghahn.

Daly, Mary. 2000. *The Gender Division of Welfare.* Cambridge: Cambridge University Press.

Douglas, Mary. 1987. *How Institutions Think.* London: Routledge and Kegan Paul.

Geissler, Birgit and Mechtild Oechsle. 2001. "Zeitordnungen des Erwerbssystems und biographische Bindungen an Andere: Verflechtung und Entkoppelung." Pp. 83–106 in *Individualisierung und Verflechtung. Geschlecht und Generation im Lebenslaufregime,* edited by C. Born and H. Krüger. Weinheim/München: Juventa.

Giddens, Anthony. 1984. *The Constitution of Society: Outline of a Theory of Structuration.* Cambridge: Polity.

Gottschall, Karin. 2000. *Soziale Ungleichheit und Geschlecht. Kontinuitäten und Brüche, Sackgassen und Erkenntnispotential im deutschen soziologischen Diskurs.* Opladen: Leske & Budrich.

Hagestad, Gunhild. 1992. "Assigning Rights and Duties: Age, Duration and Gender in Social Institutions." Pp. 261–79 in *Institutions and Gatekeeping in the Life Course,* edited by W. R. Heinz. Weinheim: Deutscher Studien Verlag.

Hakim, Catherine. 1998. "Developing a Sociology for the Twenty First Century: Preference Theory." *British Journal of Sociology* 49(1):137–43.

Han, Shin-Kap and Phyllis Moen. 2001. "Coupled Careers: Pathways Through Work and Marriage in the United States." Pp. 201–31 in *Careers of Couples in Contemporary Society: From Male Breadwinner to Dual-Earner Families,* edited by H.-P. Blossfeld and S. Drobnič. New York: Oxford University Press.

Heinz, Walter R. 1996. "Status Passages as Micro-Macro Linkages in Life-Course Research." Pp. 51–66 in *Society and Biography,* edited by A. Weymann and W. R. Heinz. Weinheim: Deutscher Studien Verlag.

Heinz, Walter R. (Ed.) 1997. *Theoretical Advances in Life-course Research,* Vol. I, 2nd ed., *Status Passages and the Life Course.* Weinheim: Deutscher Studien Verlag.

Heinz, Walter R. 1999. "Job-Entry Patterns in a Life-course Perspective." Pp. 214–34 in *From Education to Work: Cross-National Perspectives,* edited by W. R. Heinz. New York: Cambridge University Press.

Heinz, Walter R. and Helga Krüger. 2001. "The Life Course: Innovations and Challenges for Social Research." *Current Sociology* 49(2):29–53.

Heinze, Rolf G., Josef Schmidt, and Christoph Strünck. 1997. "Zur politischen ökonomie der sozialen Dienstleistungsproduktion." *Kölner Zeitschrift für Soziologie und Sozialpsychologie* 2(49):242–71.

Hochschild, Arlie R. 1997. *The Time Bind: When Work Becomes Home and Home Becomes Work.* New York: Metropolitan.

Höhn, Charlotte. 1980. "Rechtliche und demographische Einflüsse auf die Entwicklung der Ehescheidungen seit 1946." *Zeitschrift für Bevölkerungswissenschaft:* 335–71.

Huinink, Johannes. 2000. "Bildung und Familienentwicklung im Lebenslauf. *Zeitschrift für Erziehungswissenschaft* 2:209–27.

Huinink, Johannes and Elmar Brähler. 2000. "Zur Epidemiologie gewollter und ungewollter Kinderlosigkeit in Ost- und Westdeutschland." Pp. 43–54 in

Jahrbuch der Medizinischen Psychologie, Vol. 17, *Fruchtbarkeitsstörungen,* edited by E. Brähler, H. Felder, and B. Strauß. Göttingen: Hogrefe.

Kerckhoff, Alan C. 1995. "Institutional Arrangements and Stratification Processes in Industrial Societies." *Annual Review of Sociology* 15:323–47.

Klammer, Ute, Christina Klenner, Christiane Ochs, Petra Radke, and Astrid Ziegler. 2000. *WSI-FrauenDatenReport.* Berlin: Edition Sigma.

Kleinau, Elke and Christine Mayer (Eds.). 1996. *Erziehung und Bildung des weiblichen Geschlechts. Eine kommentierte Quellensammlung zur Bildungs- und Berufsbildungsgeschichte von Mädchen und Frauen.* Weinheim: Deutscher Studien Verlag.

Klement, Carmen. 2001. "Der freie Markt und seine Grenzen. Aufstiegsweiterbildung in einem geschlechtshierarchisch strukturierten Arbeitsmarkt." Pp. 139–57 in *Individualisierung und Verflechtung. Geschlecht und Generation im Lebenslaufregime,* edited by C. Born and H. Krüger. Weinheim/München: Juventa.

Knapp, Gudrun-Axeli and Angelika Wetterer (Eds.). 2001. *Soziale Verortung der Geschlechter: Gesellschaftstheorie und feministische Kritik.* Münster: Westfälisches Dampfboot.

Kohli, Martin. 1986. "The World We Forgot: A Historical Review of the Life Course." Pp. 271–303 in *Later Life: The Social Psychology of Aging,* edited by Victor W. Marshall. Beverly Hills, CA: Sage.

Kohli, Martin. 1994. "Institutionalisierung und Individualisierung der Erwerbsbiographie." Pp. 219–44 in *Riskante Freiheiten. Individualisierung in modernen Gesellschaften,* edited by U. Beck and E. Beck-Gernsheim. Frankfurt a.M.: Suhrkamp.

Krüger, Helga. 1990. "The Shifting Sands of a Social Contract: Young People in the Transition Between School and Work." Pp. 116–33 in *Childhood, Youth and Social Change: A Comparative Perspective,* edited by L. Chisholm, P. Büchner, H. Krüger, and P. Brown. London/New York/Philadelphia: Falmer.

Krüger, Helga. 1999. "Gender and Skills: Distributive Ramifications of the German Skill System." Pp. 189–228 in *The German Skills Machine: Sustaining Comparative Advantage in a Global Economy,* edited by P. D. Culpepper and D. Finegold. New York/Oxford: Berghahn.

Krüger, Helga. 2001. "Social Change in Two Generations. Employment Patterns and Their Costs for Family Life." Pp. 401–23 in *Restructuring Work and the Life Course,* edited by V. W. Marshall, W. R. Heinz, H. Krüger, and A. Verma. Toronto: University of Toronto Press.

Krüger, Helga, Claudia Born, Beate Einemann, Stine Heintze, and Helga Saifi. 1987. *Privatsache Kind—Privatsache Beruf. ". . . und dann hab' ich ja noch Haushalt, Mann und Wäsche!" Zur Lebenssituation von Frauen mit kleinen Kindern in unserer Gesellschaft.* Opladen: Leske & Budrich.

Kulawik, Teresa. 1999. *Wohlfahrtsstaat und Mutterschaft: Schweden und Deutschland 1870–1912.* Frankfurt a.M.: Campus.

Levy, René. 1996. "Toward a Theory of Life-course Institutionalization." Pp. 83–108 in *Society and Biography,* edited by A. Weymann and W. R. Heinz. Weinheim: Deutscher Studien Verlag.

Marshall, Victor W. 1995. "Social Models of Aging." *Canadian Journal on Aging* 14(1):12–34.

Mayer, Christine. 1992. ". . . und dass die staatsbürgerliche Erziehung des Mädchens mit der Erziehung zum Weibe zusammenfällt." *Zeitschrift für Pädagogik* 38(5):433–54.

Mayer, Karl Ulrich (Ed.). 1990. "Lebensverläufe und sozialer Wandel." *Kölner Zeitschrift für Soziologie und Sozialpsychologie,* Sonderheft 31.

Mayer, Karl Ulrich. 1991. "Life Courses in the Welfare State." Pp. 171–86 in *Theoretical Advances in Life-Course Research,* Vol. I, *Status Passages and Risks in the Life Course,* edited by W. R. Heinz. Weinheim: Deutscher Studien Verlag.

Mayer, Karl Ulrich. 2001. "The Paradox of Global Change and National Dependencies: Life-Course Patterns in Advanced Societies. Pp. 89–110 in *Inclusions and Exclusions in European Societies,* edited by A. Woodward and M. Kohli. London: Routledge.

Mayer, Karl Ulrich, Jutta Allmendinger, and Johannes Huinink (Eds.). 1991. *Vom Regen in die Traufe. Frauen zwischen Beruf und Familie.* Frankfurt a.M.: Campus.

McDaniel, Susan. 2001. "Born at the Right Time? Gendered Generations and Webs of Entitlement and Responsibility." *Canadian Journal of Sociology* 26(2):193–214.

McMullin, Julie Ann. 1995. "Theorizing Age and Gender Relations." Pp. 30–41 in *Connecting Gender and Aging: A Sociological Approach,* edited by S. Arber and J. Ginn. Buckingham: Open University Press.

Moen, Phyllis. 2001. "The Gendered Life Course." Pp. 179–96 in *Handbook of Aging and the Social Sciences,* 5th ed., edited by L. George and R. H. Binstock. San Diego, CA: Academic Press.

Moen, Phyllis and Mary Ann Erickson. 1995. "Linked Lives: A Trans-Generational Approach to Resiliency." Pp. 169–207 in *Examining Lives in Context: Perspectives on the Ecology of Human Development,* edited by P. Moen, G. H. Elder, Jr., and K. Lüscher. Washington, DC: American Psychological Association.

Mückenberger, Ulrich. 1989. "Der Wandel des Normalarbeitsverhältnisses unter Bedingungen einer 'Krise der Normalität.'" *Gewerkschaftliche Monatshefte* 40:211–23.

Nave-Herz, Rosemarie. 1988. *Kinderlose Ehen. Eine empirische Studie über die Lebenssituation kinderloser Ehepaare und die Gründe für ihre Kinderlosigkeit.* Weinheim/München: Juventa-Verlag.

Offe, Claus. 1984. *Arbeitsgesellschaft. Strukturprobleme und Zukunftsperspektiven.* Frankfurt a.M./New York: Campus.

Pfau-Effinger, Birgit. 1999. "Welfare Regimes and the Gendered Division of Labour in Cross-National Perspective: Theoretical Framework and Empirical Results." Pp. 69–96 in *Working Europe: Reshaping European Employment Systems,* edited by J. Christiansen, A. Kovalainen, and P. Koistinen. Aldershot: Ashgate.

Procter, Ian. 2001. "Becoming a Mother or a Worker: Structure and Agency in Young Adult Women's Accounts of Education, Training, Employment, and Partnership." Pp. 489–504 in *Restructuring Work and the Life Course,* edited by V. W. Marshall, W. R. Heinz, H. Krüger, and A. Verma. Toronto: University of Toronto Press.

Rabe-Kleberg, Ursula. 1987. *Frauenberufe: Zur Segmentierung der Berufswelt.* Bielefeld: Kleine Verlag.

Sackmann, Reinhold and Matthias Wingens (Eds.). 2001a. *Strukturen des Lebenslaufs. Übergang—Sequenz—Verlauf.* Weinheim/München: Juventa.

Sackmann, Reinhold and Matthias Wingens. 2001b. "Theoretische Konzepte des Lebenslaufs: Übergang, Sequenz und Verlauf." Pp. 17–48 in *Strukturen des Lebenslaufs. Übergang—Sequenz—Verlauf,* edited by R. Sackmann and M. Wingens. Weinheim/München: Juventa.

Schlüter, Anne. 1987. *Neue Hüte—alte Hüte? Gewerbliche Berufsbildung für Mädchen zu Beginn des 20. Jahrhunderts—zur Geschichte ihrer Institutionalisierung.* Düsseldorf: Schwann.

Seus, Lydia. 1998. "Böse Jungen—Brave Mädchen? Abweichendes Verhalten und die soziale Konstruktion von Geschlecht." Pp. 139–60 in *Kinderkriminalität. Empirische Befunde, öffentliche Wahrnehmung, Lösungsvorschläge,* edited by S. Müller and P. Hilmar. Weinheim: Leske & Budrich.

Shavit, Yossi and Walter Müller (Eds.). 1998. *From School to Work.* Oxford: Oxford University Press.

Shavit, Yossi and Walter Müller. 2000. "Vocational Secondary Education, Tracking and Social Stratification." Pp. 437–52 in *Handbook of the Sociology of Education,* edited by M. T. Hallinan. New York/Boston/Dordrecht/London/Moscow: Kluwer Academic/Plenum.

Sørensen, Annemette. 1990. "Unterschiede im Lebenslauf von Frauen und Männern." Pp. 304–21 in *Lebensverläufe und sozialer Wandel.* Sonderheft 31 der *Kölner Zeitschrift für Soziologie und Sozialpsychologie,* edited by Karl Ulrich Mayer.

Stooß, Friedemann. 1997. "Reformbedarf in der beruflichen Bildung." Expertise im Auftrag des Ministeriums für Arbeit, Gesundheit und Soziales des Landes Nordrhein-Westfalen. Pp. 47–111 in *Reformbedarf der beruflichen Bildung. Reihe: pro Ausbildung. Ausbildungskonsens NRW,* edited by Ministerium für Wirtschaft und Mittelstand, Technologie und Verkehr. Düsseldorf.

Tölke, Angelika. 1987. *Lebensverläufe von Frauen. Familiäre Ereignisse, Ausbildungs- und Erwerbsverhalten im Kontext des individuellen Lebenslaufs und der gesellschaftlichen Entwicklung.* Weinheim/München: Juventa.

Tölke, Angelika. 1996. "Berufskarrieren von Frauen und Männern: Der Einfluss von Herkunft, Bildung und Lebensform." *Zeitschrift für Frauenforschung,* 14(4):161–77.

West, Candace and Don H. Zimmerman. 1987. "Doing Gender." *Gender and Society* 1(2):125–51. Newbury Park/Beverly Hills/London/New Dehli: Sage.

Weymann, Ansgar and Walter R. Heinz (Eds.). 1996. *Society and Biography.* Weinheim: Deutscher Studien Verlag.

Witzel, Andreas and Thomas Kühn. 2001. "Biographiemanagement und Planungschaos. Arbeitsmarktplatzierung und Familiengründung bei jungen Erwachsenen." Pp. 55–82 in *Individualisierung und Verflechtung. Geschlecht und Generation im deutschen Lebenslaufregime,* edited by C. Born and H. Krüger. Weinheim/München: Juventa.

| 3 |

The Life Course in Time and Place

Glen H. Elder, Jr.

INTRODUCTION

Over forty years ago, a leading developmentalist (Bronfenbrenner 1958) wrote a thoughtful essay entitled "Socialization and Social Class Through Time and Space." When he looked back to the 1930s, he discovered that studies of class and child-rearing made sense only when they were arrayed by date of research, their historical time. Middle-class parents had become more permissive over time, while working-class parents were shifting to a more punitive, restrictive regime. Bronfenbrenner had discovered the importance of historical context. A few years later, a similar discovery occurred in the study of lives through the work of sociologists and historians, and the insights were applied to psychological studies of lives and development.

At the time, longitudinal studies were making a name for themselves in postwar America, as early studies of children became studies of adults and then the middle-aged (Elder 1998a). When investigators followed children into their adult years, they needed to know their social pathways, whether through education, military service, work experience, or family roles. Each pathway had different developmental consequences, but little was known about them, in part because the social data were not organized in terms of life experience and its chronology.

Directed by psychologists, the pioneering longitudinal studies had little interest in social pathways, social transitions, or more broadly, their institutional context. But longitudinal studies repeatedly posed challenges to this disinterest. For example, the lead investigators frequently came up short on explanations of why some people's behavior changed as they left childhood for the adult years or in other cases remained much the same

(Elder, Modell, and Parke 1993). How did troubled youth manage to find accomplishments and meaningful relationships in adulthood? How did they turn their lives around?

We understand this shortsightedness and its consequences today after a remarkable period of advance in life-course theory, method, data, and research. This is "the age of the longitudinal study" (Young, Savola, and Phelps 1991) and of methods for collecting and analyzing such data (Elder 1998b; Giele and Elder 1998; Mayer and Tuma 1990). In theory, it is also the age of contextualism (Lerner 2002). Lives are lived in specific historical times and places, and studies of them necessarily call attention to changing cultures, populations, and institutional contexts. The life course is structured by transitions, often linked in trajectories, and by systems of age-grading. If historical times and places change, they change the "way people live their lives." And this change alters the course of development and aging. Likewise, changing people and populations alter social institutions and places.

Anne Colby, an American developmentalist, noted that the controversies surrounding life-course initiatives are mostly forgotten, and "the approach is widely seen as providing an accepted set of background assumptions that guide and provide common ground for research on a great number of issues across virtually all of the social sciences" (Colby 1998:ix). She concludes that "the establishment of this approach . . . is one of the most important achievements of social science in the second half of the 20th century" (ibid.:x).

The mutual relationship between changing times and places, and changing lives and development, remains one of the most fundamental insights in life-course study (Elder and Johnson 2002; Settersten 1999). And it has special meaning to me through studies that began many years ago with "Children of the Great Depression" (Elder [1974] 1999). Keeping this core principle in mind, I shall devote my chapter to challenges, advances, and problems in this line of work. I begin with an unfinished story that has much to do with my initial studies of these depression children and then turn to challenges that lie ahead.

AN UNFINISHED STORY: GERMAN "CHILDREN OF
THE GREAT DEPRESSION"

At a conference in the late 1970s, an American historian, Rudolph Binion (1976), asked what the story of "Children of the Great Depression" might be like if the project had focused on a corresponding cohort in Germany with urban children. In historical study, this question puts to use a counterfactual method of imagining a panel study of depression-era children in

Weimar, Germany. No studies of this kind were carried out in Germany or in Europe, for that matter. He posed the question to prompt thinking about the implications of economically deprived youth in wartime and postwar Germany. What would their lives be like? Would they resemble in life experience American youth who had grown up in the Great Depression? If not, what would be the major differences?

One could well imagine this experience because the Great Depression hit Germany and Austria with greater force than the United States (Elder [1974] 1999:377). Moreover, though many families were hard pressed by the economic collapse, some were undoubtedly spared such a fate, as among doctors and educators. Even in the same community, there was substantial variation in the depression experience of Austrians (Jahoda, Lazarsfeld, and Zeisel 1971). When Marienthal's textile mill closed, the town's workers lost their only employer, but women were kept busy meeting the needs of their families. However, unemployment became a way of life for the men and they quickly lost a sense of time and structure in their lives. Some became unemployed for most of the decade, while others were spared such loss. Before we explore this diversity and its possible effects, we need some background on the American study that began so many years ago.

I examined the lives and historical context of two California birth cohorts who lived through the Great Depression: the Oakland study (birth dates 1920–1921) and the Berkeley study (birth dates 1928–1929). Note that both cohorts lived through the depression, World War II, and the postwar era of greater prosperity in the United States, but they encountered these events at very different times in their lives. Since they were born eight years apart, I assumed that they would be influenced differentially. Table 3.1 shows some of these differences.

The Oakland study included children who were exposed to the prosperous 1920s in urban America, a period of unparalleled economic growth. They entered the depression after a relatively secure phase of early development and avoided the scars of joblessness after high school as the country began to mobilize. By comparison, the Berkeley cohort encountered the vulnerable years of early childhood during hard times and the pressures of adolescence extended into the unsettled years of World War II. These risks were especially prominent in the lives of the boys.

Variations in income loss provided the point of departure for examining the differential effects of economic change on the Oakland and Berkeley study members and their families. Within the middle and working class of 1929, families were identified according to income loss (1929–1933) relative to a decline in cost of living, about 25 percent over this period. Families experienced asset losses with some frequency only when income loss exceeded 40 percent of 1929 income. As such, deprived families were defined in terms of income losses above 34 percent; all other families

Table 3.1   Age of Oakland and Berkeley Cohort Members by Historical Events

Date	Event	Age of Cohort Members	
		Oakland	*Berkeley*
1920–21		Birth	
1921–22	Depression		
1923	Great Berkeley Fire	2–3	
1923–29	General economic boom, growth of "debt pattern" way of life, cultural change in sexual mores	1–9	
1928–29			Birth
1929–30	Onset of Great Depression	9–10	1–2
1932–33	Depth of Great Depression	11–13	3–5
1933–36	Partial recovery, increasing cost of living, labor strikes	12–16	4–8
1937–38	Economic slump	16–18	8–10
1939–40	Incipient stage of wartime mobilization	18–20	10–12
1945	End of World War II	24–25	16–17
1946–49	Postwar economic growth	25–29	17–21
1950–53	Korean War and the McCarthy era	30–33	22–25
1974–	End of affluent age in postwar America: energy crisis, rising inflation	54–	46–

were categorized as nondeprived. This division proved to be equally appropriate for the Berkeley sample.

The most adverse effects of the economic downturn appeared among the Berkeley boys, more so than among girls in both cohorts and the older Oakland boys. The Berkeley boys encountered the depression crisis when they were highly dependent on parental nurturance and particularly vulnerable to family instability, emotional strain, and family conflict. Consequently, these young people were less hopeful, less self-confident, and less secure in adolescence. Nearly three out of four were drawn into World War II and the Korean War, and, despite the trauma of battle, most of the boys from deprived families gained personal competence through war experiences. Entry into higher education, supportive marriages, and the challenges of military service together accounted for their developmental well-being up to the age of forty.

By comparison, the Oakland men were less exposed to developmental risks at a young age and they took full advantage of college, marital, and service opportunities. Over 90 percent served in the military. For young women in the two cohorts, mothers played a more protective role, although deprived girls from the Oakland cohort experienced greater social deprivations in adolescence. War work, volunteer activity, getting some advanced education, and especially raising a family became their path to the adult world.

Overall, deprivation in the Great Depression generated similar changes in the family environments of both American cohorts of boys and girls (division of labor, altered family relationships, and emotional-social strains), but their developmental effects varied in ways that conform to differences in life stage and gender relative to historical forces. From another vantage point, social and economic forces of the 1930s brought mothers and daughters into the family economy and intensified their relationship. Boys were drawn into work roles in the community and they experienced an accelerated pattern of social emancipation. This proved to be costly for the youngest boys who had little nurturing from mother or father when the economy collapsed.

In this brief account we see evidence of the social diversity of historical experience in addition to cohort variation: some children were exposed to economic hardship, others were spared such hardships; some grew up in the middle class, others in the working class; and the experiences of boys and girls varied greatly. How might the lives of these young people apply to an imaginary study of German youth who were also born in the 1920s but in different regions of the Weimar Republic?

Born at opposite ends of the 1920s in urban centers of Germany, these young people experienced economic and political unrest that extended across the decade (Grunberger 1966). They grew to maturity during the Great Depression, the Nazi takeover (Schoenbaum 1971), the Holocaust, and a devastating war at home. Some were no doubt involved in the Hitler youth movement and participated in large rallies around the country (Binion 1976). With few exceptions, the boys were drawn into the military and served on one of the many war fronts. Many did not survive the war (possibly 25 percent or more of the males) and another 35 percent were POWs or were wounded in battle. The girls were mobilized into the medical corps or worked on the home front. How did these experiences affect the lives of survivors into the middle years and later life?

Using a retrospective life-history method in a sample of West Germans, Mayer (1988) found that German men born between 1915 and 1925 were almost universally involved in military service—about 97 percent of these cohorts. The men lost as many as nine years of their occupational career in the war, and many could not find employment afterward. They suffered high rates of imprisonment, both during and after the war, and only 75 percent survived the war.

The 1931 birth cohort (Mayer and Huinink 1990:220) also suffered widespread and profound hardship in the war. It disrupted their families and schooling, and the destroyed economy made stable employment illusory for many. Work experiences were, as a rule, mixed with spells of joblessness. Opportunities for advancement were unlikely up to the late 1940s. Even the economic boom of the 1950s and the 1960s did not fully compensate this younger depression cohort for its war-related losses in occupational advancement.

When the war came to an end in the spring of 1945, Germany was divided in half, the German Democratic Republic under Communist control and West Germany with its government in Bonn. The entire country faced extreme hunger, poverty, and massive human dislocation. German men and women from the 1920s encountered privation and uncertain paths to adulthood depending on their residence, east or west. We know very little about the depression experiences of the German cohorts, but the long-term impact of the war could not have been more different.

The Oakland and Berkeley men and women who survived the war years entered a booming economy. Early deficits from the war were often turned around by advanced education and occupational opportunity. The women in these cohorts frequently worked in war industries during the war or served in some capacity within the military (Campbell 1984). The end of World War II marked a period of domesticity and the beginning of what is known as the "baby boom." Young Germans faced years of poverty before the "economic miracle."

During his talk in the mid-1970s, Rudolph Binion never anticipated the reuniting of Germany over a decade later, 1989–1991. Very few of us did. For the young men and women from the 1920 cohorts, the end of a divided Germany revealed striking economic inequalities by region (Weymann, Sackmann, and Wingens 1999). This political change found stagnation and economic backwardness in East Germany, and a high level of prosperity in West Germany. Women in East Germany enjoyed full employment and a status that had not been achieved by women in the west, but wages were relatively low, as was the standard of living. Reunification often led to their loss of status as a worker.

Within a few months of reunification, the German Research Council launched a program to deepen available knowledge of societal change in Germany before and after reunification (Noack, Kracke, Wild, and Hofer 2001). Noack and his colleagues refer to reunification as "a natural experiment" of sorts and they focused on both East and West German families with adolescent sons and daughters, with emphasis on the social transformation in lives and families. (The borders between East and West Germany had been opened on November 9, 1989.)

Within the time frame of a year, the German Democratic Republic had disappeared as a political entity and West German institutions had been transferred to the eastern region of the country.

The uncertainties surrounding this dramatic change contributed to a decline of 50 percent in East German birth rates. Young people had to face changes in the system of school and occupational socialization (Vondracek,

Reitzle, and Silbereisen 1999; see also Juang, Reitzle, and Silbereisen 2000). The former mode of school organization had suddenly disappeared, and the new system of pathways and options was unfamiliar to East German youth. Their parents were handicapped in providing useful advice.

In their longitudinal study, Noack and his research team followed some aspects of my approach to children of the Great Depression (see above). In particular, they gave special attention to family perceptions of uncertainty as the "impression that things around you change so fast that you do not know how to get your bearings." This perception of change adversely affected the quality of family life and the psychosocial adaptation of members. Externalizing behavior became more common among young people, in addition to adverse somatic health, increased consumption of alcohol, and sociopolitical intolerance.

Interestingly, these outcomes were especially common among youth in the West German sample. In a related study, economic hardship and dislocation had the most adverse mental health effect on youth in West Germany (Forkel and Silbereisen 2001). The authors leave the reader without an explanation for this outcome. In any case, one of the larger questions is how reunification altered the transition to adulthood. Juang and Silbereisen (2001) found that East German girls have begun to close the gap with their West German counterparts on rate of family formation. Follow-ups into the late twenties and thirties will be most revealing of the lasting imprint of this dramatic change on lives in this younger cohort.

By thinking about depression cohorts in Germany and the United States, we identify important themes for studies of the life course in time and place (see Giddens 1984). One of the most important is the recognition that "time and place" matter greatly and must be considered together; second, the comparison highlights the value of long-term studies that view lives in context across the full life course, and not just at a point in time.

Dramatic sociopolitical change in Germany marked off distinct cultural phases for the depression cohorts:

- the Weimar republic between the world wars,
- the Nazi mobilization relative to depression hard times,
- the Second World War,
- the postwar hard times, monetary change, and eventual prosperity in West Germany
- the postwar Communist era for young adults in East Germany, compared to West Germany
- and the reunification of the country in the 1990s.

All of these phases differentiated the lives of sixty-year-olds from the 1920s. At the Max Planck-Institute in Berlin, programmatic studies directed by Karl Ulrich Mayer have investigated the social structural and occupational worlds of birth cohorts that extend back to the twenties. But we have much to learn about the life-course effect of the complex changes they have experienced up to the present. Even within a group of Germans of the same age, we should expect substantial variations. In the last quarter of the twentieth century, for example, some German youth were entering the labor market in cities with declining opportunities, such as Bremen, while youth in Munich encountered a very different economic situation marked by abundant opportunities. Heinz and his associates (1998) have been studying this strategic comparison. Similar within-country research options are available in other societies and we shall explore some prime examples.

Within a context of political continuity, American cohorts encountered the prosperity of the 1920s, the economic adversity of the 1930s, the vast mobilization of the war years, and the economic growth of the postwar era. *Children of the Great Depression* (Elder [1974] 1999) traced the impact of economic hardship across these eras, and it examined the impact of World War II, but it did not attempt to capture other contextual changes, such as the emergence of large organizations from the war, or the remarkable economic growth and migration after the war. We now have the data collection technology to obtain such information, such as survey instruments on organizations (Kalleberg 1994), and geographic data on residence from satellite readings. The challenge in longitudinal studies is to assess contextual changes across the life course and their effects. People select themselves into situations, which then shape their lives.

A third theme has to do with trajectories of resilience and their dependence on stable institutions and supportive relationships. Depression cohorts in the United States were often characterized as members of a "lost generation," but our studies typically document a life course of resilience. Military service pulled many youth out of poverty, marriage stabilized their lives, and the booming economy of the postwar era provided an opportunity to move ahead. A great many youth from deprived families managed to rise above their disadvantage—they were resilient. By contrast, there is reason to expect less evidence of resilience among the German cohorts of the 1920s. A larger percentage were wounded or had died in the war, and Germany became a battlefield that led to the destruction of towns and the economy.

This comparison illustrates a key principle of life-course theory, that of historical time and place: *The life course of individuals is embedded in and shaped by the historical times and places they experience over their lifetime.* People are born in a specific historical time, but the meaning of this location depends on the social and cultural measuring of this historical time, whether the 1930s in the United States, England, or Germany. The depression experience varied by ecological settings within these societies. The American West, for example, did not have as prolonged a depression crisis as the eastern region of aging cities.

Every project and longitudinal study is tagged with a distinct historical time and place. But no matter how consequential these social facts are, studies will no doubt continue to be carried out as if they do not exist (see Heinz et al. 1998). As Schaeper, Kühn, and Witzel assert, "Space-blindness is a traditional feature of sociological theory in general and of life-course research in particular . . . and, with few exceptions, space continues to be a neglected category" (1998:61) though there is less reason now for this indifference. Data collection can and often does include information on spatial location and characteristics. The same deficiency could be said today of the neglect of historical time and context, despite the emphasis brought to this perspective by historians and historically oriented sociologists. Theoretical change takes time.

HISTORICAL TIME AND PLACE IN BIRTH COHORTS

As early as the 1850s, demographers were viewing lives from the vantage point of birth cohorts (Sundt [1855] 1980). A surge in births in the past led to corresponding increases in subsequent marriages and births. More recently Richard Easterlin (1980) has stressed the connection between "birth and fortune." In both cases, we are encouraged to believe that birth cohorts are homogeneous on historical and ecological experience. But this account has *no connection* to reality. In fact, birth cohorts may locate people in historical time but they are typically diverse on historical and geographic experience or exposure. Membership in a birth cohort thus represents little more than an initial step toward understanding the impact of historical and ecological circumstances in the lives and life courses of individuals and birth cohorts.

Consider, for example, the Great Proletarian Cultural Revolution in the People's Republic of China, a period that extends from 1966 to 1976. One of the earliest features of this time was Chairman Mao's decision to send coastal urban youth to the countryside for reeducation (Zhou and Hou 1999). Millions of young people from the 1948–1955 birth cohort were pulled out of schools and transported to rural villages all over China. Some youth worked on the farms while others worked in the mines. Those who went to the countryside at the beginning of the revolution spent up to ten years of their lives there, though little is known about where these youth went and for how long. Both factors would make a significant difference in their lives. No study has actually investigated "the journeys" taken by these young people and their influence on their lives.

This change in residence most likely led to delays in marriage, losses in education, and postponements in careers (Gerber and Hout 1995). In June 1966, the government suspended the admission of young people to college and graduate programs for the year. This lasted throughout the Cultural Revolution, effectively denying college graduates access to postgraduate education over a twelve-year period. Two studies (Deng and Treiman 1997; Davis 1992) found that the educational advantages of coming from a privileged family declined abruptly during the Cultural Revolution. A large percentage of the young people who were closed out of graduate education were sent to rural areas to be reeducated in the mines and farms. But the duration of this sent-down experience varied widely from a few years to over a decade. Some disruptions led to the loss of education and marital delays; but other effects may have appeared in worklife and health. The occurrence of these disruptions may well have something to do with the students' destinations, pathways, and unique experiences.

Region of destination and the pathways traveled have not become a target for systematic study as yet, and we have no satisfying record of the daily life of the sent-down youth, apart from scattered diaries. Each of these unknowns has much to contribute to knowledge about how the experience influenced the life course of this cohort. But we know from personal accounts that some of the young people were welcomed to their village while others were treated more harshly.

The life-course impact of the sent-down experience stems from the total configuration of factors. These include their duration of rural experience and their escape route from their rural setting. Were other young people and adults part of this journey? How long did it take and did it lead to higher education in other countries, as was the case for many who settled in the Western world? The sent-down mandate focused on a single birth cohort in the period of youth, and yet it produced widely varied experiences, as far as we know. In any case, the sent-down experience has become a well-known generational line of demarcation in China, just as service in World War II has been for American veterans.

Consider another dramatic example of a cohort and its diverse life experience. Two decades later the Soviet Union broke apart into its component provinces, and in so doing placed the younger cohort of this country in totally different social and political systems. Fortunately, an Estonian sociologist, Mikk Titma (with Tuma, *Paths of a Generation,* 1995) managed to survey this population's students as they were completing secondary school in 1983–1985 across fifteen regions. He then followed their progress across multiple data collections up to the late 1990s. The Soviet Union collapsed after the August 1991 coup, Gorbachev was replaced by Yeltsin, and Russia was established as an independent state.

Yeltsin ended Communist rule and the state's central control of the economy. Drastic reform policies created serious problems. By 1996 the Russian economy was only three-fifths of its size four years earlier (Gerber and Hout 1998). Titma and Tuma (1995) assessed the achievements, expectations, and backgrounds of their young people before the Soviet Union dissolved, and then traced their lives into the extraordinary postcoup changes. One region retained the old command economy of the former Soviet Union (Belarus), while others adopted a market economy (e.g., Latvia, Estonia) or returned to a more primitive rural exchange system (e.g., Tajikistan). The socioeconomic lives of these young people closely resembled the changes of their region of destination in the old Soviet Union. The Estonian cohort is by far the most prosperous, whereas downward trajectories were common among youth from Belarus and the Ukraine.

Despite the profound regional differences in this cohort and widespread instability, Titma and Tuma found that the generation's future was written in large measure by its personal accomplishments, self-assessments, and goals in high school. Transitions tend to "accentuate" individual differences (Caspi and Moffitt 1993), and this study found that academic success and high aspiration were more predictive of subsequent occupational status and income in 1999 than family background. Interestingly, the young men who had become entrepreneurs with hired personnel were most visible in high school through their ambition and high self-appraisal of personal skills in the management of people.

Within this cohort, women outperformed men in education (Tuma and Titma 1998). And the difference led back to plans before secondary school graduation, to the greater effort of girls toward entering a postsecondary school, and to the successful completion of this level of education. This difference is not surprising in a society that opened up worklife opportunities for women, and it is a difference that appears in other Western societies as well. Tuma and Titma speculate that wage differentials for traditional male jobs in the skilled trades may have lured young men away from higher education. They also note that male students in secondary school receive less encouragement to achieve academically, when compared to that experienced by females.

This longitudinal study has just begun to investigate the actual life courses of its secondary school cohort of 1983–1985, and the data collected to date are limited to surveys of the former students. Ethnographies and qualitative interviews are not part of the project. Historical forces assumed a critical role in assigning youth to different social and political ecologies, though we know little about the overall impact of this cohort differentiation. Even so, the internal diversity of regions is too great to provide a precise understanding of the effects of variations in the social ecology. Rural

8

and urban variations need to be considered, along with occupations that mark off the rural areas, such as farmers.

Germany, China, and the dissolution of the former Soviet Union have provided natural experiments that have differentiated the lives of young people who were born at the same time. They demonstrate most compellingly the importance of joining historical facts with spatial location and its potential effect on how changes are experienced. This observation also applies to the comparison of cities or regions within societies.

A CONCLUDING PERSPECTIVE

When Urie Bronfenbrenner directed our attention to the historical times in which we carry out studies, his perspective was extraordinarily novel. For the most part, investigators were not studying the life course nor placing their study members in historical and geographic context. Since then we have experienced a truly remarkable growth of longitudinal studies. This development not only includes the study of young children into the adult years, but also the recognition that a full understanding of human aging requires this kind of design—that comprehensive knowledge of aging requires study that extends from the earliest moments of life across the life span. Aging cannot be fully understood when investigations begin at age fifty or sixty.

This new "age of longitudinal studies" has played an important role in focusing attention on the life course of human development and aging, and on one of its core principles—that of historical time and place. When children are followed from early childhood into adulthood and middle age, the task raises questions about their pathways and the implications of pursuing one path and not another. How lives are lived has significant developmental and aging implications.

Variations of this kind also pose the question of how to view lives through time. The age-graded life course is one response, including a thoughtful consideration of historical and ecological influences. In my brief presentation, I view the life course from this vantage point.

I close by mentioning some challenges we face in this field of study:

1. Historical and geographic influences are typically present in our longitudinal studies, and yet they are often treated as a methodological problem and not as a substantive issue worthy of study. We live in a rapidly changing world. Should we not study what that means for the research in which we are engaged?

2. Historical and geographic influences are not restricted to the early years or the later years. They occur across the life course. More effort to assess them is needed.

3. The mechanisms by which these influences affect lives and human development deserve more attention than they have received. For many years we assumed that influences assessed at a point in time represent the full story of a "social effect," but influences typically *cumulate* over time. This life-course dynamic is discussed but too rarely studied. Genetic influences are part of this story, but I leave such topics for another time.

We do indeed live in exciting times for studies of the life course. Not infrequently, I have felt like the early sociologists at Chicago who literally "ran out of students to study all of the changes taking place in their great city." My hope is that successive generations of social scientists will commit their energies to the impact of these changes, and to the influence of new cohorts on social institutions.

ACKNOWLEDGMENTS

I acknowledge support from the National Institute of Mental Health (MH 00567, MH 57549), the MacArthur Foundation Research Network on Successful Adolescent Development among Youth in High Risk Settings, a grant from the National Institute of Child Health and Human Development to the Carolina Population Center at the University of North Carolina at Chapel Hill (P01-HD31921A), and a Spencer Foundation Senior Scholar Award to Elder.

REFERENCES

Binion, Rudolph. 1976. *Hitler among the Germans.* New York: Elsevier.

Bronfenbrenner, Urie. 1958. "Socialization and Social Class Through Time and Space." Pp. 400–25 in *Readings in Social Psychology,* 3rd ed., edited by E. E. Maccoby, T. M. Newcomb, and E. L. Hartley. New York: Henry Holt.

Campbell, D'Ann. 1984. *Women at War with America: Private Lives in a Patriotic Era.* Cambridge, MA: Harvard University Press.

Caspi, Avshalom and Terrie E. Moffitt. 1993. "When Do Individual Differences Matter? A Paradoxical Theory of Personality Coherence." *Psychological Inquiry* 4:247–71.

Colby, Anne. 1998. "Foreword: Crafting Life-Course Studies." Pp. viii–xii in *Methods of Life Course Research: Qualitative and Quantitative Approaches,* edited by J. Z. Giele and G. H. Elder, Jr. Thousand Oaks, CA: Sage.

Davis, Deborah. 1992. "'Skidding': Downward Mobility among Children of the Maoist Middle Class." *Modern China* 18(4):410–37.

Deng, Zhong and Donald J. Treiman. 1997. "The Impact of the Cultural Revolution on Trends in Educational Attainment in the People's Republic of China." *American Journal of Sociology* 103(2):391–428.

Easterlin, Richard A. 1980. *Birth and Fortune: The Impact of Numbers on Personal Welfare.* New York: Basic.

Elder, Glen H., Jr. 1998a. "The Life Course and Human Development." Pp. 939–91 in *Handbook of Child Psychology,* Volume 1: *Theoretical Models of Human Development,* 5th ed., edited by Richard M. Lerner. General Editor, William Damon. New York: Wiley.

Elder, Glen H., Jr. 1998b. "The Life Course As Developmental Theory." *Child Development* 69(1):1–12.

Elder, Glen H., Jr. [1974] 1999. *Children of the Great Depression: Social Change in Life Experience,* 25th Anniversary Edition. Boulder, CO: Westview.

Elder, Glen H., Jr., and Monica K. Johnson. 2002. "The Life Course and Aging: Challenges, Lessons, and New Directions." Pp. 49–81 in *Invitation to the Life Course: Toward New Understandings of Later Life,* edited by R. A. Settersten, Jr. Amityville, NY: Baywood.

Elder, Glen H., Jr., John Modell, and Ross D. Parke (Eds.). 1993. *Children in Time and Place: Developmental and Historical Insights.* New York: Cambridge University Press.

Forkel, Ines and Rainer K. Silbereisen. 2001. "Family Economic Hardship and Depressed Mood among Adolescents from Former East and West Germany." Pp. 1955–71 in *Families and Development in Childhood and Adolescence,* edited by R. K. Silbereisen and J. Youniss. Thousand Oaks, CA: Sage.

Gerber, Theodore P. and Michael Hout. 1995. "Educational Stratification in Russia During the Soviet Period." *American Journal of Sociology* 101(3):611–60.

Gerber, Theodore P. and Michael Hout. 1998. "More Shock Than Therapy: Market Transition, Employment, and Income in Russia, 1991–1995." *American Journal of Sociology* 104(1):1–50.

Giddens, A. 1984. *The Constitution of Society: Outline of the Theory of Structuration.* Cambridge: Polity.

Giele, Janet A. and Glen H. Elder, Jr. (Eds.). 1998. *Methods of Life Course Research: Qualitative and Quantitative Approaches.* Thousand Oaks, CA: Sage.

Grunberger, Richard. 1966. *The Twelve-Year Reich: A Social History of Nazi Germany, 1933–1945.* Garden City, NY: Doubleday.

Heinz, Walter R., Udo Kelle, Andreas Witzel, and Jens Zinn. 1998. "Vocational Training and Career Development in Germany: Results from a Longitudinal Study." *International Journal of Behavioral Development* 22(1):77–101.

Jahoda, Marie, Paul F. Lazarsfeld, and Hans Zeisel. 1971. *Marienthal.* Chicago: Aldine.

Juang, Linda, Matthias Reitzle, and Rainer K. Silbereisen. 2000. "The Adaptability of Transitions to Adulthood under Social Change: The Case of German Unification." *European Review of Applied Psychology* 50(2):275–82.

Juang, Linda P. and Rainer K. Silbereisen. 2001. "Family Transitions for Young Adult Women in the Context of a Changed Germany." Pp. 1899–1917 in *Families and Development in Childhood and Adolescence,* edited by R. K. Silbereisen and J. Youniss. Thousand Oaks, CA: Sage.

Kalleberg, Arne L. 1994. "Studying Employers and Their Employees: Comparative Approaches." *Acta Sociologica* 37:223–29.

Lerner, Richard M. 2002. *Concepts and Theories of Human Development,* 3rd ed. Mahwah, NJ: Erlbaum.

Mayer, Karl U. 1988. "German Survivors of World War II: The Impact on the Life Course of the Collective Experience of Birth Cohorts." Pp. 229–46 in *Social Change and the Life Course, Volume I: Social Structures and Human Lives,* edited by M. White Riley (in association with B. J. Huber and B. B. Hess). American Sociological Association Presidential Series. Newbury Park, CA: Sage.

Mayer, Karl U. and Johannes Huinink. 1990. "Age, Period, and Cohort in the Study of the Life Course: A Comparison of Classical A-P-C Analysis with Event History Analysis or Farewell to Lexis?" Pp. 211–32 in *Data Quality in Longitudinal Research,* edited by D. Magnusson and L. R. Bergman. New York: Cambridge University Press.

Mayer, Karl U. and Nancy B. Tuma (Eds.). 1990. *Event History Analysis in Life-Course Research.* Madison: University of Wisconsin Press.

Noack, Peter, Bärbel Kracke, Elke Wild, and Manfred Hofer. 2001. "Subjective Experiences of Social Change in East and West Germany." Pp. 1798–1817 in *Families and Development in Childhood and Adolescence,* edited by R. K. Silbereisen and J. Youniss. Thousand Oaks, CA: Sage.

Schaeper, Hildegard, Thomas Kühn, and Andreas Witzel. 1998. "The Transition from Vocational Training to Employment in Germany: Does Region Matter?" Pp. 61–83 in *Restructuring Work and the Life Course,* edited by V. W. Marshall, W. R. Heinz, H. Krüger, and A. Verma. Toronto: University of Toronto Press.

Schoenbaum, David. 1971. *Hitler's Social Revolution: Class and Status in Nazi Germany, 1933–1939.* New York: Holt, Rinehart and Winston.

Settersten, Richard A., Jr. 1999. *Lives in Time and Place: The Problems and Promises of Developmental Science.* Society and Aging Series. Amityville, NY: Baywood.

Sundt, Eilert. [1855] 1980. *On Marriage in Norway* (translated by Michael Drake). New York: Cambridge University Press.

Titma, Mikk and Nancy Tuma. 1995. *Paths of a Generation: A Comparative Longitudinal Study of Young Adults in the Former Soviet Union.* Stanford, CA: Stanford University; Tallinn, Estonia: Center for Social Research in Eastern Europe.

Tuma, Nancy B. and Mikk Titma. 1998. *Educational Attainment in the Former Soviet Union: Why Women Outdid Men.* Stanford, CA: Stanford University; Tallinn, Estonia: Center for Social Research in Eastern Europe.

Vondracek, Fred W., Matthias Reitzle, and Rainer K. Silbereisen. 1999. "The Influence of Changing Contexts and Historical Time on the Timing of Initial Vocational Choices." Pp. 151–69 in *Growing Up in Times of Social Change,* edited by R. K. Silbereisen and A. von Eye. Hawthorne, NY: Walter de Gruyter.

Weymann, Ansgar, Reinhold Sackmann, and Matthias Wingens. 1999. "Social Change and the Life Course in East Germany: A Cohort Approach to Inequalities." *International Journal of Sociology and Social Policy* 19:(9/10/11):90–114. Special edition, *Understanding Social Inequality,* edited by R. M. Blackburn.

Young, Copeland H., Kristen L. Savola, and Erin Phelps. 1991. *Inventory of Longitudinal Studies in the Social Sciences.* Newbury Park, CA: Sage.

Zhou, Xueguang and Liren Hou. 1999. "Children of the Cultural Revolution: The State and the Life Course in the People's Republic of China." *American Sociological Review* 64(1):12–36.

| 4 |

Combining Methods in Life-Course Research: A Mixed Blessing?

Walter R. Heinz

INTRODUCTION

The progress of life-course research has been hampered by a false dichotomy between quantitative and qualitative approaches. As Silverman (1998) observes, in the social sciences there is a general tendency to contrast the analytical and interpretative perspectives, a tradition that tends to erect a fence between the causal or correlative explanation and the context-related understanding of social action. Solid, reliable, and valid data collection and analysis are associated with the sampling procedures and statistical tools of the quantitative framework, while the qualitative approaches are regarded as a collection of case-based, nonrepresentative methods, which are bound to lead to unfounded generalizations (cf. Bryman 1988).

Although there are examples of research that compare case-based data with survey data and the theory-generating "grounded theory approach" (Glaser and Strauss 1967; Strauss and Corbin 1990), there has been little advancement in the combination of population-based and case-oriented procedures in social research.

There is a special feature of the life course, its emergence from biographical actions and its embeddedness in social time and space, which calls for a rapprochement between the two research methodologies, which have been separated for much too long: quantitative population-oriented life-course studies and qualitative case-oriented biography studies. Both share the task of understanding the regularities and contingencies of the modern life course, the extent to which it is influenced by the restructuring of

society and how individuals, confronted with changing, short-term opportunities and constraints adapt to flexible living and working arrangements
by biographical decisions (cf. Heinz 2001).

EXPECTATIONS CONCERNING THE JOINING OF METHODS

Quantitative and qualitative researchers agree that the life course is a self-
referential process, a process that connects commitments stemming from
the individual's past decisions with the structural conditions and action
contexts of the present and the options of the future (see, e.g., Mayer 2000;
Kohli 1991). In view of an increasing destandardization of the life course,
the flexibilization of employment and marriage relations, both the event
history of cohorts and the decision-making and stock-taking criteria of
individuals are becoming an essential topic of life-course analysis. When
individuals' decisions and outcomes can no longer be explained by reference to the standard variables like age, gender, social class, or cultural
milieu, it becomes mandatory to analyze the consequences of changing
social contexts for the timing and duration of biographical transitions and
life-course sequences on the level of populations as well as on the level of
cases.

In order to come to terms with the increasing complexity of life-course
transitions and sequences, of the interrelations between biographies
within and between generations, and of the interactions between institutions and individuals, data collection and analysis must draw on the
respective strengths of quantitative and qualitative approaches instead of
pointing at each other's weaknesses—without, however, turning to a
mixed bag of methods.

While longitudinal quantitative life-course research focuses on the
macrosocial dimensions of the timing and sequencing of life events that
influence the social-status configurations of cohort members, it has difficulty illuminating the individuals' decision-making processes concerning
pathways, opportunities, and institutionally defined options. While qualitative life-history research focuses on the biography as a microsocial phenomenon by reconstructing the individuals' reasons for life plans,
decisions, and assessments of consequences in the context of their life
world, it cannot claim that its results are valid beyond the usually small
number of cases.

For instance, when we want to understand the age differences in child
birth and family formation in various cohorts, we need to find out about
the action frames that generate variations in individual meanings of
postsecondary education, economic independence, motherhood and
fatherhood, and personal autonomy. Knowing about the case-specific

configurations of social circumstances, furthermore, we get a better understanding of the quantitative relationships between social structural variables and the timing of parenthood because we are illuminating the extent
to which there is a loose coupling between social structure and biographical transitions (cf. Elder and O'Rand 1995). Thus, the combination of quantitative and qualitative methods in a longitudinal research design offers
good prospects for capturing the complex interrelationships of historical
circumstances, social location, and personal agency that are the core
dimensions which shape and direct the life paths of individuals (cf. Giele
and Elder 1998).

At first sight it seems that quantitative longitudinal approaches have
the advantage of providing data that are generalizable to populations,
cohorts, and age groups. Quantitative longitudinal studies have made
impressive progress during the last two decades in two directions. In
respect to data analysis, cohort studies, event-history analysis, sequence-
pattern analysis, and optimal matching are successful in capturing the
time dynamics of entire life trajectories with the focus on patterns of transition sequences. Their strength lies in documenting structural effects on
the life course in the sense of social bookkeeping or accounting for the
changing relationships between structural conditions and individual
behavior on the aggregate level. The statistical modeling conducted in the
framework of event-history analysis (cf. Blossfeld and Rohwer 1995) provides results that indicate which structural variables influence the timing
of life events. Such results are at least incomplete if one looks for explanations that have to take into account the actor's perspective. Here the need
for longitudinal qualitative data becomes obvious because they are the
basis for reconstructing the different meanings that life events and transitions have in subsets of a population. As I shall argue, interpretative analysis of such data, however, should not primarily aim for condensed or thick
descriptions of cases, but for theoretically guided or conceptually focused
case comparisons and systematically constructed typologies, which
improve our understanding of the variety of individually meaningful
linkages between segments of life or transitions, e.g., concerning family
life and employment (cf. Schaeper and Falk, Chapter 7 in this volume).

Qualitative life history or biography research seems to have made comparatively less visible progress. Though it has been recognized as an
important complement to life event and trajectory studies, e.g., by Giele
and Elder (1998), it has not yet become a steady companion and resides at
the margins of mainstream life-course research.

A main reason for this imbalance is the limitations concerning generalizations and causal explanations that can be derived from biographical
data. It is widely assumed that narratives only tell case-specific stories,
while variables can claim an analytical superiority because they represent

data that can be put to statistical modeling. Lieberson (1992), for instance, argues that applying the logic of causal analysis to small-N samples will lead to deterministic generalizations. This may hold for impatient and ad hoc procedures of qualitative data analysis, but must not occur when longitudinal studies manage to combine the strength of the two methodologies—the way in which the examples given below proceeded. The comparison and analysis of individual cases has recently been recommended by K. U. Mayer, a proponent of the standard event-history approach, who suggests: "By bringing the actors or rather the complexities of human lives back in, longitudinal studies could be expected to provide a bridge between the zealots of quantitative analysis and qualitative biographical studies" (2000:264).

There are signs of bringing biography from the actors' perspectives back in, for instance, by using "person-centered methods" in the study of aging (Singer and Ryff 2001) or by relating cases and biographies in research about organizations and markets (Heimer 2001). A flexible integration or pooling of evidence from standardized-quantitative and narrative-qualitative sources about the same group of people provides insights into the pathways and outcomes in life-course transitions, e.g., "on cumulative adversity relative to advantage and . . . on managing multiple challenges over the life course" (Singer and Ryff 2001:45). Narratives can be compiled into a life story from interview texts by the researchers, who start with coding interview texts according to categories serving as organizing principles, or such a story can be constructed from survey data in order to better comprehend how a respondent's life developed over time. This procedure provides hints about how life segments like social origin, education, and family impact on the timing and level of first employment or pathways with various life-course outcomes.

The combination of narratives and standard survey data has also been shown to be useful for longitudinal studies of subgroups in career pathways with diverse employment outcomes. Singer and Ryff (ibid.:55) suggest "enriched longitudinal subsamples" for which pathways can be constructed. Their examples document a combination of bottom-up and top-down analytical strategies, "for partitioning a heterogeneous population of individuals into progressively more homogeneous subgroups" (ibid.:59). They conclude from their experiences in the study of health and aging that "much of the subtlety about lives through time is revealed through focused interviews, while broader socio-demographic characteristics and facets of lives . . . are measurable with structured longitudinal surveys. It is still relatively rare to find both kinds of evidence on the same population in the study of life histories" (ibid.:62). However, there are recent advances in assembling quantitative and qualitative data, which I will turn to below, that have not been recognized in the North American life-course research community.

Another example that meets the added value that we expect from combining methods is Heimer's (2001) approach, which deals with cases and biographies in order to understand variations in routinized practices of institutions and markets: Cases are seen as targets of standard procedures, biographies as instances that do not fit easily into the scripts of institutions. Heimer argues (ibid.:49) that "particular tasks require mixes of case and biographical analysis" and suggests analyzing institutional procedures from both the perspectives of social category (population) membership and individual biographies. The latter offer insights for explaining the relationship between routine casework and the handling of unique cases, "how people react differently to cases and biographies in bureaucracies, legal settings, and markets" (ibid.:48).

From her exploration, it is possible to draw an analogy to the research procedures in our field. We localize similar and different cases in a sample in order to arrive at conclusions that are more or less anchored in routine (statistical) procedures. Individualized procedures are required to supply a coherent account of the past and present experiences of individual cases. Heimer (ibid.) argues that the coherence of a life story comes from the analysis of biography rather than an analysis of similar cases because the conceptual fabric can be reconstructed from the person's narration. For this kind of analysis, firsthand information is most important—that is, conversations in the elaborated sense of narratives, which are basic for life-course studies. Heimer's (ibid.) account highlights that institutional procedures strongly influence the meaning of life events, e.g., graduation, while life histories "support claims about identity and relationships and mark transitions. . . . In biographical analyses, documents supply the analytic context by fashioning an account of a person's past and hinting at an extended future; in case analysis, in contrast, the function of documents is to structure comparisons across case" (ibid.:72–73). As shown below, there is also the option to conduct biographical analysis with cases selected from longitudinal samples that supply the structural context.

CRAFTING CASES IN LIFE-COURSE RESEARCH

Andrew Abbott has directed our attention to the possibility of bridging the small- and large-N divide by giving a closer look at the "case" as a core unit of life-course studies: "We have all grown accustomed to think in either the causality-variables-population-analytic way or the plot-events-case-narrative way. We have a hard time imagining what it means to generalize

narratives" (1992:79). I suggest that we must not resign when being confronted with the challenge of connecting these two kinds of life-course
research because the experiences that were collected over more than a
decade in our collaborative research center on social risks and status passages in the life course demonstrate that guidelines for a sequential combination of population-variables and case-narrative methods are available.

In his introduction to a book with the deceivingly simple title *What Is a
Case?* (Ragin and Becker 1992), Charles Ragin (1992) defines cases as "comparable instances of some general phenomenon." Ragin, much like Abbott,
argues that the task of bringing greater richness to social research requires
the use of the case as a basic unit for linking quantitative and qualitative
approaches. In his comparative research methodology, cases take the center stage because they do not disembody and obscure the data, a defect that
he sees as typical of variable-oriented research, for instance in quantitative
cross-national studies. He suggests classifying the variants of case-based
research according to the dimensions empirical/theoretical and spe-
cific/general. This leads to four conceptions of what cases are: cases are
found, cases are objects, cases are made, and cases are conventions.

In our approach, cases are located in social time and institutional space,
which define life-course transitions and event sequences. Thus, our cases
are neither objects nor conventions, and they are not just found, they are
constructed at the intersection of biography, institutional regulations, and
opportunity structures. A good example for another strategy of reasoning
from organizations as cases is Victor Marshall's (1999) study of an aging
workforce in the context of seven North American corporations.

Combining the population-variable and the case-narrative strategy
becomes more and more reasonable in view of social changes that have
turned the continuous, careerlike life course into individualized and flexible biographies. Again, K. U. Mayer can be presented as a witness: "Some
might even claim that the present-day complexities defy even the monthly
fine-grained filters of life-course studies and can only be fully brought to
light in semi-observation and biographical studies" (2000:269). In our
understanding, the life course has become a flexible, time-dependent
social configuration that is co-constructed by individuals and institutions,
a configuration that evolves in a loosely coupled relationship between
social structure and personal agency. Our attempt to combine quantitative
and qualitative methods is not primarily motivated by a critique of the
standard practice of variable-oriented research or the speculative generalizations of case-based studies, but by the objectives of a research program:
status passages and risks in the life course—how individual action and
institutional regulations are interrelated over time. This called for an
approach that manages to illuminate and at least substantively explain the
kinds and outcomes of interactions of personal agency, social contexts, and

institutions at life-course transitions. We assume that the life course is constructed by active and self-reflexive actors in constraining and enabling social contexts, by actors who do not necessarily react rationally to opportunities and risks, but assess life events and transitions in terms of their biographical past and future plans. This contrasts with conventional one-method studies, be it population- or case-based; they share the drawback that the relationships between variables or between narrated events must be (re)constructed without reference to each other; we regard respondents as agents-in-contexts, who construct and reflect about transitions and events, and not just as sources of answers coded as variables. Thereby we correct the conventional approach, which assumes that respondents "follow the same narrative, which is couched as a narrative of acting variables, not of acting individuals" (Abbott 1992:63). In contrast to this assumption, we argue like Abbott, who maintains that "cases may . . . do or endure a wide variety of things, each of which may be seen as an event arising either in agency (what they do) or in structure (what they endure)" (ibid.:64). Consequently, in biographical narratives events are arranged across time in a story that includes motives, reasons, gains and losses, and references to options and constraints that cannot easily be compressed into variables and ordered by numbers, but must be coded according to meaningful categories (cf. Dey 1999).

Coding narrative interviews is not a mechanical process, but a transformation of data to another level of abstraction by comparative reasoning which presupposes that the researcher has both substantive and theoretical knowledge. While in the population-variables approach continuous plots tend to be constructed that are focused on the relationships between variables, the narrative procedure regards cases as being engaged in social contexts that are promoting or constraining individual actions. This raises the question whether narratives contain explanations for the social processes that are involved in shaping a person's life course. If we get the person's account about aspirations/expectations, circumstances, and events that co-occurred in the context of a transition, we can reconstruct his or her explanation of life-course outcomes. The researcher's plot that summarizes or condenses the actor's arrangement with opportunities and constraints, for example, at turning points of the life course, is based on the actor's narration. But the researcher's reconstruction of the narrative makes sociological sense only in comparison with other cases from the same population (cf. Strauss and Corbin 1990; Dey 1999). Such a comparative approach avoids a simplified or misleading modeling of life courses as either individualized or standardized transition sequences stated as continuous plots—one without an actor, the other without a context—and sensitizes the researcher to explore continuity and discontinuity from both an event sequence or pattern and a life history or biographical perspective.

Data collection and analysis of the social contexts and temporal dynamics of life-course transitions then develop out of what Abbott (1992:68) calls "multicase narratives." Such a database allows us to empirically ground and systematically elaborate concepts that illuminate the social embeddedness of biographies, like institutionalization, sequencing, and interrelations of life courses. These processes can be analyzed as instances of microtransformations across time on the biographical level as well as of macrochanges on the social-structural level.

In our research program, we had the opportunity to set up large-N and subsequently small-N panels and to develop a comparative process analysis using both population-variable and narrative-case data. This procedure led to a stepwise systematic generalization of heuristic concepts, which developed from confronting statistical and interpretative results over time, a process of checks and balances that is only possible with both quantitative and qualitative longitudinal data.

Thus, we were engaged in a research process that Ragin (1992) calls "casing," in order to link assumptions with evidence from two data sources that provide material for theoretical reasoning about the ways social structure and transitions as well as sequences of life events are interrelated and how actors' accounts are related to enabling and constraining social circumstances. Our task thus was to inspect quantitative and qualitative evidence by comparing cases in order to clarify or specify the extent to which a loose coupling between social structure and the life course is articulated in biographies.

Our research concerned the life course as an event history and as a biographical accomplishment, embedded in an agenda that was focused at the changes of transition patterns in regard to the institutions of family, education, work, and social security across the postindustrial life course in Germany. The life-course regimes of Anglo-American and Scandinavian societies served as comparative reference frames.

In order to narrow or focus this very general question, a dozen longitudinal studies were set up around 1988, each looking at crucial transitions, institutions, and interrelations in the fields of education and training, occupations and careers, occupation and deviance, occupation and gender, household dynamics, health and social security, poverty and the welfare state. This narrowing of the empirical focus went hand in hand with setting up panel studies that were targeted at significant populations, institutional contexts, and turning points or status transitions in the life course. This created different lenses through which the changing life course could be viewed. Each study developed its substantively grounded conceptual systematization, focusing on the triangle of actors, social opportunity contexts, and institutions over time.

Though Ragin's (2000) "fuzzy-set social science" program does not explicitly include longitudinal research designs, his suggestions to bridge the gap between the large- and the small-N camps are an ex-post support for our empirically grounded procedures. His plea for a diversity-oriented and comparative case-study approach suggests a methodological foundation for the way our research program succeeded in combining methods and process-oriented data analysis.

A fuzzy set is empirically grounded and constructed with reference to theoretical and substantive knowledge. In contrast to the conventional approach, cases are not regarded as just a source of variables, but as context-related social configurations. This is exactly the understanding of the sequential combination of methods that were developed in our research program for documenting and analyzing how cases in populations or cohorts change their status configurations and biographical action strategies over time. This presupposes substantive background knowledge of the life histories of cases, their institutional references and their opportunity contexts. We attempted to reach a compromise between insight or depth and a bird's-eye view or breadth in order to take advantage of the respective strengths of the quantitative-population and the qualitative-case approaches. Case-based data were used for discovering and generalizing biographical action patterns characteristic for the social configurations that represented a population. Confidence about the distribution of action types or decision patterns in a population or the generality of conclusions from case comparisons was sought by analyzing data from our population panels.

THE INTEGRATIVE PANEL DESIGN

The studies in our research program were based on theoretically strategic samples and a longitudinal design that permitted the assembly of standardized and narrative data in a synchronized sequence of a dialogue between quantitative and interpretative results. This program of an "integrative panel design" and its application is presented in much detail in a German publication (Kluge and Kelle 2001). Here, some examples are presented that document advantages of mixing methods on a more general level.

There are five longitudinal studies in the research program that explicitly combined standardized population panels with narrative case panels (we called them macro- and micropanels), with up to five waves each between 1989 and 2000. One study was designed as a retrospective life-history study about women and couples from three cohorts (cf. Born's and Krüger's contributions, Chapters 13 and 2, respectively, in this volume), one as a study of social assistance careers of two cohorts (cf. Leisering and Leibfried 1999), and three as prospective panel studies with youth and young adults in transition to employment and in employment careers, respectively (Sackmann and Wingens, Chapter 5 in this volume; Heinz 1999).

The guiding principle was to open observation windows that covered several years in order to pick up continuity and change in opportunity contexts, institutional regulations, and linked lives before, during, and after crucial and extended transitions. These transitions concerned labor-market entry, balancing of employment and family life, staying in or escaping from welfare dependency, pathways between education, training, employment, and also deviant behavior. Based on alternating between panels of surveys and case interviews, the research teams collected data about the social circumstances and outcomes of status sequences, about reasons why individuals initiated or postponed transitions, switched pathways, or responded to events that restructured their social contexts.

The interweaving of macro- and micropanels over time allowed internal validity checks by comparing answers to similar questions and by confronting earlier with later narrations about comparable themes or issues, e.g., occupational preferences, family plans, or the division of labor between a couple. It was also possible to systematically check whether generalizations building on qualitative observations would hold up in the analyses of standardized data, e.g., the distribution and frequency of types of coping or modes of biographical action vis-à-vis changing occupational opportunities. This procedure followed Ragin's recent recommendation:

> Accumulated case-based knowledge could be used to evaluate the results of large-N variable-oriented studies of cross-case patterns. [However] . . . this comparison of results happens only occasionally . . . because the two ways of generating knowledge produce findings that are often incompatible and sometimes contradictory.(2000, 30)

We developed two main promising ways of combining methods of data collection: a standardized macropanel as a sampling frame for a narrative micropanel, and an integrative panel design, where a series of surveys and narrative interviews follow each other (see Figure 4.1).

When analyzing the results of applying integrated methods, data can complement each other; they can be used for reciprocal validation, but they may also lead to divergent conclusions. Complementary results can fill gaps in event history and optimal matching analyses of quantitative longitudinal data. For instance, the different personal meanings of entry into, duration of, and exit from social assistance careers can contribute to unexplained variance in the timing of the escape from social welfare institutions.

Comparisons of results were facilitated across data collected with different methods because we managed to overcome the usual division of labor between the quantitative and qualitative experts to a certain degree:

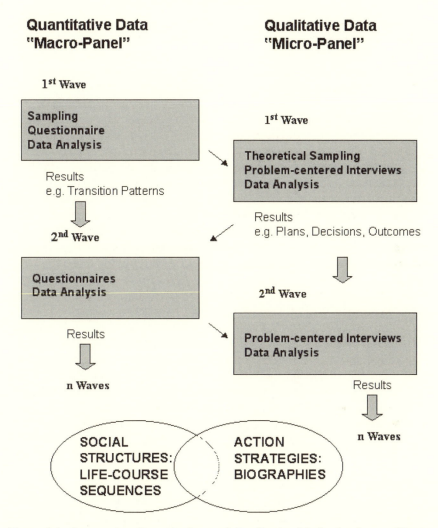

Figure 4.1 Integrating Quantitative and Qualitative Methods. *Source:* Kluge (2001:43).

Covariationists (relying on large-*N*) and configurationalists (trusting small-*N*) at the minimum listened to and learned from each other; in a few cases, however, these two styles of research were combined in one researcher. Therefore, we succeeded in finding a path to link analytic-population-centered with narrative-case-based data in a dialogue within and between our research teams. It became evident that this procedure required not only mutual openness, but also substantive knowledge about the living contexts of our panel populations in order to localize the cases for narrative interviews in comparable opportunity structures and transition pathways.

In practice, changes in the social contexts and of the biographies of cases were recorded both in an interpretative and an event-history or sequence analysis. This allowed for a flexible, process-related elaboration of heuristic concepts and their reciprocal clarification via computer-assisted (NUD-IST-software) multistage coding procedures, cluster and sequence analysis. Most of the research program's panels started with the focus on documenting changes in the structure of risks and options that persons were confronted with in status transitions, and our methodology provided the means for referring different life-course sequences to the relationships between individual decisions, opportunities, and institutionalized regulations concerning pathways. The available paths and the pathways selected in turn were documented both with macro- and micropanel data in order to have a sound basis for comparing location of cases in the social structure.

EXAMPLES FROM THE CRAFT SHOP

According to our experiences in studying the life course, results stemming from the qualitative and quantitative panels may *converge* and thus mutually support conclusions about the interaction of institutional gatekeeping and the individual's decisions concerning the timing and the duration of transitions in different opportunity contexts. Results from the macro- and micropanels, however, may *complement* each other in respect to observations about actors' biographies, social contexts, and institutional regulations, but they also may turn out to be *inconsistent*. Most interesting is an inconsistent constellation, which should not arouse defensive mechanisms but efforts to find out why this has occurred.

As indicated above, the advantage of illuminating the consequences of social change on female and male life-course patterns by using standardized and narrative data lies in improving our knowledge about the social structure and personal meaning of sequences, interrelations, and institutions that contribute to the shape of the life course. This substantive and theoretical framework developed in close collaboration with our integrated panel approach.

Concerning qualitative sampling, a combination of Glaser and Strauss's (1967; Strauss and Corbin 1990) "theoretical sampling" of similar and contrasting cases with criteria that define relevant combinations of properties (e.g., gender, level of education, occupation, labor-market region) was useful for obtaining a maximal variation of cases. Furthermore, because we had the results of standardized macropanels at our disposal, it was possible to select cases according to transition patterns and their location in the social structure: "The quantitative study serves to strategically place the qualitative sample by providing the topography of the structural conditions of the action space in question" (Kluge 2001:48).

Some examples will highlight different aspects of the integrated panel design: The study on social integration risks of educationally disadvantaged youth (Schumann 2003) shows how a well-defined sample of cases ($n = 60$) can be selected from a macrosample ($n = 732$) in order to represent a set of criteria or configurations consisting of gender, school-leaving status, and kind of training with an oversampling of cases that were expected to experience severe transition problems. A similar strategy was used in order to study pathways into employment over a period of eight years (cf. Heinz, Kelle, Witzel, and Zinn 1998), where young skilled workers ($n = 2230$) were sampled from six major occupations in a booming (Munich) and a declining (Bremen) regional labor market, in order to cover the variance of pathways within the occupational transition sequences. The microsample ($n = 91$) was selected according to case configurations consisting of gender, level of education, occupation, employment opportunities, and transition patterns from school to vocational education and training.

The following examples will illustrate ways of responding to the most challenging issue that may arise from combining methods: when results are inconsistent or contradict each other.

Survey research on women's life courses tends to find continuous patterns of transitions between family and employment. A closer look, which used quantitative and qualitative methods, revealed more discontinuity even for women who entered the labor market in Germany after the Second World War (Krüger 2001; see also Krüger, Chapter 2 in this volume). This retrospective life-history study followed a design of stepwise sampling that allowed the examination of structural dynamics as well as biographical self-reports of three cohorts of women. Since the study focused on the life-course consequences of occupational qualifications, only women with skilled worker's status were included. Looking back at their life courses, their biographical narrations referred to specific configurations of events, durations, and sequences of status positions in the separate worlds of family life and employment. By applying sequence-analytic strategies (Abbott 1995), the variety of individual sequences was reduced to a smaller number of patterns, guided by ideal types of different trajectories concerning paid and family work. Each case was then evaluated by comparing it with one of the ideal patterns. Thus, the selection of cases was finally based on different life-course patterns in a holistic sense, and not on an aggregation or combination of variables. This procedure prepared the step from the macrosample to a well-defined sample of cases who participated in narrative (problem-centered) interviews (Witzel 2000).

This study is an excellent example of the way standardized data can be put to use for structuring problem-centered, narrative interviews. It also documents pitfalls of relying on either population-analytic or narrative-case data. The researchers argue that aggregate data tend to hide the volatility of women's life courses because they produce "illusionary phase models." Pitfalls of another kind were related to narrative data. In the problem-centered interviews, women did not connect their experiences of discontinuous employment with the gendered structure of the labor market, but rather attributed discontinuity to their husbands' traditional views of the division of labor between domestic and paid work. Thus, through the combination of narrated life-history data and population-variables data it was possible to arrive at a convincing solution for discrepant results.

Another example for clarifying inconsistent results comes from the Weymann (1999) study on education-to-employment transitions in the former German Democratic Republic. The macropanel data documented that the job entry process took place according to the guidelines of centralized educational and work allocation institutions of the state. This seemed to support the notion of a highly controlled life-course regime and a restricted scope for individual choice. However, a series of problem-centered interviews occasioned the research team to reconsider their conclusions (cf. Wingens 1999): the case-based narratives pointed to a strategic arrangement. The graduates, after having built contacts with firms and negotiated their transition, used the formal procedures of the bureaucratic distribution system for legitimizing their career plans. This example shows that inconsistent results can promote the discovery of a multilayered social process that consists of balancing arrangements between institutional regulation and personal agency/autonomy of action. It also teaches us that inconsistent observations call for theoretical reformulations, in this instance concerning the role of an institution as being less an agency of control than one of ex-post legitimation.

Finally, an example that shows that quantitative longitudinal data can be a source for checking a qualitative typology that distinguishes between several modes of biographical action. This typology was translated from the small-N panel into a standardized version and validated with the large-N panel. In a job-entry study (Heinz et al., 1998) young adults' aspirations, action orientations, and evaluations of decision outcomes concerning employment and family formation were collected over a period of six years. Problem-centered interviews with ninety-one cases, which were selected from the macrosample of skilled workers in their early career years, were systematically analyzed in order to construct a typology from a property space consisting of criteria such as job security, income, skills, company loyalty, and career advancement. The resulting typology of biographical action modes consists of six configurations, which allowed us to assign all cases. Because we wanted to find out whether the relationships found between job opportunities, institutional guidelines, and the various biographical modes in the small-N sample would also hold up in the population panel, we reconstructed the dimensions and properties of the typology as items for inclusion into our fourth and last large-N–panel wave. Cluster analysis produced a partial convergence, which could be used to validate and generalize the relationships between the biographical modes, gender, and occupation. However, about a third of the respondents could not be assigned to the respective cluster or biographical mode. This partial divergence led to a systematic search for explaining the difference between case-based and variable-centered generalizations. It is likely that changes in employment contexts between the waves have led to modifications in biographical orientations. There is also the possibility that differences in the construction of a case-based and a variable-driven typology as well as differences between the construction of a holistic typology and a cluster analysis are generating discrepant results.

CONCLUSIONS

These examples, in my judgment, provide evidence that a rapprochement between the qualitative and quantitative research traditions has become possible not just as a vision but in research practice, despite statements to the contrary (cf. Mayer 2000:272). The life-course research program described can be highlighted by the following four principles:

1. In contrast to the traditional notion of using qualitative methods in an exploratory way in order to discover hypotheses that must be tested in standardized surveys and statistically modeled, the integrative panel design consists of alternating rounds of population-based surveys and case-based interviews. In longitudinal life-course studies, micro- or small-N samples should be constructed from preceding standardized macro- or large-N samples in order to interrelate sequence analysis of life events and transitions with case comparisons concerning individual actor's reasons, decisions, and assessments of outcomes.

2. Relating empirical data from quantitative and qualitative sources to each other is not a mechanical procedure. It depends on the conceptual framework and the research team's substantive background knowledge. Arriving at explanations of why results are convergent, complementary, or divergent still depends thus on what C. Wright Mills (1959) once called the "sociological imagination." This imagination, however, must be guided

and improved by a process of mutual validation, which can be promoted by alternating between interpreting case-based narratives and analyzing population-based sequences.

3. Based on the research program's experiences, methodological rules for integrating multisource results in life-course studies were summarized by Kelle and Erzberger (2001) in their discussion of the triangulation metaphor, although they warn against following these rules like a cookbook. They argue that there is no single model for integrating methods that would fit all studies which combine qualitative and quantitative methods. Depending on topic and research questions, results can be used to check for complementarity or for reciprocal validation.

4. Returning to the title of this chapter, I put forward that not just the mixing, but the sequential integration of standardized and narrative procedures is a promising way to create a dialogue between quantitative and qualitative analyses, a dialogue that enriches our insights about how structure and agency, opportunities, and restrictions on the one hand, and kinds of biographical self-management on the other hand are connected over the life course.

REFERENCES

Abbott, Andrew. 1992. "What Do Cases Do? Some Notes on Activity in Sociological Analysis." Pp. 53–82 in *What Is a Case? Exploring the Foundations of Social Inquiry*, edited by C. C. Ragin and H. S. Becker. New York: Cambridge University Press.

Abbott, Andrew. 1995. "Sequence Analysis: New Methods for Old Ideas." *Annual Review of Sociology* 21:93–113.

Blossfeld, Hans-Peter and Götz Rohwer. 1995. *Techniques of Event-History Modeling*. Mahwah, NJ: Lawrence Erlbaum.

Bryman, Alan. 1988. *Quantity and Quality in Social Research*. London: Unwin Hyman.

Dey, Ian. 1999. *Grounding Grounded Theory. Guidelines for Qualitative Inquiry*. San Diego: Academic Press.

Elder, Glen H., Jr., and Angela O'Rand. 1995. "Adult Lives in a Changing Society." Pp. 452–75 in *Sociological Perspectives on Social Psychology*, edited by K. S. Cook, G. A. Fine, and J. S. House. Needham Heights, MA: Allyn and Bacon.

Giele, Janet Z. and Glen H. Elder, Jr. (Eds.). 1998. *Methods of Life-Course Research. Qualitative and Quantitative Approaches*. Thousand Oaks, CA: Sage.

Glaser, Barney G. and Anselm L. Strauss. 1967. *The Discovery of Grounded Theory: Strategies for Qualitative Research*. Chicago: Aldine.

Heimer, Carol A. 2001. "Cases and Biographies: An Essay on Routinization and the Nature of Comparison." *Annual Review of Sociology* 27:47–76.

Heinz, Walter R. (Ed.) 1999. *From Education to Work: Cross-National Perspectives*. New York: Cambridge University Press.

Heinz, Walter R. 2001. "Work and the Life Course: A Cosmopolitan-Local Perspective." Pp. 3–22 in *Restructuring Work and the Life Course*, edited by V. W. Marshall, W. R. Heinz, H. Krüger, and A. Verma. Toronto: University of Toronto Press.

Heinz, Walter R., Udo Kelle, Andreas Witzel, and Jens Zinn. 1998. "Vocational Training and Career Development in Germany: Results from a Longitudinal Study." *International Journal of Behavioral Development* 22(1):77–101.

Kelle, Udo and Christian Erzberger. 2001. "Die Integration qualitativer und quantitativer Forschungsergebnisse." Pp. 89–133 in *Methodeninnovation in der Lebenslaufforschung*, edited by S. Kluge and U. Kelle. Weinheim/Munich: Juventa.

Kluge, Susann. 2001. "Strategien zur Integration qualitativer und quantitativer Erhebungs- und Auswertungsverfahren. Ein methodischer und methodologischer Bericht aus dem Sonderforschungsbereich 186 'Statuspassagen und Risikolagen im Lebensverlauf.'" Pp. 37–88 in *Methodeninnovation in der Lebenslaufforschung*, edited by S. Kluge and U. Kelle. Weinheim/Munich: Juventa.

Kluge, Susann and Udo Kelle (Eds.). 2001. *Methodeninnovation in der Lebenslaufforschung*. Weinheim/Munich: Juventa.

Kohli, Martin. 1991. "Lebenslauftheoretische Ansätze in der Sozialisationsforschung." Pp. 303–17 in *Neues Handbuch der Sozialisationsforschung*, edited by K. Hurrelmann and D. Ulich. Weinheim/Basel: Beltz.

Krüger, Helga. 2001. "Social Change in Two Generations. Employment Patterns and Their Costs for Family Life." Pp. 401–23 in *Restructuring Work and the Life Course*, edited by V. W. Marshall, W. R. Heinz, H. Krüger, and A. Verma. Toronto: University of Toronto Press.

Leisering, Lutz and Stephan Leibfried. 1999. *Time and Poverty in Western Welfare States*. Cambridge: Cambridge University Press.

Lieberson, S. 1992. "Small N's and Big Conclusions: An Examination of the Reasoning in Comparative Studies Based on a Small Number of Cases." Pp. 105–18 in *What Is a Case? Exploring the Foundations of Social Inquiry*, edited by C. C. Ragin and H. S. Becker. Cambridge: Cambridge University Press.

Marshall, Victor W. 1999. "Reasoning with Case Studies: Issues of an Aging Workforce." *Journal of Aging Studies* 13:377–89.

Mayer, Karl Ulrich. 2000. "Promises Fulfilled? A Review of 20 Years of Life-Course Research." *Archives Européennes de Sociologie*, 41(2):259–82.

Mills, C. Wright. 1959. *The Sociological Imagination*. Oxford: Oxford University Press.

Ragin, Charles C. 1992. "Introduction: Cases of 'What Is a Case?'" Pp. 1–17 in *What Is a Case? Exploring the Foundations of Social Inquiry*, edited by C. C. Ragin and H. S. Becker. Cambridge: Cambridge University Press.

Ragin, Charles C. 2000. *Fuzzy-Set Social Science*. Chicago/London: University of Chicago Press.

Ragin, Charles C. and Howard S. Becker (Eds.). 1992. *What Is a Case? Exploring the Foundations of Social Inquiry*. Cambridge: Cambridge University Press.

Schumann, Karl F. (Ed.). 2003. *Berufsbildung, Arbeit und Delinquenz*. Weinheim/Munich: Juventa.

Silverman, David. 1998. "Qualitative/Quantitative." Pp. 78–95 in *Core Sociological Dichotomies*, edited by C. Jenks. London: Sage.

Singer, Burton H. and Carol D. Ryff. 2001. "Person-Centered Methods for Understanding Aging." Pp. 44–65 in *Handbook of Aging and the Social Sciences*, 5th ed., edited by R. H. Binstock and L. K. George. New York: Academic Press.

Strauss, Anselm L. and Julie Corbin. 1990. *Basics of Qualitative Research*. Newbury Park: Sage.

Weymann, Ansgar. 1999. "From Education to Employment: Occupations and Careers in the Social Transformation of East Germany." Pp. 87–108 in *From Education to Work: Cross-National Perspectives*, edited by W. R. Heinz. New York: Cambridge University Press.

Wingens, Matthias. 1999. "Der 'gelernte DDR-Bürger': Biographischer Modernisierungsrückstand als Transformationsblockade?" *Soziale Welt* 50(3):255–80.

Witzel, Andreas. 2000. "The Problem-Centered Interview." *Forum Qualitative Social Research* (online journal) 1(1).

II

Life-Course Transitions and Sequences

| 5 |

From Transitions to Trajectories

Sequence Types

Reinhold Sackmann and Matthias Wingens

INTRODUCTION: ACHIEVEMENTS AND DEFICIENCIES
OF LIFE-COURSE RESEARCH

Life-course research has established itself as an empirically fruitful research perspective and conceptually innovative theoretical approach (cf. Elder, and Marshall and Mueller, Chapters 3 and 1, respectively, in this volume). Its decisive contribution to current sociology is a dynamic research perspective that allows us to study the interdependence between microsocial biographical processes and macrosocial structural change. This approach has spawned an extensive body of empirical research that has furthered knowledge in diverse realms of sociological inquiry. Beyond its empirical fruitfulness, the life-course perspective has fostered various theories of the institutionalized life while also making important theoretical contributions in general sociology.

Since the 1990s, however, a fundamental theoretical, conceptual, and methodological critique of the formal "life-course paradigm"—as conceptualized chiefly by Glen Elder—has been articulated, whereby the aspects criticized are interrelated. Theoretically, objections have been raised against the loose and undeveloped conceptual framework of life-course research, especially its focus on singular status passages and its attendant neglect of trajectories.

Methodologically, this deficiency is mirrored by the availability of a well-developed instrument for analyzing transitions, namely event-history analysis, paired with the lack of instruments for analyzing trajectories and sequences. In addition to such critiques of the formal life-course approach, substantive macrosociological theories of an institutionalization of the life course have been criticized for their inability to describe current changes in life-course regimes due to their reliance on negative concepts like the "deinstitutionalization" or "destandardization" of life courses. Moreover, the institutionalist perspective lacks further concepts and instruments for analyzing innovation and differentiation processes in different life-course regimes.

How can the theoretical and empirical hiatus between singular transitions and trajectories be bridged? And how are life courses differentiated? These guiding questions form the background of our central argument in this chapter. First, we will examine the key concepts of life-course theory, i.e., "transition" and "trajectory." Second, we will propose a formal typology of sequences as a heuristic tool for the analysis of life courses. In this context, we will discuss the general significance of "combined states" for micro- as well as macrosocial differentiation and innovation. Third, we illustrate the fruitfulness of our sequence typology by applying it to a broad range of life-course research areas. Finally, we discuss some methodological and theoretical aspects that relate to the necessary embedding of sequences in trajectories.

KEY ELEMENTS OF LIFE-COURSE RESEARCH

The formal life-course perspective developed by Elder offers a conceptual framework that continues to be widely used in life-course research. In this perspective, "the concepts of trajectory and transition [are] . . . central themes" in the study of life-course dynamics (1985:31). There is, however, a theoretical and empirical gap between the two basic concepts.

The transition concept is well defined by Elder: Transitions are "changes in state that are more or less abrupt" (ibid.:31f.). Conceptually, it is helpful to use the term "transition" in life-course research only for an individual change of state. The term "transition structure," by contrast, refers to the pattern of societal connections between two states, whereby it is of particular interest how and to what degree an institutional linkage between the two states is constructed. Transition structures exert an important effect on the number and forms of frictions and continuations between two states. Different institutional forms of transition structures tend to foster divergent outcomes in individual status passages (cf. Rosenbaum, Kariya, Settersten, and Maier 1990; Shavit and Müller 1998; Sackmann 2001). An unexplored realm in transition research is the analysis of the microdynamics of transitions (cf. Elder 1998), i.e., the breaking down of a transition into a series of biographical decisions and nondecisions. A second problem seldom discussed is the macrodynamics of transitions, which are determined by differences and changes in "state space." A "state" is defined as any (usually changeable) position in the life course or any attribute of it (e.g., "married"); a "state space" is a defined number of logically exclusive states to which an actor can move (e.g., "single," "married," "divorced," "other"). A methodological prerequisite for transition research is that the researcher frames a state space, defining which states can occur and thus defining possible changes between states, i.e., possible transitions. A state space is defined by researchers according to their specific research questions. However, each society legally institutionalizes a certain number of states, thus limiting the researcher's choice in constructing a state space to a culturally dominant state space. The problem here—especially relevant in comparative life-course research—is how legally defined state spaces differ among societies and how state spaces change historically. Despite these open questions, the concept of transition is not only clearly defined but can also be easily translated into the methodological terminology of event-history analysis. Due to its clarity and straightforward operationalization, the transition concept guides nearly all empirical life-course research (cf. O'Rand and Krecker 1990; George 1993).

By contrast, definitional problems prevail with regard to the second key concept of life-course research. The concept "trajectory" is theoretically vague. Elder refers to trajectories as a "pathway defined by the aging process or by movement across the age structure" (1985:31), whereby interdependence among different trajectories (e.g., work, family, health trajectories) within an individual life course is assumed. Elder employs, synonymously with the path metaphor, several other terms to describe trajectories: e.g., "life sphere," "life history," and "sequence of life events." The presupposition of semantic equivalence, though, is highly questionable. Beyond this terminological fuzziness, a fundamental problem concerning the relation between the two key concepts exists. Formally, "each trajectory is marked by a sequence of life events and transitions" (ibid.). At the same time, however, Elder states that, substantively, "transitions are always embedded in trajectories that give them distinctive form and meaning" (ibid.).[1] The implicit assumption is that the trajectory itself has a distinct form and meaning. But what this form is, what the content of this meaning is, and how form and meaning of a trajectory originate, are not elaborated in detail by Elder. Conceptually how transitions add up to a trajectory and how life-course research can comprehend trajectories are open questions. Methodologically, related to this deficiency, instruments that could be used for an analysis of trajectories are missing or underdeveloped.

During the past decade, mainstream life-course research has been increasingly criticized for its insufficient study of trajectories. One of the sharpest critiques was put forward by Andrew Abbott, who proceeded from the methodological reproach that a trajectory "as an actual sequence of events became almost invisible to sociological methodologies by the 1970s" (Abbott and Hrycak 1990:145) and that the prevailing method of event-history analysis had "no conception of the career as a whole" (Abbott 1990:140). For the analysis of whole trajectories, Abbott—borrowing from biological genetic analysis—introduced optimal-matching analysis to sociological research and applied it also to the analysis of life-course sequences (cf. Abbott and Hrycak 1990; Abbott 1995). Researchers who employ this method have declared it a holistic instrument for the analysis of life-course trajectories (cf. Halpin and Chan 1998). Though Abbott, too, tries to constitute the trajectory as a whole as a research object (and in doing so presents some intriguing ideas, especially on turning points and inertial segments of trajectories), he nevertheless—and contrary to the self-declared aim of the proponents of a holistic approach in life-course research—remains rather vague in defining what a whole trajectory is. He states that a trajectory is constituted by "a hooking up of a sequence of . . . inertial . . . structures into a life course" (Abbott 1997:92).

Thus far, the conceptual deficiencies of formal life-course theory have formed the background for our discussion. Besides formal approaches to life course theory—the best known of which is Elder's—there are also a number of substantive approaches. A well-known substantive and macro-sociological approach is Martin Kohli's theory of the institutionalization of the life course. Kohli (1985) distinguishes the modern standardized life course, clearly structured by school, work, and retirement, from a postmodern destandardized life course with fuzzy transitions and less predictability. This theory can be praised as well as criticized from different vantage points. One critique is that it cannot conceive of and comprehend differentiation of life-course states as a major form of innovation in life-course regimes. We elaborate on this in our discussion of combined states in the following section.

SEQUENCES IN THE LIFE COURSE: A FORMAL TYPOLOGY

In the following, we present a concept that should theoretically as well as methodologically help to overcome the life-course paradigm's problematic hiatus between the two key concepts "transition" and "trajectory." In order to do so, we elaborate a concept that serves as a linkage between single transitions and complex whole trajectories: the concept "sequence." We define a sequence as any life-course movement that includes at least two transitions between states (in a given state space). Thus, a sequence is more than a single transition, but less than a whole trajectory. The sequence approach places itself between a holistic approach focusing on trajectories and a transition approach studying single moves in isolation (cf. Pavalko 1997).

Whereas life-course research has concentrated on the analysis of either transitions or trajectories with the resulting theoretical and methodological problem of how to combine the two perspectives, the sequence concept linking them has not yet been elaborated in systematic fashion (cf. Hagestad 1991). This is remarkable from a practical point of view, too, because in dealing politically with frictions in status passages or tensions between life spheres (cf. Moen, Chapter 11 in this volume), intentional societal interventions are probably easier to carry out and more successful if they aim at changing sequences and transition structures rather than trying to change the whole institutional formation of trajectories by life-course policies and life-course regimes.[2] In the following, we develop a heuristic typology for sequences that can be applied to all fields of life-course processes, and we argue in particular for taking into account the importance of combined states for life-course theory.

The point of departure for our conception of "sequence"[3] is the assumption that the fundamental problem of the relationship between transitions and trajectories can be studied best if we limit our focus to a small number of transitions. The main reason for this restriction is to reduce the complexity of the innumerable possible combinations of states in a trajectory to a parsimonious model of sequences. In the following typology, only connections constituted by two transitions are discussed. The typology differentiates six types of sequences, which are constituted and characterized by particular sequences of states. Different states are formally represented by different letters, identical letters refer to identical states, and double letters stand for combined states (see Figure 5.1).

The first type, *rupture,* contains only one transition, e.g., from full-time work to permanent retirement, the latter state being an absorbing one. This sequence type is thus by definition not a true sequence. As a borderline case of a sequence, however, it serves the typology as a contrasting foil for the following true sequences.

The next two sequence types differ as to whether or not a certain event or state leads to a change in the initial state of a sequence. The second type, *interruption,* represents a continuation of the given state after an interlude or after an intermediate event has occurred. An example of this type could be a woman who returns to her former job after giving birth to a child. If this woman, however, feels obliged to give up her job and stay at home as a housewife, then there will be a discontinuation of the initial state. This third sequence type is labeled *change.*

The other three sequence types are of particular interest because they contain combined states. A combined state links two "pure" states. Formally, a combined state is marked by two letters of which at least one must

Sequence type		Examples
RUPTURE	A → B	Work → Retirement
INTERRUPTION	A → B → A	Work → Motherhood → Work
CHANGE	A → B → C	Work → Motherhood → Non-employment
BRIDGE	A → AB → B	Work → Parental leave (= Work + Non-employment) → Non-employment
RETURN	A → AB → A	Work → Parental leave (= Work + Non-employment) → Work
FUSION	A → B → AB	Work → Non-employment → Part-time work (= Work + Non-employment)

Figure 5.1   Sequence Typology.

represent one of the two linked states, i.e., either the initial or the concluding state. Parental leave, for example, represents such a combined state as
it links the states of work and nonemployment. A combined state is
ambivalent with respect to its linkage outcome, that is, it does not predetermine the final state of the sequence. Thus after a first transition from
full-time work to parental leave, this combined state could lead to a housewife's state of nonemployment, as in the case of the sequence type *bridge*.
Parental leave, however, can also lead back into full-time employment, a
case that is represented by the sequence type *return*.

The third sequence type containing a combined state is called *fusion*
because of its specific order of states. In this type, the combined state is the
final state of a sequence. An example could be a first transition from full-
time work to nonemployment, which is then followed by another transition into part-time work. As a combined state, part-time work links the
states of full-time work and of nonemployment.

These different sequence types generally refer to different approaches
and research questions in life-course analysis. Sequence type *rupture* corresponds to the core of traditional static analysis, which is interested in
absorbing states. By contrast, dynamic modeling from the perspective of
event-history analysis asks for the effect of an event on the duration of a
state, thus focusing on the sequence types *interruption* and *change*. The
sequence types *bridge*, *return*, and *fusion* are combined states. Since combined states are rarely invented by individuals but introduced, established, and structured on a macrosociological level, their introduction,
provision, and propagation as well as their development and transformation occupy a prominent place on the life-course policy agenda.

Methodologically, combined states constitute a challenge for comparative life-course research, for they are often not institutionalized in each country. Frequently in standardized comparisons one must decide which "pure" state resembles best a combined state (e.g., is the combined state "apprenticeship" more like "employment" or more like "in education"?). Such a research strategy, operating in a single international state space, entails a loss of information. In contrast, the sequence-typology approach accepts the singularity of state spaces (especially with regard to the formation of combined states) and compares the influence of specific state spaces on the mitigation of "universal" problems (e.g., what is the effect of an apprenticeship system compared to on-the-job training on youth unemployment?).

Theoretically, combined states are important for the study of individual as well as collective, societal processes of life-course change. They are a key locus of life-course differentiation and a significant realm of life-course innovation—and a scheme of sequence types allows to focus on these processes. A main reason for the fact that an important way in which life courses change on the micro- and macrolevel through the combination of life-course states relates to "meaning." Meaning can be understood as a form through which continuity is constructed in a frame of action (cf. Luhmann 1995).

On the microsociological level of life-course transitions the importance of combined states for continuity construction is easy to see. Role theory describes transitions as role exit and entry into a new role, a process that usually comprises feelings of ambivalence because of being exposed to conflicting role expectations and norms (cf. Ebaugh 1988).[4] From an individual perspective, combined states are important because they usually smooth what would otherwise be a rough life-course transition. They mitigate frictions between old and new roles by combining the meaning of the old state with that of the new one. Thus, combined states usually reduce feelings of subjective ambivalence and foster feelings of biographical continuity in role changes and across life-course transitions.

On the macrosociological level of life-course change combined states are also important for continuity construction. The ongoing and accelerating process of social change with its intensified differentiation of life spheres is reflected by alterations in the stock of norms as well as a reorganization of the texture of norms institutionalized in a society. In dealing with these normative changes society may construct not only new roles but it may also institutionalize multidimensional states and roles that comprise conflicting normative expectations and goals. With regard to this societal perspective—and similar to the individual perspective—combined states allow society as a whole to change its stock and texture of norms (and corresponding roles) "smoothly," thus maintaining continuity by introducing innovative norms and roles while simultaneously preserving old ones. For example, the introduction and support of part-time work in West Germany and the Netherlands during the last decades resulted from growing tensions between the old role model of "housewife" and the new role model of the "working mother." The institutionalized state "part-time work" is a societal compromise between the conflicting norms incorporated in these role models. Parental leave can be interpreted in a similar way.

Combined states are related in a complex manner to the phenomenon of ambivalence in life courses. While in microsocial perspective they usually reduce ambivalent feelings, in macrosocial perspective they principally enhance ambivalence. Merton and Barber (1976) define sociological ambivalence as conflicting ideas, wishes, and emotions that are caused by contradicting normative expectations and may result in difficulties to take a decision for action or in oscillating actions referring to different goals. According to this sociological definition[5] ambivalence is an integral part of societal state and role concepts. Being a normal by-product of the dynamic organization of norms and counternorms in society, sociological ambivalence has—indicating an ever higher complexity of life—grown in the process of societal modernization (which means a higher probability of experiencing subjective ambivalence, too). Sociological ambivalence allows for flexibility and variation in dealing with the contingencies of modern life. The institutionalization of multidimensional roles, and combined states in particular, thus enhances sociological ambivalence as a kind of appropriate answer to the complexity of life in modern society. An important macrosocial effect of the availability of combined states is that they allow for alternative biographical plans and an openness concerning these future plans. Moreover, the institutionalization of combined states gives transition processes between two states a chance to remain—at least provisionally—ambivalent because combined states do not predetermine the following state, thus allowing the individual to defer his/her decision to a later date. For example, for German women with young children, ambivalence in the decision between work and nonemployment is an important element in their situational values (cf. Engelbrech and Reinberg 1998), and the combined state of parental leave allows them to remain undecided on this issue for some time.

Combined states are not always successful life-course innovations. In Germany, for example, the combined state of part-time retirement was unsuccessful, important on paper but not in reality. The attempts to introduce apprenticeship models in the United States and Canada (cf. Heinz 1999) are another example. Thus, in order to be successful, a new combined state must be more than a mere compromise. To be successful it has to meet at least the following conditions: (a) it must relate to an important societal problem; (b) it must be innovative, i.e., it must serve as a new form, a new starting point and nucleus for negotiating this problem and it must deal with it in a way that promises to work better than existing arrangements; (c) it must be legitimate, i.e., people must—for whatever reason—accept its particular quality. Saying that people must accept the particular quality of a new combined state, however, does not mean that people must accept its intended utilization. Rather, the quality, meaning, and function of a combined state is actually constructed by individuals in their everyday practice. Given these conditions, a new combined state can become a life-course innovation.

Such life-course innovations via combined states are obviously not on the same level as the life-course changes to which the secular typology of an institutionalization and deinstitutionalization of the life course refers. They are also not on the level of a secular change from age-differentiated or age-integrated life courses in Matilda Riley's sense (cf. Riley and Riley 1994). Rather, they are on the incremental level of piecemeal reform and gradual social change. Nevertheless, these life-course innovations in the form of differentiation are important elements of social change and therefore highly relevant for life-course policy as well as theory.

APPLICATIONS OF THE SEQUENCE TYPOLOGY

In the following, we apply the sequence typology to some important fields of life-course research and discuss significant developments of combined states in their reciprocal relation to trends of life-course change.

School-to-Work Sequences

The first application refers to one of the best studied life-course sequences, the transition process from school to work (see Figure 5.2; cf. Shavit and Müller 1998; Heinz 1999).

Sequence type *rupture* marks the single transition from school to an absorbing state of work. Nowadays it is rather common for people to return to school or college after a period of work, usually in order to enhance their human capital (cf. Krahn and Lowe 1991). The type *interruption* refers to such a life-course sequence. By contrast, in sequence type *change* a first school-to-work transition is followed by a transition into some kind of nonemployment. In Germany, for example, in the 1950s and 1960s female hairdressers showed a high probability of dropping their employment careers completely after some work experience, in order to become mothers and homemakers (cf. Born, Krüger, and Lorenz-Meyer 1996).

Sequence type		School to Work Sequences
RUPTURE	A → B	School → Work
INTERRUPTION	A → B → A	School → Work → School
CHANGE	A → B → C	School → Work → Non-employment
BRIDGE	A → AB → B	School → Apprenticeship (= School + Work) → Work
RETURN	A → AB → A	School → Apprenticeship (= School + Work) → School
FUSION	A → B → AB	School → Work → Further Education (= School + Work)

Figure 5.2   School-to-Work.

A very well-known example of sequence type *bridge* is the German apprenticeship system. It links school and work and yields a rather smooth passage from the former to the latter (cf. OECD 1998; Sackmann 2001). A less well-known life-course sequence containing the combined state of apprenticeship consists in individuals returning to school or attending a university after their apprenticeship. This situation, represented by sequence type *return*, was a new mass phenomenon in West Germany in the 1980s when many young people holding a high school diploma (the *Abitur*) first did an apprenticeship and attended university thereafter. In the former socialist East Germany this sequence type has become quite popular during the last decade because of high rates of unemployment. It represents a life-course innovation, emerging as a result of several corresponding microlevel actions. It was not intentionally planned or propagated on the macrolevel. Sequence type *fusion* is best institutionalized in Great Britain, where it is quite common to take up a job first and later get comprehensive vocational training via further education courses (cf. Kerckhoff 2000). Similar sequences are common in Japan (Demes and Georg 1994).

Two trends can be observed in this field of research. One is the analysis of the "destandardization" of the life course. This destandardization is characterized by a shift away from clear-cut transitions of sequence type *rupture* to more fuzzy transitions back and forth between education and the labor market, represented here by sequence type *interruption*.[6] A second trend in the sociological literature on this field is a renewed interest in comparative analysis (cf. Shavit and Müller 1998; Green, Wolf, and Leney 1999; OECD 1998). A major theme here is that the school-to-work sequence is highly influenced by nationally specific institutional arrangements, thus producing a high interest in the sequence types *bridge, return,* and *fusion.* The German apprenticeship system is among those most intensely studied, as it became clear that its advantages (lowering youth unemployment; enhancing the qualifications of low-skilled workers) cannot be easily copied in other countries. Such experiments largely failed in the United States (cf. Lewis, Stone, Shipley, and Madzar 1998) and Great Britain (cf. Green et al. 1999). One cause for the difficulty in copying (parts of) this combined state is that any successful introduction and stabilization of this state depends on a complex institutional order supporting it and collective actors' ability to reproduce it (cf. Franz and Soskice 1994; Heinz 1999).

Work and Family Sequences

A second application of our sequence typology is to status passages concerning the interplay of occupational trajectories and family formation (see Figure 5.3). The rising labor-force participation of women and the—causally unrelated—decline of fertility rates have made "work and family sequences" and their potential influence on female employment and/or fertility patterns a focus of life-course research (cf. Brewster and Rindfuss 2000).

Sequence type *rupture* describes the female traditional pattern of completely dropping employment after family formation (e.g., marriage, childbirth). Changing female employment patterns gave rise to sequence type *interruption,* in which employment is interrupted after a family transition (usually childbirth) and resumed full-time once the child reaches a certain age. As returning to the labor force is difficult in countries with high unemployment rates, sequence type *change*—characterized by unemployment following a family interruption—has become quite common there.

Widely discussed in West Germany (cf. Schaeper and Falk, Chapter 7 in this volume) is the effect of the combined state "parental leave" on female labor-market participation. In sequence type *bridge,* parental leave appears to be a first step for women leaving the labor market, for in this case the state "housewife" follows parental leave. Yet one political intention accompanying the introduction of parental leave was to make it easier for women to return to work after a nonemployment phase, as in sequence type *return.* An instrument to achieve this goal was a guarantee that women could return—within a given period—to their former job after taking parental leave. Another sequence type, especially fostered in countries with a traditionally high number of housewives like the Netherlands, West Germany, or Great Britain, is the type *fusion:* here, part-time work (also a combination of full-time work and nonemployment) allows—

Sequence type		Family and Work Sequences
Rupture	A → B	Full-time work → Non-employment
Interruption	A → B → A	Full-time work → Non-employment → Full-time work
Change	A → B → C	Full-time work → Non-employment → Unemployment
Bridge	A → AB → B	Full-time work → Parental Leave (= Full-time work + Non-employment) → Non-employment
Return	A → AB → A	Full-time work → Parental Leave (= Full-time work + Non-employment) → Full-time work
Fusion	A → B → AB	Full-time work → Non-employment → Part-time work (= Full-time work + Non-employment)

Figure 5.3   Family and Work.

ceteris paribus—mothers a smooth return into employment after a family break. The extent of the institutionalization, use, and propagation of part-time work differs widely among Western countries (cf. Blossfeld and Hakim 1997).

While there is a general trend toward more equalization of women's and men's employment patterns, especially in the United States and Scandinavia, OECD countries still vary greatly in their degree of equalization, with institutional arrangements for combined states exerting a profound influence on the diversity of gendered employment patterns. It seems to be no coincidence that in some countries such combined states are in part a product of active family policy. Indeed, parental leave has been shown to affect fertility behavior, especially with regard to second- and higher-order births (cf. Huinink 2002).

Separation Sequences

A third field for application of our typology is potential turning points in family trajectories. Family sociologists have paid greater attention to separation processes in light of an accelerating trend toward higher divorce rates in most OECD countries (see Figure 5.4; cf. Cherlin 1992; Goode 1993).

A traditional approach concentrates on the sequence type *rupture*, in which the state "divorced" is an absorbing one. In this case divorces indicate a "disruption of families." However, most countries with high divorce rates also have high remarriage rates, leading to numerous sequences of

Sequences type		Separation Sequences
RUPTURE	A → B	Married → Divorced
INTERRUPTION	A → B → A	Married → Divorced → Remarried
CHANGE	A → B → C	Married → Divorced → Cohabitation
BRIDGE	A → AB → B	Married → In Separation (= Full-time work + Non-employment) → Divorced
RETURN	A → AB → A	Married → In Separation (= Full-time work + Non-employment) → Stay Married
FUSION	A → B → AB	

Figure 5.4   Separation.

the type *interruption*. Particularly in the United States and the former German Democratic Republic, a high rate of new family formations through remarriage to some extent balances out the "disruption of families" by divorce. In some countries, especially in the Nordic countries and the former GDR, sequence type *change*—in which cohabitation follows divorce—has gained relevance (this sequence type implies a high acceptance of cohabitation as an alternative to marriage). Whether combined states of separation exist depends on the divorce laws of a country. In the former GDR, for example, a divorce was a simple legal act for which there were hardly any institutionally mandated preconditions. By contrast, in most countries, especially Catholic ones, divorce has historically been either completely prohibited (as in Ireland) or made conditional on some evidence of "family disruption" (as in West Germany prior to 1976). Many countries that liberalized divorce law during recent decades introduced a new legal state of "living in separation," which represents a combined state meaning "still married, but intending divorce." If it results in a divorce after the legally defined minimum duration of "living in separation," this combined state represents sequence type *bridge*. If "living in separation" leads to the spouses' reconciliation, it represents sequence type *return*.[7]

Combined states in this field are related to institutional mechanisms that, on the one hand, facilitate divorce, but on the other raise the individual costs of divorce. The term "costs" is used here in the sense of sociological rational choice theory; it encompasses subjective costs (e.g., implementing an intended transition) as well as objective costs (e.g., legal fees). The introduction of the state "living in separation" as a precondition for divorce in East Germany in the wake of German unification raised these costs and thus was there a major cause for declining frequencies of divorce since 1990.[8]

Criminal Sequences

Most life-course theory focuses on the structure and transformation of the education, work, and family sequences through which most people in a society move. In recent decades, however, profound changes have transformed sequences through which only a minority of the population passes. Eliza Pavalko (1997) has demonstrated this with respect to mental-illness sequences, in which hospitalization has become only a minor part of more complex and varied pathways leading people into and out of psychiatric care. Whereas efforts to dynamically restructure psychiatric sequences have been important since the 1970s, similar endeavors have a long history in the treatment of criminal offenders, especially in the United States. In our last application the sequence typology is applied to passages in and out of prison (see Figure 5.5).

Sequence type *rupture* characterizes a criminal sequence in which the state "prison inmate" is an absorbing state separating convicted from "decent" people. Penal reforms introduced the alternative sequence types *interruption* and *change*. In these cases, prison either has no positive effect and reinforces criminal behavior or it achieves some kind of "resocialization" constituting a turning point in a criminal trajectory.

As early as in the middle of the nineteenth century, John Augustin introduced a new combined state called "probation." Probation offers an alternative to a prison term by placing criminals under special surveillance, while also providing them with assistance (cf. Petersilia 1997). This new combined state was first introduced by a private person (and his charity); over time, it became legally instituted in all American states. Following this example, most Western countries proceeded to introduce this combined state as well (e.g., Germany in the second half of the twentieth century). To formally construct an intended sequence of the type *bridge* for the combined state "probation," at least three transitions are needed (turning criminal, getting probation, and becoming "decent" thereafter). An alternative course is marked by sequence type *return*, meaning recidivism after probation. Much empirical research on the effects of "probation" focuses on the probabilities of these two sequence types (cf. Kerner, Dolde, and Mey 1996). Sequence type *fusion* shortens prison terms by introducing the combined state of "being out on parole," also a combination of the threat of prison with some kind of special surveillance (and assistance).

In the period since the late nineteenth century, social trends in the treatment of criminal offenders have been diverse. The introduction and

Sequence type		Criminal Sequences
RUPTURE	A → B	Criminal Behavior → Prison
INTERRUPTION	A → B → A	Criminal Behavior → Prison → Criminal Behavior
CHANGE	A → B → C	Criminal Behavior → Prison → Non-deviant Behavior
BRIDGE	A → AB → B	Non-deviant Behavior → Criminal Behavior → Probation (= Non-deviant Behavior + Prison) → Non-deviant Behavior
RETURN	A → AB → A	Non-deviant Behavior → Criminal Behavior → Probation (= Non-deviant Behavior + Prison) → Prison
FUSION	A → B → AB	Non-deviant Behavior → Criminal Behavior → Prison → Parole (= Non-deviant Behavior + Prison)

Figure 5.5   Criminal Behavior.

spread of the combined states "probation" and "parole" may be interpreted as paralleling a trend of massive decriminalization since the late nineteenth century (cf. Haferkamp 1985). They are thus part of a liberalization in criminal law (and are so perceived, e.g., in Germany). In recent decades, however, a countertrend toward toughening criminal law (and treatment of offenders) has emerged, especially in the United States and Great Britain. Surprisingly, the combined states of "parole" and "probation" do not lose their importance in this new context. "Tough" U.S. states like Texas show high rates both of imprisonment and probation. Criminological literature indicates that the meaning of the combined state "probation" may change in this context, the emphasis being on "probation" as a tougher alternative to prison (cf. May 1994).

CONCLUDING THEORETICAL AND METHODOLOGICAL CONSIDERATIONS

One guiding question in this chapter refers to the problematic gap between transitions and trajectories. Our argument is that a well-defined concept of sequences can bridge this hiatus. We proposed a parsimonious formal model (connecting only two transitions) of six sequence types. Supplementing current static and dynamic modeling approaches to life courses, our sequence typology highlights the importance of combined states both for individuals' bridging of transitions and for institutions' attempts to modify transition structures that initiate social changes in the life course. The introduction of combined states is a means of innovative life-course policy. Our heuristic sequence typology serves as a methodological instrument. As it is kept formal, it can and must be adapted to specific research questions. The briefly sketched application sequences (school-to-work, family and work, separation, criminal sequences) prove the adaptability of the typology. Whether the typology can be improved by empirical research in the numerous areas of life-course analysis, however, remains an open question.[9]

A second guiding question relates to the problematic conceptual lack in theories of the institutionalized life course concerning differentiation processes in life-course regimes. It can be stressed that the introduction and diffusion of combined states are important elements in the differentiation and innovation of the state space of sequences. In most cases they represent macrosocial, institutionalized forms of life-course policy, addressing specific frictions in transition moves. In many instances they are intended to bridge tensions between life spheres. Combined states can strike a complex balance between continuity and change management. Whether there are regularities in the evolution (and nonevolution) of combined states still remains an open research question. With regard to the modernization process in life courses, it remains to be studied in detail whether the systemic differentiation of life spheres and the tensions among them result in a growing importance of combined states in individual life-course sequences, or whether the globalization process causes a growing uniformity of the state space framing individual life-course decisions (cf. Weymann, Chapter 8 in this volume).

Several theoretical and methodological aspects of the sequence concept need to be considered, elucidated, and formulated before it can be readily employed in empirical research. An important point is that sequences (like transitions) merely constitute one part of larger trajectories. Sequences—like transitions—acquire additional form and meaning through their embeddedness in trajectories. The theoretical and methodological problem of embedding sequences in trajectories thus merits careful consideration. Of particular concern here are, theoretically, the temporal structure of trajectories and, methodologically, the possibilities and limits of different instruments of analysis.

The Temporal Structure of Trajectories

Sequences are temporally embedded in trajectories in three dimensions: relative to past states, to the duration of states in a sequence, and to the expected duration of future states. First, sequences—like transitions and states—are not without history; each sequence is, in Lawrence Hazelrigg's (1997:100) terms, "memory-endowed": "Sequencing is usually 'memory-endowed' in the sense that a later state in the sequence remembers information in earlier states, which means that states are not independent" (ibid.). This "memory of the process" consists of individual experiences and identities as well as of collected resources (e.g., human capital and social networks). Sequence analysis, therefore, has to take into account the prehistory of a sequence. Second, the individual and social meaning of a state within a sequence is also a product of the state duration. In general, a longer participation in a social field implies a stronger attachment to a certain state, for this allows individuals to learn field-specific knowledge, to build and intensify networks, and to develop state-connected self-images and identities. As a rule of thumb, the longer a person participates in a social field, and the longer he or she remains in a state, the less likely a change of state becomes ("state-dependency"). Third, the expected future duration of a state is also a relevant factor for the analysis of sequences. Individuals make investments in expectation of future profits (e.g., they invest in human capital, new roles, new relationships, or new skills). Their investment behavior is—ceteris paribus—influenced by the expected time horizon for the return on investments. The latter is dependent on "discount rates," i.e., future returns of an investment are discounted relative to current costs—implying discount curves of different shapes. One can assume that discount rates change over the life course. Empirically based sociological knowledge concerning the nature and change of these expectations across the life course is still rather limited, however.

Methodological Approaches to Sequences

Various methodological approaches can be marshaled for the heuristic analysis of sequences in the life-course perspective. Four methods in particular recommend themselves: qualitative analysis, event-history analysis, optimal matching, and combinations of these methods.

Qualitative analyses seek to ascertain the meaning of the relationship between the entry and exit of different states. Event-history analysis still is the main avenue for the quantitative study of life courses, as it allows an adequate multivariate analysis of the time dependence of social processes. Although this method is limited by its focus on transitions, its potential is not yet exhausted. Approaches with considerable promise include the precise modeling of time-variant covariates standing for macrostructural processes, and the modeling of interdependencies between different spheres of life and between persons. Especially important are the effects of the incidence and duration of certain states on the speed of transitions (e.g., "institution effects") (cf. Wingens, Sackmann, and Grotheer 2000).

Sequence type		Examples
FREEZE	A → AB → AB#	Work → Parental Leave (= Work + Non-Employment) → Part-time Work (= Work + Non-Employment)
MISHAP	A → AB → C	Work → Parental Leave (= Work + Non-Employment) → Unemployment

Figure 5.6   Additional Sequence Types.

Optimal matching analysis enables us to study the typical form of whole trajectories. It thus allows us to overcome the analytical isolation of transitions and sequences within trajectories.

Obviously, each of these methods has limitations that can be reduced through a combination of methods. Indeed, initial attempts have been made to combine methods for the analysis of sequences in life courses. The fruitfulness of methodological combinations has been both theoretically (cf. Pavalko 1997) and empirically (cf. Han and Moen 1999) demonstrated. The latter used sequence types defined by optimal matching analysis as predictors for transitions. Such studies suggest that new opportunities arise methodologically when optimal matching is employed as an additional instrument in life-course research. Theoretically, the conceptual widening of the dichotomous "transition-trajectory" frame of the life-course paradigm to the triangular one of "transition—sequence—trajectory" will further our knowledge of the societal embeddedness of life courses as well as of the production of social structure by life courses.

ACKNOWLEDGMENTS

This research was supported by the Deutsche Forschungsgemeinschaft Special Collaborative Centre 186. We thank Walter R. Heinz and Victor W. Marshall for helpful suggestions on early drafts.

NOTES

1. Elder (1998) refers to the central role of the timing of transitions (together with their sequence and the duration of states) for their meaning in trajectories. Off-time transitions, he agrees, produce asynchronies in trajectories and therefore have potentially negative consequences for individual development. However, a theory of off-time transitions presupposes reliable knowledge of age norms for transitions—and whether the theory of age norms (cf. Settersten 1999) is sufficiently elaborated to play a key role in life-course research seems questionable (as Elder seems to concede).

2. Comparative life-course policy is discussed by Mayer (1997, 2001) and Lei-sering and Leibfried (1999). The limits of life-course policy are already pointed to by Heclo (1988).

3. The term "sequence" is used with various meanings in life-course research. In contrast to Abbott, who uses the term to characterize whole trajectories, we restrict its meaning to only parts of trajectories. There exists an older tradition of sequence analysis that refers only to the normative order of states. An empirical analysis of sequences of a young adult cohort showed, for example, that "orderly," standardized and/or institutionally underpinned sequences are more common than others, but more than half of the respondents showed "disorderly" sequences (cf. Rindfuss, Swicegood, and Rosenfeld 1987). If one differentiates only three states, checked at annual intervals over a twelve-year period, a quarter of nearly eleven thousand respondents show a singular sequence of transitions (cf. Rindfuss 1991). Substantively, one can conclude that—as this study on longer life-course segments demonstrates—there are no "average life-course patterns": "Life-course experiences of individuals are almost as unique as their fingerprints—no two being identical" (Uhlenberg and Chew 1986, cited in Hagestad 1991:37).

4. Feelings of ambivalence may be intensified by an individual's different ref-erence groups that pull him/her in different directions (cf. Coser 1966). Such feel-ings may also be accentuated if a role change simultaneously means a change from the hitherto dominant life sphere and its normative structuring of the old state to a new dominant life sphere that structures the new state by different or even con-tradicting norms (as it is the case in the school-to-work transition).

5. Recent discussion in sociology on the concept of ambivalence ignores this classic insight into the value-neutral nature of sociological ambivalence. For exam-ple, Smelser (1998) holds on to a restricted psychological conception of ambiva-lence and confines its social meaning to ambivalent feelings in situations of dependency, whereas Connidis and McMullen (2002) broaden the definition of ambivalence to the point of a pejorative alternative to open social conflict.

6. Similar trends are discussed in the field of the changing transition from work to retirement away from abrupt exit to blurred exit [cf. Mutchler, Burr, Pienta, and Massagli (1997); see also Marshall, Clarke, and Ballantyne (2001) for an examina-tion of the impact of blurred exits on well-being].

7. We are not aware of any institutional arrangement defining sequence type fusion in separation processes.

8. In the area of family sequences, one could also elaborate on the introduction, propagation, and spread of combined states concerning family formation. During recent decades most OECD countries have developed some institutional arrange-ment for "cohabitation" as a legally defined state combining elements of "married" and "single."

9. For example, one may add two further sequence types with a different logic (see Figure 5.6).

Sequence type *freeze* is quite common in parental leave sequences in Germany, where the combined state "parental leave" is followed by a second combined state ("part-time work"; "#" denotes that this is a different combined state). In this case, the second combined state in particular is held for a long time, thus postponing a transition either back to full-time work or to nonemployment. Thus, in some instances the transition process is "frozen," for the combined state can turn into an absorbing state.

Sequence type *mishap* belongs to a different class of sequences, for the third state "C" (in our example, "unemployment" after insolvency of the former employer) is not part of an intended, planned movement of the individual. "Mishap" sequences are quite common in life courses. Illnesses, a spouse's death, a change of social circumstances, etc. affect one's trajectory and can constitute turning points in a trajectory. However, one has to take into consideration that people usually try to cope with "mishaps" by actively redirecting their path and "repairing" their trajectory. Thus, a "mishap" often becomes the starting point of a new sequence. The individual logic of coping in life courses is discussed in some detail in Elder's control cycle concept (cf. Elder 1985). For an interesting empirical comparison of coping movements and institutional coping arrangements following unemployment and divorce, see DiPrete and McManus (2000).

REFERENCES

Abbott, Andrew. 1990. "Conceptions of Time and Events in Social Science Methods." *Historical Methods* 23:140–50.

Abbott, Andrew. 1995. "Sequence Analysis: New Methods for Old Ideas." *Annual Review of Sociology* 21:93–113.

Abbott, Andrew. 1997. "On the Concept of Turning Point." *Comparative Social Research* 16:85–105.

Abbott, Andrew and Alexandra Hrycak. 1990. "Measuring Resemblance in Sequence Data: An Optimal Matching Analysis of Musicians' Careers." *American Journal of Sociology* 96:144–85.

Blossfeld, Hans-Peter and Catherine Hakim (Eds.). 1997. *Between Equalization and Marginalization*. Oxford: Oxford University Press.

Born, Claudia, Helga Krüger, and Dagmar Lorenz-Meyer. 1996. *Der unentdeckte Wandel. Annäherung an das Verhältnis von Struktur und Norm im weiblichen Lebenslauf*. Berlin: Edition Sigma.

Brewster, Karin L. and Ronald R. Rindfuss. 2000. "Fertility and Women's Employment in Industrialized Nations." *Annual Review of Sociology* 26:271–96.

Cherlin, Andrew J. 1992. *Marriage, Divorce, Remarriage*. Cambridge, MA: Harvard University Press.

Connidis, Ingrid Arnet and Julie Ann McMullin. 2002. "Sociological Ambivalence and Family Ties: A Critical Perspective." *Journal of Marriage and the Family* 64:558–67.

Coser, Rose Laub. 1966. "Role Distance, Sociological Ambivalence, and Transitional Status Systems." *American Journal of Sociology* 72:173–87.

Demes, Helmut and Walter Georg (Eds.). 1994. *Gelernte Karriere. Bildung und Berufsverlauf in Japan*. Munich: Iudicium.

DiPrete, Thomas A. and Patricia A. McManus. 2000. "Family Change, Employment Transitions, and the Welfare State: Household Income Dynamics in the United States and Germany." *American Sociological Review* 3:343–70.

Ebaugh, Helen Rose Fuchs. 1988. *Becoming an Ex: The Process of Role Exit*. Chicago: Chicago University Press.

Elder, Glen H., Jr. 1985. "Perspectives on the Life Course." Pp. 23–49 in *Life-Course Dynamics. Trajectories and Transitions*, 1968–1980, edited by G. H. Elder, Jr. Ithaca, NY: Cornell University Press.

Elder, Glen H., Jr. 1998. "The Life Course and Human Development." Pp. 939–91 in *Handbook of Child Psychology*, Vol. 1: *Theoretical Models of Human Development*, edited by R. M. Lerner. New York: Wiley & Sons.

Engelbrech, Gerhard and Alex Reinberg. 1998. "Erwerbsorientierung und Beschäftigungsmöglichkeiten von Frauen in den neunziger Jahren." Pp. 39–92 in *Beschäftigungsrisiko Erziehungsurlaub*, edited by Gesellschaft für Informationstechnologie und Pädagogik am IMBSE. Opladen: Westdeutscher Verlag.

Franz, Wolfgang and David Soskice. 1994. "The German Apprenticeship System." *WZB Discussion Paper* FS I:94–302. Berlin.

George, Linda K. 1993. "Sociological Perspectives on Life Transitions." *Annual Review of Sociology* 19:353–73.

Goode, William J. 1993. *World Changes in Divorce Patterns*. New Haven, CT: Yale University Press.

Green, Andy, Alison Wolf, and Tom Leney. 1999. *Convergence and Divergence in European Education and Training Systems*. London: Institute of Education, University of London.

Haferkamp, Hans. 1985. "Leistungsangleichung und Individualisierung." *Zeitschrift für Rechtssoziologie* 6:45–69.

Hagestad, Gunhild O. 1991. "Trends and Dilemmas in Life-Course Research. An International Perspective." Pp. 21–48 in *Theoretical Advances in Life-Course Research*, edited by W. R. Heinz. Weinheim: Deutscher Studien Verlag.

Halpin, Brendan and Tak Wing Chan. 1998. "Class Careers as Sequences." *European Sociological Review* 14:111–30.

Han, Shin-Kap and Phyllis Moen. 1999. "Clocking Out: Temporal Patterns of Retirement." *American Journal of Sociology* 105:191–236.

Hazelrigg, Lawrence. 1997. "On the Importance of Age." Pp. 93–128 in *Studying Aging and Social Change*, edited by M. A. Hardy. Thousand Oaks, CA: Sage.

Heclo, Hugh. 1988. "Generational Politics." Pp. 381–412 in *The Vulnerable*, edited by J. L. Palmer, T. Smeeding, and B. Boyle Torrey. Washington, DC: Urban Institute Press.

Heinz, Walter R. (Ed.). 1999. *From Education to Work. Cross-National Perspectives*. New York: Cambridge University Press.

Huinink, Johannes. 2002. Polarisierung der Familienentwicklung in europäischen Ländern im Vergleich. In *Elternschaft heute*, edited by N. Schneider and H. Matthias-Bleck. Opladen: Leske and Budrich.

Kerckhoff, Alan C. 2000. "Transition from School to Work in Comparative Perspective." Pp. 453–74 in *The Handbook of the Sociology of Education*, edited by M. T. Hallinan. New York: Kluwer.

Kerner, Hans-Jürgen, Gabriele Dolde, and Hans-Georg Mey (Eds.). 1996. *Jugendstrafvollzug und Bewährung*. Bonn: Forum.

Kohli, Martin. 1985. "Die Institutionalisierung des Lebenslaufs." *Kölner Zeitschrift für Soziologie und Sozialpsychologie* 37:1–29.

Krahn, Harvey and Graham Lowe. 1991. "Transitions to Work." Pp. 130–70 in *Making Their Way*, edited by D. Ashton and G. Lowe. Milton Keynes, UK: Open University Press.

Leisering, Lutz and Stephan Leibfried. 1999. *Time and Poverty in Western Welfare States*. Cambridge: Cambridge University Press.

Lewis, Theodore, James Stone III, Wayne Shipley, and Svjetlana Madzar. 1998. "The Transition from School to Work." *Youth and Society* 29:259–92.

Luhmann, Niklas 1995. *Social Systems*. Stanford, CA: Stanford University Press.

Marshall, Victor W., Philippa J. Clarke, and Peri J. Ballantyne. 2001. "Instability in the Retirement Transition: Effects on Health and Well-Being in a Canadian Study." *Research on Aging* 23(4):379–409.

May, Tim. 1994. "Probation and Community Sanctions." Pp. 861–87 in *The Oxford Handbook of Criminology*, edited by M. Maguire, R. Morgan and R. Reiner. Oxford: Clarendon.

Mayer, Karl U. 1997. "Notes on a Comparative Political Economy of Life Courses." *Comparative Social Research* 16:203–26.

Mayer, Karl U. 2001. "The Paradox of Global Social Change and National Path Dependencies." Pp. 89–110 in *Inclusions and Exclusions in European Societies*, edited by A. Woodward and M. Kohli. New York: Routledge.

Merton, Robert K. and Elinor Barber. 1976. "Sociological Ambivalence." Pp. 3–31 in *Sociological Ambivalence and Other Essays*, edited by R. K. Merton. New York: Free Press.

Mutchler, Jan E., J. A. Burr, A. M. Pienta, and M. P. Massagli. 1997. "Pathways to Labor Force Exit: Work Transitions and Work Instability." *Journal of Gerontology: Social Sciences* 52B(1):13–26.

O'Rand, Angela M. and Margaret L. Krecker. 1990. "Concepts of the Life Cycle." *Annual Review of Sociology* 16:241–62.

OECD. 1998. *Education Policy Analysis*. Paris: Author.

Pavalko, Eliza K. 1997. "Beyond Trajectories. Multiple Concepts for Analyzing Long-Term Process." Pp. 129–47 in *Studying Aging and Social Change*, edited by M. A. Hardy. Thousand Oaks, CA: Sage.

Petersilia, Joan. 1997. "Probation in the United States." *Crime and Justice* 22:149–200.

Riley, Matilda White and John W. Riley, Jr. 1994. "Structural Lag: Past and Future." Pp. 15–36 in *Age and Structural Lag*, edited by M. White Riley, R. L. Kahn, and A. Foner. New York: John Wiley & Sons.

Rindfuss, Ronald R. 1991. "The Young Adult Years: Diversity, Structural Change, and Fertility." *Demography* 28:493–512.

Rindfuss, Ronald R., C. Gray Swicegood, and Rachel A. Rosenfeld. 1987. "Disorder in the Life Course: How Common and Does It Matter?" *American Sociological Review* 52:785–801.

Rosenbaum, James E., Takehito Kariya, Richard A. Settersten, Jr., and Tony Maier. 1990. "Market and Network Theories of the Transition from High School to Work." *Annual Review of Sociology* 16:263–99.

Sackmann, Reinhold. 2001. "Age and Labour-Market Chances in International Comparison." *European Sociological Review* 17(4):373–89.

Settersten, Richard A., Jr. 1999. *Lives in Time and Place. The Problems and Promises of Developmental Science*. Amityville, NY: Baywood.

Shavit, Yossi and Walter Müller (Eds.). 1998. *From School to Work*. Oxford: Clarendon.

Smelser, Neil J. 1998. "The Rational and the Ambivalent in the Social Sciences." *American Sociological Review* 63:1–16.

Uhlenberg, P. and K. S. Chew. 1986. "The Changing Place of Remarriage in the Life Course." Pp. 23–52 in *Current Perspectives on Aging and the Life Cycle*, Vol. 2, edited by D. L. Kertzer. Greenwich, CT: JAI.

Wingens, Matthias, Reinhold Sackmann, and Michael Grotheer. 2000. "Berufliche Qualifizierung für Arbeitslose: Zur Effektivität AFG-finanzierter Weiterbildung im Transformationsprozess." *Kölner Zeitschrift für Soziologie und Sozialpsychologie* 52:60–80.

| 6 |

Dynamics of Women's Employment Careers

Labor-Market Opportunities and Women's Labor-Market Exit and Reentry

Marlis Buchmann, Irene Kriesi, Andrea Pfeifer,
and Stefan Sacchi

INTRODUCTION

This chapter examines the causes affecting women's labor-market exits and reentries. Some women are continuously employed, while others interrupt their labor-market careers and resume them after shorter or longer periods. Some women, however, leave the labor market and never return. From a theoretical point of view, both supply-side factors and demand-side factors are expected to have an impact on women's withdrawal from the labor force. This chapter focuses on the ways in which labor-market structures impinge upon women's extended employment interruptions, taking into account women's family situation and their human capital. Referring to labor-market segmentation theories, organizational theories, and theories of segregation, we derive hypotheses specifying both the conditions under which women are likely to exit the labor market and to reenter it. The analyses are based on a representative sample of Swiss men and women in the German-speaking part of Switzerland, who were born between 1949–1951 and 1959–1961, respectively. The data set provides retrospective biographical information on respondents' educational careers, family histories, and labor-market experiences. This enables us to examine women's employment interruptions and labor-market reentries from a life-course perspective. The great advantage of this approach is the disentanglement of the causal processes involved by taking into account the sequential order of the events of interest. Using event history analysis, we limit ourselves to examining women's first extended employment exit and first reentry.

THEORETICAL CONSIDERATIONS

From a life-course perspective women's employment careers can be conceptualized as a sequence of job and nonemployment spells that are linked by transitions into a job, between jobs, or into nonemployment. Individual spells are not independent of each other but are strongly influenced by previous spells and transitions in education, family life, and employment. From recent research analyzing women's labor-market exits and reentries it is well-known that women's labor-market behavior is greatly affected by family events and their human capital. Many studies show that getting married or giving birth often leads to labor-force withdrawal. Employment patterns are also strongly influenced by the type of education women received before labor-force entry (Buchmann, Kriesi, Pfeifer, and Sacchi 2002; Drobnič, Blossfeld, and Rohwer 1999; Lauterbach 1994). Such findings are most often explained by employing Becker's (1975, 1991) human capital theory and new home economics approach or resource theory (e.g., Blood and Wolfe 1960). Given the limited length of this contribution we will not elaborate on these well-known and widely applied approaches but focus on theories conceptualizing the demand side of the labor market.

Compared to individual attributes, much less is known about how *contextual* factors influence women's labor-market careers. This reflects, in part, the dominance of individual-centered theorizing (as exemplified by the neoclassical and functionalist paradigms), and in part the difficulties of measuring contextual factors. The few studies that account for labor-market opportunities and constraints in assessing women's market interruptions are hampered by some limitations. Most of them limit themselves to such relatively easy-to-measure attributes as work time regulations, working conditions, and private or public sectors (see Kurz 1998; Lauterbach 1994; Born 1991; Krüger and Born 1991). Others are purely descriptive in character (see Engelbrech 1991a, 1991b). The predominantly qualitative study conducted by Born, Krüger, and Lorenz-Meyer (1996) is based on a relatively small sample ($N = 220$) and limits itself to the analysis of the five most important occupations. In the more recent literature, the study conducted by Glass and Riley (1998) is an exception as they pay attention to job characteristics. Given the relative neglect of labor-market opportunities in empirical studies investigating women's labor-market careers, this chapter attempts to assess the significance of the employment context for women's labor-market interruptions and reentries. We make use of several theoretical approaches associated with structural labor-market research. In particular, we refer to labor-market segmentation theory and organizational theory.[1] Although these theories have not been developed to primarily explain women's labor-force attachment, they provide important insights into the ways in which labor-market opportunity structures shape women's employment behavior.

Labor-Market Segmentation Theory

Taking into account that some workers are equipped with highly specialized skills that cannot be easily substituted, segmentation theory posits that firms attempt to secure these employees by offering them higher salaries, better working conditions, and favorable upward mobility chances. The emergent property emanating from the recruitment and reward policies applied by individual firms is the splitting of the labor market into numerous segments, each of which exhibits strong mobility barriers. Hence, segmentation theory attributes income inequalities and unequal mobility chances to firms' recruitment and reward policies. In addition, we assume that labor-market segmentation affects women's labor force attachment. In particular, we suspect that the costs of extended employment interruptions vary across labor-market segments. Furthermore, the quality of employment, with regard to work-family compatibility especially, is expected to differ between labor-market segments and thus affect women's labor-force attachment. Among the various variants of labor-market segmentation theory, we choose Sengenberger's concept of the tripartite labor market (Sengenberger 1987; for Switzerland, see Levy, Joye, Guye, and Kaufmann 1997). Given the tight linkages between the labor market and the Swiss educational system (Buchmann and Sacchi 1998), this approach captures best the particularities of the Swiss labor market.[2] A major characteristic of the Swiss labor market is the strong segmentation along skill lines.

According to this approach, the labor market is subdivided into three segments, namely, the internal labor market, the occupation-specific labor market, and the peripheral labor market for unskilled labor. The segment of the *internal labor market* shows great resemblance with the core segment of the labor market specified by the theory of the dual economy. Recruited for entry ports at the lower levels of the organizational hierarchy, skilled workers climb up the institutionalized career ladders acquiring firm-specific knowledge. Consequently, the ties between workers and firms become strong as firms provide good career advancement chances and workers acquire firm-specific skills not easily transferable to other companies. Access to the *occupation-specific labor market* is predicated on the appropriate educational certificate. Hence, this labor-market segment is subdivided into numerous subsegments. *Within* particular occupation-specific subsegments, skills can be easily transferred between firms. Mobility *between* the subsegments is limited, however, as it requires the additional acquisition of an occupation-specific credential. Moreover, the occupation-specific labor market tends to discriminate against women because of its close link to the gender segregation of the occupational structure. Women are almost completely cut off from a substantial number of industrial and crafts-related subsegments of the occupation-specific labor market given that the respective apprenticeships are strongly dominated by men (e.g., mechanics). Vice versa, men are excluded from some female-dominated subsegments of the occupation-specific labor market (e.g., nursing). The *peripheral labor market* is dominated by unskilled tasks to be performed by workers with no specific educational credentials. Resembling the peripheral segment of the dual labor-market theory, the exchange of workers does not result in substantial replacement costs. Hence, working conditions are not very attractive and salaries are rather low.

The core idea of Sengenberger's (1987) theory, namely that the strength of the ties between firms and workers varies by labor-market segment, may be helpful in explaining women's labor-force attachment. In particular, we suspect that the costs of extended employment interruptions (e.g., deskilling, reduced mobility chances, income losses) differ by labor-market segment. Likewise, labor-market segments vary in the degree to which they enable family-work compatibility.

1. Women's access to the *internal labor-market segment* is limited because employers stereotype women as having low aspirations and exhibiting low labor-force attachment due to anticipated family responsibilities. In the interest of minimizing replacement costs, firms prefer to hire men for jobs located in the internal labor-market segment (Blossfeld 1991). Hence, women who attempt to enter this labor-market segment are likely to be confronted with statistical discrimination (Bornschier 1982; Blossfeld and Mayer 1988). If they nonetheless manage to get access to the internal labor market, we suspect that employment interruptions or reduction of working hours will be difficult because *firms expect continuous and full-time employment*. Given these norms, the propensity to withdraw from the internal labor-market segment is expected to be *high*. Moreover, the withdrawal is likely to result in the permanent exclusion from this attractive segment of the labor market accompanied by substantial costs related to income loss, deskilling, and the loss of an attractive occupational position

(Blossfeld 1991). Labor-force reentry by women formerly employed in the internal labor market is expected to result in downward mobility, be it to an entry port position in the internal labor market or to the occupation-specific segment of the labor market (Borkowsky and Streckeisen 1982).

2. Within the numerous subsegments of the *occupation-specific labor market* we expect the likelihood of extended employment exits to depend on the occupation-inherent work-family compatibility. Occupations characterized by flexible work arrangements and ample part-time opportunities are likely to lower the rate of women's employment exits and, vice versa, to increase the rate of women's employment reentry.

3. For women, the *peripheral segment* of the labor market is expected to provide a big pool of unskilled (part-time) jobs characterized by flexible working arrangements. As women are often relegated to these relatively unattractive jobs because of statistical discrimination, they are often forced to stay in these jobs due to economic necessity. Women's extended employment exits are therefore rather unlikely. If they do occur, employment reentry is expected to follow frequently and rapidly.

Sengenberger's (1987) conceptualization of the tripartite labor market shows two shortcomings. First, by focusing on the private sector of the economy, it neglects the significance of the public sector for the distribution of labor-market opportunities. Second, it fails to grasp the unequal development of employment opportunities by economic sectors. For these reasons, we expand the notion of the tripartite labor market by introducing, first, the distinction between private and public segments of the labor market; and, second, the distinction between the service sector and the other economic sectors.

1. Becker (1993) has shown that the public sector in Germany represents a labor-market segment of its own characterized by rather strong mobility barriers. Although resembling occupational careers located in the internal labor market of private firms, public service careers follow to an even greater extent institutionalized rules pertaining to seniority, internal recruitment, and well-defined lifelong career ladders. Consequently, public sector employment is rather secure and the respective occupational careers are stable. In stark contrast to the private sector, institutionalized rules regarding employment conditions and career advancement chances are not limited to individual establishments. Rather, they apply to all branches of a given public service institution. Hence, it makes sense to conceive of the public sector as a separate segment of the labor market embracing all public service branches. Compared to the private sector, the favorable employment conditions in the public sector, such as greater employment stability, ample part-time opportunities, and better work-

family compatibility are likely to result in less frequent employment interruptions. Should they occur, more frequent and rapid employment reentry is to be expected.

2. When examining women's labor-force attachment, differences between economic sectors in employment opportunities in general and those related to the prevalence of flex-time work arrangements in particular need to be taken into account. In this respect, the service sector greatly differs from the other economic sectors. The growth of the service sector greatly spurred women's employment opportunities. The supply of typically female jobs increased rapidly in education, administration, sales, and services, in the health sector and in social work (Höpflinger, Charles, and Debrunner 1991). The expansion of the service sector was also accompanied by the rapid dissemination of flex-time arrangements attributable in part to technological and organizational changes, in part to the shortage of skilled labor. Flex-time work is particularly widespread in office jobs where the organization of work is determined to a lesser degree by technological constraints (ibid.). Hence, opportunities for part-time work vary with occupations *and* economic sectors. Against this background we assume that—even *within* given occupations—flex-time work is more widespread in the service sector compared to agriculture and industry. Greater job opportunities coupled with ample flex-time work offers are likely to lower the rate of female employment interruptions and, in case they do occur, to increase the rate of reentry.

Organization Theory

Neostructural theory advanced some criticism of segmentation theory (e.g., Baron and Bielby 1980). First, the neglect of the internal heterogeneity of labor-market segments was critiqued. The second critique refers to the exclusion of firm-level processes responsible for the unequal distribution of employment opportunities. According to organization theory, job opportunities, income, and mobility chances depend on the firm-specific division of labor and the concomitant recruitment and reward policies.

Basically, two approaches within organization theory refer to the relations between organizational processes and individual labor-market outcomes. First, *organizational ecology* focuses on firm foundations, mergers, and closures as well as organizational growth and decline and stresses their effects on workers' careers (Carroll, Havemann, and Swaminathan 1990; Haveman and Cohen 1994; DiPrete et al. 1997). Second, *organizational demography* examines the significance of firm-specific structures on individual labor-market outcomes (Stewman and Konda 1983; Rosenbaum 1981, 1984; Brüderl, Preisendörfer, and Ziegler 1993). In this perspective, structural factors refer to the distribution of employees across hierarchical levels and cohorts, and the number and types of vacancies.[3] For reasons of empirical practicability, our theoretical considerations of organizational characteristics are limited to two factors, namely, *firm size* and *position in the organizational hierarchy* (Carroll et al. 1990).[4]

The theoretical status of firm size differs between the two organizational approaches. According to *organizational ecology*, the number of new jobs created by small firms is large; the survival rate, however, is rather low (OECD 1994). Workers employed in small firms are thus exposed to strong structural fluctuations (i.e., high job turnover rate). They run a greater risk of losing their jobs (Kalleberg and Mastekaasa 1998). *Organizational demography* assumes increasing opportunity costs of labor-force interruptions as the size of the organization grows, thus creating an incentive for women's continuous employment. This link is expected because many organizational characteristics relevant for upward mobility and income chances depend on firm size. These characteristics are hierarchical differentiation, institutionalization of career ladders, job profiles, and opportunities for skill updating as well as the number of higher level vacancies. Empirical evidence supports the expected link between firm size and opportunity costs insofar as income, upward mobility chances, and employment stability increase with organizational size (see Preisendörfer 1987; for Switzerland, see Lewin 1982 and Bundesamt für Statistik 1996). To date, however, it is still disputed whether the expected link is really attributable to *organizational processes*. Arguments advanced by Sengenberger's (1987) *segmentation theory* offer an alternative interpretation. Big firms create internal labor markets, for which strong ties between workers and the organization are characteristic due to the good career advancement prospects and the acquisition of firm-specific skills. Hence, opportunity costs of employment interruptions increase with firm size. Nevertheless, organization theory and segmentation theory suggest *different* hypotheses regarding the link between firm size and women's labor-force attachment. From an organizational perspective, women employed in big firms are expected to exit the labor market *less* often due both to lower rates of fluctuations and more favorable rewards. By contrast, segmentation theory led us to the hypothesis that women employed in internal labor markets of big firms are *more* likely to exit the labor force.

The propensity of working women to withdraw from the labor force is also affected by their position in the organizational hierarchy. There are two sides to the coin, however. One side implies that the opportunity costs of employment exits increase with the rank in the organizational hierarchy. Hence, the higher the position the less likely women are to give up their jobs. Should they nevertheless exit the labor force, a great proportion of these women is expected to reenter employment rapidly. The other side implies that jobs in the higher echelons of the organizational ladder typically show a "male profile." Gendered organizations (see Acker 1991; Müller 1993; Heintz and Nadai 1998) implicitly presuppose a traditional division of labor between the sexes, enabling men to fully concentrate on their jobs while women care for the family. Hence, higher positions offer few opportunities for flex-time and part-time work as well as job sharing. Against this background, the exit rate from these jobs should be higher. And when women formerly employed in high-status jobs reenter the labor force, they are likely to experience downward mobility. However, the expected rates of employment exits and reentries need to be qualified in several respects. First, employees in high-status jobs enjoy considerable autonomy regarding working hours. This helps women to juggle their work and family obligations. Second, the high salaries that come with jobs in the higher echelons of the organizational hierarchy allow women to hire domestic help and pay for their small children's day care. Despite the various counteracting factors involved, we expect that such attributes of high-status jobs as high salaries coupled with the financial opportunity for hiring domestic help, autonomous working hours, and last but not least interesting work are more important in determining women's labor-force attachment than long working hours and male job profiles. By and large, we therefore expect the rate of employment exits to decrease as the job status increases. Because employment reentry may result in downward mobility for women formerly working in high-status jobs, the rate of labor-force reentry should be lower and slower the higher the position of the former job was.

DATA AND METHODS

The data are taken from a mailed retrospective life-history survey *"Berufsverlauf im sozio-technischen Wandel,"* carried out in 1989 (Buchmann and Sacchi 1997). It is representative of Swiss citizens of both sexes in the German-speaking part of Switzerland, who were born between 1949–1951 and 1959–1961, respectively.[5] The survey includes detailed biographical information on education, occupation, and the family, and provides exact dates of family and labor-force transitions. Consideration of employment histories is limited to jobs held after the completion of formal education, but respondents were directed to report only those jobs that lasted a minimum of four months. We define women's employment exit as a labor-force withdrawal lasting a full year at least. Given that 82 percent of the women who withdrew from the labor force during the observation period ($N = 481$) did it only once ($N = 395$), we limit our analysis to *first* employment exit and, consequently, to *first* employment reentry.[6]

To estimate the effects of contextual factors on the rates of women's employment exit and reentry, we employ event history analysis. We choose the semiparametric Cox regression model, which does not specify any assumptions about the time dependency of the hazard rate (Allison

1984). This serves our purpose, as we are mainly interested in the effects of the explanatory variables on the occurrence of the events and not in the distribution of the timing of the events. However, the Cox model presupposes proportional hazard rates among relevant subgroups (e.g., birth cohorts). To determine whether the data are consistent with the proportionality assumption of the Cox regression model, we ran graphical and statistical tests (Blossfeld, Hamerle, and Mayer 1986). The statistical tests allow for interactions between the covariates of interest and duration.[7] The tests suggest that the hazard rates of both employment exit and reentry significantly differ between *cohorts* and *educational groups.* To address the violation of the proportionality assumption we specify the Cox regression model by including interaction terms between education and duration and cohort and duration, respectively (ibid.).

To include time-varying covariates, we employed the technique of episode splitting (see Brüderl and Ludwig-Mayerhofer 1994).[8] For the *exit model,* we split the employment episode, first, into the *job spells* a respondent experienced during the observation period (i.e., the duration between labor-force entry and the time of the survey in 1989) and, second, according to the timing of family events (e.g., marriage, divorce, pregnancy, births, children's entry into and exit from schooling).[9] For the *reentry model,* we use the same procedure except that we leave aside the splitting by job spells.[10] Preparation of the event-history data file according to the procedures described here yielded 3917 episodes for the exit model and 1688 episodes for the reentry model.[11]

For the exit and the reentry models, we use the same covariates. The *labor-market segments* to which jobs are allocated are measured by *occupation, occupation-specific part-time opportunities, economic sectors,* and the *private and public sectors.* These covariates are *time-varying* for the exit model and *time-constant* for the reentry model. Based on the international classification of occupations (ISCO-88), we specify seventeen occupational groups in order to differentiate occupation-specific labor-market segments. Clerical work serves as reference category. Occupation-specific part-time opportunities are measured as the proportion of women within a given occupation holding jobs characterized by employment levels of less than 90 percent. These computations are based on the 1990 Swiss Census data. A dummy is used to differentiate service sector jobs from industrial and agricultural jobs. Another dummy distinguishes public sector jobs from private sector ones. The *organizational context* characteristics we consider in this study are *firm size, hierarchical position* defined as *formal authority* and *occupational prestige,* and *employment level.* Again, these job attributes are *time-varying* covariates in the exit model and *time-constant* covariates in the reentry model as they refer to the last job held before withdrawing from the labor force. Firm size is defined as the number of employees. We distinguish four categories specifying 1–9, 10-49, 50–99, and above 100 employees. Small firms serve as reference group. A dummy is used to differentiate jobs that are vested with formal authority from those that are not. Occupational status is measured with Treiman's occupational prestige scale (Treiman 1977). Employment level (i.e., the number of weekly hours worked by the respondents) distinguishes full-time from part-time jobs. The latter are defined by the range of 1–35 working hours per week. Due to the sample size and many missing values on working hours, it was not feasible to distinguish between several types of part-time work.[12] In addition, we include a category indicating missing values. Finally, *regional context* measures whether firms are located in urban areas or in the countryside. Again, we include a category for missing values.

We now turn to the control variables. As empirical evidence amply documents the importance of family situation, human capital, and financial circumstances for women's labor-force attachment, both our models control for family attributes, human capital factors, and potential individual earnings (based on a full-time job) in order to determine the net effects of contextual covariates.[13] A dummy was used to differentiate the two cohorts with the older one (1949–1951) being the reference group. Another dummy indicates whether the information on some characteristics of jobs women held *after* the fifth job is missing.[14] Finally, our models include the above-mentioned interaction terms (education and duration; cohort and duration) to handle the violations of the proportionality assumptions in the Cox model.[15]

RESULTS

Figures 6.1 and 6.2 depict the survival functions of women's employment exit and reentry. Figure 6.1 shows that approximately 3.5 years after first labor-force entry 75 percent of the women are still occupationally active. After 8 years, the proportion of those who have not yet withdrawn from the labor force is estimated to be 50 percent. Fifteen years later, the estimation is roughly 30 percent. Figure 6.2 illustrates that, approximately 2.5 years after withdrawal from the labor force, the estimated proportion of employment reentry amounts to roughly 25 percent. After 8 years, approximately 50 percent of the women have returned to the labor market and 15 years later the estimated proportion is two-thirds.

As we are interested in the contextual causes affecting women's propensity to exit the labor force and, vice versa, to reenter the labor market after an extended period of nonemployment, we ran the Cox regression models for labor-force withdrawal and reentry. The multivariate analyses are presented in Table 6.1. The major finding is that, net of many individual attributes and circumstances, job-related opportunity structures associated with

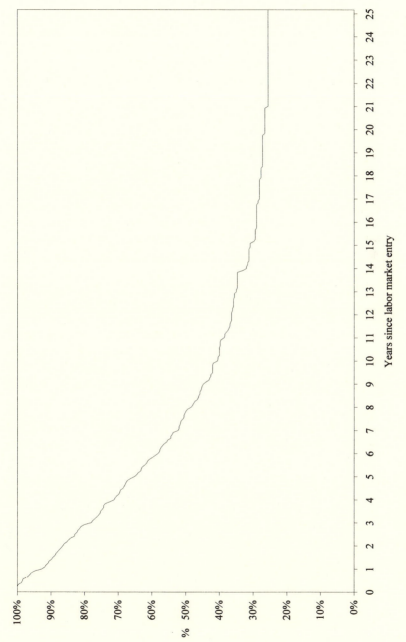

Figure 6.1 Employment Exit: Survival Function.

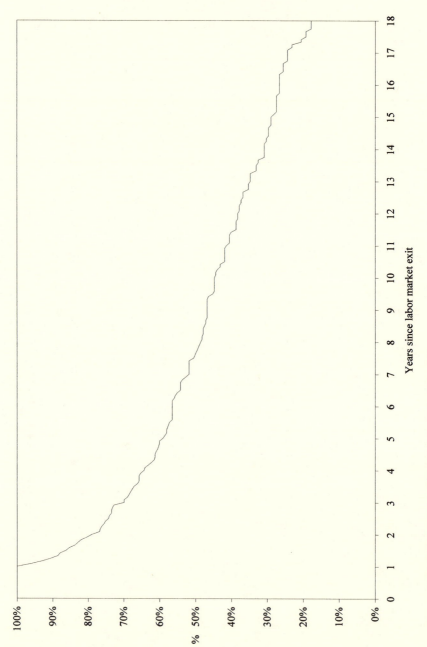

Figure 6.2 Employment Reentry: Survival Function.

Table 6.1 Determinants of Employment Exit and Reentry

Cox Regression	B		exp B	(se B)	B		exp B	(se B)
			Exit				*Reentry*	
Labor Market Context								
Occupation[a] (office clerks)		**						
Teachers: sec. level & up	1.04	*	2.83	(0.52)	−1.01	+	0.37	(0.63)
Professions	0.99	*	2.70	(0.41)	−0.53		0.59	(0.48)
Finance assoc. professionals	1.43	***	4.18	(0.36)	−1.20	+	0.30	(0.66)
Customer service clerks	0.16		1.17	(0.29)	0.47		1.60	(0.41)
Teachers: kindergarten/elem.	0.85	*	2.33	(0.38)	−0.74	+	0.48	(0.44)
Mod. health & nursing APs	0.13		1.14	(0.26)	−0.45		0.64	(0.34)
Cosmetic body care	−0.49		0.61	(0.34)	−0.39		0.68	(0.48)
Personal health and child care	0.79	**	2.19	(0.27)	−0.73	+	0.48	(0.38)
Phy./eng. science APs	0.10		1.11	(0.31)	−1.01	*	0.36	(0.49)
Restaurant service workers	−0.51	+	0.60	(0.29)	−0.18		0.84	(0.37)
Salespeople	−0.04		0.96	(0.19)	−0.63	*	0.54	(0.30)
Trade/artisans	0.20		1.23	(0.33)	0.25		1.28	(0.43)
Skilled agricultural workers	−0.23		0.79	(0.44)	0.35		1.41	(0.65)
Machine operators	0.37		1.44	(0.42)	0.23		1.25	(0.54)
Unskilled laborers	−0.69	+	0.50	(0.40)	0.29		1.34	(0.52)
Other occupations	−0.00		1.00	(0.31)	−0.76	+	0.47	(0.45)
Part-time opportunities[a,b]/10	−0.17	*	0.85	(0.07)	0.02		1.02	(0.12)
Sector: service sector[a,c]	0.08		1.08	(0.15)	0.19		1.21	(0.22)
Type of firm: public service[a,c]	0.36	**	1.44	(0.14)	0.16		1.17	(0.18)
Position: job authority[a]	−0.87	+	0.42	(0.46)	1.50	**	4.50	(0.60)
Occupational status[a]	−0.08	**	0.92	(0.03)	0.08	*	1.08	(0.04)
Employment level[a] (full-time)		+						
Part-time	−0.36	*	0.70	(0.16)	0.09		1.09	(0.21)
Missing values	−0.04		0.96	(0.21)	−0.16		0.85	(0.27)
Firm size[a] (1–9 employees)						+		
10–49 employees	0.16		1.17	(0.15)	0.01		1.01	(0.21)
50–99 employees	−0.12		0.89	(0.21)	0.55	*	1.73	(0.27)
≥100 employees	−0.03		0.97	(0.15)	−0.13		0.87	(0.23)
Region[a] (urban)		*						
Rural	−0.19	+	0.83	(0.12)	−0.07		0.94	(0.18)
Missing values	0.28	+	1.33	(0.18)	0.21		1.23	(0.23)
Control Variables								
Domestic Characteristics								
Pregnancy/birth[a,c]	1.80	***	6.06	(0.14)	−2.37	***	0.09	(0.62)
No. of children 0–6 years[a]	0.09		1.09	(0.14)	−0.65	***	0.52	(0.12)
No. of children 7–14 years[a]	0.46	+	1.59	(0.25)	−0.11		0.90	(0.11)
No. of children 15–25 years[a]	/		/	/	0.58	*	1.79	(0.28)
Marital status: married[a,c]	1.51	***	4.55	(0.13)	−0.71	**	0.49	(0.23)
Marital status: formerly married[a,c]	1.18	*	3.27	(0.49)	1.74	***	5.68	(0.41)

Table 6.1 Determinants of Employment Exit and Reentry (*continued*)

		Exit				Reentry		
Cox Regression	B		exp B	(se B)	B		exp B	(se B)
Human Capital								
Education (voc. training)		***				***		
Lower secondary education	−0.51	**	0.60	(0.19)	0.57	**	1.76	(0.23)
Vocational college	−0.67	**	0.51	(0.22)	0.73	**	2.08	(0.24)
Univ. entrance exam (baccal.)	−1.05	***	0.35	(0.32)	1.03	***	2.81	(0.30)
Higher vocational diploma	−2.10	***	0.12	(0.58)	1.19	**	3.30	(0.48)
University	−2.09	**	0.12	(0.72)	2.20	***	8.99	(0.67)
Labor market experience[a]	−0.42	**	0.66	(0.16)	0.32	+	1.38	(0.20)
Labor market experience2[a]	0.01		1.01	(0.01)	−0.02	+	0.98	(0.01)
Potential individual earnings[a,d]	0.11	+	1.12	(0.06)	−0.17	*	0.84	(0.08)
Birth cohort: 1959–61[c]	−1.02	***	0.36	(0.14)	0.56	**	1.75	(0.18)
In training[a,c]	0.24		1.27	(0.19)	0.05		1.05	(0.23)
Values after fifth job: missing[c]	0.47	*	1.60	(0.24)	0.35		1.42	(0.34)
Interaction Terms								
Lower sec. educ. × time	−1.35	***	0.26	(0.14)	−1.68	***	0.19	(0.21)
Vocational school × time	−1.31	***	0.27	(0.20)	−1.89	***	0.15	(0.27)
Baccalaureate × time	−1.45	***	0.24	(0.19)	−1.22	***	0.30	(0.25)
Higher voc. training × time	−1.71	***	0.18	(0.33)	−1.03	+	0.36	(0.56)
University × time	−1.58	***	0.21	(0.43)	−1.61		0.20	(1.51)
Birth cohort × time	−1.07	***	0.34	(0.12)	−1.10	***	0.33	(0.20)
-2 Log likelihood	5274				2759			
Modell chi-square	1372.01	***			693.69	***		
Df	50				51			
Episodes	3637				1688			
Events	431				259			

[a]Time-dependent.
[b]In occupations.
[c]Dichotomous variable.
[d]Per 100 SFr.
+, $p = .10$;   *, $p = .05$;   **, $p = .01$;   ***, $p = .001$.

occupation, type of firm, firm size, and *organizational position* affect women's labor-market attachment.

The first contextual covariate, *occupation,* shows a significant total effect for women's propensity to exit the labor force. For employment reentry, the differences between occupational groups are similar in magnitude; they are not significant, however, due to the smaller sample of episodes reducing the power of the statistical test. The findings provide support for our expectation that occupation-specific labor-market segments greatly affect women's labor-force attachment. The opportunities for continuous employment vary considerably between occupational groups. When interpreting the effects of particular occupational groups, we must keep in mind that *clerical work* is the reference category. The effect coefficients thus reflect the differences between the hazard rates observed for given occupational groups and the rate observed for clerical work. As clerical jobs offer relatively favorable conditions for combining work and family due to the large number of widely spread job offers and the broad dissemination of flex-time work, the great majority of the significant negative effects shown for both the exit and reentry models make sense. Most occupation-specific labor-market segments provide fewer opportunities for attaching women to paid work when compared to clerical work. In order not to go beyond the scope of this chapter, we limit our discussion to selected occupation-specific labor-market segments.

Women in *professions*, such as medical doctors, architects, computer scientists, and chemists, are more likely to exit employment compared to women in clerical work. In these highly skilled, male-dominated occupations, the myth of work-family incompatibility is expected to be particularly strong (for the sciences, see Nowotny 1986; for computer scientists, see Heintz, Nadai, Fischer, and Ummel 1997). Accordingly, commitment to work is still seen as a "calling" (Weber) incompatible with other time- and energy-consuming activities, such as raising a family. Reduction of working hours due to family obligations is therefore regarded as a violation of professional norms. Hence, the cultural constraints prevailing in the professions force women to withdraw from paid work when they become mothers.

Kindergarten and *elementary school teachers* show a higher rate of employment exit and a lower rate of employment reentry. Against the background of common beliefs, this is somewhat surprising (see Kurz 1998). These beliefs involve the notion that teaching provides considerable flexibility and autonomy with regard to working hours, thus enhancing work-family compatibility. We attribute the high exit rate observed in our data to the increasing demands expressed over the last two decades by parents, pupils, and the school administration. Permanent school reforms, conflicting expectations between the parties involved, as well as rising emotional and communicative problems with pupils combine to evoke burnout syndromes (Barth 1992; Forneck and Schriever 2000), finally resulting in withdrawal from the labor force. Previous employment as kindergarten or elementary school teacher does not encourage employment reentry after an extended period out of the labor force. The decreasing attractiveness of these occupations, the lack of opportunities for upward mobility, combined with the particularly high costs of retraining due to occupation-specific mobility barriers help explain the low propensity to resume paid work.

Occupation-specific opportunity structures also refer to the chances of engaging in *part-time work*. As expected, Table 6.1 shows that women remain more often continuously employed when they work in occupations that provide a sizable share of part-time jobs. First of all, part-time work makes it easier to combine paid work with family obligations. Second, occupations offering a substantial proportion of part-time jobs enhance the opportunities for switching to part-time work when women expect children. The extent of part-time work opportunities offered by the occupations in which women held jobs before they withdrew from the labor force does not affect the rate of employment reentry, however.

The next two findings shown in Table 6.1, namely, the effects of *economic sectors* and *public versus private sectors*, must be seen in the light of the amendments to Sengenberger's (1987) concept of the tripartite labor market (see section on theoretical considerations). Against our expectations, women working in service sector jobs are not more likely to be continuously employed compared to their counterparts holding either industrial or agricultural jobs. And women employed in public sector jobs are even more likely to withdraw from the labor force than their colleagues in the private sector. The former group's likelihood of exiting employment is 44 percent higher compared to the latter one (see *exp B* in Table 6.1). This finding may be attributable to civil servants' anticipation of few difficulties when reentering employment. The greater efforts made by the public sector to establish gender-egalitarian work opportunities may even encourage women to temporarily exit employment because they can more firmly count on equivalent jobs when they intend to resume paid work. Since these women do not have to fear skill depreciation and income losses often associated with extended periods away from paid labor, they might be more willing to interrupt employment compared to their counterparts in the private sector. If this argument holds, the reentry rate observed for women previously employed in the public sector should be higher compared to women who worked in the private sector before withdrawing from the labor force. Although not significant, the direction of the finding is in line with the argument provided here. All in all, the higher exit rate observed for public sector employees suggests better reentry conditions.

We now turn to the findings in Table 6.1 pertaining to the *organizational context* of women's labor-force attachment. The significant negative effects of *formal authority* and *occupational status* quite impressively show that women working in high-status jobs and in jobs vested with authority are much less likely to withdraw from the labor force compared to their respective counterparts. If they do nonetheless interrupt their work careers, they reenter employment much more often than women previously holding low-status jobs or jobs without formal authority. Women formerly employed in superior positions are 4.5 times as likely to return to paid work compared to their low-status counterparts (see *exp B in Table*

6.1). This is in line with our expectations. We argued that higher positions in the organizational hierarchy enhance women's labor-force participation by offering not only greater prestige and responsibility but also interesting work, and considerable flexibility and autonomy with regard to working hours. The "male profile" of these jobs discussed above apparently does not impede women's continuous employment, whether these positions are reserved exclusively for women who are not burdened with family obligations, or whether these women have learned to reduce their household obligations (see Wright, Baxter, and Birkelund 1995).[16] As mentioned before, women previously employed in the higher echelons of the organizational hierarchy are also more likely to reenter employment. We suspect that their strong work commitment brings them back to the labor force despite the danger of downward mobility coupled with income losses.

The ways in which *employment level* affects the rate of employment exit corresponds with our expectations. Women working in part-time jobs are less likely to withdraw from the labor force than women holding full-time jobs. Part-time work gives more leeway for combining work and family obligations. Our findings thus show that both the part-time opportunities provided by the *occupation* and the *individual engagement* in part-time work affect the rate of exiting the labor market. Table 6.1 shows no relationship between employment level and reentry into paid work. This finding is in line with those reported by Lauterbach (1994) as well as Klein and Braun (1995). According to Hakim's (1997) expectation of low work commitment associated with part-time work, the rate of employment exit among women holding part-time work should be higher and, vice versa, the rate of employment reentry of women previously employed in part-time work should be lower. Apparently, this is not the case (for similar findings, see Kurz 1998).

The total effects of *firm size* differ between employment exit and reentry. The likelihood of exiting employment does not seem to be affected by the size of the firm in which respondents hold jobs. However, the size of the firm in which women worked before exiting the labor force significantly influences employment reentry. Women previously employed in medium-sized firms (50–99 employees) are much more likely to return to paid work compared to their counterparts who held jobs in small firms of less than 10 employees (reference group). This finding is in line with our hypothesis derived from organizational demography (see section on theoretical considerations). According to the arguments presented there, larger firms provide more favorable conditions for skill updating. Women previously employed in such firms may therefore be attractive to future employers, thus encouraging women's employment reentry. This positive effect does not hold for firms with more than 100 employees, however. The reentry rate of women previously employed in these large firms (compared to the average size of Swiss enterprises) does not significantly differ from the rate observed for women coming from small firms (1–9 employees). The negative direction of the finding lends itself to an interpretation based on segmentation theory. In large firms, entry barriers may keep women away from returning to the internal labor markets. After an extended period out of the labor force, these women must fear being relegated to the entry ports of internal labor markets or to experience downward mobility to the occupation-specific segment of the labor market. As both options are not very favorable, women formerly holding jobs in large firms with internal labor markets may decide to stay away from paid work.

Regional disparities may also play a role for women's labor-force attachment. The findings show that the reentry rate is not affected by the regional context of women's last job before exiting the labor force. Women whose jobs were in urban areas are not more likely to return to paid work than their counterparts in rural areas. The exit rate, however, does vary by the regional context of the job. Urban working women are more likely to withdraw from the labor force compared to women whose jobs are in rural areas. Likewise, the exit rate is higher for women for whom the information on the regional context of their jobs is missing. The last finding is hard to interpret and the lower exit rate observed for rural women runs against our expectations. We may speculate about the causes responsible for the lower rate, for example, regional disparities in salaries with lower levels in rural areas (see Bauer 1998).

The second part of Table 6.1 shows the effects of various individual attributes. In the theoretical context of the present chapter, individual characteristics serve as control variables. For this reason, we do not comment the respective findings extensively. Not surprisingly, family attributes have a very strong impact on women's propensity to exit and reenter the labor force. Education exerts a strong effect as well. It is not constant across time, however (see the interaction terms).

Compared to women of the older cohort (women born between 1949 and 1951), the exit rate is lower among members of the younger cohort (women born between 1959 and 1961). Younger women also reenter the labor force more often and faster after a labor-force exit. These findings indicate an intergenerational change in employment patterns and a substantial increase in women's labor-force integration, which cannot be explained by the contextual and individual characteristics we control for in our models. It seems plausible, however, that changing attitudes, especially with respect to gender roles, the division of household labor, and the importance of employment in women's life course have strongly contributed to the observed change.

Finally, the variable indicating whether the information on some characteristics of jobs women held *after* the fifth job is missing shows a significant effect on the exit rate.[17]

CONCLUSIONS

Our findings indicate that labor market opportunities affect women's labor-force attachment *net* of the family situation, human capital factors, and financial resources. In particular, higher positions in the organizational hierarchy greatly lower women's propensity to exit the labor force. Employment in the higher echelons of the organizational hierarchy before exiting the labor force also helps women to return to paid work. These findings strongly support our expectations derived from organizational theory. By offering prestige, responsibility, interesting work, and considerable autonomy with regard to working hours, high-status jobs, and those vested with formal authority enhance women's work commitment, thus lowering the exit rate. In case women employed in such jobs interrupt their work careers, they reenter employment quickly, because of anticipated skill depreciation and income loss. Employment in part-time work also helps women to stay in the labor force thanks to the greater work-family compatibility. In line with organizational arguments is the finding that women with jobs in medium-sized firms before exiting the labor force are more likely to return to paid work than their counterparts who held jobs in small firms. Jobs allocated in larger firms provide more opportunities for skill updating. For this reason, women previously employed in such firms may therefore be attractive to future employers, thus helping these women to return to the labor force. As suspected, the influence of firm size may also be interpreted in the framework of segmentation theory. Our findings support this view, as large firms do not provide more favorable conditions for women's employment reentry compared to small firms. Entry barriers to internal labor markets may be at work and keep former employees of large firms away from returning to the labor force, as they may fear being relegated to entry ports of the internal labor market or even to the occupation-specific labor-market segment. In general, our findings show that arguments based on segmentation theory are pertinent to understanding women's labor-force attachment. In particular, women's opportunities for continuous employment and their propensity to exit and reenter the labor force vary considerably between occupation-specific labor markets. One important characteristic of these labor markets is the availability of part-time jobs, which greatly helps keep women in the labor force. Moreover, the opportunity structures also differ between the private and public sectors of the economy. Interestingly enough, segmentation arguments hold in that the two sectors are indeed different, but the results do not show the expected direction. Jobs in the public sector are associated with higher rates of employment exits. We attributed this to more favorable conditions of employment reentry prevailing in this sector. All in all, the findings presented in this chapter provide evidence that organizational arguments and those based on labor-market segmentation theory greatly help us understand women's labor-force attachment.

NOTES

1. In addition, our book (Buchmann et al. 2002) presents the arguments provided by structural approaches of gender segregation. Given that the variables measuring sex-specific occupational segregation did not substantially improve the explanatory power of our model, we do not discuss these theoretical approaches here.

2. Initially, we also considered the concept of the dual labor market (Averitt 1968). However, the explanatory power of a variable included in the model and measuring the core and peripheral labor-market segments revealed to be minimal. We therefore decided not to present the theoretical arguments related to the concept of the dual labor market.

3. The second approach, especially, supplements the concept of the tripartite labor-market segmentation advanced by Sengenberger.

4. Information on organizational characteristics collected in personal interviews or with questionnaires administered to employees is not very reliable (Preisendörfer 1987).

5. The German-speaking part of Switzerland comprises about 65 percent of the population.

6. Over the observation period (i.e., first labor-force entry after completion of formal education to the time of the survey), 40 percent of the women in our sample were continuously employed ($N = 309$) and 60 percent left the labor market once or several times ($N = 481$).

7. The interaction term is defined as follows: $z = z_c\, x_g\, (\ln v - \ln c)$, where x_g is the covariate of interest, $\ln v$ the log of duration and $\ln c$ the log of average duration.

8. This implies that we split the data into two subepisodes each time a time-varying covariate changes its state. To include the number of children as time-varying covariate, for example, the total employment spell is subdivided into subspells each time a child is born.

9. The attributes that change with each job, such as human capital indicators, earnings, organizational characteristics, and region, can thus be assessed

10. Here, job attributes are time-constant covariates because they always refer to the job held immediately before withdrawal from the labor force.

11. The number of episodes in the exit model was reduced to 3637 because of missing data for covariates. A missing value for one subepisode resulted in the exclusion of all subepisodes of the respective respondent. This procedure ensures that we examine complete histories only.

12. Although we define part-time work by the range of 1–35 working hours per week, the distribution clusters around particular weekly working hours (e.g., 20 working hours). This is so because, in most instances, the weekly working hours of part-time jobs cannot be chosen at liberty. Very often, employers offer jobs with pre-fixed weekly working hours (Stephan 1995). Hence, there are only a few job spells included in part-time jobs with more than 30 weekly working hours).

13. To assess the family situation, we include the following time-varying covariates. A dummy is used to assess a *pregnancy,* assuming the value of 1 during a nine-month period before birth. The *number of children* is differentiated by age group referring to children 0–6, 7–14, and 15–25 years of age. The variable referring to children 15 years and older is omitted from the exit model. At the time of labor-force withdrawal, the number of women with children of that age is practically nil. *Two dummies measure marital status.* The first one includes married women and those who get married within a six-month period. The second one includes divorced and widowed women and those who get divorced within a six-month period. *Human capital* is measured by *education and labor-market experience*. Education is defined by six categories, referring to lower secondary education, vocational college, apprenticeship, baccalaureate, higher vocational training, and university. Apprenticeship serves as the reference category. Labor-market experience is measured as years worked before the event. We additionally include the squared term of labor-market experience in order to acknowledge the expected curvilinear effect of work experience on employment decisions. Finally, a dummy is included to assess whether the respondent is in training. This dummy assumes the value of 1 for the duration of the training, including two months before and four months after the training period. Respondent's *financial circumstances* are defined as potential individual earnings (based on a full-time job) as information on household income has not been collected in the survey.

14. The data sets provide information on most time-varying covariates for the first five jobs only. This is not a major problem as the great majority of respondents held less than five jobs. However, in order not to exclude respondents who held more than five jobs during the observation period from the analysis, we substituted the missing values by assigning the modus. By including a dummy indicating the substitution of values, we are able to assess whether this procedure results in any bias.

15. In order to determine to what extent the influence of individual attributes varies with the labor-market context, it would be instructive to include in our models interaction effects between *individual and contextual characteristics*. Due to insufficient statistical power we refrain from estimating such models.

16. Wright, Baxter, and Birkelund (1995) find these mechanisms of self-selection at work in Canada.

17. This suggests that women whose work careers are characterized by numerous job shifts show a higher propensity to withdraw from the labor force. Numerous job changes may reflect a low commitment to one's occupation, which goes hand in hand with many employment interruptions. Although this interpretation is plausible and in line with the results of the reentry-model, the finding might also indicate that our estimates of the contextual factors are slightly distorted by the necessary substitution of missing values (see DATA AND METHODS).

REFERENCES

Acker, Joan. 1991. "Hierarchies, Jobs, Bodies: A Theory of Gendered Organizations." Pp. 162–79 in *The Social Construction of Gender,* edited by J. Lorber and S. A. Farrell. London: Sage.

Allison, Paul D. 1984. *Event History Analysis. Regression for Longitudinal Event Data.* Beverly Hills/London/New Delhi: Sage.

Averitt, Robert T. 1968. *The Dual Economy. The Dynamics of American Industry Structure.* New York: Norton.

Baron, James N. and William T. Bielby. 1980. "Bringing the Firm Back In: Stratification, Segmentation, and the Organization of Work." *American Sociological Review* 45:737–67.

Barth, Anne-Rose. 1992. *Burnout bei Lehrern: Theoretische Aspekte und Ergebnisse einer Untersuchung.* Göttingen und Zürich: Hogrefe Verlag für Psychologie.

Bauer, Tobias. 1998. "Familie, Zeitverwendung und Lohnmöglichkeiten. Eine Analyse der Zusammenhänge nach Geschlecht anhand der SAKE 1995." *SAKE-News* 98(1):1–26.

Becker, Gary S. 1975. *Human Capital.* New York/London: Columbia University Press.

Becker, Gary S. 1991. *A Treatise on the Family.* Cambridge, MA/London: Harvard University Press.

Becker, Rolf. 1993. *Staatsexpansion und Karrierechancen. Berufsverläufe im öffentlichen Dienst und in der Privatwirtschaft.* Frankfurt a.M.: Campus.

Blood, Robert O., Jr., and Donald M. Wolfe. 1960. *Husbands & Wives: The Dynamics of Married Living.* New York/London: Free Press.

Blossfeld, Hans-Peter. 1991. "Der Wandel von Ausbildung und Berufseinstieg bei Frauen." Pp. 1–22 in *Vom Regen in die Traufe: Frauen zwischen Beruf und Familie,* edited by K. U. Mayer, J. Allmendinger, and J. Huinink. Frankfurt a.M.: Campus.

Blossfeld, Hans-Peter, Alfred Hamerle, and Karl Ulrich Mayer. 1986. *Ereignisanalyse. Statistische Theorie und Anwendung in den Wirtschafts- und Sozialwissenschaften.* Frankfurt a.M./New York: Campus.

Blossfeld, Hans-Peter and Karl Ulrich Mayer. 1988. "Arbeitsmarktsegmentation in der Bundesrepublik Deutschland. Eine empirische Überprüfung von Segmentationstheorien aus der Perspektive des Lebenslaufs." *Kölner Zeitschrift für Soziologie und Sozialpsychologie* 40:262–83.

Borkowsky, Anna and Ursula Streckeisen. 1982. "Wiedereinstieg von Frauen in den Beruf. Theoretische Überlegungen zu Determinanten im domestikalen Arbeitsbereich und im Lohnarbeitsbereich." *Schweizerische Zeitschrift für Soziologie* 8:279–310.

Born, Claudia. 1991. "Zur Bedeutung der beruflichen Erstausbildung bei der Verbindung von Familien- und Erwerbsarbeit in weiblichen Lebensläufen." Pp. 19–31 in *Lebensläufe von Frauen und ihre Benachteiligung im Alter,* edited by C. Gather. Berlin: Edition Sigma.

Born, Claudia, Helga Krüger, and Dagmar Lorenz-Meyer. 1996. *Der unentdeckte Wandel. Annäherung an das Verhältnis von Struktur und Norm im weiblichen Lebenslauf.* Berlin: Edition Sigma.

Bornschier, Volker. 1982. "Segmentierung der Unternehmen in der Wirtschaft und personelle Einkommensverteilung." *Schweizerische Zeitschrift für Soziologie* 8:519–39.

Brüderl, Josef and Wolfgang Ludwig-Mayerhofer. 1994. "Aufbereitung von Verlaufsdaten mit zeitveränderlichen Kovariaten mit SPSS." *ZA-Information* 34:79–105.

Brüderl, Josef, Peter Preisendörfer, and Rolf Ziegler. 1993. "Upward Mobility in Organizations: The Effects of Hierarchy and Opportunity Structure." *European Sociological Review* 9(2):173–88.

Buchmann, Marlis, Irene Kriesi, Andrea Pfeifer, and Stefan Sacchi. 2002. *Halb drinnen—halb draussen. Analysen zur Arbeitsmarktintegration von Frauen in der Schweiz.* Zürich/Chur: Rüegger.

Buchmann, Marlis and Stefan Sacchi. 1997. *Berufsverlauf und Berufsidentität im sozio-technischen Wandel: Konzeption, Methodik und Repräsentativität einer retrospektiven Befragung der Geburtsjahrgänge 1949–51 und 1959–61.* Zürich: Eidgenössische Technische Hochschule (ETH).

Buchmann, Marlis and Stefan Sacchi. 1998. "The Transition from School to Work in Switzerland: Do Characteristics of the Educational System and Class Barriers Matter?" Pp. 407–42 in *From School to Work: A Comparative Study of Educational Qualifications and Occupational Destinations,* edited by Y. Shavit and W. Müller. Oxford: Clarendon.

Bundesamt für Statistik (Ed.). 1996. *Die Schweizerische Lohnstrukturerhebung 1994. Kommentierte Ergebnisse und Tabellen.* Bern: Bundesamt für Statistik.

Carroll, Glenn R., Heather Havemann, and Anand Swaminathan. 1990. "Karrieren in Organisationen. Eine ökologische Perspektive". Pp. 146–78 in *Lebensverläufe und sozialer Wandel,* edited by K. U. Mayer. Sonderheft 31 der *Kölner Zeitschrift für Soziologie und Sozialpsychologie.* Opladen: Westdeutscher Verlag.

DiPrete, Thomas A., Paul M. de Graaf, Ruud Luijkx, Michael Tåhlin, and Hans-Peter Blossfeld 1997. "Collectivist versus Individualist Mobility Regimes? Structural Change and Job Mobility in Four Countries." *American Journal of Sociology* 103(2):318–58.

Drobnič, Sonja, Hans-Peter Blossfeld, and Götz Rohwer. 1999. "Dynamics of Women's Employment Patterns over the Family Life Course: A Comparison of the United States and Germany." *Journal of Marriage and the Family* 61(1):133–59.

Engelbrech, Gerhard. 1991a. "Berufsausbildung, Berufseinstieg und Berufsverlauf von Frauen. Empirische Befunde zur Erklärung beruflicher Segregation." *Mitteilungen aus der Arbeitsmarkt- und Berufsforschung* 24(3):531–58.

Engelbrech, Gerhard. 1991b. "Frauenspezifische Restriktionen des Arbeitsmarktes—Situationsberichte und Erklärungsansätze zu Phasen des Berufsverlaufs anhand von IAB-Ergebnissen." Pp. 91–118 in *Vom Regen in die Traufe: Frauen zwischen Beruf und Familie,* edited by K. U. Mayer, J. Allmendinger, and J. Huinink. Frankfurt a.M.: Campus.

Forneck, Hermann J. and Friederike Schriever. 2000. *Die individualisierte Profession. Untersuchung der Lehrer/-innenarbeitszeit und -belastung im Kanton Zürich.* Zürich: Bildungsdirektion des Kantons Zürich.

Glass, Jennifer L. and Lisa Riley. 1998. "Family Responsive Policies and Employee Retention Following Childbirth." *Social Forces* 76(4):1401–35.

Hakim, Catherine. 1997. "A Sociological Perspective on Part-Time Work" Pp. 22–70 in *Between Equalization and Marginalization. Women Working Part-Time in Europe and the United States of America,* edited by H.-P. Blossfeld and C. Hakim. Oxford: Oxford University Press.

Haveman, Heather A. and Lisa E. Cohen. 1994. "Ecological Dynamics of Careers: The Impact of Organizational Founding, Dissolution, and Merger on Job Mobility." *American Journal of Sociology* 100(1):104–52.

Heintz, Bettina and Eva Nadai. 1998. "Geschlecht und Kontext. De-Institutiona-lisierungsprozesse und geschlechtliche Differenzierung." *Zeitschrift für Soziologie* 27(2):75–93.

Heintz, Bettina, Eva Nadai, Regula Fischer, and Hannes Ummel. 1997. *Ungleich unter Gleichen. Studien zur geschlechtsspezifischen Segregation des Arbeitsmarktes.* Frankfurt a.M.: Campus.

Höpflinger, François, Maria Charles, and Annelies Debrunner. 1991. *Familienleben und Berufsarbeit: Zum Wechselverhältnis zweier Lebensbereiche.* Zürich: Seismo.

Kalleberg, Arne L. and Arne Mastekaasa. 1998. "Organizational Size, Layoffs, and Quits in Norway." *Social Forces* 76(4):1243–73.

Klein, Thomas and Uwe Braun. 1995. "Der berufliche Wiedereinstieg von Müttern." *Zeitschrift für Soziologie* 24(1):58–68.

Krüger, Helga and Claudia Born. 1991. "Unterbrochene Erwerbskarrieren und Berufsspezifik: Zum Arbeitsmarkt- und Familienpuzzle im weiblichen Lebenslauf." Pp. 142–61 in *Vom Regen in die Traufe: Frauen zwischen Beruf und Familie,* edited by K. U. Mayer, J. Allmendinger, and J. Huinink. Frankfurt a.M.: Campus.

Kurz, Karin. 1998. *Das Erwerbsverhalten von Frauen in der intensiven Familienphase. Ein Vergleich zwischen Müttern in der Bundesrepublik und in den USA.* Opladen: Leske and Budrich.

Lauterbach, Wolfgang. 1994. *Berufsverläufe von Frauen. Erwerbstätigkeit, Unterbrechung und Wiedereintritt.* Frankfurt a.M.: Campus.

Levy, René, Dominique Joye, Olivier Guye, and Vincent Kaufmann. 1997. *Tous egaux? De la stratification aux representations.* Zürich: Seismo.

Lewin, Ralph. 1982. *Arbeitsmarktsegmentierung und Lohnstruktur. Theoretische Ansätze und Hauptergebnisse einer Überprüfung am Beispiel der Schweiz.* Zürich: Schulthess.

Müller, Ursula. 1993. "Sexualität, Organisation und Kontrolle." Pp. 97–114 in *Transformationen im Geschlechterverhältnis: Beiträge zur industriellen und gesellschaftlichen Entwicklung,* edited by B. Aulenbacher and M. Goldmann. Frankfurt a.M./New York: Campus.

Nowotny, Helga. 1986. "Über die Schwierigkeiten des Umgangs von Frauen mit der Institution Wissenschaft." Pp. 17–30 in *Wie männlich ist die Wissenschaft?* edited by K. Hausen and H. Nowotny. Frankfurt a.M.: Suhrkamp.

OECD (Organisation for Economic Cooperation and Development). 1994. "Job gains and Job Losses in Firms." *Employment Outlook* 12:103–34.

Preisendörfer, Peter. 1987. "Organisationale Determinanten beruflicher Karrieremuster." *Soziale Welt* 38(2):211–26.

Rosenbaum, James E. 1981. "Careers in a Corporate Hierarchy: A Longitudinal Analysis of Earnings and Level Attainment." Pp. 95–124 in *Research in Social Stratification and Mobility, Volume 1,* edited by D. J. Treiman and R. V. Robinson. Greenwich, CT: JAI.

Rosenbaum, James E. 1984. *Career Mobility in a Corporate Hierarchy.* New York: Academic Press.

Sengenberger, Werner. 1987. *Struktur und Funktionsweise von Arbeitsmärkten. Die Bundesrepublik Deutschland im internationalen Vergleich.* Frankfurt a.M.: Campus.

Stephan, Gesine. 1995. *Zur Dynamik des Arbeitsangebots von Frauen. Vollzeit-, Teilzeit- und Nichterwerbstätigkeit.*" Frankfurt a.M./New York: Campus.

Stewman, Shelby and Suresh L. Konda. 1983. "Careers and Organizational Labor Markets: Demographic Models of Organizational Behaviour." *American Journal of Sociology* 88(4):637–85.

Treiman, Donald J. 1977. *Occupational Prestige in Comparative Perspective.* New York: Academic Press.

Wright, Erik Olin, Janeen Baxter, and Gunn Elisabeth Birkelund. 1995. "The Gender Gap in Workplace Authority: A Cross-national Study." *American Sociological Review* 60:407–35.

| 7 |

Employment Trajectories of East and West German Mothers Compared

One Nation—One Pattern?

Hildegard Schaeper and Susanne Falk

INTRODUCTION

Between 1945 and 1990 two politically, economically, and—in part—culturally different societies coexisted in Germany. This situation changed fundamentally when upon unification in 1990 the West German institutional order was transferred to the territory of the hitherto German Democratic Republic (GDR). Assuming that institutions play a significant role in the shaping of the life course (cf. Heinz 1992), the question arises as to how and in which ways this transformation affected East German life courses. In order to answer this question it seems particularly promising to compare the employment trajectories of East and West German women, which differed markedly prior to unification.

Our theoretical point of departure is the idea that life courses are doubly embedded: in culture *and* in social structure—or, with regard to gender relations, in a "gender culture" *and* a "gender order." Compared to approaches that limit their focus to either the structural shaping of life courses or the cultural dimension, this perspective has a decisive advantage: It allows us to expose asynchronous and contradictory elements in the development and composition of culture and social structures and to investigate their effects on life courses—thereby addressing the issue of institutional (in-)consistencies and their implications (cf. Leisering and Schumann, Chapter 9 in this volume). In particular, we seek to answer the following questions: Did the adoption of the West German gender order result in an adaptation to West German life-course patterns? Or did the GDR gender culture, which to a large extent did not correspond with the West German gender order, have such an enduring hold that a convergence has been delayed? In what way do the differing opportunity structures in East and West Germany influence the assimilation of German lives?

Empirically, our research questions will be examined by analyzing the duration of the homemaking period after the birth of a child.

THE DOUBLE EMBEDDEDNESS OF LIFE COURSES

According to life-course theories that refer to structural sociology or, more precise, to differentiation theory and that proposed the concept of the "social structure of the life course," the structure of the life course results from the mapping of institutional differentiation onto the life course (cf. Mayer 1991; Mayer and Müller 1986). Formal governmental institutions play a decisive role in the shaping of life courses as they set age limits and regulate access and entitlements. Cultural conceptions of biographical sequences, i.e., informal or cultural institutions,[1] are of secondary significance. At best, they reinforce the effects of formal institutions. Cultural-sociological approaches (e.g., Meyer 1992), in contrast, focus on the life course as a cultural construct and emphasize the role of collective patterns of interpretations, norms, and role expectations.

The work of Kohli (1986) and Levy (1996a, 1996b) integrates the structural and cultural dimension. Kohli, for example, conceptualizes the life course as an institution that controls the temporal order of life and that at the same time structures the knowledge stock of the everyday world. Thus, he takes into account both material and symbolic aspects. Levy's concept of the life course as a "sequence of participation-position-role configurations," too, comprises structure and culture. The structural aspect refers to the participation in social fields, to the positions people occupy in these fields, and to the corresponding life chances. Because participation and position are subject to social evaluations, expectations, norms, and interpretations, the life course at the same time is a cultural phenomenon.

The analysis of female life courses under conditions of change benefits from Levy's approach for two reasons: (1) His concept of the life course as a sequence of participation-position-role configurations takes into account that most members of a society participate simultaneously in several subsystems or social fields. This idea is especially important for the analysis of female life courses to which the employment-centered three-phase model of Kohli (preparatory phase (i.e., education), active phase (i.e., gainful employment), retirement) does not apply. (2) According to the double nature of the life course as a structural and cultural phenomenon, Levy distinguishes between a structural and a cultural institutionalization of life courses that may be or not may be congruent.

Structural institutionalization of life courses means stable links between participation, status positions, status configurations, and status sequences, which emerge from the effect of various institutions such as the labor market, the education system, and the welfare state. A typical example of structural institutionalization is the link between participation in the labor market and income, which are both tied to education. Cultural institutionalization of life courses refers to the degree of diffusion and dissemination of life-course models or, more generally speaking, of life-course relevant conceptions, interpretations, and evaluations. Such processes of institutionalization yield—universal or group-specific, e.g., male and female—"normal biographies," which are structurally institutionalized and/or culturally institutionalized, thus having normative, cultural validity.

The various organizations and institutions relevant to the life course may operate consistently and in harmony; life-course patterns may be structurally as well as culturally institutionalized—thereby exerting more influence on the construction of biographies than models that are only culturally well established (cf. Levy 1996a:95). In times of fast social or cultural change, however, such a conformity is an exception, and frictions are the rule. It is thus possible that the culturally anchored constructions of life courses deviate from those which are carried by formal institutions, organizations, and social structure. Agreeing with Levy (1996b:87) we assume that in this case an adjustment will occur. In contrast to Levy, however, who supposes that structure will adapt to culture, we leave it open to empirical investigation whether structure or culture will change.

Levy (1996a), among others, stresses the existence of different coexisting life-course models, especially for the genders. Gender is a segregation principle that is embedded in every societal institution. Institutions presuppose a male and female "master status," a status that dominates all status positions (cf. Krüger 1995:204). This "doing gender of institutions" takes place at the structural as well as at the cultural level and generates gender-specific life courses and life-course patterns. In order to characterize the gender specificity of culture and structure we refer to the concepts "gender culture" and "gender order," which were proposed by Connell (1987), Ostner (1993), and Pfau-Effinger (2000).

Following Pfau-Effinger (2000), *gender culture* comprehends the prevalent values, norms, interpretive patterns, and role models concerning the family, the gender-specific division of labor, the maternal and paternal roles, the societal spheres attributed to men and women, and—related to the cultural construction of motherhood—conceptions of childhood. With regard to the life cycle, a society's gender culture implies collectively shared life-course designs that differ according to gender and that consist of general ideas concerning the sequence of life phases and the relationship between different life domains (cf. Geissler and Oechsle 1990). In addition, the gender culture also includes culturally dominant female and male "normal biographies" with more concrete schedules for the timing and duration of life periods.

The *gender order* refers to the objective structural relationships between the two genders (cf. Becker-Schmidt 1993), which is, according to Connell (1987), determined by three parameters: division of labor, power, and "cathexis," that is, the emotional and sexual relationship. In addition, the term "gender order" refers to the "gender regime" of institutions and organizations, which presupposes a gender-specific division of labor. The labor market and the system of social security, for example, are based on the construct of the so-called normal employment relationship, which is characterized by continuous full-time employment and usually assumes a second person in the background who relieves the full-time worker of family and household responsibilities. Another example for gender-structured institutions is the family, with its specific demands on the availability of the parents. These gender-structured institutions and organizations have effects not only on specific life phases, but on the entire life course. In this way, gender-specific life-course patterns can become structurally institutionalized as "normal biographies."

As with social structure and culture in general, the relationship between gender order and gender culture may vary. Social structure and culture can be considered as two sides of the same coin; social structure always is based on an underlying cultural "subtext." Formal institutions, too, resort to and are shaped by cultural constructions of normality. By doing so, these institutions regularly take into account the culturally prevalent role models, interpretive patterns, and values. In equilibrium the cultural constructions inherent in formal institutions are identical to the informal, cultural institutions. Ideally, culture and social structure are homologous. In modern societies, however, which are characterized by a high dynamic of change, we cannot assume this homology to be the rule. Instead, we have to reckon with asynchronous developments on both levels triggering more or less severe frictions and tensions between gender order and gender culture. Depending on which level lags behind, we speak of a "cultural lag" (cf. Ogburn 1964) or a "structural lag."

The analytical distinction between gender order and gender culture, hence, is a precondition for focusing our attention on contradictions and asynchronies in the constitution and development of gender order and gender culture and for posing the question how under these circumstances biographies are constructed. It is true that in West Germany, too, the development of gender culture and gender order did not run parallel. In East Germany after unification, however, the discrepancies are much more pronounced. In order to substantiate this assertion we will in the next sections first outline the GDR's and West Germany's gender cultures and gender orders and second describe the relationship between gender order and gender culture in East Germany after unification.

TWO GERMAN NATIONS: TWO CULTURES, TWO ORDERS, TWO LIFE-COURSE PATTERNS

The gender culture of the *GDR* can be briefly described as a "dual breadwinner/state childcare model" (Pfau-Effinger 1999).[2] It was based on the female role model of the working housewife and mother, which envisioned full integration of women into gainful employment, yet left intact their traditional responsibility for the reproductive sphere. Parallel to this, a social construction of childhood prevailed, which defined childhood as a separate phase requiring special care and support. Childcare and child-rearing were hereby understood, however, as largely public responsibilities.

In the early years of the GDR these cultural constructions were not collectively shared and had to be propagated intensively by state authorities and the socialist party. The fact that within two generations the new role models gained widespread acceptance, however, cannot be attributed solely to the massive propaganda. To a large extent it is the result of a wide range of accompanying regulative and organizational provisions by which these cultural patterns became materialized and structurally institutionalized.

The law conferred the right but also the obligation to gainful employment on both men and women. Step by step, childcare leave was extended ultimately to twelve months, the so-called baby year. Leave from work upon the birth of a child was socially and financially well safeguarded: The carer was compensated for loss of earnings associated with childcare, social insurance contributions were paid, and job retention was guaranteed. The maximum period of twelve months, however, was relatively short by West German standards, and with a few exceptions only mothers were entitled to take childcare leave. Parallel to this, the system of public childcare was fostered to such an extent that all-day care was guaranteed for children of nearly all ages. Part-time work was possible only to a limited extent. Ultimately, wage levels, the tax system, and divorce law all conspired to favor the dual-earner family.

This encompassing institutionalization of women's gainful employment was accompanied by a cultural as well as structural institutionalization of a specific female "normal biography"—the so-called pendulum model (Trappe 1995), which is characterized by a continuous full-time employment, interrupted only by brief family phases. The vast majority of East German mothers took the baby year, but additional family-related employment interruptions, the housewife status, or part-time work when returning to the workplace[3] virtually were unknown in the younger generation.

The gender culture of *West Germany* is characterized by a modernized version of the "male breadwinner/female childcare provider model" (Pfau-Effinger 1999) in which marriage is most clearly conceived as a "male breadwinner marriage" during the phase of active parenthood. As in the GDR, childhood is constructed as a separate phase requiring intensive childcare. In contrast to the GDR, however, childcare should ideally be provided at home. It is true that the traditional, family-centered female role model has been replaced by that of the "double conduct of life," in which women's and mothers' employment is understood to be normal. At the same time, however, the traditional image of the mother has remained culturally dominant: A "good mother" belongs with her child, at least while it is small (Oechsle 1998:190ff.). Consequently, a new ideal developed of the employed mother who allocates her working time to gainful employment according to the degree of care her child needs.

At the level of the gender order these modernized female role models were taken into account only to a limited extent. In institutions and organizations the sharp separation between labor market and the family, which presupposes a gender-specific division of labor, continues to prevail (cf. Krüger 1995:202). The labor market assumes the existence of a second person—typically the female partner—in the background. Correspondingly, family-related organizations such as school and childcare facilities offer almost exclusively half-day care (cf. Bauereiss, Bayer, and Bien 1997), thus requiring that one of the parents be exempt from regular employment obligations. Furthermore, the tax system does not reward dual-earner households. Parental leave, which in 1992 was increased from eighteen months to three years, indeed reduces the labor market and career risk associated with family-related employment interruption. Yet the means-tested amount of childcare allowance, which is not designed to compensate for loss of earnings, but to acknowledge childcare and child-rearing as an important societal task, again presupposes the existence of a breadwinner.

In this way, a specific maternal "normal biography" was structurally supported, the so-called three-phase model. In the past this model was culturally and empirically less common than generally assumed (cf. Born, Krüger, and Lorenz-Meyer 1996). Gainful employment of married women was not seen as desirable, but it was accepted in case the family needed the wife's income to maintain an acceptable standard of living. In younger generations, however, the three-phase model attained cultural and structural prevalence and can be regarded as structurally and culturally institution-alized. Almost every mother (and virtually no father) entitled to parental leave interrupts gainful employment up to the maximum duration of three years or even longer (cf. Engelbrech and Reinberg 1998; Engelbrech 1997). When reentering the labor market West German mothers, in addition, assume part-time rather than full-time work (Schneider and Rost 1998:226).

Comparing the normal biography in the GDR and West Germany it becomes obvious that the distinctive feature is not the phase pattern but the duration of employment interruption and the employment patterns upon labor market reentry.

ONE GERMAN NATION: ONE CULTURE, ONE ORDER, ONE LIFE-COURSE PATTERN?

Upon unification of the two German nations, the West German regulatory provisions in the fields of family, social, labor-market, and tax policy were transferred, without modifications, to the new German *Länder* (federal states). As a result, a new institutional framework for employment deci-sions of mothers came into existence, favoring longer periods of employ-ment interruptions. At the same time, the unification process with its radical political and economic changes evoked changes in opportunity structures, too. The labor market was by no means reorganized in gender-neutral fashion. The massive drop in employment opportunities affected women far more than men (cf. Engelbrech and Reinberg 1998:47): their unemployment rate in 1995 was nearly 20 percent, twice the male rate (ibid.:49). Female employment in typically male sectors was increasingly obstructed; in addition, phenomena of social closure also occurred in gender-mixed or typically female labor-market segments. For example, contrary to the situation in West Germany, where women profited from the increase of employment opportunities in the tertiary sector, employers in East Germany prefer to appoint men to the newly created jobs in the ser-vice sector. In other words, the reconstruction of the East German labor market followed a logic that was not restricted to economic and labor mar-ket criteria, but that also made use of the social category of gender as an additional structuring principle.

Changes in opportunity structures also occurred in the realm of public childcare. With the exception of after-school centers, there had been a mas-sive cutback of public childcare supply, paired with a rise in prices. Between 1991 and 1994 the supply of childcare opportunities for children aged three to six decreased by 23 percent (cf. Bauereiss et al. 1997:90). In the same period childcare opportunities for children aged less than two

Table 7.1   Attitudes of East and West German Women Aged 18 to 30 toward
            Maternal Employment Activity, 1991 and 1996[a]

	1991		1996	
	East	*West*	*East*	*West*
A small child surely suffers if his/her mother is employed.	49	64***	46	66***
A working mother can have a just as affectionate and trusting relationship with her children as a mother who is not employed.	93	76***	87	80
It is indeed good for a child when his/her mother is employed and does not simply concentrate on the household.	63	44***	68	49***

[a]Percent in agreement; value 1, "agree completely"; value 2, "tend to agree" in a four-step answer scale combined.
***East-West difference significant at $p < 0.01$ (chi-square test).
Source: ALLBUS; own calculations

years were reduced by 59 percent. In comparison to West Germany, however, the supply in East Germany remains numerically superior.

Due to the unilateral transfer of the West German regulatory provisions to the East, an all-German gender order indeed came into existence. Gender culture is a different matter, however. As far as can be concluded from the attitudes toward maternal employment and the gender-specific division of labor, no complete convergence of the different gender cultures occurred. In 1996, East German women perceived the effects of maternal employment on the well-being of the child to be far less negative than did West German women (Table 7.1). In addition, the differences between East and West Germany only changed marginally when compared to 1991.

When it comes to attitudes toward the gender-specific division of labor, the East-West differences are less pronounced but still existent (cf. Falk and Schaeper 2001). An equal majority of East and West German women reject the idea that the employment sphere should be exclusively men's place and the reproductive sphere women's place. Among East German women this disagreement is more marked. At the same time gainful employment is more important for East German than for West German women: In 1994, 60 percent of the young East German women and 30 percent of the young West German women agree with the statement that gainful employment is a central domain of life, 88 percent (vs. 78 percent in West Germany) would like to go to work even if the money is not needed.

Summarizing these findings, East German women continue to orient themselves toward a public construction of childhood, they consider motherhood and gainful employment not as mutually exclusive but as goals that can be synchronically combined. They reject more often than West German women do the exclusive localization in the family, and they have a strong orientation toward gainful employment, which is not solely instrumentally motivated by economic necessity. Thus, there is much evidence for the assumption that the biographical designs that were internalized during the GDR era remain prevalent and that no assimilation of the East and West German gender culture has occurred. In other words: The GDR gender culture remained relatively resistant to externally induced changes. In East Germany a "cultural lag" emerged, a contradiction between the culturally prevalent female normal biography and the new gender order.

What are the possible consequences of this constellation for female employment trajectories? In light of the complex interplay between gender order, gender culture, and opportunity structures, we cannot put forward an unambiguous hypothesis. Instead, we would like to present evidence for two possible alternatives:

1. A convergence of East and West German employment trajectories could be occurring for two reasons. First, due to the new gender order the responsibility for childcare now is imposed on East German mothers. Second, the opportunity structure changed in two relevant aspects: (a) the reduction in and increased costs of external childcare options, hindering the synchronous reconcilability of work and family; (b) the limited labor market opportunities for East German women, especially mothers.

2. Equally plausible would be a continuation of the difference in employment trajectories between East and West German women. This difference could result not only from the persisting East German gender culture, but also from unequal opportunity structures. The lower household income of partners in East Germany—due to lower wage levels and/or unemployment of the partner—could make maternal employment economically necessary.

DATA AND METHODS

In order to investigate which of these alternatives is presently empirically supported, we analyze longitudinal data from two projects conducted at the Bremen Special Research Programme (Sonderforschungsbereich 186). the study "Managing Occupational Status and Forming a Family: Skilled Workers Ten Years after Leaving School" and the study "Occupational Trajectories in East Germany." The West German sample consists of young skilled workers who completed their vocational training in Bremen and Munich in 1989/1990 and who were followed until 1997/1998. The selected group of the East German sample is composed of young skilled workers who completed their apprenticeship training in 1985 and 1990 in Leipzig and Rostock. The final panel wave took place in 1997.

Our analyses focus on women's behavior upon unification and examine the duration of the "homemaking episode" or "family phase" after the birth of a child. Therefore, from the East German sample in all but one analysis, births were excluded that occurred before 1 October 1990, the official date of unification. As a result, the window of observation spans the period 1989/1990 to 1997/1998 in West Germany and 1990 to 1997 in East Germany. In addition, all analyses are limited to births that occurred after graduation. For the purposes of our study, we included all mothers independently of their activity prior to the birth of a child,[4] meaning that we did not examine employment interruptions but rather, more generally, interruptions of the previous activity.

"Duration of the homemaking episode" was operationalized as follows: The process we observed starts with the month in which the child was born. For all birth episodes we assumed a two-month interruption period. This time span corresponds to the statutory maternity leave that all employed mothers have to take. Longer periods of interruptions occur when the mother takes parental leave or performs household labor. The criteria for the end of the interruption are not limited to the resumption of a full-time or part-time employment position, but can also include the transition to education or to unemployment.[5] Marginal—i.e., insurance-exempt—employment, however, is treated as family work.

Based on the above selection criteria, 202 birth episodes of 185 West German mothers and 119 birth episodes of 113 East German mothers formed the basis for our investigation, in which primarily event-history analysis (cf. Blossfeld and Rohwer 1995) was employed. This analytical tool is especially designed to analyze time-dependent processes, which are right-censored, i.e., are not completed, and to examine the effect of both time-dependent and time-constant covariates.

FINDINGS

The Duration of the Homemaking Period: East and West German Mothers Compared

The length of time women interrupt their previous activity when giving birth to a child is shown by the survivor functions displayed in Figure 7.1. The survival analysis, which estimates how long it takes the mothers to leave their status as a homemaker (how long they survived in this status), show clear and significant differences between West and East German mothers: East German women end the family phase more quickly than their West German counterparts. At the end of the three-year childcare

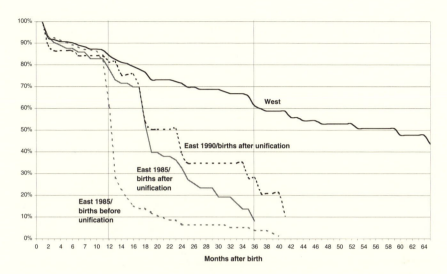

Figure 7.1 Duration of the Homemaking Episode of West German and East German Mothers Before and After Unification (Product-Limit Estimation).

leave the majority (approximately 60 percent) of West German mothers do not resume another activity, and roughly half of the women do not end the homemaking episode until their child reaches the age of six, i.e., school age.

Differences in the duration of interruption were also found within the group of East German mothers. To investigate this we did a "pre-post unification" comparison and included in our analysis—for this question only—births prior to 1 October 1990 as well. It is not surprising that the vast majority of East German women who gave birth to a child during the GDR period finished their family phase in the twelfth month, i.e., within the statutory leave period. By contrast, vocational training graduates who gave birth to a child after unification interrupted their employment for considerably longer periods.

The shape of the survivor functions suggests that there are certain points in time when the likelihood of realizing occupational reentry rises considerably. The curves for the East German women whose children were born after unification (the solid grey line and the dashed black line), for example, fall steeply between seventeen and nineteen months. In order to examine in more detail the time-dependency of the process under investigation we estimated period-specific hazard rates of reentry (transition rates), which can be understood as the present inclination to end the homemaking episode (Figure 7.2).[6]

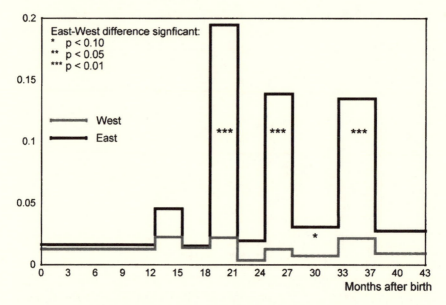

Figure 7.2   Transition out of Homemaking in East and West Germany: Estimated Hazard Rates (piecewise constant exponential model with period-
specific East-West effect).

The course of the transition rates reveals clear time-dependent patterns
or, put differently, age-specific "threshold values." In the period before the
child reaches the age of one year, West and East German women alike
exhibit little propensity to end the family phase, and the reentry rate of
East German mothers equals that of their West German counterparts. The
"baby year" is thus taken equally often in both the old and the new German states. Among both West and East German mothers, the transition
rate rises when the child reaches one year, one-and-a-half, two, and three
years in age, respectively. These "threshold values" are much more pronounced in the Eastern sample, and the East-West difference is highly significant—except in the interval of twelve to fourteen months.

The Duration of the Homemaking Period: The Formative Strength of Parental Leave Regulations

The results of another multivariate model suggest, however, that the
increased transition rates of East and West German women during the
intervals eighteen to twenty and thirty-three to thirty-six months can

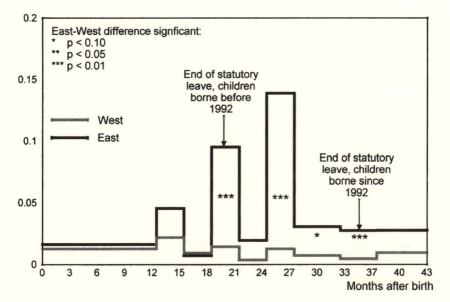

Figure 7.3 Transition out of Homemaking in East and West Germany: Estimated Hazard Rates (piecewise constant exponential model with period-specific East-West effect, controlling for expiry of statutory parental leave).

essentially be attributed to the ending of the statutory leave periods. If one controls for the expiry of parental leave, the hazard rates during the said periods for the most part no longer rise, or if they do, only marginally. Only in the Eastern sample does the tendency to end the family phase remain strong when the child is 18 months old (Figure 7.3).

This finding indicates that the end of the statutory leave period itself has a strong positive impact (see Table 7.2)—a result that was also obtained by Bird (2001)[7] and Braun and Klein (1995). Since the job retention guarantee expires when the family phase extends beyond the childcare leave period, there is a strong tendency to carry out the institutionally foreseen occupational reentry. This incentive has a more marked effect in the new German states than in the old. Yet as common estimation models showed, the difference is not significant (model not reported).

As regards the effect of the duration of statutory parental leave, which was extended from eighteen to thirty-six months in 1992, we observe that East German as well as West German mothers ended the homemaking episode more quickly when the 18-month regulation was in effect (Figure

Table 7.2   Factors Affecting the Transition out of Homemaking: Separate Piece-wise Constant Exponential Models (β-Coefficients)

Time period/covariate	West Germany		East Germany	
	Model 1	Model 2	Model 1	Model 2
0–11	–4.10***	–3.18**	–4.32***	–5.42***
12–14 (1 year)	–3.51**	–2.57	–3.15**	–4.40***
15–17	–4.27***	–3.02*	–5.05***	–5.48***
18–20 (18 months)	–3.79***	–2.50	–2.42*	–2.68*
21–23	–5.19***	–4.25**	–3.92***	–4.87***
24–26 (2 years)	–3.90**	–2.95*	–1.91	–2.85**
27–32	–4.32***	–3.36*	–3.33**	–4.26***
33–36 (3 years)	–4.18**	–2.10	–3.30**	–2.77*
>36	–3.62**	–2.61	–3.15**	–4.50***
Prestige of training occupation	–0.00	–0.00	0.01	0.01**
Employment prior to birth of the child[a]	0.01	0.04	0.20	0.34
Unemployment rate[b]	–0.12	–0.22	–0.06	0.01
Birth of subsequent child[c]	–1.32**	–1.24**	–15.45	–15.48
Position of child in sequence of births	0.93**	0.93**	0.41	0.42
Expiry of parental leave[d]	2.03***		2.46***	
Length of parental leave entitlement[e]		0.13		–0.78***
LL null model	–362.94	–362.94	–330.59	–330.59
LL estimated model	–345.48	–351.64	–260.97	–277.11
Cases	185		113	
Events	68		77	
Episodes (after splitting)	694		327	

*$p < 0.1$;   **$p < 0.05$;   ***$p < 0.01$.
[a]Employment activity three months prior to birth; 1 = employed; 0 = other.
[b]Women's unemployment rate; time-dependent on a yearly basis.
[c]Time-dependent dummy variable; 1 = birth of another child in interruption episode, 0 = no other child.
[d]Time-dependent dummy variable, defined in relation to parental leave entitlement; 1 = months 35 to 37 when entitled to 36-month parental leave, months 17 to 19 when entitled to 18-month parental leave, months 14 to 16 when entitled to 15-month parental leave; 0 = other.
[e]Statutory leave entitlement; 1 = 36 months; 0 = 15/18 months.

7.4). The differences between the two survivor functions of West German mothers and the effect of parental leave regulations on the transition rate (see Table 7.2, model 2 for West Germany), however, are not significant. West German mothers with an eighteen-month entitlement to parental leave did not reenter the labor market significantly sooner than those entitled to a three-year leave period. In other words, they prolonged their homemaking phase far beyond the statutory leave period.

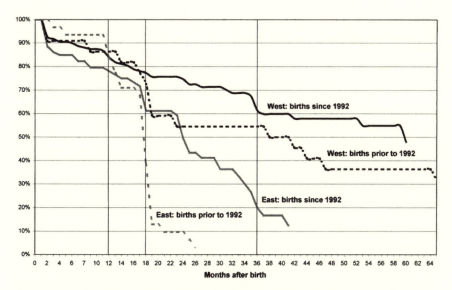

Figure 7.4 Duration of the Homemaking Episode in East and West Germany Before and After the Extension of Statutory Parental Leave from 18 to 36 Months (product-limit estimation).

In contrast to West Germany, the differences in East Germany are much more pronounced, and they are significant. This holds also true in multivariate estimation models (see Table 7.2, model 2 for East Germany), which yielded a clear negative effect of the new parental leave regulation, indicating that the introduction of the long parental leave led to an actual increase in the duration of family-related employment interruptions. Hence we conclude that in East Germany parental leave regulations serve the function of strongly steering mothers' labor-market participation.

The comparison of the survivor functions for the two East German groups reveals another interesting phenomenon: Few mothers who gave birth to a child before 1992 exit from homemaking during the first twelve months of leave. The point in time when the child is one year old, however, marks a turning point in the behavior and sends a strong signal to return to the labor market. East German mothers who gave birth to a child in 1992 or later, in contrast, more often quit homemaking within the first twelve months, but their inclination to end the family phase does not increase when the child reaches the age of one year. It follows that the dominant GDR model of the baby year markedly affected the behavior of mothers shortly after unification, yet thereafter began to weaken.

The Duration of the Homemaking Episode: The Impact of the Labor Market and the Family Constellation

In the multivariate models, no empirical evidence can be found for the proposition that either employment status prior to birth or the unemployment rate influences the end of the family phase (see Table 7.2). Contrary to the supposition voiced at the outset, then, the unfavorable labor market situation in East Germany did not lead East German women to opt for a longer baby break.

Family events, by contrast, do matter—at least in West Germany. The birth of another child within the interruption period significantly reduces the likelihood of exiting from homemaking (by 70 percent as compared to mothers without a further birth during the leave episode). In West Germany, hence, a further birth is of considerable relevance for the duration of the family phase. On the one hand, the birth of another child results in a prolongation of the interruption period. On the other hand, it is also reasonable to assume that due to the long leave episodes associated with the birth of the first child in West Germany, the likelihood of having a second child rises within the same period.

The effect estimated for East Germany points in the same direction. However, due to the small number of East German women who give birth to a further child within one and the same interruption episode, the parameter estimate does not prove significant. The observation that in East Germany several births within a homemaking period are less common than in West Germany provides additional evidence of a quite distinct interruption behavior: East German women interrupt employment upon childbirth for a relatively short period and reenter the labor market prior to the birth of a second child.

In accordance with the findings of Braun and Klein (1995), a first-born child causes a longer baby break than a second- or third-born—a phenomenon that Braun and Klein attribute to the increasing financial demands caused by additional children. The effect of the variable "position of the child in the sequence of births" proves strong and significant in West Germany (see Table 7.2); not surprisingly, it is weaker (and insignificant) in East Germany. As East German mothers take a relatively short baby break when their first child is born, it meets our expectation that with further children no notable additional reduction of the leave period is observed.

Activities Following the Homemaking Period

At the end of the observation period a majority of West German mothers (66 percent) had not finished their baby break, whereas a majority of

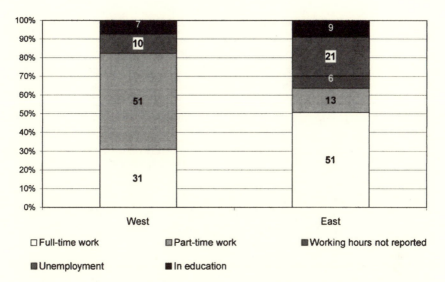

Figure 7.5 Activities Following the Homemaking Episode (percentage distribution).

East German mothers (65 percent) had resumed activities other than homemaking. Focusing on those women who carried out the transition out of homemaking, we once again observe quite different patterns. Due to the unfavorable labor market conditions in East Germany, the proportion of unemployed East German mothers exceeds the percentage of unemployed West German mothers considerably (Figure 7.5).

The second finding worth mentioning refers to the proportion of full-time workers, which in East Germany is far beyond the corresponding proportion found in West Germany (51 vs. 31 percent). Taking into account that a large fraction of East German part-time workers actually prefer full-time employment (cf. Kreckel and Schenk 2001), the East-West difference would be even more pronounced under less depressed labor-market conditions. As Kreckel and Schenk (2001) point out, we, of course, cannot rule out the possibility that the employment preferences and decisions are inspired by financial considerations. However, such materialistic motives, which partly are based on economic necessity, are accompanied by a strong subjective attachment to being fully integrated into gainful employment.

CONCLUSION

Based on the analyses presented here, the answer to the question posed at the outset—whether female employment trajectories in East and West

Germany have converged—can be summarized as follows: Convergence *and* persistent difference.

The employment trajectories of East German women have approximated those of their West German counterparts to the extent that the family phase is now longer than it was prior to unification. When contrasting the employment trajectories of East with those of West German skilled workers in their late twenties, however, it becomes evident that this convergence is still far from complete.

Not only do East German mothers more often resume full-time work when reentering the labor market, but they also end the family phase more quickly. In doing so, East German mothers strongly base their behavior on the new parental leave provisions; statutory childcare leave has thus become a major formative factor in female life courses in East Germany and is partly responsible for the partial convergence with West German patterns. Yet we see signs of the emergence of new age-specific thresholds *prior* to the end of statutory childcare leave, at which East German mothers exhibit a strong inclination to end the family phase. The "baby year," which in the GDR defined the maximum duration of the period of employment interruption, appears to be increasingly replaced by one-and-a-half or two baby years. The gender order imported from the West, we conclude, constitutes a formative framework for East German life courses as well, yet its effects are mitigated by a specifically East German gender culture, which was fashioned in the GDR era and which has survived the rapid transformation of the gender order.

Nevertheless, we cannot rule out that in addition to these gender-cultural influences, unfavorable opportunity structures have also contributed to shorter employment interruptions. This study has been able to show, however, that the disadvantageous labor market situation in East Germany after unification, with limited employment opportunities, has led neither to a prolongation of the family phase nor to an adoption of the housewife model.

NOTES

1. By referring to culture as an informal institution, we follow Zintl (1999) and go beyond the pragmatic and narrow notion employed by Leisering and Schumann (Chapter 9 in this volume). Instead of distinguishing between formal and informal institutions, Jepperson (1991:150ff.) identifies different "carriers" of institutions: central authority systems ("regimes") consisting of explicitly codified rules and sanctions, culture and, in addition, organizations.

2. The characterization of the GDR's gender culture and gender order draws, in addition, on the description given by Braun, Jasper, and Schröter (1995), Braun and Klein (1995), Schäfgen and Spellerberg (1998), and Schenk and Schlegel (1993).

3. Female part-time work was mainly performed by older women and, hence, was a means of gradual transition into retirement (cf. Kreckel and Schenk 2001).

4. In multivariate estimation models, however, we controlled for the employment status prior to birth.

5. There may be some objections to this procedure. Since the status of a housewife was not socially accepted in the GDR, we cannot rule out the possibility that East German women described themselves as being unemployed while actually performing housewife duties without actively seeking a job. On the other hand, to be a housewife is more legitimate in West Germany. This might have had the result that West German mothers who were looking for a job actually classified themselves as housewives. When this is the case, the duration of the family phase would have been overestimated in West Germany and—due to the higher percentage of unemployed East German mothers—underestimated in East Germany. However, we can prove that West German mothers who classified themselves as housewives were not looking for a job. In addition, in view of the strong orientation of East German women toward gainful employment it seems reasonable to assume that their self-categorization of being unemployed is not biased by social desirability.

6. The time periods were chosen on the basis of theoretical considerations as well as explorative analyses (cf. Falk and Schaeper 2001).

7. See also Gottschall and Bird (2003).

REFERENCES

Bauereiss, Renate, Hiltrud Bayer, and Walter Bien. 1997. *Familienatlas II. Lebenslagen und Regionen in Deutschland. Karten und Zahlen.* Opladen: Leske and Budrich.

Becker-Schmidt, Regina. 1993. "Geschlechterdifferenz—Geschlechterverhältnis: soziale Dimensionen des Begriffs 'Geschlecht.'" *Zeitschrift für Frauenforschung,* 11(1+2):37–46.

Bird, Kate. 2001. "Parental Leave in Germany—An Institution with Two Faces?" Pp. 55–87 in *Institutionen und Lebenslauf im Wandel. Institutionelle Regulierung von Lebensläufen,* edited by L. Leisering, R. Müller, and K. Schumann. Weinheim and Munich: Juventa.

Blossfeld, Hans-Peter and Götz Rohwer. 1995. *Techniques of Event History Modeling.* Mahwah, NJ: Erlbaum.

Born, Claudia, Helga Krüger, and Dagmar Lorenz-Meyer. 1996. *Der unentdeckte Wandel. Annäherungen an das Verhältnis von Struktur und Norm im weiblichen Lebenslauf.* Berlin: Edition Sigma.

Braun, Anneliese, Gerda Jasper, and Ursula Schröter. 1995. "Rolling Back the Gender Status of East German Women." Pp. 139–66 in *German Unification: The Destruction of an Economy,* edited by H. Behrend. London: Pluto.

Braun, Uwe and Thomas Klein. 1995. "Der berufliche Wiedereinstieg der Mutter im Lebensverlauf der Kinder." Pp. 231–52 in *Kinder in Deutschland. Lebensverhältnisse von Kindern im Regionalvergleich,* edited by B. Nauck und H. Bertram. Opladen: Leske and Budrich.

Connell, Robert W. 1987. *Gender and Power: Society, the Person and Sexual Politics.* Cambridge: Polity.

Engelbrech, Gerhard. 1997. *Erziehungsurlaub—und was dann? Die Situation von Frauen bei ihrer Rückkehr auf den Arbeitsmarkt. Ein Ost/West Vergleich.* IAB-Kurzbericht Nr. 8. Nürnberg: Institut für Arbeitsmarkt- und Berufsforschung.

Engelbrech, Gerhard and Alexander Reinberg. 1998. "Erwerbsorientierung und Beschäftigungsmöglichkeiten von Frauen in den neunziger Jahren. Wirtschaftliche Umstrukturierung und frauentypische Arbeitsmarktrisiken in Ost- und Westdeutschland." Pp. 41–91 in *Beschäftigungsrisiko Erziehungsurlaub,* edited by Gesellschaft für Informationstechnologie und Pädagogik am IMBSE. Opladen: Westdeutscher Verlag.

Falk, Susanne and Hildegard Schaeper. 2001. "Erwerbsverläufe von ost- und westdeutschen Müttern im Vergleich: ein Land—ein Muster?" Pp. 181–210 in *Individualisierung und Verflechtung. Geschlecht und Generation im deutschen Lebenslaufregime,* edited by C. Born and H. Krüger. Weinheim and Munich: Juventa.

Geissler, Birgit and Mechtild Oechsle. 1990. *Lebensplanung als Ressource im Individualisierungsprozess.* Working paper No. 10. Bremen: Sonderforschungsbereich 186 der Universität.

Gottschall, Karin and Kate Bird. 2003. "Family Leave Policies and Labor-Market Segregation in Germany: Reinvention or Reform of the Male Breadwinner?" *Review of Policy Research 20(1):115-34.*

Heinz, Walter R. (Ed.). 1992. *Institutions and Gatekeeping in the Life Course.* Weinheim: Deutscher Studien Verlag.

Jepperson, Ronald L. 1991. "Institutions, Institutional Effects, and Institutionalism." Pp. 143–63 in *The New Institutionalism in Organizational Analysis,* edited by W. W. Powell and P. J. DiMaggio. Chicago and London: University of Chicago Press.

Kohli, Martin. 1986. "Social Organization and Subjective Construction of the Life Course." Pp. 271–92 in *Human Development and the Life Course: Multidisciplinary Perspectives,* edited by A. B. Sørensen, F. E. Weinert, and L. R. Sherrod. Hillsdale, NJ: Erlbaum.

Kreckel, Reinhard and Sabine Schenk. 2001. "Full Time or Part Time? The Contradictory Integration of the East German Female Labour Force in Unified Germany." Pp. 159–76 in *Restructuring Work and the Life Course,* edited by V. W. Marshall, W. R. Heinz, H. Krüger, and A. Verma. Toronto, Buffalo, and London: University of Toronto Press.

Krüger, Helga. 1995. "Dominanzen im Geschlechterverhältnis: Zur Institutionalisierung von Lebensläufen." Pp. 195–219 in *Das Geschlechterverhältnis als Gegenstand der Sozialwissenschaften,* edited by R. Becker-Schmidt and G.-A. Knapp. Frankfurt a.M. and New York: Campus.

Levy, René. 1996a. "Toward a Theory of Life-Course Institutionalization." Pp. 83–108 in *Society and Biography. Interrelationships Between Social Structure, Institutions and the Life Course,* edited by A. Weymann and W. R. Heinz. Weinheim: Deutscher Studien Verlag.

Levy, René. 1996b. "Zur Institutionalisierung von Lebensläufen. Ein theoretischer Bezugsrahmen." Pp. 73–113 in *Kritische Übergänge. Statuspassagen und sozialpolitische Institutionalisierung*, edited by J. Behrens and W. Voges. Frankfurt a.M. and New York: Campus.

Mayer, Karl Ulrich. 1991. "Life Courses in the Welfare State." Pp. 146–58 in *Theoretical Advances in Life-Course Research*, edited by W. R. Heinz. Weinheim: Deutscher Studien Verlag.

Mayer, Karl Ulrich and Walter Müller. 1986. "The State and the Structure of the Life Course." Pp. 217–46 in *Human Development and the Life Course-Multidisciplinary Perspectives*, edited by A. B. Sørensen, F. E. Weinert, and L. R. Sherrod. Hillsdale, NJ: Erlbaum.

Meyer, John W. 1992. "The Life Course as a Professionalized Cultural Construction." Pp. 83–95 in *Institutions and Gatekeeping in the Life Course*, edited by W. R. Heinz. Weinheim: Deutscher Studien Verlag.

Oechsle, Mechtild. 1998. "Ungelöste Widersprüche: Leitbilder für die Lebensführung junger Frauen." Pp. 185–200 in *Die ungleiche Gleichheit. Junge Frauen und der Wandel im Geschlechterverhältnis*, edited by M. Oechsle and B. Geissler. Opladen: Leske and Budrich.

Ogburn, William F. 1964. *On Culture and Social Change*. Selected Papers. Chicago: University of Chicago Press.

Ostner, Ilona. 1993. "'Immer noch wartet die Frau zu Hause . . .' Zur sozialpolitischen Regulierung weiblicher Lebenschancen in der Bundesrepublik." Pp. 99–115 in *Moderne Lebensläufe im Wandel: Beruf—Familie—Soziale Hilfen—Krankheit*, edited by L. Leisering et al. Weinheim: Deutscher Studien Verlag.

Pfau-Effinger, Birgit. 1999. "Change of Family Policies in the Socio-Cultural Context of European Societies." *Comparative Social Research*, 18:135–59.

Pfau-Effinger, Birgit. 2000. *Kultur und Frauenerwerbstätigkeit in Europa. Theorie und Empirie des internationalen Vergleichs*. Opladen: Leske and Budrich.

Schäfgen, Katrin and Annette Spellerberg. 1998. "Kulturelle Leitbilder und institutionelle Regelungen für Frauen in den USA, in West und Ostdeutschland." *Berliner Journal für Soziologie*, 8(1):73–90.

Schenk, Sabine and Uta Schlegel. 1993. "Frauen in den neuen Bundesländern—Zurück in eine andere Moderne?" *Berliner Journal für Soziologie* 3(3):369–84.

Schneider, Norbert F. and Harald Rost. 1998. "Von Wandel keine Spur—warum ist Erziehungsurlaub weiblich?" Pp. 217–36 in *Die ungleiche Gleichheit. Junge Frauen und der Wandel im Geschlechterverhältnis*, edited by M. Oechsle and B. Geissler. Opladen: Leske and Budrich.

Trappe, Heike. 1995. *Emanzipation oder Zwang? Frauen in der DDR zwischen Beruf, Familie und Sozialpolitik*. Berlin: Akademie Verlag.

Zintl, Reinhard. 1999. "Institutionen und gesellschaftliche Integration." Pp. 179–98 in *Soziale Integration. Sonderheft der Kölner Zeitschrift für Soziologie und Sozialpsychologie*, No. 39, edited by J. Friedrichs and W. Jagodzinski. Opladen: Westdeutscher Verlag.

III

Institutions and the Life Course

| 8 |

The Life Course, Institutions, and Life-Course Policy

Ansgar Weymann

TRANSITIONS, SEQUENCES, TRAJECTORIES, AND INSTITUTIONAL REGIMES

Life-Course policy shapes opportunity structures through institutions that define the spectrum of individual control over transitions, sequences, and trajectories. An example from educational life courses elucidates this. The stratification, vocational specificity (i.e., occupation-centeredness), and standardization of educational institutions are regulated very differently across Western nation-states. Moreover, educational systems are organized either on a national, federal, regional, or quasi-market basis. This, in turn, has a major impact on the accessibility of the educational system to various individuals, on the range of educational paths available to them, and, ultimately, on transitions into the labor market. Analogous examples of the institutional shaping of the life course can be found in family policy, in labor-market and employment policy, as well as in health care, pensions, and social assistance. The study of transitions, sequences, and trajectories brings such historically evolved institutions into focus and renders differences in life-course policy across countries and time visible.

Life-Course research has only marginally concerned itself with life-course policy, for it takes a predominantly microsociological approach to the analysis of social structure. For example, event-history analysis or panel research observes, describes, and analyzes the linkage between individual life events and transitions, sequences, or trajectories as a chain of transition probabilities. These transition probabilities differ both among individuals and among aggregate groups according to gender, educational attainment,

partnership status, and occupation. The indicators of the latter are introduced into the model as time-dependent or independent covariates, measured on different levels of aggregation. In this manner, a life course or
cohort is perceived proceeding through a society's institutions and social
structure.

Institutions, social structures, and societies are subject to historical
change. The observation, description, and analysis of life courses and
cohorts thus shed light on the impact of changes in macrosociological
structures such as the influence of new family/partnership forms,
reformed educational institutions, modified labor-market and employment regimes, or welfare-state institutions. Such research can have a comparative and/or longitudinal design.

Life-Course research and cohort analysis are a successful partial solution of the micro-macro problem. Cohort analyses focus on birth cohorts,
entrance cohorts, and exit cohorts that are embedded in the flux of historical events, to use Mannheim's (1952) or Ryder's (1965) formulation.
Mannheim speaks of "generations" rather than cohorts when, embedded
in the historical stream of societal events, a cohort develops a consciousness of its own identity as a distinct social and historical group, to the
extent that this self-perception is also confirmed by a matching external
perception. Compared with the concepts "life course" and "cohort," the
term "generation" adds the dimension of the subjective meaning of action
and collective interpretation patterns of the symbolic world.[1] Furthermore, the concept of generation includes the idea of a cohort's potential
collective action. And finally, if we study life courses as biographies, we
are interested in the temporal reflection and symbolization of one's own or
of another's identity by use of the interpretative cultural models of a society or a group.[2] In all these cases, the analysis of the dynamic unfolding of
transitions, sequences, and trajectories has the dual objective first of gaining a better understanding of the dynamic of the life course, and second,
of taking life-course dynamics as indicators of the present condition of—
and change in—the social structure.

What is insufficiently present or sometimes completely missing in life-
course, cohort, and biographical research is the direct observation, description, and theoretical analysis of the institutions and social structure of one
or more societies. Social structure is the historically evolved institutional
world of a specific society at a specific time. It is the product of historical
struggles and embedded in a particular culture and civilization. As a rule
the state and the market, politics and economy, legal system, culture, and
collective historical identity as well as a society's vast array of institutions
are all peripheral to the perspective of life-course research. Yet these "holistic," macrosociological objects are foci of classical sociological research and
the aim of sociology has always been their analysis and comprehension as

social facts (Durkheim [1895] 1961). The price of life-course research's methodological innovation has been a weakening of its grounding in social and institutional theory.[3]

In contemporary Western societies, life-course regimes are buttressed largely by the life-course policy of the nation-state. For this reason, we describe the nation-state as the framework within which life-course policy shapes a society's institutions. The argumentation follows neoinstitutionalist assumptions. It thus assumes an interest among actors in the calculability of decisions and the minimization of transaction costs, and also assumes the path dependency of trajectories. The life-course policy of the nation-state, which had been institutionalized progressively since the nineteenth century, has been called into question by processes of globalization and historical rupture. The latter process will be examined using the case of the German Democratic Republic (GDR) and its life-course policy inheritance. Globalization and supranationalization of life-course regimes in the fields of the welfare state and education will be considered using the case of the European Union (EU).

LIFE-COURSE INSTITUTIONS AND THE NATION-STATE

In the course of centuries of occidental modernization, *Gemeinschaft* (community) has been replaced with *Gesellschaft* (society).[4] In modern society, the individual life course is no longer predominantly conditioned by shared values, norms, and everyday life experience of traditional communities, but by personal interest, i.e., utilitarian principles. Since people are free and (nearly) equal in their physical and mental abilities and conceive of themselves as equals, they compete for their share of coveted scarce objects, particularly for property, power, and pleasure. The state of modern society is thus the struggle of all against all. Political thinkers such as Machiavelli, Hobbes, and Marx—with Italian Renaissance states, Cromwell's Britain, and nineteenth-century class struggles in mind, respectively—conceived of this omnipresent competition as a permanent state of civil war; while social scientists such as Adam Smith, Schumpeter, Hayek, or Coleman (1990) viewed competition in liberal society as a great source of innovation and prosperity. In societies of the Western type, high labor productivity, high employment rates, strong inputs of capital and science, and the accumulating utilization of capital produce more wealth than necessary for subsistence. Additionally, free trade in expansive markets creates opportunities for specialization in areas of comparative advantage. Despite an extremely unequal distribution of wealth, this is the only society in the history of humankind that has enduringly generated grand surpluses.

However, *liberté* and *egalité* (plus *productivité*) do not foster *fraternité*, as a revised formulation of the famous slogan of the French revolution would have it. In small communities, it is not difficult to reconcile the striving for individual gain with the need for reliable cooperation. In larger ones, on the other hand, the tendency to sacrifice fair cooperation for even minor individual gains is strong (Olson 1965, 1982). Whereas communities impose life-course arrangements on their members according to religious rules and cultural norms of tradition, in modern society life-course policy becomes necessary to provide institutional support for the conduct of individualized lives. Institutional arrangements and entitlements to education, family support, health insurance, unemployment insurance, and old-age provision are key elements of life-course policy in modern society—shaping, supporting, or enabling transitions, sequences, and trajectories in the course of life. Life-Course policy lays the foundations for rational life conduct and helps to stabilize transitions, sequences, and trajectories—in nationally specific ways (Esping-Anderson 1990, cf. 1999; de Swaan 1988; Leisering 2003; Mayer 2001; Heinz 2001).

Life-Course policy is anchored in the contemporary nation-state and shaped by the market, constitutional liberalism, and the type of welfare regime.

The *liberal tax state* is a machine of community ends that is confronted by manifold, economizing individual ends.[5] It can deprive privately economizing individuals of the fruits of their economic performance only up to the point where they stop investing their utmost energies (Schumpeter 1918). This rationale presupposes that modern humankind has been transformed into *homines oeconomici:* a type of person who privileges the pursuit of profit and remunerated labor, who creates specialized, differentiated economic institutions, and perpetually strives for cost minimization (Polanyi 1995). The universal competition in modern society points to the first condition prerequisite to peaceful and prosperous exchange and coexistence: agreement on a *contrat social*. Civil and political rights constitute the primary and essential foundation of life-course policy in liberal, noncommunitarian society.

With the supplementary establishment of the *welfare state*, individuals and population groups became linked in new, far-reaching networks that are deeply rooted and enduring. Only in the context of the secure institutional framework provided by the welfare state can the majority of the population undertake long-term life planning. The status of citizenship, however, harbors a conflict between its constitutive civil (freedom and liberty), political (participation), and social rights (entitlements to welfare and social security) (cf. Marshall 1992a, 1992b; Dahrendorf 1992). Social rights limit the economic freedom of actors and reduce the influence of the market and its relative prices. Furthermore, the granting of social rights to an individual or group can mean inclusion in the form of access to certain privileges for the beneficiary, but at the same time exclusion for all others. Examples are tax regimes that offer selective entitlements to economic sectors, branches, professions, and regions, and welfare regulations that target carefully defined groups.

In sum, society's members are bonded together in three principal ways: as *market subjects* (*bourgeois*) through antagonistic cooperation within the institutional framework of the marketplace; as *citizens* (*citoyens*) through contract, law and constitution, and by the *welfare state* regime. Modern nation-states have established a legal framework for conflict resolution and a constitution (with the exception of Britain) that grants civil and political rights. Further, they have developed a welfare regime that provides minimal or adequate benefits and entitlements. This legal, fiscal, and institutional framing and support of life through life-course policy profoundly enhances the rationality and reliability of individual life-course choices by providing the necessary institutions as collective goods (Hardin and Baden 1977; Ostrom 1990).

INSTITUTIONS AND LIFE-COURSE DECISIONS

We have argued that the nation-state establishes and develops institution regimes that guide or support transitions, sequences, and trajectories in the course of life. At the theoretical center of this analysis is the concept of individual choices within institutional constraints and resources. This paradigm involves integrating the assumption of purposive action with comparative institutional analysis. "The core process . . . central to social structure is the choice between socially structured alternatives. This differs from the choice process of economic theory, in which the alternatives are conceived to have inherent utilities" (Brinton and Nee 1998:xii). Concepts central to understanding choices within institutions are bounded rationality, externalities, social embeddedness and networks, human capital, social capital, trust, and transaction costs.

Institutions are a means to reduce the double contingency of exchange and human interaction, i.e., the unlimited freedom of individual actors.[6] Institutions represent the rules of society or, more generally, they are self-imposed restrictions on human action. They define and limit the scope of legitimate decision-making. Institutions provide models of successful and self-confident behavior in a complex and chaotic environment, and they improve the limited capacity of the individual actor for rational decision-making. Furthermore, institutions set and regulate incentives to purposefully stimulate economic, social, and political exchange.

Institutions are not simply "given" as natural social facts. They exist because—and when—they reduce uncertainty in human interaction by setting up formal or informal rules. This can be observed in families, firms or the state, on the micro-, meso-, and macrolevel of institutional analysis. The *raison d'être* of institutions is their utility in reducing transaction costs. This capacity is especially important in the case of extended exchange. Exchange, expanding in time, space, and scope in modern times, permanently stimulates a growing demand for adequate institutions that can transform incalculable insecurity into calculable risks. For example, a growing economy with spatially expanding markets and complicated, long-term fiscal transactions requires legal regulations, reliable sanctions, effective governance regimes, rationalization, and civilization.[7]

Due to the central role of institutions, their change determines the development of societies over time. Institutional change is the key to understanding social change (North 1990). Therefore, special attention should be given to the emergence and change of institutions. "A closer attention to questions of institutional origin is a prerequisite for comprehensive explanations of maintenance and stability, on the one hand, and emergence and change, on the other" (Knight and Sened 1998:2). The evolution of institutions yields no final, optimal form. "Evolutionary accounts of institutional change employ a collective benefits focus to explain a variety of institutional forms" (ibid.:3).

What are these collective benefits? Besides the capacity to reduce transaction costs, and to transfer uncertainty into risk, institutions contribute effectively and efficiently to the problem of creating collective goods. Institutions provide groups of individuals with the means to resolve collective action problems and they render collective action beneficial. The benefits may be the allocation of scarce resources, social optimization, and stability, or a desired collective activity. Institutions can establish an opportunity structure whose incentives for individual actors are framed in such a way that individually profitable action leads simultaneously to collective benefits. This can be achieved through the market as well as by public choice (Buchanan 1975).

Institutional analysis can contribute to an understanding of collective life-course policy and, similarly, of the individual life course. The problem is to explain why individual actors should be willing to agree voluntarily with social or public choice decisions concerning institutions that impose restrictions on the maximal freedom of individual life-course options by setting up rules of conduct. Again, the answer is the individual's interest to reduce the transaction costs of decision-making over her or his course of life, especially over extended periods of time and within complex networks of social interaction.

Individuals have an interest in making plans for a successful life: a life in which one benefits from one's own previous life-course decisions. Life-Course decisions are made step by step and successively, beginning with the negotiation of discrete transitions that cumulate into a series of sequences and then ultimately constitute long-term trajectories. The individual at $t1$ is the product of his or her decisions made at $t0$. The chance for making beneficial and rational life-course decisions profoundly depends on having reliable and valid expectations of gainful exchange and interaction in the future. Such expectations are predicted and calculated on the basis of previous life experiences. The past life course provides the individual with previously acquired information and resources and simultaneously restricts options for future decision-making due to the lack of information and resources not acquired. In this sense, the individual creates her- or himself over the course of life, developing from decision to decision (Brennan and Buchanan 1985; cf. Heinz 2002).

For this reason, the individual is not "naturally" inclined to comply with rules imposed by social or public choice, because these rules restrict the freedom of future decision-making. At the same time, an individual's interest in maximum free choice conflicts with his or her interest in coping successfully with the problem of double contingency. Only effective rules imposed by institutions that have been established by social or public choice can transform incalculable uncertainty into calculable risks. Similarly, only institutions with effective rules can provide a basis for rational life-course planning and reduce uncertainty and transaction costs in individual life courses. If the individual knows that other individuals are subject to the same set of rules, and if the public choice process of setting up institutions is itself bound to the rules of constitution and law, the individual can rationally make plans for his or her transitions, sequences, and trajectories over the course of life. If this were not the case, any individual could only situationally maximize benefits from transition to transition. This would lead to a Hobbesian life—nasty, brutal, and short—because the outcome of passages through sequences and trajectories would become incalculable and costly.

The neoinstitutionalist argument, thus, is that although self-imposed rules represented by institutions restrict options for maximizing benefits, these same institutions and rules can reduce transaction costs of exchange and social interaction. Rational decision-making in the course of life is dependent on institutions and rules. And this is the reason why rational, self-reflexive actors can agree to set rules collectively for the game of life, rules represented by institutions. They prefer collaborative long-term gains to individual situational maximizing.[8] Obviously, a disadvantage of this strategy is a strong path dependency of life-course policy and life-course conduct.[9]

In the modern era, however, effective life-course policy—the policy of providing institutions that support and guide individual transitions, sequences, and trajectories over the course of life—depends on the nation-state, its market rules, constitution, and legal system, and on welfare state entitlements. Substantive and profound historical ruptures like the post-1989 transitions of the former socialist East Bloc countries or ongoing processes of globalization challenge the effective life-course regime of the modern state to which we have grown accustomed since the nineteenth century.

In the following two sections we will first investigate some aspects of East Germany's transformation and life-course policy heritage. Second, we will deal with the multitiered life-course policy of the European Union as a new kind of inter- and supranational life-course regime.

EAST GERMANY'S LIFE-COURSE POLICY HERITAGE

We will outline two examples of East German life-course policy heritage. The first example is the institutional regulation of the transition from education to work; the second is maternal protection and parental leave policy. In both cases, the social transformation has led to a radical reform of life-course policy. Yet at the same time, surprising path dependency can be observed in both life-course policy and life-course conduct.[10]

Peculiarities of the GDR's Life-Course Regime

In the German Democratic Republic educational, employment, and welfare institutions strongly influenced life-course transitions. Individual choices concerning life-course direction were politically restricted. The youth organization *Freie Deutsche Jugend*, the trade union *Freier Deutscher Gewerkschaftsbund*, and the socialist party *Sozialistische Deutsche Einheitspartei* were powerful gatekeepers in strategic life-course status transitions like university enrollment, employment, and career advancement (Krüger and Pischke 1995). With unification, this dominant role of institutions has vanished. A prime example of this rapid change is the loss of the state-regulated linkage between education and employment. Employment after graduation is now no longer guaranteed. The hitherto unknown problem of unemployment emerged as did pressures for higher occupational mobility. Further, the labor market and occupational structure underwent a profound reorganization, and many educational qualifications and vocational skills were de- or revalued.

The post-1989 structural upheavals and radical institutional changes have affected millions of life courses and given rise to new inequalities. Whereas the West German educational, labor market, and employment systems offer individuals far more opportunities for a self-determined life course, they supply much weaker institutional guidance than did the centralized, socialist German Democratic Republic.

The decay and collapse of the German Democratic Republic were caused mainly by the failure to solve economic problems of productivity, innovation, and adaptation to the world market. The decision to join the Federal Republic became the preferred means of problem-solving and the declaration of adoption of the West German constitution finally established legal integration. Whereas the transformation of the legal and economic system—achieved by introducing the Western model in the East—happened within just a few months, it would take much longer to assimilate cultural patterns, milieus, and identity. One can use the classic sociological term "cultural lag" to describe the delay between *system integration and social integration* (Lockwood 1964).

The German Democratic Republic has been described as a "work society" (Kohli 1994) both because of the long period of time within the life course during which people worked and because firms were not merely sites of production, but also important actors in social policy and in social life in general. Full-time employment was the norm for both women and men. The government ensured the continuity of female employment, for example, by allowing only short-term employment interruptions in case of maternity and by providing a fully developed day-care system. In view of the fact that unemployment insurance was eliminated and benefits in case of widowhood or divorce rescinded in the 1970s, the "right" to work in the German Democratic Republic was in fact a duty.

The transition from a socialist system to a market economy profoundly changed the institutional setting and opportunity structures in which life-course agency was embedded. With the introduction of the West German political, legal, and economic institutions, life-course options proliferated but at the same time became more uncertain and risky. The imported market rationality forced rationalization of many sectors of society as well as of individual life conduct. When life conduct is rationalized, biographical expectations and decision-making and particularly human capital investment are embedded far more than before in a context of scarcity of resources under conditions of strong competition. Human capital has now to be acquired and invested according to market rules, which penetrate many spheres of personal life. At the same time, support from the state has waned and institutional direction in the transition from one status to another has largely disappeared.

After reunification, social, political, and civil rights were reequilibrated in favor of liberty and at the expense of social rights and state providence. The state's hegemony in life-course policy was eliminated or attenuated. *A new horizon of life conduct had to emerge step by step in the course of biographical reflection on trials and errors in everyday life.* This transition was harder for older cohorts who had been socialized and had acquired their human capital under socialist social and cultural conditions. The younger generation,

on the other hand, can be expected to be able to address problems more successfully after having acquired a new horizon of everyday life suited to the
new opportunity structure's resources and restrictions.

The Transition from Education to Work

In the German Democratic Republic, the state provided job placement
for graduates of all educational institutions. In West Germany and unified
Germany, no comparable system of state guidance of the transition from
education to work has existed. One must distinguish here between two
kinds of graduates, however: graduates from vocational schools—the so-
called Dual System—on the one hand, and graduates of higher educational institutions on the other. Traditionally, vocational school graduates
in Germany have been provided with considerable institutional guidance.
Germany's time-honored Dual System, which combines classroom learning with work-based training over a period of three years, enables the
majority of apprentices to achieve direct occupational entry (often into
the firm where they did their apprenticeship) upon completion of their
vocational training.[11] The Dual System is responsible for the relatively low
rate of youth unemployment in Germany compared with other European
countries (Franz, Inkmann, Pohlmeier, and Zimmermann 1997). The German Democratic Republic, when founded in 1949, did not abolish the Dual
System. For this reason, the history of the school-to-work transition among
vocational school graduates is characterized by institutional continuity in
both the East and the West. For higher-educational graduates, on the other
hand, no such links between education and employment have ever existed
in the West, whereas in the German Democratic Republic direct state
placement of higher educational graduates not only existed but was
mandatory.

*With unification, West German educational and employment policy were
introduced into the former East Germany. If one examines education-to-work
transition patterns and subsequent occupational career patterns in the New German States, an interesting effect of the legacy of the East German regime can be
observed.* Over the short term, i.e., within the first twelve months after
graduation, vocational school graduates benefit greatly from the continuity of the Dual System. The life-course policy of guiding this transition
enables nearly all graduates to find employment within a short period. For
graduates of colleges and universities, no comparable effective life-course
guidance of transitions from education to work exists any longer. This
results in a very dramatic increase in the duration of graduates' job search
and thus in the frequency and duration of postgraduate unemployment.

Over the longer term, beginning with the second year after graduation,
the effect of life-course policies guiding the transition from education to

work is reversed. Two years after graduation, more than 95 percent of graduates from colleges and universities have found a job—without the benefit of institutional guidance of this transition. Human capital accumulation and individual job search proves to be a successful recipe for initial job entry. The carefully guided graduates of vocational schools, meanwhile, face severe employment problems over the longer term. After being hired rapidly, many lose their jobs within the first years of work. Their lower level of human capital—relative to academic graduates— reduces their job opportunities on a very competitive labor market. Life-Course policy developed to guide the transition from education to work cannot provide any enduring support for the employment careers of skilled workers.

Upon examining occupational entries in East and West Germany it becomes clear that in shaping the transition from school to work, institutional structures like the Dual System can reduce considerably the risks associated with occupational entry even in extraordinary circumstances of rapid and profound social change as in the case of system transformation. However, the same life-course policy institution is unable to offer enduring support for life-course trajectories. The "head start" of the guided group of apprentices is followed by a disadvantage over the longer run due to their lower level of individual human capital. The extended and risky transition period of academic graduates, however, is followed by successful job search and career sequences. We may call this an unintended or latent effect of a life-course policy institution designed to guide the transition from education to work.

The Compatibility of Work and Family

A second example of a lasting impact of East Germany's life-course regime is the institutional support of child rearing, intended to increase the compatibility of work and family (see also Schaeper and Falk, Chapter 7 in this volume).

The institutional arrangements supporting the compatibility of work and family have differed in the German Democratic Republic and in the Federal Republic of Germany. In the German Democratic Republic, a "baby break" after the birth of the first child was introduced in 1986; the maximum length of this employment interruption was twelve months. A comprehensive state system of child care—consisting of crèches, nursery schools, and after-school daycare—made it possible for mothers with small children to pursue occupational and family work simultaneously after the "baby break." In West Germany, too, parental leave was introduced in 1986, at first for up to ten months. In the ensuing years, the maximum period of leave was gradually increased. Since 1992, parental leave can be taken for up to three years per child. In contrast to the German Democratic Republic, West Germany considers primarily the family to be in charge of raising children. This has consequences for state institutional support. The state supply of crèche places for children under three years of age is insufficient, and nursery and elementary schools often supervise children only half the day. The lack of places in childcare institutions makes employment and family difficult to reconcile. For this reason they are often not pursued simultaneously, but sequentially: periods of maternal leave are followed at first by a "housewife" phase. The reentry into the work force usually does not happen until the children have reached school age (age six).

After 1989, the female graduates of the East German Dual System frequently entered a second training program, in the form of an additional apprenticeship or higher educational degree program. The great interest in education can be understood as an adaptation to the educationally meritocratic Western society. In the GDR, income distribution was far more equal than in West Germany (Kohli 1994), and educational degrees had only minor social differentiating effects. Since unification, however, higher education has opened the door to occupational advancement and higher income. Moreover, the increased rate of higher education can be seen as a product of pent-up demand. The supply of apprenticeship positions was centrally managed in the GDR. In collaboration with firms, the government developed "apprenticeship registries." In many cases the available apprenticeship positions did not match individual preferences (Hille 1990). Finally, the interest in educational improvement can be attributed to the fact that certain training and educational programs in the GDR lost some or most of their value in the new social order. This applied mainly to persons who had received their occupational training in sectors and branches in which labor demand declined after unification as a consequence of postponed tertiarization of the economy.

With unification, familial and occupational life cycles became much harder to combine. The life-course policy of the GDR, which sought to make work and family life more compatible, vanished. The much weaker institutional support in unified Germany leads us to expect a rising share of "housewives" among women in the East, an assimilation to the Western level. But in fact this is not the case. While among West German female apprenticeship graduates the rate of "housewives" rises two years after graduation and reaches 15 percent five years after graduation, among East German female apprenticeship graduates the rate of "housewives" lies well under 5 percent. Compared to their West German counterparts, a much smaller proportion of East German female graduates of both higher educational institutions and apprenticeship programs became "housewives." In West Germany the share of "housewives" among female higher educational graduates rises markedly three years after graduation, while in East Germany it remains low.

A different picture can be seen with regard to the take-up of *maternal leave*. The origin of this might well be that in the GDR, too, since 1986 a one-year, paid "baby year" was available for employed women. Thus, the West German form of parental leave adopted after unification was familiar and accepted.

In summary, whereas maternal leave is widely appreciated and accepted in East and West Germany, and despite the institutional bias toward the "housewife" role experienced by all women in unified Germany, Eastern mothers with a small child are far less likely to assume the "housewife" role than their Western counterparts.[12] Moreover, fewer East German women claim parental leave, and parental leave is claimed for shorter periods of time. An explanation for the lesser assumption of "housewife" status lies in the internalized GDR life-course model, which in family phases foresaw continuous employment.

Path Dependency of Institutions and Biographical Self-Concepts

The individual life course rests firmly on the persistence of institutions. A new life-course path will be accepted individually (and in the longer run by social and public choice) only under the condition that the expected gains from institutional innovation grossly exceed the transaction costs of switching to a new regime.

The German Democratic Republic's joining the Federal Republic of Germany brought with it the introduction of a completely new system of institutions. The institutional pillars of individual life-course paths in East Germany were thus transformed from one day to the next. The restructuring processes that had accompanied unification generated new opportunities, chances, and risks and have led to revisions of rational life conduct. As in a great experiment, in the case of this rapid societal transformation one can observe the interrelations between individual agency and institutional settings. A particular role in the interaction of society and biography is played by the institutional guidance provided by life-course policy.

Life courses are the product of the interactions between individual decisions and given institutional settings. However, *institutional bridges*, like those offered by the Dual System, help overcome labor-market impediments. But this only works at the point of first occupational entry. Over the longer term, the better *human capital investment of individuals* proves its worth. University graduates' occupational trajectories converge in the East and the West after one year, whereas apprenticeship graduates' life courses do not, even though the East German higher educational graduates experienced a worse, delayed start. A marked difference in East- vs. West German life

paths can be seen in the continuing disparity in female employment trajectories. Even after ten years there has been no convergence. Upon giving
birth to their first child, fewer women in the East than in the West become
"housewives." *Parental leave*, on the other hand, which was an available and
widely claimed state benefit in the German Democratic Republic, finds
broad acceptance.

Biographical self-conceptions survive changes in institutions. The biographical model of the working woman and mother, internalized in the German
Democratic Republic era, still guides women's behavior.[13] Furthermore,
the value-rational behavior to which East German women became accustomed in the German Democratic Republic era has been reinforced since
unification by an instrumentally rational motivation. Since employment
prospects now worsen after long phases of nonemployment, and since in
light of high divorce rates the "housewife" role is no longer an alternative
to earning a living through employment, value-rational socialization in
the old life world and instrumentally rational decision-making in the new
life world go hand-in-hand.

THE MULTITIERED PATTERN OF THE EUROPEAN UNION'S LIFE-COURSE POLICY

In *The Consequences of Modernity*, Anthony Giddens (1990) designates
modernization as a project of Western civilization, and globalization as its
youngest offspring. Globalization creates new risks of unparalleled
dimensions and tends to undermine trust and confidence in the course of
history and individual life. This thesis corresponds with the argumentation of Pierre Bourdieu (1993) in *La Misère du Monde (The Weight of the
World: Social Suffering in Contemporary Society)*, a collection of life-course
interviews.

Life-Course policy provides public goods in the fields of family support, education, health care, employment, social assistance, and old-age
provision. In an era of globalization, can these ends still be sufficiently
attained by national governments following their own particular pathways—or is inter- or supranational life-course policy the better solution?[14]

The nation itself is a product of modernization, a contingent configuration whose elements are an industrial-capitalist economy, a military, a
bureaucratic administration, a (democratic) state, and ethnosymbolism
(Mann 1993; Smith 1998; cf. Hanagan and Tilly 1999). The nation-state is a
response to the decay of the premodern, hierarchical polyethnic type of
religious and feudal society. Will the nation-state disappear with the dawn
of globalization? Will this in turn lead to the destruction of the welfare
state and citizenship? Will national life-course regimes in education, public health, old-age provision, and social assistance vanish?

The answer depends on how we understand globalization. The most radical and simplest idea is that all (advanced) industrial countries will converge toward common methods of production and economic life as a consequence of best practice, free trade, and free capital mobility. More sophisticated research shows a strong persistence of national pathways (Crouch and Streeck 1997; Hall and Soskice 2001; Kenworthy 2002). National (or regional) collocation of multinational corporations; public goods like education, infrastructure, research and development, law, and constitution; and tacit knowledge of language, culture, and norms—which facilitate interaction—are strong forces contributing to a reduction in the transaction costs of conducting international activities (Berger and Dore 1996).

Diagnoses of the powerlessness of governments in the face of transnational capital, the obsolescence of the nation-state as an organizing principle, the collapse of the welfare state, the death of industrial policy, and the end of national diversity are exaggerated. What matters is the transformative capacity of modern states, the ability to adapt to external shocks and pressures (Boyer and Drache 1996; Hollingsworth and Boyer 1997; Weiss 1998).

Are international regimes the better solution? Can they serve as a more effective buffer against the impact of the global economy? Will international regimes stabilize the nation-state and strengthen its transformative capacity (Krasner 1983; cf. Sally 1998)? Are inter- and supranational regimes of life-course institutions developing (Boje, Steenbergen, and Walby 1999; Sandholtz and Sweet 1998; Woodward and Kohli 2001)?

The recent history of an emerging life-course policy in European countries and the European Union may suggest a preliminary answer. We will focus our attention on social policy and education.

Social Policy

In a comparative study, Abram de Swaan (1988) has investigated the development of what he terms "state care" in the realms of health, education, and welfare over centuries of modernization in England, France, Germany, and Holland (and to a certain extent the United States). Beginning with measures against vagabondage, the care of the state grew to include social assistance and welfare, education and a national curriculum, health care and public health, health and retirement insurance, old-age provision, and family assistance. The driving force behind this process was that individuals, peasant families, villages, local governments, and religious and worldly authorities alike had been overwhelmed by the looming problems of industrialization and the free market. Increasingly, poverty, starvation, epidemics, mass migration, violence, and anomie were overburdening the coping capacity of premodern individual and corporate actors. Only a new collective actor, the caring (nation-) state, could deal effectively with the problems of modern society. The care of the state was in the interest of the suffering population, and at the same time the birth of the nation-state became an attractive instrument for the ascendant new elite: entrepreneurs, social movements, political parties, administrators, scientists, and intellectuals.

Today, step by step, the European Union is becoming an important instrument for dealing with the challenge of a global economy. The mobility of goods, services, and capital was of course followed by the mobility of persons, and this has created a need for European life-course policy. The EU converts globalization (partly) into an internal process of supranational institution building (Cousins 1999).

In the field of social policy, Stephan Leibfried and Paul Pierson (1995) have argued that the European Union is a response to shared problems, a spillover from the common market of goods, services, and capital. Social policy, originally a nation-state domain, is affected by the European Union in many fields, including health insurance, safety regulations, employment and industrial policies, maternity laws, long-term care, education and vocational training, family assistance, immigration rules, provision for disability, poverty and old age, gender and equal opportunity policy, etc. "The process of European integration has eroded both the sovereignty (by which we mean legal authority) and autonomy (by which we mean de facto capacity) of member states in the realm of social policy" (ibid.:44). Social policy as a central means of life-course policy is being shaped more and more by supranational institutions of the EU, e.g., the European Parliament, the European Commission, and the European Court of Justice. Benefit access, portability, and consumption have become issues of supranational life-course policy.

Education

Another field of European life-course policy is education, especially higher education, vocational training, and retraining. Can the emergence of a common European educational policy be observed? Are the diverse national patterns of governance assimilating into a European pattern? And are indicators of educational input (capital, law, institutions) and output (quantity, qualifications, credentials) converging? Can these indicators serve as reliable and valid measures of comparative effectiveness and efficiency? What are the impacts of European policy, benchmarking, and networks on national educational policies and institutional performance? Do these bring about a homogenization of educational ideas, regimes, and institutions? Finally, what impact do the national diversity of policies and institution regimes as well as an emerging European life-course policy have on the individual life course in European countries? Specifically, what is their impact on careers in education and work, including the transition from education to work?

To fully answer these questions, a longitudinal or historical perspective on educational policymaking is needed (cf. Vinovskis 1999). At this point, however, we can offer only some preliminary observations.

Empirical life-course research has demonstrated the impact of governance patterns, institutions, and curricula on educational and professional careers. Presently, transitions and trajectories are not homogenized across EU or OECD nations (Breen and Jonsson 2000; Shavit and Blossfeld 1993; Shavit and Müller 1998; Heinz 1999; cf. Heidenheimer 1997). "What then are the reasons for the apparent international variations in the association between educational qualifications and occupational destinations?" (Shavit and Müller 1998:2). Shavit and Müller attribute such variations primarily to differences in the degree of stratification and standardization in national systems of education. The authors hold that these two variables, together with whether a "Dual System" of vocational training exists and whether a "qualificational" or "organizational" employment market predominates, account for the observed heterogeneity of the transitions and trajectories among the thirteen nations studied. National differences of this kind could well become a focus of educational life-course policy by the European Union.

Other objects of European life-course policy in the field of education could be human capital investment in new generations (Coleman 1996; Schultz 1981; Becker 1976, 1981), gender inequality in the context of family and social policy (DiPrete and McManus 2000), international competitiveness in technology and economics (Schofer, Ramirez, and Meyer 2000), and the interrelation of education and employability (Groß 2000). All of these are closely related to economic and research policy, already a supranational domain of the EU, and to social policy, a EU domain in the process of development.

Thus far, examinations and certificates have become mutually acknowledged across EU member states; regulations and restrictions have been imposed on fees, tuition, scholarships, and grants; exchange programs for students and scholars have been established (Barblan, Reichert, Schotte-Kmoch, and Teichler 2000); and comparative studies of standards and effectiveness have been launched (Deutsches PISA-Konsortium 2001; Education in Europe 1999; Goedegebuure et al. 1994; Vink 1997). "These common trends arise not only from the policies of the European Commission . . . but also . . . from the common structural problems which most states in the EU face" (Green, Wolf, and Leney 1999).

The development of European policies will have an impact on the traditional national diversity of relationships between the state and education (Henkel and Little 1999). The educational life-course regime is tending toward a new model of mixed governance: supranational EU, the market, and the local community are gaining influence at the expense of the nation-state. This is a pattern of governance that gives priority to individual market participation and to market mechanisms and supply over extended citizenship rights (Crouch 1998). Will the British model of educational life-course policy become the common European pattern, stimulating a transition to quasi-markets at the expense of traditional communities and welfare state entitlements (Braun and Merrien 1999)?

The European Union began as a common market for a restricted range of products, but this common market has steadily expanded to encompass virtually all products and services. This historical process stimulated and facilitated the mobility of persons within the European Union. In the wake of this development, legal regulations had to be homogenized and the European Union has progressively acquired jurisdiction over many fields of policy. Initially, article 128 EWGV gave supranational EU institutions some authority over national educational systems. This was originally restricted to vocational qualification, training, and retraining schemes. But the European court extended EU jurisdiction to other fields of educational policy, arguing that higher education also constitutes vocational qualification and training. Articles 126 and 127 of the Maastricht Treaty prescribe the development of a European dimension in education, the promotion of mobility of students and scholars, the cooperation of the educational institutions of the member states, information exchange, benchmarking, and the expansion of correspondence courses and universities (Lassahn and Ofenbach 1994).

CONCLUSION

Life-Course research has a long tradition of analyzing passages of individuals and cohorts through institutions and social structure. This approach can be applied to investigate the impact of life-course policy on life courses. We have outlined two central fields of life-course policy research: the historical transformation of the former GDR, and the supranationalization of life course in the European Union.

Neoinstitutionalism provides a theoretical rationale for life-course policy studies and life-course analysis. We have argued that institution regimes guide and support transitions, sequences, and trajectories in the course of life. At the theoretical center of this analysis is the concept of individual choice within the framework of institutional constraints and resources. Institutions are a means to reduce the double contingency of exchange and human interaction. They represent the rules of society or, more generally, self-imposed restrictions on (and guidelines for) human action. Institutions exist because they reduce uncertainty and transaction costs in human interaction by setting up formal or informal rules, and because they contribute effectively and efficiently to the problem of creating collective goods.

Institutional analysis can contribute to the study of life-course policy and to life-course analysis for the same reasons. Individuals have an interest in reducing the transaction costs of decision-making in the course of life, especially over extended periods of time and within complex networks of social interaction. Only institutions with effective rules can provide a basis for rational life-course planning and reduce uncertainty and transaction costs. If the individual knows that other individuals are subject to the same set of rules, and if the public choice process of setting up institutions is itself bound to the rules of constitution and law, then the individual can rationally plan transitions, sequences, and trajectories. In particular, extended sequences and long-term trajectories depend on effective institution regimes provided by life-course policy.

The life-course regime of the nation-state to which we are accustomed has been challenged, however, by substantive and profound historical breaks like the post-1989 transitions of former socialist societies or ongoing processes of globalization. Globalization as a long-term historical process will progressively encompass all societies of the world and all population segments. For this reason, longitudinal and comparative studies of life-course policy are a prime objective of life-course analysis. Furthermore, neoinstitutionalism provides explanatory theoretical arguments that apply well to both fields of research.

An interesting task for life-course research would be to explore whether a European dimension in life-course policy is emerging in the form of institution regimes that guide and support transitions, sequences, and trajectories in a diversity of fields. The rationale of European life-course policy again would be its greater capacity to reduce transactions costs in the course of life compared to the politics of national, regional, and local institutions, as well as its capacity to facilitate rational life-course decision-making with respect to extended chains of sequences and long-term trajectories.

NOTES

1. On generations and the economy of the individual life in the flux of history see Weymann (1996).

2. In empirical research this theoretical shift of emphasis coincides with the transition to qualitative, interpretive methods, which can also be combined with quantitative and representative data sets (see Heinz, Chapter 4 in this volume; Kluge and Kelle 2001).

3. Thus comparisons among societies or across historical time have been made without considering that the indicators used in the macrodata sets might stand for very different social realities. Are liberal professionals, the self-employed, civic associations, unions, or political parties really the same in liberal societies, under socialism, and in the Third World (cf. Curtis, Baer, and Grabb 2001; Paxton 2002)?

4. One of the best definitions can be found in Tönnies (1979:34).

5. Market and constitutional liberalism should be clearly distinguished (Vanberg 1999:234).

6. Some of these arguments coincide with those found in discussions in social anthropology (Gehlen 1961, 1988), symbolic interactionism (Berger and Luckmann 1966), and system theory (Luhmann 1995).

7. Institutions have been a prime concern in the classical texts of Adam Smith, Karl Marx, Max Weber, Norbert Elias, and others. For a state-of-the-art perspective see Scott (2001).

8. Coleman (1990) further distinguishes "conjoint" (institutional) and "disjoint" (organizational) relations.

9. We will not address here the problems of path dependency—e.g., social rigidity, and utilization of institutions by special-interest groups.

10. For a more in-depth treatment of these issues see Falk and Weymann (2002), Weymann (1999), and Weymann, Sackmann, and Wingens (1999).

11. As a rule, Germany's Dual System (like several other European countries' systems of occupational training) takes three years and proceeds simultaneously in a firm and in a vocational school; that is, each week a certain number of hours are spent in each setting. The Dual System thus provides an institutional bridge between education and employment.

12. The rejection of the "housewife" role can also be explained by the high divorce rate and the high number of single-parent families. A further factor is the tense labor-market situation, in which the chances of a woman reentering her occupation after leaving it rapidly declined (cf. Granovetter 1974).

13. The persistent impact of socialist socialization is analyzed also by Lewin-Epstein, Stier, Braun, and Langfeldt (1999).

14. For more see Leisering (2003) and Weymann (2003).

REFERENCES

Barblan, Andris, Sybille Reichert, Martina Schotte-Kmoch, and Ulrich Teichler. 2000. *Implementing European Policies in Higher Education Institutions*. Kassel: University of Kassel.

Becker, Gary S. 1976. *The Economic Approach to Human Behavior*. Chicago: Chicago University Press.

Becker, Gary S. 1981. *A Treatise on the Family*. Cambridge, MA/London: Harvard University Press.

Berger, Peter and Thomas Luckmann. 1966. *The Social Construction of Reality*. Garden City, NY: Doubleday.

Berger, Suzanne and Ronald Dore. 1996. *National Diversity and Global Capitalism*. Ithaca, NY: Cornell University Press.

Boje, Thomas P., Bart van Steenbergen, and Sylvia Walby. 1999. *European Societies. Fusion or Fission?* London/New York: Routledge.

Bourdieu, Pierre. 1993. *La Misère du Monde.* Paris: Edition du Seuil. (Published in English in 1999 as *The Weight of the World: Social Suffering in Contemporary Society.* Stanford, CA: Stanford University Press).

Boyer, Robert and Daniel Drache. 1996. *States Against Markets. The Limits of Globalization.* London: Routledge.

Braun, Dietmar and François-Xavier Merrien. 1999. *Towards a New Model of Governance for Universities?* London/Philadelphia: Jessica Kingsley.

Breen, Richard and Jan O. Jonsson. 2000. "Analysing Educational Careers: Multinomial Transition Model." *American Sociological Review* 65:754–72.

Brennan, Geoffrey and James M. Buchanan. 1985. *The Reason of Rules. Constitutional Political Economy.* Cambridge: Cambridge University Press.

Brinton, Mary C. and Victor Nee. 1998. *The New Institutionalism in Sociology.* New York: Russell Sage Foundation.

Buchanan, James M. 1975. *The Limits of Liberty: Between Anarchy and Leviathan.* Chicago/London: University of Chicago Press.

Coleman, James S. 1990. *Foundations of Social Theory.* Cambridge, MA/London: Belknap Press of Harvard University Press.

Coleman, James S. 1996. "Bringing New Generations into the New Social Structure." Pp. 175–90 in *Society and Biography: Interrelations Between Social Structure, Institutions and the Life Course,* edited by A. Weymann and W. R. Heinz. Weinheim: Deutscher Studienverlag.

Cousins, Christine. 1999. *Society, Work and Welfare in Europe.* London/New York: St. Martins.

Crouch, Colin. 1998. "Staatsbürgerschaft und Markt. Das Beispiel der neueren britischen Bildungspolitik." *Berliner Journal für Soziologie* 8:453–72.

Crouch, Colin and Wolfgang Streeck. 1997. *Political Economy of Modern Capitalism.* London/Thousand Oaks/New Delhi: Sage.

Curtis, James E., Douglas E. Baer, and Edward G. Grabb. 2001. "Nations of Joiners: Explaining Voluntary Association Membership." *American Sociological Review* 66(6):783–805.

Dahrendorf, Ralf. 1992. *Der moderne soziale Konflikt. Essays zur Politik der Freiheit.* Stuttgart: Deutsche Verlagsanstalt.

Deutsches PISA-Konsortium. 2001. *PISA 2000. Basiskompetenzen von Schülerinnen und Schülern im internationalen Vergleich.* Opladen: Leske and Budrich.

DiPrete, Thomas A. and Patricia A. McManus. 2000. "Family Change, Employment Transitions, and The Welfare-State: Household Income Dynamics in the United States and Germany." *American Sociological Review* 65:343–70.

Durkheim, Emilie. [1895] 1961. *Regeln der soziologischen Methode.* Neuwied/Berlin: Luchterhand.

Education in Europe. 1999. *Statistics and Indicators.* Luxembourg: Eurostat.

Esping-Andersen, Gösta. 1990. *Three Worlds of Welfare Capitalism.* Princeton, NJ: Princeton University Press.

Esping-Andersen, Gösta. 1999. *Social Foundations of Postindustrial Economies.* Oxford/New York: Oxford University Press.

Falk, Susanne and Ansgar Weymann. 2002. "Social Change, the Life Course, and

Socialization. Biographies of Labor-Market Entrants after Unification." Pp. 501–26 in *Advances in Life-Course Research: New Frontiers in Socialization*, Vol. 7, edited by R. A. Settersten, Jr., and T. J. Owens. London: JAI/Elsevier.

Franz, Wolfgang, Joachim Inkmann, Winfried Pohlmeier, and Volker Zimmermann. 1997. *Young and Out in Germany: On the Youths' Chances of Labor-Market Entrance in Germany.* NBER Working paper series No. 6212. Cambridge, MA: National Bureau of Economic Research.

Gehlen, Arnold. 1961. *Anthropologische Forschung. Zur Selbstbegegnung und Selbstentdeckung des Menschen.* Reinbek: Rowohet.

Gehlen, Arnold. 1988. *Man, His Nature and Place in the World.* New York: Columbia University Press.

Giddens, Anthony. 1990. *The Consequences of Modernity.* Oxford: Polity/Basil Blackwell.

Goedegebuure, Leo, Frans Kaiser, Peter Maassen, Lynn Meek, Frans van Vught, and Egbert de Weert. 1994. *Higher Education Policy. An International Comparative Perspective.* Oxford/New York/Seoul/Tokyo: Pergamon.

Granovetter, Mark S. 1974. *Getting a Job: A Study of Contacts and Careers.* Cambridge, MA: Harvard University Press.

Green, Andy, Alison Wolf, and Tom Leney. 1999. *Convergence and Divergence in European Education and Training Systems.* London: University of London.

Groß, Martin. 2000. "Bildungssysteme, soziale Ungleichheit und subjektive Schichteinstufung. Die institutionelle Basis von Individualisierungsprozessen im internationalen Vergleich." *Zeitschrift für Soziologie* 29:375–96.

Hall, Peter A. and David Soskice. 2001. *Varieties of Capitalism: The Institutional Foundations of Comparative Advantage.* Oxford/New York: Oxford University Press.

Hanagan, Michael and Charles Tilly. 1999. *Extending Citizenship, Reconfiguring States.* Lanham: Rowman and Littlefield.

Hardin, Garret and John Baden. 1977. *Managing the Commons.* San Francisco: Freeman.

Heidenheimer, Arnold J. 1997. *Disparate Ladders: Why School and University Policies Differ in Germany, Japan, and Switzerland.* New Brunswick/London: Transaction.

Heinz, Walter R. (Ed.) 1999. *From Education to Work: Cross-National Perspectives.* Cambridge: Cambridge University Press.

Heinz, Walter R. 2001. "Work and the Life Course: A Cosmopolitan-Local Perspective." Pp. 3–22 in *Restructuring Work and the Life Course*, edited by V. W. Marshall, W. R. Heinz, H. Krüger, and A. Verma. Toronto/Buffalo/London: University of Toronto Press.

Heinz, Walter R. 2002. "Self-Socialization and Post-Traditional Society." Pp. 41–64 in *New Frontiers in Socialization*, Vol. 7, edited by R. A. Settersten and T. J. Owens. Oxford: JAI/Elsevier.

Henkel, Mary and Brenda Little. 1999. *Changing Relationships Between Higher Education and the State.* London/Philadelphia: Jessica Kingsley.

Hille, Barbara. 1990. "Jugend und Beruf in beiden deutschen Staaten." Pp. 37–74 in *DDR-Jugend. Politisches Bewusstsein und Lebensalltag*, edited by B. Hille and W. Jaide. Opladen: Leske and Budrich.

Hollingsworth, J. Rogers and Robert Boyer. 1997. *Contemporary Capitalism: The Embeddedness of Institutions.* Cambridge/New York: Cambridge University Press.

Kenworthy, Lane. 2002. "Corporatism and Unemployment in the 1980s and 1990s." *American Sociological Review* 67(3):367–88.

Kluge, Susann and Udo Kelle. 2001. *Methodeninnovation in der Lebenslaufforschung. Integration qualitativer und quantitativer Verfahren in der Lebenslauf- und Biographieforschung.* Weinheim/Munich: Juventa.

Knight, Jack and Itai Sened. 1998. *Explaining Social Institutions.* Ann Arbor: University of Michigan Press.

Kohli, Martin. 1994. "Die DDR als Arbeitsgesellschaft? Arbeit, Lebenslauf und soziale Differenzierung." Pp. 31–61 in *Sozialgeschichte der DDR*, edited by H. Kaelble, J. Kocka, and H. Zwahr. Stuttgart: Klett-Cotta.

Krasner, Stephen D. 1983. *International Regimes.* Ithaca/London: Cornell University Press.

Krüger, Alan B. and Jörn-Steffen Pischke. 1995. "A Comparative Analysis of East and West-German Labor Markets: Before and After Unification." Pp. 405–45 in *Differences and Changes in Wage Structures*, edited by R. B. Freeman and L. F. Katz. Chicago: University of Chicago Press.

Lassahn, Rudolf and Birgit Ofenbach. 1994. *Bildung in Europa.* Frankfurt a.M.: Peter Lang.

Leibfried, Stephan and Paul Pierson. 1995. *European Social Policy. Between Fragmentation and Integration.* Washington DC: Brookings.

Leisering, Lutz. 2003. "Government and the Life Course." In *Handbook of the Life Course*, 205–25, edited by J. T. Mortimer and M. L. Shanahan. New York: Kluwer.

Lewin-Epstein, Noah, Haya Stier, Michael Braun, and Bettina Langfeldt. 1999. "Family Policy and Public Attitudes in Germany and Israel." *European Sociological Review* 16(4):99.1–99.17

Lockwood, David. 1964. "Social Integration and System Integration." Pp. 244–57 in *Explorations in Social Change,* edited by G. K. Zollschan and W. Hirsch. London: Houghton Mifflin.

Luhmann, Niklas. 1995. *Social Systems.* Stanford, CA: Stanford University Press.

Mann, Michael. 1993. *The Sources of Social Power.* Vol. II. *The Rise of Classes and Nation States, 1760–1914.* Cambridge/New York: Cambridge University Press.

Mannheim, Karl. 1952. "The Problem of Generations." Pp. 276–320 in K. Mannheim, *Essays on the Sociology of Knowledge,* edited by P. Kecskemeti. London: Routledge & Kegan Paul.

Marshall, Thomas H. 1992a. *Bürgerrechte und soziale Klassen.* Frankfurt a.M./New York: Campus.

Marshall, Thomas H. 1992b. *Citizenship and Social Class.* London/Concord, MA: Pluto.

Mayer, Karl Ulrich. 2001. "The Paradox of Global Social Change and National Path Dependencies: Life-Course Patterns in Advanced Societies." Pp. 89–110 in *Inclusions and Exclusions in European Societies,* edited by A. Woodward and M. Kohli. London/New York: Routledge.

North, Douglass C. 1990. *Institutions, Institutional Change and Economic Performance.* Cambridge, MA: Cambridge University Press.

Olson, Mancur. 1965. *The Logic of Collective Action. Public Goods and the Theory of Groups.* Cambridge, MA: Harvard University Press.

Olson, Mancur. 1982. *The Rise and Decline of Nations: Economic Growth, Stagflation and Social Rigidities.* New Haven/London: Yale University Press.

Ostrom, Elinor. 1990. *Governing the Commons. The Evolution of Institutions for Collective Action.* Cambridge: Cambridge University Press.

Paxton, Pamela. 2002. "Social Capital and Democracy: An Interdependent Relationship." *American Sociological Review* 67(2):254–77.

Polanyi, Karl. 1995. The Great Transformation. Politische und ökonomische Ursprünge von Gesellschaften und Wirtschaftssystemen. Frankfurt a.M.: Suhrkamp.

Ryder, Norman. 1965. "The Cohort as a Concept in the Study of Social Change." *American Sociological Review* 30:843–61.

Sally, Razeen. 1998. *Classical Liberalism and International Economic Order: Studies in Theory and Intellectual History.* London/New York: Routledge.

Sandholtz, Wayne and Alec Stone Sweet. 1998. *European Integration and Supranational Governance.* Oxford/New York: Oxford University Press.

Schofer, Evan, Francisco O. Ramirez, and John W. Meyer. 2000. "The Effects of Science on National Economic Development, 1970 to 1990." *American Sociological Review* 65:688–887.

Schultz, Theodore W. 1981. *Investing in People.* Berkeley: University of California Press.

Schumpeter, Joseph A. 1918. "Die Krise des Steuerstaates." *Zeitfragen aus dem Gebiet der Soziologie* 4:3–75.

Scott, W. Richard. 2001. *Institutions and Organizations.* Thousand Oaks/London/New Delhi: Sage.

Shavit, Yossi and Hans-Peter Blossfeld. 1993. *Persistent Inequality. Changing Educational Attainment in Thirteen Countries.* Boulder/San Francisco/Oxford: Westview.

Shavit, Yossi and Walter Müller (Eds.). 1998. *From School to Work: A Comparative Study of Educational Qualifications and Occupational Destinations.* Oxford: Clarendon.

Smith, Anthony D. 1998. *Nationalism and Modernism: A Critical Survey of Recent Theories of Nations and Nationalism.* London/New York: Routledge.

Swaan, Abram de. 1988. *In Care of the State: Health Care, Education and Welfare in Europe and the USA in the Modern Era.* New York: Oxford University Press.

Tönnies, Ferdinand. 1979. *Gemeinschaft und Gesellschaft.* Darmstadt: Wissenschaftliche Buchgesellschaft. (Published in English in 2001 as *Community and Civil Society,* edited by J. Harris. Cambridge/New York: Cambridge University Press.)

Vanberg, Victor V. 1999. "Markets and Regulations. On the Contrast Between Free-Market Liberalism and Constitutional Liberalism." *Constitutional Political Economy* 10:219–43.

Vink, Mark J. C. 1997. *Efficiency in Higher Education: A Comparative Analysis on Sectoral and Institutional Level.* Utrecht: Elsevier/De Tijdstroom.

Vinovskis, Maris A. 1999. *History and Educational Policymaking*. New Haven/London: Yale University Press.

Weiss, Linda. 1998. *The Myth of the Powerless State*. Ithaca, NY: Cornell University Press.

Weymann, Ansgar. 1996. "Modernization, Generational Relations and the Economy of Life Time." *International Journal of Sociology and Social Policy* 16:37–57.

Weymann, Ansgar. 1999. "From Education to Employment: Occupations and Careers in the Social Transformation of East Germany." Pp. 87–108 in *From Education to Work: Cross-National Perspectives*, edited by W. R. Heinz. Cambridge: Cambridge University Press.

Weymann, Ansgar. 2003. "Future of the Life Course." Pp. 703–14 in *Handbook of the Life Course*, edited by J. T. Mortimer and M. J. Shanahan. New York/Boston/Dordrecht/London/Moscow: Kluwer-Plenum.

Weymann, Ansgar, Reinhold Sackmann, and Matthias Wingens. 1999. "Social Change and Life Course in East Germany. A Cohort Approach to Inequalities." *International Journal of Sociology and Social Policy* 19:90–114.

Woodward, Alison and Martin Kohli. 2001. *Inclusions and Exclusions in European Societies*. London/New York: Routledge.

| 9 |

How Institutions Shape the German Life Course

Lutz Leisering and Karl F. Schumann

INTRODUCTION: LIVES AND INSTITUTIONS

In industrial and postindustrial societies the labor market and the institutions of education to a large extent structure individual lives. In Germany, as in other West and North European countries, the welfare state additionally shapes lives by way of a range of institutions that deal with risks in the individual life course. Correspondingly, European life-course researchers put a stronger emphasis on the role of institutions in shaping individual lives than American researchers do, at least with regard to formal and governmental institutions (Marshall and Mueller, Chapter 1 in this volume; Leisering 2003a). The sociological concept of "institution" refers to relatively stable normative patterns of individual behavior. The concept implies the existence of agencies that regulate behavior as well as models of normality that function as background expectations for such regulations.

In this chapter we focus on formal agencies and organizations that provide a regulatory framework for individual lives. These agencies are imbued by normative patterns of what ought to happen in a life course and at what age. Models of a "normal" working life function as orientations for regulating status passages and for helping in problematic life situations.

Today citizens are able to plan their life course in a more individualized way than their ancestors a century ago (Beck 1992). The expanding range of options includes education, occupational training, gainful employment, family life, unemployment benefit, social assistance, and retirement. The welfare state comes in especially with regard to transitions in the life course and situations of risks. In addition to work-related risks like accidents, disability, and unemployment, the welfare state provides assistance in situations of illness, parenthood, divorce, etc. Some of these provisions are gendered, that is, different options are offered to men and women or the same options may mean something different to the two sexes. In this way gender-specific models of a "normal" life are implemented and continually reaffirmed by the institutions that regulate the life course.

HOW INSTITUTIONS AND INDIVIDUALS NEGOTIATE THE LIFE COURSE

We distinguish four regulative mechanisms and related provisions (cf. Kaufmann 2002):

(1) resources: transfer payments during illness, child benefit, social assistance payments, etc.,

(2) credits like tax exemptions for married persons or earned income tax credits,

(3) personal social services, e.g., in social assistance, health services or psychiatric care,

(4) protective rights and privileges like guarantees of jobs for women on maternity leave, job security for handicapped persons.

What we call regulations are in fact negotiated arrangements between the institutions and the individuals. The way in which such options are used to manage transitions in the spheres of family and partnership, education and vocational training, occupation and work, illness and therapy as well as social security and social control depends on the individual. Persons may neglect those options and prefer to take care of risks alone without recurrence to social services and assistance. For example, some persons who are entitled to receive social assistance will not apply for it because of pride; they want to be able to see to themselves throughout their whole life (Hartmann 1985). Other reasons for the occasional mismatch between options and demands are that the practices of the agencies start from outdated assumptions of normality or that they lack acceptance for other reasons. However, the regulative power of institutions normally persists even if some persons under certain conditions refuse to make use of payments and rights.

American readers may be puzzled by the strong emphasis on the role of institutions in shaping the life course. Is not the individual biography the genuine sphere for idiosyncrasies, the core of autonomy? Is it not possible to escape from societal expectations and live a life according to own standards: as hermit for example or as hippie? Yes, but the very examples illustrate the normality of institutionally prestructured patterns of work and family life. The life course is organized predominantly around the occupational career, as Kohli (1986) has argued, but other aspects of the life course are regulated as well. Particularly in welfare states various intermissions of the occupational career have stimulated options for intervention and assistance. Still, the individual may neglect those options or use them only selectively. Thus it is adequate to assume a loose coupling of social-structural preconditioning and individual construction of the biography. However, inasmuch as the individual depends on the agreement of gatekeepers for the realization of personal goals, their criteria for eligibility for particular options are binding. It is in that sense that life courses are regulated by institutions.

HOW INSTITUTIONS SHAPE THE LIFE COURSE

The regulation of the life course has been investigated by various research projects of the Bremen Life-Course Research Center (Sfb 186) since 1988. Four research questions have come to the fore in most projects:

1. How do institutions acquire *responsibility* for particular phases or transitions in the life course of individuals?
2. What are the *guiding principles* of those institutions, principles that function as orientations or models for regulating the life courses of people?
3. What *interactions* are there *between institutions*, for example, division of responsibility or adaptation of guidelines?
4. How is the *interaction between individuals and institutions* organized? What negotiating strategies and definitions of situations are being used? How important are those negotiations for institutional change?

In this section we depict some results of the research projects of the Sfb 186 to illustrate the fruitfulness of this research agenda.

THE ACQUISITION OF RESPONSIBILITY

Some of the institutions that regulate the life course, for example, the school system, are accountable by law for almost the entire citizenry. These institutions constitute one end of a spectrum that ranks various institutions according to the scope of their responsibility for society members. On the other end one may think of welfare institutions that gain accountability only when requested by the individual. Social assistance, for example, comes into play only if a poor individual applies for it. As a consequence of the passive responsibility of welfare agencies in Germany, an estimated 50 percent of the impoverished population that would be entitled to support does not apply for it (Hauser, Cremer-Schäfer, and Nouvertné 1981).

Whether an institution becomes accountable for a particular individual has been analyzed in the Sfb 186 as a problem of gatekeeping. Research projects have looked at the negotiations of inclusion in or exclusion from the services of a particular organization or the realm of responsibility of an institution (cf. Heinz 1992). Several studies have identified the varying degrees of formality and intensity of gatekeeping depending on whether the gatekeeper is a professional or a family member. Many research results stress the fact that gatekeeping is essentially influenced by the sex of the access-seeking individual. Here again it becomes evident that gender is a structural category, that is, a social status that is connected with distinct regulations and normative patterns. Based on those distinctions the different options for the life courses of men and women are continuously reproduced.

From this point of view Helga Krüger (1995) has investigated the dual system of occupational training in Germany. Historically those occupations that make it possible to support a family have been considered the domain of boys, while the so-called natural vocations like nursing and assisting in medical care have been excluded from the dual system and turned into full-time schooling, predominantly for girls. Notwithstanding the fact that some of those vocations have been incorporated into the dual system in the meantime, the transition from school to work requires girls to accommodate to those inequalities. Their applications for trade and craft apprenticeships are likely to be turned down, and they are more or less pressed to attend full-time vocational education without being paid.

The rather smooth functioning of selective gatekeeping practices within the system of vocational training in Germany has also been studied by the research project conducted by Schumann and his coworkers. The study has focused on the transition from school to work and the relation between occupational trajectories and delinquency. One aspect is the gendered selection into apprenticeships: How do girls whose attempt to get an apprenticeship as carpenter or auto mechanic has failed, accommodate to that rejection? It was discovered that among the most powerful agents in the "cooling out"—process (Goffman 1952), that is, in the process to help adapt to the failure, are the male partners of those girls. They argue that the so-called natural occupations for women may better combine with the tasks of women to care for a family. Thus they help to absorb tendencies to resist the gender-related inequality (Seus 1993).

GUIDING PRINCIPLES OF INSTITUTIONAL REGULATIONS

The principles that guide the institution's regulating activity can be observed best in situations of change. For example, in the juvenile justice system, which tries to prevent juveniles from drifting into a criminal career, the idea of "diversion" became the dominant guiding principle during the 1980s and 1990s. "Diversion" denotes a life-course perspective on delinquency by viewing it as an episode during adolescence that will disappear in most cases; if not, delinquency may be attributed to the intrusive way the juvenile justice system has handled it, e.g., by imprisonment, or secondary deviation, as it is called by Lemert (1967). Diversion from the formal juvenile justice procedure then implies that after police and courts have demonstrated their potential to punish, they forego further formal sanctioning and rather dismiss the case after having cautioned the offender or demanded some disciplinary measure to be completed. Thus, the juvenile justice system based on the principle of diversion postpones any responsibility for controlling the life course of young offenders as long as other institutions like the family, the school, or the apprentice's work place may informally control the behavior, until a pattern of recidivism has occurred (cf. Heinz and Storz 1992).

Quite similar tendencies are apparent in the welfare institutions. Social assistance is available only if support by kin (parents or children) is not available. While for a long time it was considered a long-term benefit, since the 1990s assistance has been seen more and more as a device to bridge a situation of risk until the person can once again support him- or herself. In a way social assistance, as the research project led by Stephan Leibfried and Lutz Leisering has shown, helps recipients to develop a new perspective on life and make an attempt at further education with the prospect of later employment (Leisering and Leibfried 1999). While such an approach may inform policymakers to reduce the number of persons dependent on social assistance, it also highlights the agency of the recipients and their potential to actively create their own biography.

COORDINATION BETWEEN INSTITUTIONS

Is there any consistency between the patterns and the modalities of operation of different institutions? Again social welfare provides a good illustration by its principle of subsidiary competence: Only after other societal institutions, primarily the family, have lost the ability to support a poor person, will social assistance offices take responsibility. The underlying principle of subsidiarity is based on the priority of self-help and help by informal social networks. Restoring the ability of self-help or reinstituting the responsibility of social networks is among the aims of welfare case management.

A similar orientation is at work in the health system, which has recently turned to concepts like restoring one's capability to work and achieve. These are, of course, the guiding principles of the labor market. Moreover, interventions of the juvenile justice system are also guided by those principles. The research conducted in Sfb 186 has confirmed the importance of the principle of work ethics, much like Max Weber understood it in his analysis of the spirit of capitalism, as a link between the guiding principles of various institutions. For example, as long as adolescent or young adult offenders show a strong work ethic in their apprenticeship or on their job, the juvenile court will restrict its interventions to the lowest possible level. It does not want to interfere with the occupational trajectory (Panter, Prein, and Seus 2001). In fact, the idea of rewarding a belief in the work ethic seems to be the common denominator for many institutions.

INTERACTIONS BETWEEN INDIVIDUALS AND INSTITUTIONS

As mentioned earlier, the regulation of the life course by institutions is predominantly indirect. Institutions open up options that may expand the scope within which the life may be planned, but at the same time they generate constraints. The balance will determine the modalities of interaction between institutions and individuals, e.g., the scope available for negotiating further collaboration.

There may be situations in which the element of force involved in the relations becomes stronger. Currently in Germany we experience an example of this tendency. A model for social assistance practiced in the United States, "Wisconsin Works," looms large in the German discussion. This has strengthened the tendency to merge the system of unemployment insurance with welfare assistance in joint case management: monitoring and counseling social assistance recipients to determine their abilities and to find the most adequate job or education to reintegrate them into the labor force while threatening them with reduction or even loss of payments if they do not cooperate. This is a thoroughgoing institutional regulation of the life course.

There are also indications that institutions may become open to the views of the individuals. A good example seems to be the public health sector. Research results by Marstedt, Milles, and Müller (2001) on health insurance and rehabilitation clinics point out that the health insurance schemes have in the last decade changed their approach from a more administrative orientation toward a customer-oriented stance. By becoming more interested in improving public health rather than simply reimbursing treatment the sickness funds have developed an orientation toward the potentially ill, aiming to prevent illness. Such an orientation has not only created a concern of the sickness funds for preventive measures, but it also has led them to play more the role of a pilot (Schwarze 2001), by suggesting appropriate ways of treatment as well as of prevention.

The degree to which institutions regulate the life course may be hidden or the outcome may be interpreted by individuals as autonomous acts. This can be illustrated by results from research on the transition from school to work. While the normal pattern for that transition would imply entering the dual system of apprenticeship, there are those who fail to obtain an apprenticeship contract. Among them especially are pupils who fail to graduate from the *Hauptschule*. If failing to graduate becomes apparent the pupils are contacted by special teachers and persuaded to register for particular *Ausbildungsvorbereitungsjahre* (preparatory vocational classes), which provide basic training in areas like metal- or woodworking. In addition those classes also offer a second chance to get a *Hauptschule* equivalency *degree*. This option, rather than the types of work offered, makes such classes attractive for young people: Those who eventually graduate believe that they have gained a chance for an apprenticeship (Dietz, Matt, Schumann, and Seus 1997). In reality only a minority of them manages to enter the dual system eventually. Others spend year after year in a kind of waiting spiral before eventually entering the labor force mostly at an unskilled level. From the point of view of the vocational system, preparatory classes are a measure to avoid adolescent unemployment. From the perspective of the individual, these classes are seen as an important step toward a working career. Young persons especially tend to interpret personal developments in a rather optimistic way, thereby turning institutional guidance into self-made success. Or, to paraphrase Walter Heinz (2002), socialization becomes to a large degree self-socialization.

To sum up, the interactions between institutions and individuals constitute a process of negotiating different goals on both sides. The individuals bargain for appropriate options, and the institutions for compliance as well as acceptance of what they have to offer. While individuals essentially live their life autonomously, they perceive their developing life course as self-made. If in the negotiations with institutions their request for particular options is accepted or rejected, they take responsibility for that as a consequence of the way they conducted their previous lives.

THE GERMAN LIFE-COURSE REGIME

In Germany the institutional formation of the life course is particularly pronounced. What are the key elements of the German "life-course regime"? (For a critical discussion of the term "life-course regime" see Leisering 2003a.) We propose that three elements characterize the German life-course regime:

- high regulation
- curb on wage labor
- inequality structured by status and gender.

High Regulation

Germany has a strong and active state as a source of legislation and regulatory powers. It is a federal state but in many ways the autonomy of the states (*Länder*) is limited, or, in the case of education, only used to a limited extent. Besides the state, German society is firmly structured by corporatist actors and arrangements, above all trade unions and employers, who are organized in a unitary way and rely on unitary collective labor agreements. The field of health care is dominated by collective agreements between medical doctors and sickness funds. If we were to choose one normative principle that characterizes German society it would be security, stability, and continuity. This applies to the regulation of the labor market, to provisions against social risks through the welfare state, to the "production regime," and to society at large. Soskice and others have described Germany as a "flexibly coordinated corporate system," contrasted to "deregulated, open systems" (for a discussion of such characterizations see Mayer 1997:219–22). Germany is a "high-trust society" (as compared to low-trust societies), with "trust" pertaining to the social relationship between the corporate actors and within society at large: Society is conceived by its citizens as a community of shared solidarity to attend collectively to individual risks.

As mentioned earlier, several institutions combine and interact to create a certain life-course regime. In the German case all key institutions—labor market, education, family, and welfare state—add up to a tight regulatory framework for social life. The underlying idea is a wide-ranging responsibility of government for the well-being of its citizens enshrined in the notion of "welfare state" (in German: "social state").

Curb on Wage Labor

Compared to many other countries Germany might be called a "reluctant work society." In his classical work *The Three Worlds of Welfare Capitalism*, Esping-Andersen (1990) has distinguished three "welfare regimes"—liberal, conservative, and social democratic, each of which gives rise to a certain "labor-market regime." Germany, a conservative welfare regime, clearly exhibits features of the related labor-market regime: In all phases of the life course labor-market participation is low (see Table 9.1 for a comparison with other OECD countries). People enter the labor market late because periods of education are long, while, at the other end of the life course, people exit from the labor market through retirement at an early age. As a former longstanding German minister of labor and social order, Norbert Blüm, once remarked: Germany has the oldest students and youngest pensioners. For many years this has been the German way of coping with unemployment, a strategy, though, that failed to reach its aim.

Table 9.1   Labor-Force Participation Rates in OECD Countries, 2001 (Percentage of Economically Active Persons in Each Group)

	Young People (15–24 Years)	Old People (55–64 Years)	Men (15–64 Years)	Women (15–64 Years)
Norway	63.1	68.5	84.0	76.4
Switzerland	67.8	68.2	89.2	73.0
Sweden	54.3	70.4	81.4	77.1
Japan	46.5	65.8	85.0	60.1
New Zealand	63.5	62.9	83.4	68.5
United States	64.6	60.2	83.4	70.5
Denmark	67.2	58.9	83.3	75.0
Great Britain	61.1	54.0	82.2	67.6
Portugal	47.9	52.0	79.4	64.6
Canada	64.7	51.3	82.1	70.8
Ireland	50.1	47.9	79.0	56.0
Australia	69.4	48.6	81.7	65.8
Finland	50.4	50.3	76.7	72.5
Netherlands	73.6	39.9	84.2	66.9
Spain	46.8	41.9	79.8	51.6
Germany	52.2	41.5	79.3	63.8
France	29.9	38.8	74.3	61.8
Austria	54.7	29.0	79.0	62.3
Belgium	33.6	26.0	72.7	54.5
Italy	37.6	19.4	74.2	47.3

Source: OECD (2002).

In the middle phase of life a low labor-market participation of women, especially married women, also curbs labor. In the German Democratic Republic, however, the sexes did not differ with regard to labor-market participation, and since German unification East German women continue to have higher employment rates (see Schaeper and Falk, Chapter 7 in this volume). Another curb on labor in the middle phase of life is the small size of the low-wage sector. The service sector is underdeveloped and there is a good system of social assistance as an alternative source of income. Generally, in Germany the aim of fighting poverty prevails over the aim of fighting unemployment.

Structured Inequality

While inequality obviously is not peculiar to German society, the structuring of inequality by status and gender is particularly pronounced. For the citizens this is an equivocal situation. On the one hand many groups enjoy a high degree of security, institutional support, and protection in their lives. On the other hand this security is granted on unequal terms. Inequality is institutionalized by law and culture. Certain groups enjoy privileges and particular powers, which give rise to vested interests by which the privileged successfully defend their privilege in the political process. First, educational certificates are closely linked to status hierarchies in the occupational system. Certificates largely determine the start and even the further progress of a career. Second, there is a segmented system of occupational status. Civil servants are a class on their own, as are vocational groups like medical doctors and lawyers. Within firms seniority is a key principle of status and wage. Third, gender is more than a sociodemographic characteristic of persons. It is enshrined in all social institutions, becoming an institution in itself that pervades all spheres of social life (see the contributions by Krüger and by Born, Chapters 2 and 13, respectively, in this volume). Fourth, the dividing line between the employed and the unemployed is also very sharp. Switching between the two groups is difficult, and as a result long-term unemployment is widespread.

Much of what has been said applies to conservative welfare regimes in general. Conservative regimes are characterized by a high degree of "decommodification" (higher than in liberal regimes, though lower than in social democratic regimes), with decommodification denoting the degree to which the state enables its citizens to live independently of the labor market. Conservative regimes are also characterized by corporatist structures and a strong emphasis on the family. As regards labor-market participation, other conservative regimes like France, Italy, Belgium, and Austria also rank low (Table 9.1). Table 9.2 characterizes the life course in the three welfare regimes with special reference to the temporal structure of working lives.

Table 9.2 confirms the three elements of the German life-course regime that we have described: The high degree of standardization of vocational training and the low degree of job mobility hint at extensive regulation. Late labor-market entry and early retirement testify to the curb on wage labor. The high degree of stratification of the educational system and the low degree of both job mobility and class mobility indicate structured inequality.

Restructuring or Immobility?

Esping-Andersen's typology is based on data from around 1980. Has the German life-course regime changed since, are its peculiarities fading? Table 9.1, which gives current figures, does not suggest a thoroughgoing change. But the question of whether change has occurred has also to be put in institutional terms. Are we witnessing a "deinstitutionalization" of the German life course? This question has been much debated in German social science since Kohli's seminal article of 1986. Kohli himself, almost

Table 9.2   Life Courses in Three Welfare Regimes: The Temporal Structure of Working Lives[a]

	Liberal Welfare Regime	Conservative Welfare Regime	Social Democratic Welfare Regime
Stratification of educational system	low [high]	high	[low]
Standardization of vocational training	low	[high]	[low]
Labor-market entry	early	late	early
Job mobility	high	low	low [high]
Class mobility	[low]	[low]	[high]
Retirement	variable	early	late

Source: Leisering (2003a), based on Mayer (2001:102) and Allmendinger and Hinz (1998:78).
[a][. . .]: from Allmendinger and Hinz (1998).
Mayer's and Allmendinger and Hinz's results differ on two accounts (cells "low [high]").
Mayer's results are derived from theoretical hypotheses about the three welfare regimes in general, whereas Allmendinger and Hinz's findings are based on empirical data from Mayer's *Eurocareers* project for Britain, Germany, and Sweden.

fifteen years later, still sees a highly institutionalized life course as an integral part of the (German version of the) work society (Kohli 2000). In the international political debate Germany is often seen as a laggard, as overregulated and overbureaucratized (for a critical assessment of this debate with regard to the labor market see Fuchs and Schettkat 2000), combined with an inability to break up these institutional structures. But empirical indicators with regard to changes in the three elements of the German life-course regime—regulation, curb on wage labor, structured inequality—are ambivalent (see Table 9.3).

Regulation.   There is strong resistance by privileged and powerful groups to deregulating the labor market. Chancellor Schröder's coalition government of social democrats and the Green Party, in power since 1998 (and reelected in 2002), has only cautiously changed ingrained labor laws, which make it difficult to lay off workers. Standardized collective labor agreements that do not account for the particular economic situation of a company have become somewhat more flexible in practice. All in all, deregulation is limited, even if, for example, temporary working contracts have been facilitated by statute, and the reorganization of the labor exchanges to speed up reentry of unemployed persons is high on the agenda of Schröder's second-term coalition government after the election in September 2002. Unemployment benefit has also been reduced and stricter criteria for eligibility have been imposed over the last twenty years.

There are a number of substantial, though less perceived changes that go beyond the crude dichotomy of regulation versus deregulation. These

Table 9.3   The German Life-Course Regime

Key Elements	Relevant Institutions	Changes
High regulation	Education, labor market, family, welfare state	Resistance to change, but limited deregulation alongside needs for new regulation; "activation" as new strategy
Curb on wage labor	Education, labor market, family, welfare state	Moderate extension of wage labor; incentives for family care
Inequality structured by status and gender	Education, labor market, family, welfare state	Slow change (institutional inertia), but quest for change

changes combine deregulation with needs for new regulation in new settings. Examples include privatization in the field of old-age security—the pension reform act of 2001 formally established a public-private mix—and in the field of long-term care—the reform act of 1994 opened the gate for private care services under a newly created care insurance. These reforms have reduced the scope of state provision. At the same time new demands for state regulation of the privatized spheres have been created.

Another example is "activating" policies related to what Giddens and Blair have termed the "Third Way." The activating approach has been changing labor-market policy and social security especially in the field of social assistance and health (Schwarze 2001). Public provision of services is supplemented by and partially substituted by measures designed to enable people to help themselves. New forms of counseling, case management, and increased client-orientation under New Public Management (Leisering 2003b) strengthen the role of individuals as agents. In this way, the new measures create more flexibility in the labor market and foster the process of individualization through increased options (and obligations). In the process, new sanctions and controls are being introduced and new agencies installed that manage activating policies. Activating policy, therefore, is not an outright deinstitutionalization of the life course but rather a refinement of "life-course policy" in a highly institutionalized welfare state [for the concept of life-course policy see Leisering and Leibfried (1999), Leisering (2003a), Schwarze (2001), Weymann, Chapter 8 in this volume].

Curb on Wage Labor.   The figures in Table 9.1 do not reveal that there have been recent (moderate) changes toward loosening the curb on wage labor. This applies to all phases of the life course. Legislative measures make for later retirement. The age of retirement for women is currently being raised from sixty to sixty-five years (laid down in advance in the reform act of 1992) and the 2001 reform act makes early retirement less attractive by lowering pension benefits before the age of sixty-five. Still the great reform act of 2001 all in all provided weak incentives to retire late (Viebrok 2001). Moreover, under collective labor agreements an estimated 80 percent of employees are subject to compulsory retirement at the age of sixty-five. Unlike the United States, this is not unconstitutional in Germany. There are also attempts at cutting the length of education, by introducing Anglo-Saxon academic degrees (bachelor, master) and through the growing role of polytechnics, which lead to graduation after three years, while at universities the first degree normally requires five to seven years.

Increasing the number of low-paid jobs is hotly debated but there are only first departures. Retrenching unemployment benefit and introducing welfare-to-work measures induce more people to take jobs they would not take otherwise. A recalibration of the relationship between the three parameters: social assistance benefits, level of wages, and taxation is also widely debated. A start has been made in a tax reform that has rendered incomes below the level of subsistence tax-free. A major social assistance reform is scheduled for 2003 (Leisering 2003b). New service jobs in the field of long-term care are growing at a slow rate.

But there is a countermovement, a strong move toward enhancing family policy propagated by all political parties since the mid-1980s. Entitlements to old-age pensions for mothers purely based on earlier childcare were introduced in 1985 and have been extended massively since. Child benefit has been raised considerably in Schröder's first term (1998–2002), along with tax relief for families. There is evidence of a marked change of normative models from redistributive class policies to family policy, which redistributes from the childless to families. On the one hand these family policies aim to fight child poverty and to increase the incomes of families, including single parents. On the other hand women are induced to stay at home and devote their lives to family care. The extension of maternity leave has indeed had this effect (Bird 2001). The alternative to raising cash benefits, namely, expanding personal social services to enable women better to coordinate wage labor and family care, however, is pursued only in a hesitant way. Despite the pressure on the German economy to become more competitive in a globalizing world and despite the alleged hegemony of neoliberalism, a very German conservative notion of family and gender is still going strong.

Structured Inequality.   With regard to equality, the change in the German life-course regime is slowest. There is a strong quest for change but inertia seems to prevail. On the level of debates, citizens and politicians are groping for new norms. The women's movement has grown since the 1970s and nondiscrimination has become a standard legal guideline for employers. The EU, both the European Court of Justice and gender mainstreaming policy guidelines, are increasingly influencing German law and politics. The increase in family values has had an ambivalent effect as described above. New issues of equality and social justice refer to the growing number of migrants, to justice between successive generations ("sustainable policies" in old-age security), and to the dividing line between the living conditions of West and East Germans that still exists more than ten years after unification.

The following are four examples of cautious attempts at breaking up the ingrained structure of inequality by status: First, a reform of civil servants' old-age pensions has started with the aim of containing and restructuring those pensions along the same lines as workers' pensions under the 2001 act. Second, it remains to be seen how the stratified occupational system reacts to the introduction of the American-style academic degrees of bachelor and master. These new certificates challenge the traditional institutionalized career ladders that mirror the traditional German degrees. Third, the boundary between employment and unemployment is to be made more permeable through a *Kombilohn*, which combines wages and social assistance benefits in the low-wage sector of the labor market. Pilot schemes in some states (*Länder*), however, have been to little avail. Fourth, over the last decades the medical profession has lost some of its power. The health reform bill of 2003 is a first step toward breaking the supply monopoly of the corporatist medical association.

CONCLUSION

In the previous section we illustrated how life courses in Germany are subject to strong institutional regulation. The institutional fabric has been loosening recently, though it is not disappearing but rather being reshaped. Institutions are changing not to the degree deemed necessary by some observers but more than perceived in popular debates. The actors that constitute the German life-course regime—state, bureaucracies, corporatist actors, and pressure groups—also make for its political support and persistence. However, while social and political change in Anglo-Saxon countries tends to be more discontinuous and fueled by great rhetoric of change, evolutionary change prevails in Germany (for the evolutionary change of the German welfare state see Leisering 2001). In this way the institutions of German society become more similar to those in other countries but there is no break with ingrained basic structures ("path dependence").

However, other life-course regimes are also changing. Contrary to views voiced in the early 1990s the process of globalization does not imply a wholesale deregulation of the economy nor a sweeping deinstitutionalization of other spheres of life outside the market. The revival of neoinstitutionalism has shown that ingrained institutions do not easily dissolve but rather adapt gradually within their "path." New economic, demographic, and social challenges require new institutions. As regards the welfare state, for example, we are not facing its end or its wholesale downsizing to a residual welfare state. Rather, recent research inquires into the "new politics of the welfare state" (Pierson 2001). The partial privatization of old-age pensions generates new needs for the state to regulate financial markets and private providers. In this way new arenas of political conflict over the institutional shaping of life courses are opened up (Myles and Pierson 2001, Leisering 2002). New insecurities in a globalized world require new securities, a recent catchword being "flexicurity"—combining security of social protection with flexibility in the labor market. Prospects are that the emerging world society will also be a work society that goes along with an institutionally structured life course.

Also less regulated and more flexibly coordinated societies encompass more institutional regulation than imagined by neoliberal politicians. The instructional regulation of the life course is particularly pronounced in Germany but it is a vital component of the life course in all advanced Western societies, even or especially in an age of globalization.

REFERENCES

Allmendinger, Jutta and Thomas Hinz. 1998. "Occupational Careers under Different Welfare Regimes: West Germany, Great Britain and Sweden." Pp. 63–84 in *The Dynamics of Modern Society: Poverty, Policy and Welfare*, edited by L. Leisering and R. Walker. Bristol: Policy.

Beck, Ulrich. 1992. *Risk Society: Towards a New Modernity*. London/Newbury Park/New Delhi: Sage.

Bird, Katherine. 2001. "Parental Leave in Germany—An Institution With Two Faces." Pp. 55–87 in *Institutionen und Lebensläufe im Wandel*, edited by L. Leisering, R. Müller, and K. F. Schumann. Weinheim/Munich: Juventa.

Dietz, Gerhard-Uhland, Eduard Matt, Karl F. Schumann, and Lydia Seus. 1997. *Lehre tut viel ... Berufsbildung, Lebensplanung und Delinquenz bei Arbeiterjugendlichen*. Münster: Votum.

Esping-Andersen, Gøsta. 1990. *The Three Worlds of Welfare Capitalism*. Princeton, NJ: Princeton University Press.

Fuchs, Susanne and Ronald Schettkat. 2000. "Germany: A Regulated Flexibility." Pp. 211–44 in *Why Deregulate Labour Markets?*, edited by G. Esping-Andersen and M. Regini. Oxford: Oxford University Press.

Goffman, Erving. 1952. "On Cooling the Mark Out: Some Aspects of Adaptation on Failure." *Psychiatry* 15:451–63.

Hartmann, Helmut. 1985. "Armut trotz Sozialhilfe. Zur Nichtinanspruchnahme von Sozialhilfe in der Bundesrepublik." Pp. 169–89 in *Politik der Armut und die Spaltung des Sozialstaats,* edited by S. Leibfried and F. Tennstedt. Frankfurt a.M.: Suhrkamp.

Hauser, Richard, Helga Cremer-Schäfer, and Udo Nouverné. 1981. *Armut, Niedrigeinkommen und Unterversorgung in der Bundesrepublik Deutschland.* Frankfurt a.M.: Campus.

Heinz, Walter R. 1992. "Institutional Gatekeeping and Biographical Agency." Pp. 9–27 in *Institutions and Gatekeeping in the Life Course,* edited by W. R. Heinz. Weinheim: Deutscher Studien Verlag.

Heinz, Walter R. 2002. "Self-Socialization and Post-Traditional Society." Pp. 41–64 in *New Frontiers in Socialization,* edited by R. A. Settersten and T. J. Owens. Amsterdam/London/San Diego: Elsevier.

Heinz, Wolfgang and Renate Storz. 1992. *Diversion im Jugendstrafverfahren der Bundesrepublik Deutschland.* Bonn: Bundesministerium der Justiz.

Kaufmann, Franz-Xaver. 2002. "Elemente einer soziologischen Theorie sozialpolitischer Intervention." Pp. 69–106 in *Sozialpolitik und Sozialstaat.* Soziologische Analysen, edited by F.-X. Kaufmann. Opladen: Leske and Budrich.

Kohli, Martin. 1986. "The World We Forgot: A Historical Review of the Life Course." Pp. 271–303 in *Later Life: The Social Psychology of Aging,* edited by V. W. Marshall. Beverly Hills, CA: Sage.

Kohli, Martin. 2000. "Arbeit im Lebenslauf: Alte und neue Paradoxien." Pp. 362–82 in *Geschichte und Zukunft der Arbeit,* edited by J. Kocka, C. Offe and B. Redslob. Frankfurt a.M./New York: Campus.

Krüger, Helga. 1995. "Dominanzen im Geschlechterverhältnis." Pp. 195–219 in *Das Geschlechterverhältnis als Gegenstand der Sozialwissenschaften,* edited by R. Becker-Schmidt and G.-A. Knapp. Frankfurt a.M./New York: Campus.

Leisering, Lutz. 2001. "Germany—Reform from Within." Pp. 161–82 in *International Social Policy: Welfare Regimes in the Developed World,* edited by P. Alcock and G. Craig. London: Macmillan.

Leisering, Lutz. 2002. "Entgrenzung und Remoralisierung—Alterssicherung und Generationenbeziehungen im globalisierten Wohlfahrtskapitalismus." *Zeitschrift für Gerontologie und Geriatrie* 35:343–54.

Leisering, Lutz. 2003a. "Government and the Life Course." Pp. 205-25 in *Handbook of the Life Course,* edited by J. T. Mortimer and M. J. Shanahan. New York and others: Kluwer.

Leisering, Lutz. 2003b. *Die Kreativität des lokalen Sozialstaats. Die Modernisierung der kommunalen Sozialhilfeverwaltungen in Deutschland (1990–2000) und internationale Reformerfahrungen.* With contributions by B. Hilkert et al. Opladen: Leske and Budrich, forthcoming.

Leisering, Lutz and Stephan Leibfried. 1999. *Time and Poverty in Western Welfare States. United Germany in Perspective.* Cambridge: Cambridge University Press.

Lemert, Edwin. 1967. "The Concept of Secondary Deviation." Pp. 40–64 in *Human Deviance, Social Problems, and Social Control,* edited by E. Lemert. Englewood Cliffs, NJ: Prentice Hall.

Marstedt, Gerd, Dietrich Milles, and Rainer Müller. 2001. "Eine neue Wohlfahrts-kultur? Lebenslaufpolitik und Risikobearbeitung in der Sozialversicherung." Pp. 91–118 in *Institutionen und Lebensläufe im Wandel,* edited by L. Leisering, R. Müller, and K. F. Schumann. Weinheim: Juventa.

Mayer, Karl Ulrich. 1997. "Notes on a Comparative Political Economy of Life Courses." *Comparative Social Research* 16:203–26.

Mayer, Karl Ulrich. 2001. "The Paradox of Global Social Change and National Path Dependencies. Life-Course Patterns in Advanced Societies." Pp. 89–110 in *Inclusions and Exclusions in European Societies,* edited by A. Woodward and M. Kohli. New York: Routledge.

Myles, John and Paul Pierson. 2001. "The Comparative Political Economy of Pension Reform." Pp. 305–55 in *The New Politics of the Welfare State,* edited by P. Pierson. Oxford: Oxford University Press.

OECD. 2002. *OECD Employment Outlook.* July, Vol. 1(7).

Panter, Rosl, Gerald Prein, and Lydia Seus. 2001. "Per Doppelpass ins Abseits. Zur Kontinuität von Interpretations- und Handlungsmustern in Arbeitsmarkt und Strafjustiz und deren Konsequenzen." Pp. 157–85 in *Institutionen und Lebensläufe im Wandel,* edited by L. Leisering, R. Müller, and K. F. Schumann. Weinheim: Juventa.

Pierson, Paul. Ed. 2001. *The New Politics of the Welfare State.* Oxford: Oxford University Press.

Schwarze, Uwe. 2001. "Aktivierende Sozialpolitik." Pp. 119–54 in *Institutionen und Lebensläufe im Wandel,* edited by L. Leisering, R. Müller, and K. F. Schumann. Weinheim/Munich: Juventa.

Seus, Lydia. 1993. *Soziale Kontrolle von Arbeitertöchtern.* Pfaffenweiler: Centaurus.

Viebrok, Holger. 2001. "Die Bedeutung institutioneller Arrangements für den Übergang in den Ruhestand." Pp. 215–50 in *Institutionen und Lebensläufe im Wandel,* edited by L. Leisering, R. Müller, and K. F. Schumann. Weinheim/Munich: Juventa.

|10|

Growing Up in American Society

Income, Opportunities, and Outcomes

Frank F. Furstenberg

INTRODUCTION

The organization of childhood and early adulthood experience is by no means unique in the United States. Yet, growing up in the United States is uniquely tinged by certain distinctive features, namely, the extremely high premium that Americans place on individual choice; the diverse nature of the population; the large level of inequality that exists in America; and the peculiar constellation of American institutions that touch portions of the population as a result of the unequal life chances of children and adolescents. This chapter discusses both these common and disparate features of the American life course with an eye toward the way that particular social institutions and perhaps absence of others shape the experience of growing up, American-style.

The main part of the chapter describes the typical demographic and social experiences of today's children and youth, focusing on the distinction between the life courses of those who grow up in affluent families and those who do not. While my primary aim is to contrast the life circumstances of the rich, those of modest means, and those of very limited means, I will also occasionally refer to the special situation of minority groups and immigrants, as well as the different experiences of males and females. Gender has a decreasing significance in the early part of the life course compared to economic standing or social class. I will argue that institutions support and sustain the affluent, while for working-class and poor youth, they are much less supportive and often undermining. Social class matters more in the United States than in most countries with advanced economies and it matters more now than it did a half-century ago in shaping the life chances of young people. The reason why may well be because of the ever-shrinking role of the public sphere in family life (Furstenberg 1997). The contraction of government support for social welfare services in recent decades has imposed limits on the life choices of those without the means to purchase daycare, early education, after-school care, and high-quality schooling (Garfinkel, Hochschild, and McLanahan 1996).

At the risk of some oversimplification, I will attempt to describe the modal experience for those of high privilege, those with modest means, and the poor and near poor. Admittedly, no neat way exists for drawing the boundaries between these three economic groupings, and I give too little attention to the important variations that occur within each economic category. Nonetheless, economic position clearly creates vastly different social experiences that I will attempt to describe at least in a broad-brush fashion in the main part of this chapter. This fairly stark picture of the opportunity structure does not offer an adequate account of subcultural differences in religion, region, ethnicity, and immigration. And I will virtually ignore individual-level differences within families that may affect how individuals manage the opportunities available to them, a topic that attracts considerable attention by social scientists (Furstenberg, Eccles, Elder, and Sameroff 1999).

Before starting, I must say something about the distribution of social class in the United States. Looked at comparatively, the United States has a much higher level of inequality than most other countries with developed economies (Vleminckx and Smeeding 2001). Researchers who have calculated various measures of inequality among households or families across nations with highly developed economies have consistently shown that the United States has the largest spread between rich and poor. While we are among the wealthiest countries in the Western world in per capita income, we have the highest level of poverty and, accordingly, the greatest spread between the top and bottom of the income distribution. In other words, we have the most rich and poor of any of our counterparts and the smallest level of families comfortably situated in the middle of the income distribution.

For the purpose of this discussion, privileged families will be defined as those in the upper fifth of the income distribution, which stood at slightly under $100,000 in 2000 (U.S. Census Bureau 2002a, 2002b), though many families in the top quintile hardly view themselves as well-off. Indeed, one could easily argue that privilege requires a standard of living that only is attained by the top decile. In 2000, poverty levels were officially defined for a family of four at $17,463. But families can barely get by with incomes twice that standard, and in 1999, more than 30 percent of Americans were in households with incomes below 200 percent of the official poverty level for their family size (Dalaker and Proctor 2000). In the middle lies the vast majority of Americans who are neither rich nor poor.

The distinctive shape of the U.S. income distribution is partly a by-product of the strong American belief that everyone has equal opportunity and is free to rise above our station at birth (Hochschild 1981). Paradoxically, at the same time Americans resist redistribution mechanisms through tax and social welfare programs that are designed to level the playing field while holding firmly to the idea that parents are responsible for managing their children's life chances. It is up to parents to find appropriate neighborhoods, schools, and social institutions that afford their children opportunities for advancement. The government is expected to provide some assistance, but many Americans believe that government programs may undermine parental authority and therefore rob parents of the initiative that is required to guide their children's moral, social, and academic education. The primacy of the family as a mechanism of allocation of resources and responsibilities in the United States is especially ironic and problematic given the high levels of marital instability that are characteristic of our kinship system. I return to this structural anomaly later in the chapter.

GROWING UP PRIVILEGED

The accumulation of privilege for children begins before birth and extends into early adulthood. The most obvious and blatant expression of privilege is the much higher likelihood that children will be born into marital unions that have a high likelihood of survival (Ellwood and Jencks 2001). In the middle of the last century, divorce rates were actually higher among the more affluent. The situation sharply reversed several decades ago and now higher-status parents are far more likely to have children within marriage and far less likely to divorce after marriage (Goldstein and Kenney 2001). Huge differences in the likelihood of being raised by both biological parents exist by social class, and minorities, especially blacks and Puerto Ricans, are less likely to enjoy the benefits of growing up with two parents in the home regardless of social class (McLanahan and Sandefur 1994; Cherlin 1992; Bumpass 1990).

Marriage typically occurs in the late twenties in upper-class or privileged families, virtually all of whom are well-educated professionals, high-level managers, and successful entrepreneurs. This segment of the population rarely marries before the graduate school years and only then when the end of schooling is in sight. Childbearing only occasionally occurs outside marriage (Hoffman and Foster 1997). When it does, it usually happens by design in consensual unions following a lengthy period of cohabitation or by single women who intend to have a child outside marriage. This means that children are generally planned and couples have often undergone lengthy deliberations about when to begin childbearing. They start when they have the means to do so and when relationships have been time tested. Thus, the children of privileged unions are typically wanted *before* conception.

Once conception occurs, affluent couples often speak about "our pregnancy."[1] Fathers are expected to take interest in the development of the fetus by visits to the doctor, helping to monitor precautionary measures such as no or a low intake of alcohol, and attending birthing classes. The choice of an obstetrician, if not jointly made, is at least a topic of mutual consultation. Of course, it is taken for granted that parents will do their utmost to prepare for the birth by selecting appropriate medical care, infant equipment, and plans for the postpartum period. In short, parenthood is managed jointly and a high premium is placed on anticipating the baby's wants and needs. And it goes almost without saying that these parents have the resources to make appropriate choices, and they generally display a great willingness to consume them on behalf of their child.

Commitments to careful management and high investment are evidenced even more once a child is born. Deliberation begins with the selection of a child's name and continues to the choice of appropriate toys, feeding routines and later food selection, baby equipment, picking playmates and arranging for play dates, and so on. All these decisions are designed to cultivate the child's human, cultural, and social capital (Lareau 1989, forthcoming; Lamont 1992). Needless to say, the choice of childcare arrangements, daycare, and preschool are not left to chance. Both parents are expected to deliberate and discriminate among possible choices. As much time and attention is given to the selection of a preschool program as used to be given to the choice of a college. The responsibilities of management have grown as parents in the upper classes have fewer offspring and as children have become more and more the object of consumption and cultivation in the free-market economy that dominates American society.

Many parents, usually mothers, in upper-class families curtail their work hours after their first child is born. Many are able to take advantage of employment benefits that provide paid leave or at least are able to afford to take time off because of their high-income employment (Sanchez and Thomson 1997). When women return to work, as they typically do after a stay at home, enormous care is given to the choice of alternative arrangements for infant and toddler care until the child reaches full-time preschool. Almost all affluent parents now elect to send their children to nursery school by age three or four, mostly to a privately run center. Before then, when parents work full-time, it is not uncommon to rely on a care-giver in the home (Snyder and Hoffman 2001). Rigorous standards are applied to assure the child's safety and development. Privileged parents expect auxiliary childcare agents to be more than custodians; they must be able to contribute to the child's cognitive and emotional development. It is not uncommon for parents to recruit childcare workers who can expose the preschooler to a second language or some other special skill.

As in other social classes, close kin are trusted surrogates, but even kin are likely to uphold the strong values placed on cultivation of talents and skills. The older generation of privileged parents often expresses the view that the current generation has become overly managerial and excessively attentive to their children's needs compared to the more casual styles of childrearing practiced in their day. Privileged parents perceive that the stakes are rising and that they have an obligation to give their children every possible advantage in making their way into an elite education (Lareau and Horvat 1999).

A growing number of privileged families, especially in large urban areas, are opting out of the public school system (U.S. Census Bureau 2001). Professional and affluent families are attempting to preserve the economic status of their children through private education, much as the tiny group of upper-class families have long attempted to preserve their social stand-ing by sending their children to private boarding schools.

In suburban and nonurban areas, parents are more likely to use resi-dential location as a means of gaining advantage for their children through schooling. In the United States, where local property taxes are a primary source of school funding, communities vary enormously in the quality of their public schools. Consequently, parents with school-age children pick their residence according to the quality of the schools, and hence purchase high-quality public education by locating in affluent communities that can only be afforded by families with means (Maddaus 1987). So residential selection becomes a major mechanism for maintaining intergenerational advantage.

Whether children attend public or private school, affluent parents lib-erally supplement formal schooling with after-school classes and activities explicitly tailored to nurture talents and build skills. Children are rarely left to their own devices; their time is scheduled between schoolwork and classes or athletic programs during the school year (Lareau forthcoming). At younger ages, parents schedule play dates for their children, screening the quality of their children's peers as carefully as they screen the quality of their own social activities. When children get older, they are sent to camps in the summertime that are carefully selected to provide recre-ational education. These days, adolescents are often sent abroad to gain language skills and knowledge of different cultures.

Childhood is seen as progressive and a time of development. Privileged parents are likely to be attentive about what their children eat at mealtime, what they watch on television or at the movies, and their children's friends. When children display problems, parents are quick to seek professional help. Their contacts in the professional classes make them aware of the advantages of prevention and early intervention. Thus, children in upper-class families are mentored, tutored, counseled, and medicated if they show any tendencies to veer off course.

All but a tiny fraction of the children of privileged families complete high school and most go on to college immediately thereafter. A small but growing minority, however, pause to travel or work for a year before entering college, but they typically do so after gaining admission (Jeppson 2002). In many respects, it is fair to say that college—the four-year program that leads to a Bachelor's degree—is the pivotal moment in the life course of Americans. There is a yawning gap in social and economic status between the roughly one-third of American youth who complete college and those who do not.

A vast majority of privileged youth will complete college; indeed, many will continue beyond college to gain a professional degree. The question facing youth in upper-class families is not *whether* but *where* one attends college (McDonough 1997). It is generally assumed, without a large amount of evidence, that the choice of college has a powerful effect on later economic and social standing (Hill 2002). Grooming children for acceptance into an elite college begins early and continues through the adolescent years. Parents and youth are remarkably conversant in college rankings, and as children enter high school, they are encouraged to begin thinking about where they might want to attend.

While we have a limited amount of good ethnographic work on the college selection process, it involves careful screening (McDonough 1997). College visits are now a common rite of passage in upper-class families, where parents and children visit numerous campuses to narrow down choices (Kantrowitz 2002). Most parents are intensely involved in the selection process, and it is increasingly popular to bring paid coaches and consultants to advise the student and assist in the application process (Heyn and Cohen 2002). Families routinely pay for private lessons to prepare applicants for College Board Tests, the national tests that assess credentials. Parents also use their social networks to garner recommendations to elite institutions. Since colleges give strong preference, all things being equal, to accepting the kin of alumnae, it is not uncommon for the offspring to attend the same institutions that were attended by their parents, siblings, or extended kin.

The children of upper-class families almost always attend residential colleges, generally beyond commuting distance from their parents' home.

Geographical mobility is encouraged in the upper classes; though some children eventually return to live near where they grew up, typically this is neither expected nor highly desired by young adults. College prepares children for this separation.

In many respects, the four-year residential college is the most highly developed institution for young adults in American society. Unlike in Europe where students typically attend universities in their locality while residing in their natal family, the children of affluent Americans leave home at eighteen and often do not return except for brief visits or possibly for more extended stays during the summer months. Consequently, the college campus becomes a young adult's home away from home. Youth develop strong loyalty to these institutions and frequently form their main friendships during their college years. The social networks developed in college are a large part of social capital acquired in early adulthood. Elite colleges provide a rich stock of cultural and social capital that is drawn upon in early adulthood and later life.

The residential college resembles a total institution (Goffman 1961). In addition to college classes, it offers a full range of educational recreation in the form of clubs, music, theater, and even a newspaper. Students receive health services on campus and no college is complete without a counseling service to aid students with academic, social, or psychological troubles. In short, the residential college is a microcosm of the larger society, training students to be independent and able to function outside the family. Once upon a time, college was a major mating market. While it still provides opportunities for mate selection, marriage among the upper class typically occurs long after college is completed. Consequently, college is a time for sexual experimentation. In contrast to the openly prudish standards of American society, most college dorms are coeducational and few make efforts to control sexual behavior.

College experience is not the only form of social capital acquired during this period of life. From early adolescence into early adulthood, it is common for children from privileged families to work. Work is seen as a necessary experience for all American youth regardless of social class, but children from well-off families are likely to spend time in government internships, working in hospitals or law offices, or assisting in research projects (Cottle 1998; Altschuler 2002; Kinsman 2002; Song 2002). Again, family and school contacts are used to locate work experiences that may build skills, experience, and knowledge necessary to make informed professional choices following college graduation.

Many students move directly from college into postgraduate training programs, but it is not uncommon to spend a period of one to five years working and traveling between college and entrance into graduate education. During this period, youth may be encouraged by their families to become economically independent or they may be subsidized by their families while they explore the world, volunteer for community service, or simply experience a period of limbo (Ligos 2002).

American youth are not expected to develop strong professional commitments until their early twenties, and even then, many do not before they turn thirty. Youth from upper-class families are given great latitude in the timing of important identities. Finding oneself is a central task of late adolescence and early adulthood. Thus, youth are generally encouraged to experiment in employment, personal relationships, living situations, and the like as part of the quest for finding meaningful work and satisfying emotional relationships.

Eventually, the majority of young adults from well-off families enter postbaccalaureate programs to prepare for their specific job. This training generally occurs in elite universities, more often than not, different from where they attended college even if their undergraduate degree was from an elite university. Switching places is part of the process of building social capital: graduate training programs are carefully screened and consciously selected for the quality of students and faculty who may offer sponsorship and contacts necessary for later employment. The quality of institutions and personal recommendations count heavily in the placement of young professionals as well as in business.

Settling down among the children of the affluent typically occurs in their late twenties and early thirties, by which time most have completed their professional training and begun working in earnest. It is at this point in the life course that most will form permanent partnerships and begin the process of family formation. Young adults continue to relocate residentially, usually until their children are settled in school, when geographical mobility declines. Thus, community ties among the affluent are often not strong. Americans tend to be less committed to place-based strategy than to functional communities organized around work, worship, or leisure time pursuits (Lamont 1992).

I have said little about gender differences in the experiences of children growing up in the upper classes. Undeniably, gender differences remain; however, the gap between male and female experiences has been steadily diminishing, so much so that the careers of boys and girls in affluent families differ only modestly. Rates of educational attainment, the timing of first sexual experience, cohabitation, and marriage are remarkably similar for males and females. Gender differences become more conspicuous once parenthood occurs, when mothers bear a larger burden of childcare and childrearing responsibilities. These differences, which have a powerful affect on professional advancement, are evident in all social classes.

The ranks of the affluent are gradually becoming more ethnically diverse. Asians, Hispanics, and African Americans are more likely than they were a generation ago to be attending private schools and far more likely to be admitted to elite colleges and universities, largely as a result of affirmative action programs that explicitly mandated opportunity for minority groups (Bowen and Bok 1998). While the advantages conferred by economic standing continue to favor European Americans, talented minorities have a much greater chance of being recruited into elite educational institutions than was true several decades ago. On the other hand, patterns of residential segregation produce high levels of segregation in public schools, restricting opportunities for minorities and the less advantaged, especially in large metropolitan areas (Rivkin 1994).

NEITHER RICH NOR POOR: GROWING UP IN THE MIDDLE

Studies of working-class and lower-middle-class families who make up the vast bulk of the American population used to be far more common in sociology than is true in the present era (Gans 1962; Komarovsky 1962; Lynd and Lynd 1956; Seeley, Sim, and Loosley 1956). We have relatively few qualitative studies about growing up in families with modest means today. Using the rough yardstick mentioned earlier, about half of U.S. families are neither well-off nor poor or near poor. Yet sociological studies on the family life of this population are sparse compared to the vast amount of work that has been done on families living in poverty or the working poor.

Typically, family members in this middle stratum have completed high school and received some college or training after graduation. Some have completed a four-year college degree, but probably most have not attended a residential college. Jobs may vary from skilled laborer to semi-professional or in sales, the service sector, or low-level management. Parents uniformly consider themselves members of the middle class; almost no one in America describes themselves as working class. But those in this economic grouping are likely to stress their ability to manage without government assistance and to be able to provide for their offspring (Lamont 2000). It is not unusual for families in the middle class to get occasional help from kin, but mostly they are less rather than more likely than families in the privileged classes to receive regular assistance. Thus, many families in this stratum are likely to have few assets beyond home ownership. Most are just getting by and fear of falling into the ranks of the working poor is a dominant concern for many families who are neither privileged nor underprivileged.

Family formation generally begins earlier in the middle than it does among the more privileged though not so early as occurs among the poor. Depending on region of the country and religious values, cohabitation is often a prelude to marriage, but middle-class families often hold the more disapproving attitudes toward premarital sex, nonmarital childbearing, and divorce than do those who are privileged or poor (Trent and South 1992).

Working- and middle-class families are vulnerable partly because of a powerful belief in the autonomous nuclear family and the virtues of the market economy. Insufficiently protected by government and community supports, families in the middle have a difficult time managing economically. While many government and union jobs provide good health benefits and pensions, those in the private sector may be offered only meager benefits through their work and most have incomes too high to qualify for means-tested government support programs. Families in the middle are likely to look for church or community daycare and aftercare programs. Typically, they do not have the luxury of being discriminating about the quality of services and programs for their children.

Working- and lower-middle-class families stress obedience and deference to parents rather than early autonomy and self-regulation (Alwin 1988; Kohn 1977). It seems likely, however, that the childrearing practices of the privileged are beginning to diffuse downward and more leeway is given to children to determine their own preferences in the middle class than occurred in the previous generation. Still, life is more focused on the household, the extended family, and the proximate community than is true for the privileged class. Parents select communities to minimize the risk of bad things happening to their children rather than the possibility of promoting opportunity (Furstenberg et al. 1999). However, parents want to do a little better for their children than their parents were able to do for them. This leads them to try to conserve the values that were handed down by their parents. Attachment to family, a strong commitment to religious institutions, and local community are the bedrock values of Middle America (Lamont 2000).

Education as a route to social mobility is strongly endorsed as well, but more emphasis is placed on classroom control and mastering the basics than among privileged families. Parents are likely to be far less discriminating in the choice of a school district than is true among families at the top. They are both less well informed about educational choices and they often lack the means to move to the more affluent areas that contain the best public schools (Ryan et al. 1995).

Children of middle-income families are somewhat less likely to attend preschool programs than more privileged families, though almost all now attend kindergarten (Zill and West 2000). Except for those who attend parochial schools that are subsidized by religious organizations, children in the middle will go to public schools. Since there is great variation in the quality of public schools, their prospects for postsecondary education depend tremendously on where they reside. School districts, which are funded by a combination of federal, state, and local taxes, offer a wide range in the quality of academic and extracurricular programs that span from unacceptably poor to very demanding and rich in services.

While parental investment has probably increased in terms of time spent with children and money spent on children, the gap between the middle and the upper classes in resources available to children has probably increased because families in the middle are squeezed both for time and money. Parents work to better their children's chances, but by working they are not as available for after-school care or on the weekends (Mattox 1990; Gibbs 1989). And the rising demands for household goods prompted by advertising and the growth of a consumer economy may have made families feel poorer relative to those who are well-off.

Parents with more modest means regard college, especially a four-year residential program, as a luxury rather than a necessity. Many more families aspire to state or community colleges that are local and far more affordable (McDonough 1997). The cost of one year of private college is close to the annual after-tax income of most families in the middle. While scholarships are available for academically (or more often athletically) talented children in the middle, only a small percentage end up in private colleges or universities. High-quality state education is the most common route to social mobility from the middle to the privileged classes.

But many children from families with limited means do not end up completing a four-year degree. More often, they take courses part-time and extend their education well beyond the normal college years. This means that for many youth in the middle class, schooling is combined with full-time employment, and often marriage and parenthood. This combination leads many youth to compromise their educational goals in favor of short-term economic gain from employment.

Middle-class jobs do offer some mobility paths in the United States. Workers move sometimes from skilled labor or from sales and service to middle-management positions if they have the talents and the educational credentials. Government and public sector jobs typically provide career routes up the ranks, allowing those in the middle class to reach the privileged sectors. At the same time, more recent evidence increasingly portrays an hourglass-shaped labor market, in which middle-class jobs are scarce and the jobs at the top demand higher educational credentials for advancement (Massey and Hirst 1998).

One area where public policy has contributed to social mobility for minorities is through fair employment and affirmative action programs. Federal and state legislation established over the past several decades to promote minority hiring has effectively increased the diversity of the labor force at both entry-level and middle-management positions. Practices to increase diversity through fair housing or school busing have been far less successful. Economic and racial segregation has actually increased in both neighborhoods and schools since the 1970s, restricting access to quality education for children in the middle, not to mention underprivileged youth (Orfield and Ashkinaze 1991).

Gender equality within families and in the larger society has grown in conspicuous ways. It is difficult to say whether these changes have occurred evenly in all classes. Clearly, women in the middle class have begun to shoulder a large share of family support. It is less clear whether men have increased their domestic obligations. Recent data on time use indicates that men are doing a larger share of childcare, but their contribution to housework remains very modest (Bianchi et al. 2000). Rather than men doing more, women are doing less. This means that more services are being purchased outside the home, adding to the income burden on families in the middle. Little is known about the power sharing within families in the middle. Continuously high rates of divorce in the middle classes suggest that power arrangements may not have realigned to take account of women's changing political, social, and economic status. It will be interesting to see if divorce rates drop as men become accustomed to the idea of gender equality. For the time being, family life remains a testing ground for new ideas about gender relations.

One conspicuous subgroup of families in the middle is single-parent families who are temporarily or even permanently downwardly mobile (Newman 1988; Arendell 1986). They are interestingly situated for purposes of examining class differences because the parents may orient their children to the privileged class but often lack the means to support them in the fashion to which they were born. While the literature on single-parent families shows that these children are likely to fare less well than their counterparts from higher income households, we know relatively little about the strategies that middle-income parents who dropped from privilege use to maintain their children's social class position.

FAMILIES AT THE BOTTOM

An outpouring of studies of highly disadvantaged families has appeared in sociology and developmental psychology over the past several decades (Ambert 1997; Brooks-Gunn, Duncan, and Aber 1997). We probably know more about this segment of society than we do about any other. New research on the effects of welfare reform legislation has focused attention on this segment of the population during the past ten years (Chase-Lansdale and Brooks-Gunn 1995). And there has been a tremendous amount of interest among sociologists and demographers in the patterns of family formation of the poor, in large measure because of the high rates of early childbearing and nonmarital childbearing to single mothers that distinguishes the United States from all other industrialized nations (Wu and Wolfe 2001; Cherlin 1992).

Since the 1960s, the pattern of early family formation has become problematic because many younger fathers were not in a position to assume child support, as well-paying manufacturing jobs for the less-educated shrank in the postwar period. The decline of union jobs also reduced the possibility of men earning a family wage, eroding the marital prospects of males with less than a high school education and, more recently, even those who completed high school. The hardest hit economically have been minority males, whose real wages fell steeply while minority females were able to hold their own economically (Danziger and Gottschalk 1995).

In real terms, the minimum wage has steadily decreased since reaching a high point in the 1960s (Halperin 1998; Levy 1988). Families at the bottom are worse off today than they were in 1970 before the period of hyperinflation and economic stagnation. Figure 10.1 shows the drop in real income for men and women who do not complete high school or whose highest educational level is high school graduation. Generally speaking, wage growth, or the lack thereof, has undermined the traditional sequence of family formation among the poor and working poor.

There is growing evidence that lower-class men and women, especially, regard marriage as a luxury good that is increasingly elusive (Edin 1998; Furstenberg, Sherwood, and Sullivan 1992). This is certainly one source of the relatively high rate of early childbearing that occurs especially among poor and near-poor families. The inability to imagine a stable family in the near future leads many couples to risk pregnancy by not using contraception and to allow unplanned conceptions go to term (Hayes 1987). Evidence suggests that many women who bear children do believe that the father will provide support and may eventually enter marriage, though this in fact usually does not occur. While a small minority of young couples do eventually marry, most unions dissolve quickly in the face of new family responsibilities. In sharp contrast to the privileged class, and to a lesser extent families in the middle, children are often unplanned and born into unstable unions of parents who are ill-prepared to assume the financial and childcare obligations of parenthood.

Typically, children born into these circumstances begin family life with one full-time parent, and, if they are fortunate, have another committed parent living outside the household or a grandparent, who assumes financial and childcare support within the household (Garfinkel, McLanahan, Tienda, and Brooks-Gunn 2001). Evidence suggests that the support of extended kin is critical in fostering opportunities for low-income children; the role of nonresidential fathers is less clear. Surprisingly, most evidence

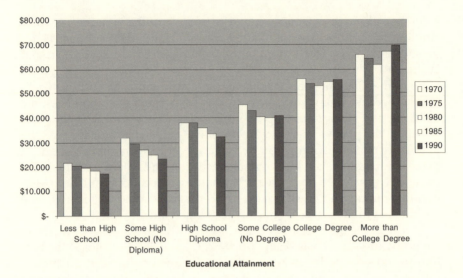

Figure 10.1   Mean Real Income by Educational Attainment, Males Aged 25 Years and Older, Selected Years 1970–1990. *Source*: U.S. Census Bureau (2002b).

points to the importance of child support but not paternal visitation in shaping the child's cognitive and emotional development. Some researchers have speculated that childcare by nonresidential parents is too thin to make much difference, or possibly that it often accompanies great conflict between the custodial and noncustodial parent (McLanahan 2000). In any event, lower-class children frequently have to rely on a network of relatives inside and outside the family—often the kin of the residential parent—to provide sponsorship, mentoring, and direct child supervision.

Family liabilities are not necessarily the worst problems faced by low-income children. Evidence suggests that most lower-class parents—even teen mothers—are capable and caring enough, but they face unusual amounts of stress in coping with daily life. Income sufficiency is a major problem for single parents and, close to 40 percent of household in the lowest income quintile reported experiencing at least one instance of difficulty in meeting basic needs in 1995 (Bauman 1999). While the government offers medical care for children, it does not provide care for the adults who take care of them. Shifts in welfare policy for the poor have made childcare more available to working parents, but many experts question the adequacy of childcare that is frequently delivered informally by unskilled caregivers. Higher quality programs, such as Head Start, are available to some, but government support is inadequate to offer places in formal programs to all preschool children.

The low levels of parental education and the inadequacy of daycare and preschool education mean that a high proportion of low-income children enter school lacking the skills that predict educational success (Guo and Harris 2000). Their lack of preparation is aggravated once they are in school by a number of factors, the most important of which are high geographical mobility and poor schools. Low-income families in the United States have extremely high rates of residential instability owing to their economic and family circumstances (Astone and McLanahan 1994). In many schools, most students who begin the school year have left by the following summer. This creates a certain level of chaos in classrooms because teachers are unable to get to know many of their students during the school year. Add to that the poor state of most schools that are attended by low-income students. The teachers receive lower pay if the schools are in poorer districts, and there are fewer resources available to help children such as computers or science equipment. Moreover, the schools generally lack supportive services that are routinely offered to children with problems in more affluent school districts. Not surprisingly then, most studies show that poor students, especially urban minorities, lose ground once they enter the school system (Entwisle, Alexander, and Olson 1997). The education gap, which is relatively small at the beginning of school, grows steadily with time so that by high school, lower-income students are many grades behind in their educational attainment compared to well-off students.

Public education, many critics in the United States claim, is a failing institution (Tyack and Cuban 1995). In fact, it appears to fail primarily the children of lower-class families, especially those who reside in poor school districts. While the government offers modest support for low-income school districts, this support is largely consumed by students in federally mandated special education programs. The poor-quality educational programs create a poorly trained population that is largely relegated to unskilled and low-income jobs.

Many social scientists in the United States have come to believe that conditions in the neighborhood where poor schools are located independently affect children's chances of social mobility. Stimulated by the writing of William Julius Wilson (1987), researchers have examined Wilson's hypothesis that a "ghetto-specific culture" emerges in communities with very high rates of poverty, unemployment, and female-headed households. While scores of studies over the past decade have sought to test this theory, the preponderance of evidence seems to be that neighborhoods have a rather puny impact on children's life chances independent of their family background and schooling (Plotnick and Hoffman 1999). True, it can be shown that neighborhood conditions influence parental strategies of childrearing, and the particular management strategies that parents employ to protect their children from immediate dangers as well as locate opportunities for their intellectual and social development do have some effect on the life chances of poor children (Pittman and Chase-Lansdale 2001; Bluestone and Tamis-LeMonda 1999; Walker and Furstenberg 1994). Skilled parenting contributes to social mobility, but skilled parenting is relatively independent of neighborhood status.

It is not so much the quality of parenting but parental expectations and parents' ability to garner social capital that affects children's chances of rising out of poverty. Parents who know how to work the system, getting their children into better schools or out of the public school system, are more likely to see them succeed in later life. Lower-class parents are at a distinct disadvantage in their cultural capital about how to manage schooling opportunities compared to middle-income and privileged families (Diamond 1999–2000). For example, many parents simply do not know the course requirements for entrance into a four-year college; even if their children are able academically, they often do not accumulate credits in higher level math and science (Useem 1992).

By and large, the only recourse for low-income families is to opt out of the system altogether and send their children to parochial schools or to get their children into one of the small number of magnet schools that attract better teachers and hence more of the middle-income families (Neild 1999). Certain low-income parents exhibit much greater initiative and skill than others in navigating the educational system. This is especially true of some immigrant groups, who effectively pool their knowledge of good schools and teachers within schools. But it is also true for other underprivileged parents who are determined to see their children escape poverty (Furstenberg et al. 1999).

School performance is closely linked, especially in high school, to the risk of other kinds of problematic behaviors: sexual risk taking, substance use and abuse, and delinquency (Gruber and Machamer 2000; Voelkl, Welte, and Wieczorek 1999; Swaim 1991). Of course, all of these behaviors occur among youth in privileged and middle-income families as well. However, the consequences of these behaviors are distinctly different depending on social class. Parents with more resources have the opportunity to secure treatment, and they are better able to fend off the adverse reactions of teachers or representatives of the criminal justice system.

Over the past two decades, harsh and punitive responses to juvenile offenses have become widespread at the federal, state, and local levels. This is especially true for drug offenses, which are treated severely and often lead to incarceration. Low-income, minority males in particular have extraordinarily high rates of involvement in the criminal justice system (Sampson 1987). Upward of 25 percent of black and 15 percent of Latino males will spend some time in a correctional facility, with many having their first encounter with the criminal justice system before the age of eighteen (Bureau of Justice Statistics 2002). Of course, this means that many of these young men will not complete high school and will suffer in the labor market.

The sharp gender differences in educational and economic attainment among low-income youth strongly affect the relations between young men and women as they move through adolescence and enter adulthood. Minority women especially, and low-income women more generally, have come to see men as lacking in marriage potential. Women describe men as exploitative, unreliable, and controlling; in turn, men see women as demanding, disloyal, and unreasonable. This culture of gender distrust leads younger women to consider childbearing before marriage as a prudent strategy for testing the commitment of potential partners in marriage. Men typically fail the test, and single parenthood has become the normal, if not desired, sequence of family formation in the lower-class. The sharply gendered pattern of life creates high rates of antagonism between men and women, with men asserting traditional authority but with few of the resources, other than physical force, of retaining their status advantage.

THE U.S. CLASS SYSTEM IN COMPARATIVE PERSPECTIVE

My task in this chapter has been to describe some of the distinctive features of American society that structure the early part of the life course up through the transition to adulthood. The powerful belief that parents should be held primarily responsible for the fate of children conceals a class bias that strongly favors the privileged and deters mobility among the disadvantaged. Families with wealth use their resources to take advantage of the checkerboard nature of school systems. Because education is primarily funded through property taxes, huge differences exist in the quality of education from one locality to the next. Those with the means to do so reside in areas with good schools or send their children to private school. Those with modest means must make do and highly disadvantaged families are relegated to inferior education.

The strong reliance on the family as the primary mechanism of allocation for children ultimately erodes family stability because parents are almost entirely left to their own devices for supporting their children. Marital instability, long a feature of American society, wreaks special havoc because children whose parents elect to separate almost automatically suffer a huge economic penalty and hence are much more prone to remain poor as adults. Parents without stable employment are less likely to plan childbearing, less willing and able to marry, and more prone to divorce when marriage occurs. Hence, family instability is a powerful mechanism of stratification, especially in a society that provides little public support to children outside the family. In this sense, marital instability can be expected to have particularly pernicious consequences for children in American society, compared to countries that offer considerable public support and services to children of single parents.

Interestingly, no good comparative study of the consequences of marital instability in industrialized countries exists (Heuveline, Timberlake, and Furstenberg 2002). Some countries may cushion some of the shock of work/family conflict by offering support packages for working parents (Jacobs and Gornick 2002). Paid parental leave, universal childcare and pre-school programs, after-school care, flex-time, and other support services for working parents may help families deal with the routine stress of working outside the home. Do these efforts to support the family through government interventions pay off in greater well-being of parents and children? As of yet, there has been rather little research designed to test whether the availability of these services reduces role strain among parents and helps to fend off, what the sociologist Lewis Coser (1974) once referred to as the demands of "the greedy workplace."

I have claimed in this chapter that the sharp inequalities in schooling in the United States lead to immense disparities in the opportunities for children of privileged families, compared to both those of modest means, and especially children from economically disadvantaged families. State-funded systems, especially when they are accompanied by strong and universal preschool education, should moderate the class inequalities. Again, the comparative evidence in support of this assumption is relatively weak even though the data are now available to put this proposition to an empirical test.

More difficult to examine is the dark shadow cast by the criminal justice system on the development of adolescents in the United States, where substantial minorities of low-income youth spend time in a correctional institution. Comparative research on this topic is lacking altogether, in part because no other nation has adopted this punitive strategy for dealing with delinquent behavior. Nonetheless, creative research strategies may exist for looking at the consequences of delinquent behavior in the United States and other countries, perhaps Canada or Britain, which have not used the criminal justice system so liberally to deter delinquent behavior.

It is an exciting time for sociologists and developmental psychologists who are interested in the conditions that produce successful development in children, youth, and young adults. The data are becoming available for the first time to examine how social and economic inputs by families, schools, neighborhoods, media, health, and welfare systems affect the process of growing up in different societies that share certain features in common but differ in political culture and public policies. This is exactly the kind of work that has been pioneered by Walter R. Heinz and his colleagues at Bremen. They have created a promising future for their intellectual heirs in the twenty-first century.

NOTE

1. Fathers-to-be can find numerous books to help them make the most of their role during pregnancy. Such titles include Heinowitz and Chamberlain's *Pregnant Fathers: Entering Parenthood Together* (1995) and Mungeam and Gray's *A Guy's Guide to Pregnancy: Preparing for Parenthood Together* (1998).

REFERENCES

Altschuler, Glenn C. 2002. "College Prep: A Tryout for the Real World." *New York Times*, 14 April, sec. 4A, p. 20.

Alwin, Duane. 1988. "From Obedience to Autonomy: Changes in Traits Desired in Children." *Public Opinion Quarterly* 52:33–52.

Ambert, Anne-Marie. 1997. *The Web of Poverty: Psychosocial Perspectives*. New York: Haworth.

Arendell, Teresa. 1986. *Mothers and Divorce: Legal, Economic, and Social Dilemmas*. Berkeley: University of California Press.

Astone, Nan Marie and Sara S. McLanahan. 1994. "Family Structure, Residential Mobility, and School Dropout: A Research Note." *Demography* 31:575–84.

Bauman, Kurt J. 1999. *Extended Measures of Well-Being: Meeting Basic Needs*. Washington, DC: U.S. Census Bureau.

Bianchi, Suzanne M., Melissa A. Milkie, Liana C. Sayer, and John P. Robinson. 2000. "Is Anyone Doing the Housework? U.S. Trends and Gender Differentials in Domestic Labor." *Social Forces* 79:191–228.

Bluestone, Cheryl and Catherine S. Tamis-LeMonda. 1999. "Correlates of Parenting Styles in Predominantly Working- and Middle-Class African American Mothers." *Journal of Marriage & the Family* 61:881–93.

Bowen, William G. and Derek Bok. 1998. *The Shape of the River: Long-Term Consequences of Considering Race in College and University Admissions*. Princeton, NJ: Princeton University Press.

Brooks-Gunn, Jeanne, Greg J. Duncan, and J. Lawrence Aber (Eds.). 1997. *Neighborhood Poverty: Policy Implications in Studying Neighborhoods*. New York: Russell Sage.

Bumpass, Larry L. 1990. "What's Happening to the Family? Interactions between Demographic and Institutional Change." *Demography* 27(4):483–98.

Bureau of Justice Statistics. 2002. *Criminal Offender Statistics*. Washington, DC: U.S. Justice Department. 2 June. http://www.ojp.usdoj.gov/bjs/crimoff.htm.

Chase-Lansdale, P. Lindsay, and Jeanne Brooks-Gunn. 1995. *Escape from Poverty: What Makes a Difference for Children?* Cambridge: Cambridge University Press.

Cherlin, Andrew J. 1992. *Marriage, Divorce, Remarriage*, rev. and enl. edition. Cambridge, MA: Harvard University Press.

Coser, Lewis A. 1974. *Greedy Institutions; Patterns of Undivided Commitment*. New York: Free Press.

Cottle, Mark. 1998. "Working: The Importance of Internship." *New York Times*, 13 December, sec. 3, p.1.

Dalaker, Joseph and Bernadette D. Proctor. 2000. *Current Population Reports, Series p-60, Consumer Income*. Washington, DC: U.S. Bureau of Census.

Danziger, Sheldon H. and Peter Gottschalk. 1995. *America Unequal*. Cambridge, MA: Harvard University Press.

Diamond, John B. 1999–2000. "Beyond Social Class: Cultural Resources and Educational Participation Among Low-Income Black Parents." *Berkeley Journal of Sociology* 44:15–54.

Edin, Kathryn. 1998. "Why Don't Poor Single Mothers Get Married (or Remarried)?" Paper presented at the Russell Sage Foundation, New York.

Ellwood, David T. and Christopher Jencks. 2001. "The Growing Differences in Family Structure: What Do We Know? Where Do We Look for Answers?" Paper prepared for the New Inequality Program, supported by the Russell Sage Foundation.

Entwisle, Doris R., Karl L. Alexander, and Linda Steffel Olson. 1997. *Children, Schools, and Inequality*. Boulder, CO: Westview.

Furstenberg, Frank F., Jr. 1997. "Family-State Relations and the Well-Being of Children." Pp. 187–91 in *Monitoring and Measuring the State of Children: Beyond Survival*, edited by A. Ben-Arieh and H. Wintersberger. Eurosocial Report 62. Vienna: European Centre for Social Welfare and Policy Research.

Furstenberg, Frank F., Jr., Jacquelynne Eccles, Glen H. Elder, Jr., and Arnold J. Sameroff. 1999. *Managing to Make It: Urban Families in High-Risk Neighborhoods*. Chicago: University of Chicago Press.

Furstenberg, Frank F. Jr., Kay Sherwood, and Mercer L. Sullivan. 1992. *Caring and Paying: What Fathers and Mothers Say About Child Support*. Report prepared for MDRC project Parents' Fair Share Demonstration. New York: MDRC.

Gans, Herbert. 1962. *Urban Villagers*. New York: Free Press of Glencoe.

Garfinkel, Irwin, Jennifer L. Hochschild, and Sara S. McLanahan (Eds.). 1996. *Social Policies for Children*. Washington, DC: Brookings Institution.

Garfinkel, Irwin, Sara S. McLanahan, Marta Tienda, and Jeanne Brooks-Gunn. 2001. "Fragile Families and Welfare Reform." *Children and Youth Services Review* 23:277–301.

Gibbs, Nancy. 1989. "How America Has Run Out of Time; Workers Are Weary, Parents Are Frantic and Even Children Haven't a Moment to Spare: Leisure Could Be to the '90s What Money Was to the '80s" *Time* 133(17):58.

Goffman, Erving. 1961. *Asylums: Essays on the Social Situation of Mental Patients and Other Inmates*. Chicago: Aldine.

Goldstein, Joshua and Catherine T. Kenney. 2001. "Marriage Delayed or Marriage Forgone? New Cohort Forecasts of First Marriages for U.S. Women." *American Sociological Review* 66(4):506–19.

Gruber, Enid and Ann Marie Machamer. 2000. "Risk of School Failure as an Early Indicator of Other Health Risk Behaviour in American High-School Students." *Health, Risk & Society* 2:59–68.

Guo, Guang and Kathleen M. Harris. 2000. "The Mechanisms Mediating the Effects of Poverty on Children's Intellectual Development." *Demography* 37(4):431–47.

Halperin, Samuel (Ed.). 1998. *The Forgotten Half Revisited: American Youth and Young Families, 1988–2008.* Washington, DC: American Youth Policy Forum.

Hayes, Cheryl D. 1987. *Risking the Future: Adolescent Sexuality, Pregnancy, and Childbearing.* Washington, DC: National Academy Press.

Heinowitz, Jack and David B. Chamberlain. 1995. *Pregnant Fathers: Entering Parenthood Together.* Parents as Partners.

Heuveline, Patrick, Jeffrey Timberlake, and Frank F. Furstenberg, Jr. 2002. "Shifting Childrearing to Single Mothers: Results from 17 Western Nations." *Population and Development Review* 29(1):47–71.

Heyn, Eve and Katherine Cohen. 2002. "College Try: Admissions Counselor Katherine Cohen Offers Kids Expert Tips for Getting into the School of Their Dreams (In Her Own Words)." *People Weekly,* 22 April, v. 57, i.15.

Hill, Michael. 2002. "Racing to Make It to the Head of the Class: There's No Proof That a Prestigious Education Leads to Success in Life, But That Doesn't Stop Students from Applying." *Los Angeles Times,* 19 May, part 5, p. 4.

Hochschild, Jennifer L. 1981. *What's Fair? American Beliefs about Distributive Justice.* Cambridge, MA: Harvard University Press.

Hoffman, Saul D. and E. Michael Foster. 1997. "Economic Correlates of Nonmarital Childbearing Among Adult Women." *Family Planning Perspectives* 29: 137–40.

Jacobs, Jerry A. and Janet C. Gornick. 2002. "Hours of Paid Work in Dual-Earner Couples: The U.S. in Cross-National Perspective." *Sociological Focus* 35:169–87.

Jeppson, Jake. 2002. "Take a Break, Jake; What I Learned From Not Going to College." *Washington Post Magazine,* 21 July, p. W38.

Kantrowitz, Barbara. 2002. "The New College Game: Roll the Dice, Pick a Card. Will Ditch-Digging in Peru or Perfect SATs Let You Skip a Turn and Go Straight to Harvard?" *Newsweek,* 8 April, p. 46.

Kinsman, M. 2002. "No Time for a Job; Teens Passing up Work to Prepare for College—or Just Hang Out." *San Diego Union-Tribune,* 26 July, p. C1.

Kohn, Melvin L. 1977. *Class and Conformity: A Study in Values,* 2nd edition. Chicago: University of Chicago Press.

Komarovsky, Mirra 1962. *Blue Collar Marriage.* New York: Random House.

Lamont, Michele. 1992. *Money, Morals, and Manners: The Culture of the French and American Upper-Middle Class.* Chicago: University of Chicago Press.

Lamont, Michele. 2000. *Dignity of Working Men: Morality and the Boundaries of Race, Class and Immigration.* New York: Russell Sage Foundation.

Lareau, Annette P. 1989. *Home Advantage: Social Class and Parental Intervention in Elementary Education.* New York: Falmer.

Lareau, Annette P. Forthcoming. *Inside Families: The Importance of Social Class in Children's Daily Lives.* Berkeley: University of California Press.

Lareau, Annette P. and Erin McNamara Horvat. 1999. "Moments of Social Inclusion and Exclusion: Race, Class, and Cultural Capital in Family-School Relationships." *Sociology of Education* 71:37–53.

Levy, Frank. 1988. *Dollars and Dreams: The Changing American Income Distribution.* New York: Norton.

Ligos, Melinda. 2002. "Personal Business; First the College Diploma, Then the Internship." *New York Times,* 9 June, sec. 3, p. 10.

Lynd, Robert S. and Helen M. Lynd. 1956. *Middletown: A Study in American Culture.* New York: Harcourt, Brace & World.

Maddaus, John S. 1987. *Residential Mobility and School Enrollment.* Paper presented at annual meeting of the New England Educational Research Organization, Stratton Mountain, VT, April.

Massey, Douglas S. and Deborah S. Hirst. 1998. "From Escalator to Hourglass: Changes in the U.S. Occupational Wage Structure 1949–1989." *Social Science Research* 27:51–71.

Mattox, William R., Jr. 1990. "America's Family Time Famine." *Children Today* 19(6):9(4).

McDonough, Patricia M. 1997. *Choosing Colleges. How Social Class and Schools Structure Opportunity.* Albany: State University of New York Press.

McLanahan, Sara. 2000. "Family, State, and Child Well-Being." *Annual Review of Sociology* 26:703–06.

McLanahan, Sara and Gary Sandefur. 1994. *Growing Up with a Single Parent.* Cambridge, MA: Harvard University Press.

Mungeam, Frank and John Gray. 1998. *A Guy's Guide to Pregnancy: Preparing for Parenthood Together.* Hillsboro, OR: Beyond Words.

Neild, Ruth C. 1999. "Same Difference: School Choice and Educational Access in an Urban District." Ph.D. dissertation, University of Pennsylvania. *Dissertation Abstracts International* 60:2441.

Newman, Katherine S. 1988. *Falling from Grace: The Experience of Downward Mobility in the American Middle Class.* New York: Free Press.

Orfield, Gary and Carole Ashkinaze. 1991. *The Closing Door: Conservative Policy and Black Opportunity.* Chicago, IL: University of Chicago Press.

Pittman, Laura D. and P. Lindsay Chase-Lansdale. 2001. "African American Adolescent Girls in Impoverished Communities: Parenting Style and Adolescent Outcomes." *Journal of Research on Adolescence* 11:199–224.

Plotnick, Robert D. and Saul D. Hoffman. 1999. "The Effect of Neighborhood Characteristics on Young Adult Outcomes: Alternative Estimates." *Social Science Quarterly* 80:1–18.

Rivkin, Steven G. 1994. "Residential Segregation and School Integration." *Sociology of Education* 67:279–92.

Ryan, Bruce A., Gerald R. Adams, Thomas P. Gullotta, Roger P. Weissberg, and Robert L. Hampton (Eds.). 1995. *The Family-School Connection: Theory, Research and Practice.* Thousand Oaks, CA: Sage.

Sampson, Robert J. 1987. "Urban Black Violence: The Effect of Male Joblessness and Family Disruption." *American Journal of Sociology* 93:348–82.

Sanchez, Laura and Elizabeth Thomson. 1997. "Becoming Mothers and Fathers: Parenthood, Gender, and the Division of Labor." *Gender & Society* 1:747–72.

Seeley, John R., R. Alexander Sim, and Elizabeth W. Loosley. 1956. *Crestwood Heights, a Study in the Culture of Suburban Life.* New York: Basic Books.

Snyder, Thomas D. and Charlene M. Hoffman. 2001. *Digest of Education Statistics, 2000, NCES 2001-034.* Washington, DC: U.S. Department of Education, National Center for Education Statistics.

Song, Sora. 2002. "Summer Slummin'." *Time* 160(4, 22 July):63.

Swaim, Randall C. 1991. "Childhood Risk Factors and Adolescent Drug and Alcohol Abuse." *Educational Psychology Review* 3:363–98.

Trent, Katherine and Scott J. South. 1992. "Sociodemographic Status, Parental Background, Childhood Family Structure, and Attitudes toward Family Formation." *Journal of Marriage and the Family* 54:427–39.

Tyack, David B. and Larry Cuban. 1995. *Tinkering toward Utopia: A Century of Public School Reform.* Cambridge, MA: Harvard University Press.

U.S. Census Bureau. 2001. "School Enrollment—Social and Economic Characteristics of Students: October 2000 (PPL-148). Table 6. Enrollment Status of Primary Family Members 3 to 17 Years Old, by Family Income, Level of Enrollment, Control of School, Sex, Race, and Hispanic Origin: October 2000." 1 June. http://www.census.gov/population/www/socdemo/school/ppl-148.html.

U.S. Census Bureau. 2002a. "Historical Income Tables—Families, (Table) F-1. Income Limits for Each Fifth and Top 5 Percent of Families (All Races): 1947 to 2000." 16 April. http://www.census.gov/hhes/income/histinc/f01.html.

U.S. Census Bureau. 2002b. "Historical Income Tables—Families, (Table) P-19. Years of School Completed—People 25 Years Old and Over by Mean Income and Sex: 1967 to 1990." 21 March. http://www.census.gov/hhes/income/histinc/p19x1.html.

Useem, Elizabeth L. 1992. "Middle Schools and Math Groups: Parents' Involvement in Children's Placement." *Sociology of Education* 64:264–79.

Vleminckx, Koen and Timothy. M. Smeeding (Eds.). 2001. *Child Well-Being, Child Poverty and Child Policy in Modern Nations. What Do We Know?* Bristol, UK: Policy.

Voelkl, Kristin E., John W. Welte, and William F. Wieczorek. 1999. "Schooling and Delinquency among White and African American Adolescents." *Urban Education* 34:69–88.

Walker, Karen E. and Frank F. Furstenberg, Jr. 1994. "Neighborhood Settings and Parenting Strategies." Paper presented at the annual meeting of the American Sociological Association, Los Angeles, August.

Wilson, William J. 1987. *The Truly Disadvantaged.* Chicago: University of Chicago Press.

Wu, Lawrence L. and Barbara Wolfe. 2001. *Out of Wedlock: Causes and Consequences of Nonmarital Fertility.* New York: Russell Sage.

Zill, Nicolas and Jerry West. 2000. *Condition of Education, 2000.* Washington, DC. Office of Education Research and Improvement.

IV

Interrelations and the Life Course

|11|

Linked Lives

Dual Careers, Gender, and the Contingent Life Course

Phyllis Moen

INTRODUCTION

Societies, institutions, and groups develop expectations about behavior associated with particular positions at different ages and stages (Heinz 1991; Turner 1978; Weymann and Heinz 1996). Throughout the twentieth century we have seen the development of cultural norms and institutionalized practices related to career development as a lockstep process of first education, then full-time, continuous employment on a track of upward mobility, or at least movement toward seniority associated with particular occupations, and eventually total and irreversible retirement from the workforce (e.g., Spilerman 1977; Wilensky 1961). I label this the *life course* or *career regime:* the institutionalized rules, routines, and regulations shaping occupational trajectories and transitions, as well as the adult life course (of men at least).

Simultaneously, individuals also develop expectations about their own occupational paths. In times of social stability, members of each new generation acquire a sense of their own future biographies by looking at the lives of their parents or rather their same sex parent, given that lives play out in very gendered ways. In the twentieth century, governments, schools, and workplaces in North America—as in Europe—developed policies and practices that institutionalized the life course, so that most middle-class white men (at least) did in fact follow the lockstep blueprint—from schooling through occupational careers to retirement (see Hagestad and Neugarten 1985; Kohli 1986; Marshall, Heinz, Krüger, and Verma 2001; Moen and Han 2001a, 2001b). In the United States, universal schooling, medical advances, public health, occupational career ladders, seniority, the Fair Labor Standards Act, Unemployment Insurance, Social Security, an expanding economy—all converged to standardize the life course. Such standardization presumed a gendered division of labor, captured in the breadwinner/homemaker career template (Moen 2003; Williams 2000). This template provided cultural guidelines and structural options and constraints related to occupational careers and family "careers" that effectively *decoupled* paid work from unpaid family work. This became the "ideal-typical" "Ozzie and Harriet" family, perceived by most Americans in the middle of the twentieth century as the "best" arrangement, even for those who could not afford or fit its parameters. ("Ozzie and Harriet" were roles in a popular television situational comedy in the United States in the 1950s, depicting a white, middle-class family in which the father was a breadwinner and the mother was a full-time homemaker.)

However, in times of large-scale social upheaval, old templates become obsolete, and the only thing that is clear to one generation is that their lives will not resemble those of their parents. The life-course paradigm locates individual career development in the *historical context* of major social transformations—such as war, economic downturns or prosperity, shifts to a service (or so-called dot.com) economy, immigration, the civil rights movement, the women's movement, the globalization of the economy, and the changing contract between employers and employees (e.g., Elder 1974; Forest, Moen, and Dempster-McClain 1995; Moen 1989, 1992). Life-course scholars also investigate the *dynamics of lives* (e.g., Hogan 1981; Guillemard and Rein 1993; Han and Moen 1999b; Moen and Forest 1990; Mortimer et al. 1996; O'Rand and Henretta 1999; Pavalko and Smith 1999; Quick and Moen 2002; Sampson and Laub 1993; Zhou and Moen 2001; Zhou, Tuma, and Moen 1995, 1997): how experiences (such as schooling, disability, cohabitation, job shifts, marriage, retirement, divorce, downsizing, parenting) and their pacing (when they occur in one's life biography) shape the life courses of individuals, families, and cohorts.

In this chapter I emphasize two additional contributions of life-course analysis: a focus on *linked lives* and *institutional embeddedness*. My theme is that individual occupational career development is *co-constructed*, shaped by multiple layers of social relations and social institutions. We at the Cornell Careers Institute (e.g., Han and Moen 2001; Moen 2003; Moen, Sweet, and Townsend 2001; Tolbert and Valcour 2001) investigate couples and careers, showing the ways contemporary career templates, opportunities, and constraints, as well as individual choices, continue to reproduce gender distinctions and inequalities. Studying the patterning of couples' career biographies is key to understanding the strategic choices behind that patterning. Despite the institutionalization of the lockstep template, with its focus on workers as individual decision-makers whose "decisions" are more or less already prescribed, contemporary occupational career development is increasingly a conjoint process between marital partners. It is also a *gendered* process, embedded in existing and frequently outdated institutional arrangements predicated on a gendered division of labor. Contemporary career development, for the majority of the American workforce, now involves three interrelated lines of decision-making, consisting of each partner's occupational career goals and paths, as well as their conjoint family or relationship "career" path (Christensen and Gomory 1999; Hertz 1986; Moen 2003). Moreover, these decisions now take place on a moving platform of social, economic, technological, and organizational changes including increased risk of layoffs and forced early retirement, producing a sense of changes accompanied by uncertainty, ambiguity, and ambivalence at both individual and cultural levels.

Typically, scholars studying work/family issues do not consider occupational career paths, while occupational scholars focus exclusively on the career lines of individuals (Arthur, Hall, and Lawrence 1989; Moen 1998; Rosenfeld 1992). Thus, neither set of researchers examines the interrelationships between husbands' and wives' (or nonmarried partners') occupational careers. It is here where life-course scholarship can make a real contribution. In the remainder of this chapter I discuss contemporary career paths as they are institutionalized in the United States, locating them as well within the backdrop of ongoing social change. I then move on to models of dual-career strategies of adaptation. As European scholars (e.g., Blossfeld and Drobnič 2001; Blossfeld and Hakim 1997; Buchmann 1989; Guillemard and Rein 1993; Heinz 1991; Heinz and Krüger 2001; Settersten and Mayer 1997; Weymann and Heinz 1996) point out, a life-course theoretical lens is especially useful precisely because these are times of remarkable dislocations in taken-for-granted rules and roles shaping life in the twenty-first century. How individuals—and couples—are managing in these times of uneven change and an increased sense of risk is crucial to understanding both contemporary career development and the changing demography of the workforce.

INSTITUTIONALIZED CAREER LINES

I find the "career" concept a useful one, since it incorporates a number of twin ideas: *transitions* and *trajectories, individuals* and *organizations, subjective identities* and *objective paths* (e.g., Arthur and Rousseau 1996; Hall 1996;

Rosenfeld 1992). It is also a useful frame for linking change in lives with large-scale changes in culture and in society (see also Barley 1989; Han and Moen 2001; Moen and Han 2001a, 2001b; Moen 2003).

The notion of career typically depicts an internal organizational ladder (e.g., Wilensky 1961; Spilerman 1977), but it also stands for an institution-alized life path and a series of choice processes. It is, therefore, potentially useful in seeking to understand both stability and change in individual lives, organizations, and society. As Barley points out, the career concept can be used as a "lens for peering at larger social processes known as insti-tutions" (1989:49). Sewell (1992:16) notes that there are a multiplicity of structures shaping society and individual lives, existing and operating at different levels and in different modalities, with different logics and dynamics. This multiplicity of structures is endemic to the concept of career. First, occupational career paths are a function of the ways education, training, credentialing, jobs, work, seniority, occupational advancement, retirement, and pensions are structured by both public- and private-sector policies and practices. As Kohli (1986) reminds us, existing structures pre-sume a lockstep pattern, from full-time schooling to full-time, continuous employment throughout much of adulthood, to a one-way, irreversible exit into retirement. Governments, businesses, professional organizations, and unions all have policies and practices that constrain occupational and workforce entry and exit portals, as well as the design and timing of, along with incentives associated with, particular occupations and employment patterns.

Second, embedded in these structural arrangements, and in the rewards of conforming to them, is the assumption of workers as "unencumbered" [see Williams (2000), as well as Moen (2001, 2003)], able and willing to devote their full attention and effort to their jobs. Even more deeply embedded is the cultural presumption that most of these "unencum-bered" workers are male, each with someone else, a wife, able and willing to devote her time and talents to taking care of day-to-day family and per-sonal challenges, thereby removing them from the worker's radar screen and even facilitating each unencumbered worker's own occupational career progression.

Third, existing family structures also rest on the foundation of this breadwinner/homemaker template. Family members who occupy "good" jobs (with benefits, raises, security, and possibilities for advancement) are also the family providers. Other adults in the household may work for pay, but often scale back their occupational goals and investments when faced with a time squeeze of combining employment with parenting, or con-fronting a geographic move to advance their partner's career. The ones doing the scaling back are, typically, women (Becker and Moen 1999; Hochschild 1989).

What is fundamental to understanding contemporary occupational career development is the fact that individuals are simultaneously members of both families and workplace organizations, even as careers are simultaneously attributes of individuals, occupations, and organizations. Individuals are also located in, and perpetuate, the larger opportunity structure of "enduring inequalities" (e.g., Tilly 1999) associated with such personal characteristics as gender, race/ethnicity, social class background, religion, nationality, and age. This confluence of overlapping role and status memberships—each with a set of distinctive goals, expectations, patterning, constraints, and possibilities—provides the backdrop against which people in intimate relationships, and even those *anticipating* such relationships, make vocational and occupational career choices.

THE UNEVENNESS OF SOCIAL CHANGE

Having scholars shift from an *individual* to a *couple* theoretical unit of strategic career decision-making is insufficient to understanding the mechanisms leading to particular occupational pathways, absent recognition of their embeddedness in multiple social and cultural dislocations. Economies, nations, families, workplaces, and occupational career lines are themselves in the process of change—producing uncertainty, ambiguity, and ambivalence regarding occupational career intentions, timing, and choice (see also Krüger 1996; Marshall et al. 2001; Moen and Orrange 2002). In order to understand the choices and experiences of contemporary individuals and couples, it is essential to examine the trends and forces shaping the nature of work, career paths, gender, families, and the life course, and the gaps between what has and has not changed.

For example, the demise of the traditional employer/employee contract (trading long hours and commitment for mobility or at least security) in the United States has come about in response to globalization and concomitant corporate mergers, downsizing, and restructuring. What is particularly striking is that such restructuring (typically resulting in layoffs and forced early retirements) now takes place in good economic climates as well as bad, and affects white-collar as well as blue-collar workers. Even managers and professionals with considerable seniority are no longer immune from such displacement. Workers who "survive" their firms' downsizing find themselves doing their laid-off coworkers' jobs as well as their own, increasing the demands of their jobs as well as their own insecurity and uncertainty about the future. The traditional lockstep career path, characteristic of many middle-class men in the middle of the twentieth century, is clearly becoming a shaky proposition, even for white, educated, male professionals, as the (often implicit) social contract between employer and employee is being rewritten. Workers of all ages and stages in the United States find themselves vulnerable to job and/or income loss, with seniority no longer necessarily meaning security, and without the protections available to many Europeans. Young, new entrants to the U.S. workforce can no longer plan to stay in the same job or with the same company for very many years. As a consequence, many American workers feel they must signal their commitment (and value to their employer) by putting in long hours on the job (e.g., Clarkberg and Moen 2001; Jacobs and Gerson 1998; Moen and Sweet 2003). Many others are required to put in overtime hours even when they do not wish to do so. The growing incidence of recurrent job shifts as well as those in nonstandard employment (e.g., contract work) means a growing disjuncture between career as a cultural ideal and career as experienced reality.

At the same time, few American workers now have full-time homemakers to assist them with the domestic aspects of their lives and thereby facilitate their career development. Not only are most women, wives, and mothers entering and remaining in the workforce, but most men, husbands, and fathers no longer have partners available to take care of their personal and family needs and responsibilities. And few can afford to pay for someone to perform these services. In the United States, most employees live in homes in which all adults (who are not in school and not retired) are in the workforce, in neighborhoods where all adults are away at work during most of the workday, most of the workweek (see discussion in Moen 2001; Moen et al. 2001). "Breadwinning" is increasingly defined as a joint responsibility among marital partners. While the division of paid work in U.S. households is not necessarily shared equally between husbands and wives, having both partners in the labor force has become the norm. The twenty-first century "Ozzie and Harriet" family icon will be a dual-earner couple.

In such times of rapid social change in roles and relationships, old norms and templates are no longer relevant, but new ones have yet to emerge. This is particularly striking in the case of gendered career paths (see, for example, Blair-Loy 1999; Krüger and Baldus 1999; Moen 1992, 2003). For example, many American women have been socialized to believe that: (1) they can (and should) pursue and move up career ladders, and (2) they can (and should) simultaneously have a successful marriage and family life. Similarly, many "new age" American men have come to believe that (1) they can (and should) continue to be the family breadwinners, following the traditional linear, lockstep career path and (2) they can (and should) actively participate in child rearing and domestic work on the home front. But real jobs (as opposed to temporary jobs) seldom provide people with the time to function effectively both at home and at work, even as wage scales have failed to keep pace with the cost of living. Members of the new American workforce—men as well as women—are increasingly without any backup (such as full-time homemakers, relatives, stay-at-home neighbors) on the domestic front (for Germany, see Krüger, Chapter 2 in this volume).

In this half-changed world, the routines and norms associated with traditional career paths are no longer guideposts (see Moen 2001; Moen and Orrange 2002; Orenstein 2000). Rather, career development is increasingly a process of ad hoc decision-making taking place in a climate of ambiguity, uncertainty, and outdated scripts. Not only do the media, parents, and teachers offer mixed messages, but political practices, along with the structure of contemporary institutions (work, family, gender, retirement, and the life course), lag behind societal and personal expectations related to them.

Synchronizing two occupational careers along with a relationship or family "career" is a formidable feat in a world fashioned for unencumbered workers "backed up" by homemakers. The existing social organization of work, occupational career paths, and household divisions represent a *structural lag,* with policies and practices changing more slowly than has the demography of the workforce (Moen 1994; Riley, Kahn, and Foner 1994). What Merton (1968) calls the "social givens": the range of established or institutionalized alternatives—such as the forty-hour (or more) work week, and the lockstep model of occupational career development—continues to constrain choices, even though these "social givens" may be out of date.

Americans, therefore, are increasingly engaging in the construction of their own customized career paths and life courses in a world characterized by conflicting cultural signals. The life-course focus on human agency—that is, goal-oriented behavior aimed at strategies of adaptation to new situations and/or outmoded constraints (e.g., Elder 1998; Giele and Elder 1998; Heinz and Krüger 2001; Marshall et al. 2001; Moen and Wethington 1992)—becomes especially salient in such times of social change.

As Bronfenbrenner (1979) points out, location in different ecologies may render the same experience—such as becoming a parent—individually distinctive. Thus, parenthood—or marriage or geographical moves—typically produces quite different occupational career effects for men and women, husbands, and wives. What is not captured in the individualistic models of this process is the negotiation and realignment of couples' roles and relationships following such transitions.

CONSTRAINED BUT INTENTIONAL DECISION-MAKING

Gender and occupational status shape not only life pathways but the subjective side of life as well, coloring expectations, self-concepts, goals, and affinities in ways that permeate and interrelate with shifts in roles and relationships over the life course (Krüger 1996; Moen 2001; O'Rand 1996). The institutionalized nature of careers and the life course provides individuals with available lists of reasons, motives, and aspirations, such as expectations regarding career paths (Meyer 1986:205). Consider, for example, the implicit contracts between employer and employee and between family members regarding division of labor (at home and at work), job security, and job progression. These "contracts" color individuals' views of their experiences and transitions both at home and at work, affecting habits, choices, preferences, and strategies of action (Bourdieu 1984; Breiger 1995; Swidler 1986). What contemporary Americans experience is the dissolution of these contracts, with no clear-cut alternatives replacing them.

Thus, career development in men's and women's lives cannot be separated from intentions about and control over occupational trajectories, including decisions of whether, and when, to move, enter or leave the workforce, to change jobs or work hours, or to retire. But control itself is a function of both the nature of jobs and family/biographical history. Planned or expected changes in roles and resources are more easily adapted to than unanticipated crisis events. Most research on career development assumes that individuals are active, purposive agents in planning their occupational careers, but in fact their degree of control may be limited. For example, increasingly frequent episodes of corporate mergers, downsizing, and restructuring means that some individuals have little control over their career development; and contract or temp jobs mean that a growing number of individuals may even lose control over their career development, and that their preferences are also shaped by their work and family history/biography.

Preferences are shaped by the existing organizational and institutional environment as well as family history, personal experiences, and the nature of one's work. As March and Olsen (1989) recognize, intentions are often both ambiguous and embedded in an existing structure of beliefs and aspirations that changes in tandem with institutional change. Thus career intentions are both *reflective* of broader beliefs and dispositions and *discovered* and *constructed* even as they are acted on. When choices are made they frequently serve to redefine preferences.

Nevertheless, individuals do have a varying sense of control over their lives, as well as actual control over their career paths. Bandura (1982:140) points out that having little ability to influence significant events and the circumstances of one's life can produce feelings of anxiety, futility, and despondency. This matters because young Americans are having to make educational, occupational, relational, and family choices in the absence of clear options with identifiable consequences (Moen and Orrange 2002); and midcourse Americans find few clear options around retirement, second or third careers, or purposive activity more generally in the second half of adulthood.

DUAL-CAREER STRATEGIES

A focus on the couple rather than the individual as a key component of career decision-making follows a long tradition in life-course analysis emphasizing the theoretical significance of *linked lives* (e.g., Elder 1995; Elder, George, and Shanahan 1996; Giele and Elder 1998). Individuals make choices in the context of the couple's relations and resources, as well as goals, needs, opportunities, and constraints. But this is a gendered process, as underscored by the paradigm of the social construction of gender, emphasizing how women's "choices" are often constrained by their husbands' circumstances (Krüger and Baldus 1999; Moen 2003; Risman 1998).

Another life-course theme, that of *adaptive strategies*, points to the ways couples seek to manage the often conflicting and overwhelming demands of two occupational careers along with their family (or relationship) career. One can visualize a number of strategic actions as couples cope with the dilemmas and dislocations brought about by a world in which occupational career paths remain structured as if workers are without family or personal lives, when in fact very few contemporary workers have the time, opportunity, or inclination to devote themselves exclusively to furthering their occupational careers. And even those who can do so must synchronize both partners' career paths. As Moen and Wethington (1992) point out, the notion of strategic action encompasses both deliberate choices and normative, culturally prescribed ways of behaving. These two lines of adaptation can be separated conceptually but are more difficult to separate empirically. For example, couples may "decide" that the woman and not the man will reduce work hours, based on the man's comparative advantage in earnings and advancement (e.g., Becker 1981). But this "decision" is grounded in a structural and cultural environment fraught with gender expectations and structural constraints on women's earnings and advancement, expectations, and constraints that invariably color the decision-making process (e.g., Becker and Moen 1999; Bielby and Bielby 1992; Brines 1994; England and Farkes 1986; Feldberg and Glenn 1979; Hakim 1997; Hiller and Philliber 1986; Risman 1998).

It is also grounded in the structure of work. Jobs and career paths come *prepackaged* in ways that presume that workers are without family responsibilities, reducing the options for "good" part-time jobs, for example. Many supposedly full-time jobs, moreover, demand far more than the traditional forty-hour workweek (Clarkberg and Moen 2001).

A third issue concerns theories of family process. There may well be differences in the degree to which couples strategize as a unit. Constantine (1986), for example, describes three family types: negotiating (which we assume here), ordered (for instance, couples who see the husband's job as the most important and always act accordingly), and individualized (in

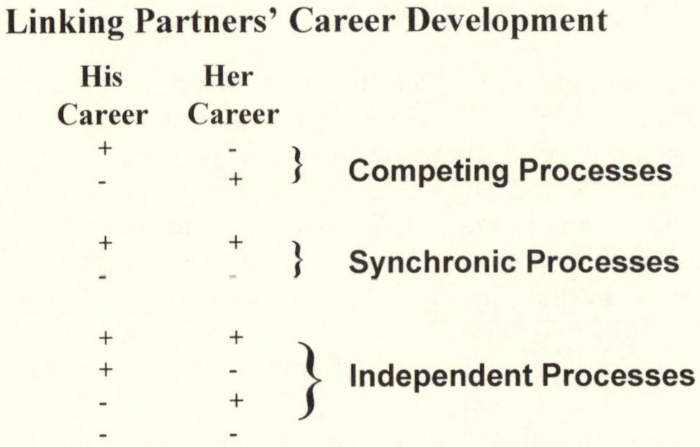

Linking Partners' Career Development

His Career	Her Career		
+	-	}	Competing Processes
-	+		
+	+	}	Synchronic Processes
-	-		
+	+		
+	-	}	Independent Processes
-	+		
-	-		

Figure 11.1   Theoretical perspectives on the dual-career interface.

which individuals make independent decisions, regardless of the circumstances of the other spouse).

There are various theoretical models of dual career development (see Figure 11.1). For example, partners may find that their occupational career goals and successes *compete* or *compensate* with one another. Another model is one of *parallel* tracks, *synergistic* with one another. Still another model would be that these are *independent processes,* with each spouse a separate actor, meaning that individualistic theories are appropriate.

Couples make occupational career decisions under the constraint of the structure and culture of both occupational and family goals, needs, and resources as these are experienced at different life stages (e.g., Becker and Moen 1999; Clarkberg and Moen 1999; Han and Moen 1999a; Hays 1996; Moen and Wethington 1992). Most people follow strategies that bend their personal lives to their occupational careers, rather than the reverse. Consider, for example, two (related) family strategies that have been adopted culturewide: postponing marriage and/or childbearing and reducing family size (cf. Clarkberg 1999; Pittman and Blanchard 1996). Both serve to reduce the family demand side of the work career/family career equation. The rising number of nannies and au pairs points to another strategy for those who can afford it: in essence, hiring a "wife" (Hochschild 1999; Moen and Yu 2000).

These strategies are frequently variants of the gendered, outdated, but still institutionally grounded and culturally prescribed breadwinner/homemaker template. However, some couples are deliberately devising their own mechanisms of adaptation (see Hertz 1986; Presser 1994; Risman 1998).

HIS JOB, HER JOB

In our analyses at the Cornell Careers Institute we focus on *work-related* lines of adaptation, considering the couple as the theoretical unit of interest. To summarize the discussion thus far: the disjuncture between the two-earner family form and the organization of both work and family (grounded on the male as breadwinner/wife as homemaker template) constitutes an enormous structural lag (Moen 2001; Riley et al. 1994) requiring creative strategies of adaptation. Couples can follow various alternative pathways, especially in terms of their temporal and emotional investment in their occupational careers. Dichotomizing each spouse's degree of occupational career investment produces a two-by-two table of hypothetical arrangements (see Table 11.1).

First, couples can actively seek to maximize both of their careers (the *dual committed* in quadrant A). Those in this category are typically characterized as on the "fast track" of professional and/or managerial careers. Both spouses in this arrangement can be expected to put in long hours on the job, hold high-status (professional or managerial) jobs, and accord high priority to each of their jobs.

A second strategy is to put both careers on the "back burner," giving primacy to the private aspects of their lives (those with *alternative commitments* in quadrant D). This can be either a deliberate choice or the situation of couples lacking the human capital and/or opportunity to do otherwise. This category includes couples in nonprofessional occupations as well as those in a variety of jobs who deliberately choose to work (at most) a regular "full-time" workweek. Couples with *alternative commitments* may see both spouses' jobs as having equal (low) priority in their lives. However, this option is likely to be rare, given the way jobs, careers, pay scales, and consumption patterns are structured (Blau, Ferber, and Winkler 1998; Han and Moen 1999a; Schor and Holt 2000).

In some cases only one partner has low career aspirations or has "scaled back" career plans. This "compensatory" strategy occurs when one spouse invests more in paid work while the other spouse invests more in the domestic aspects of their lives (quadrants B and C). When husbands are heavily invested in their jobs and their wives are not, we see a modified form of the traditional breadwinner/homemaker template (the *neotraditionalists* in quadrant C). This follows the classic "job" versus "gender" model developed by Feldberg and Glenn (1983) and reflects the ongoing

Table 11.1   Theoretical Model of Working Couples' Potential Strategies
of Adaptation

		Husbands' Career Investment	
		High	Low
Wives' Career Investment	High	A: Dual Committed	B: Crossover Commitments
	Low	C: Neo-traditionalists	D: Alternative Commitments

Source: Moen and Yu (2000).

social construction of gender (e.g., Hochschild 1989; Risman 1998). By contrast, when wives are the ones exclusively on a demanding occupational career track, couples are very much at odds with contemporary gender norms (those with *crossover commitments,* quadrant B).

The evidence suggests that a model of compensatory action (quadrant C—the *neotraditionalists*) is typical of most dual-earner couples (e.g., Becker and Moen 1999; Blossfeld and Hakim 1997; Blossfeld and Drobnič 2001; Moen and Yu 2000). For example, husbands with highly absorptive jobs are apt to have wives who carry more of the emotional burden at home (e.g., Bolger, DeLongis, Kessler, and Wethington 1989; Repetti 1989; Repetti and Wood 1997). This, along with findings on the gendered division of household labor (see Coltrane and Ishii-Kuntz 1992; Shelton and John 1996) and theories of the social construction of gender (e.g., Risman 1998), reinforces the *neotraditional* couple career strategy. However, a considerable minority of couples have both spouses highly invested in their jobs (the *dual committed* in Table 11.1), and many of them are effectively managing two major occupational career paths along with their family careers (see Barnett and Rivers 1996; Hertz 1986; Hochschild 1997; Moen and Yu 2000; Risman 1998). Our data suggest that these couples are less likely to have children than those pursuing other dual-earner arrangements.

Research at the Cornell Careers Institute (Moen and Yu 2000; Moen and Sweet 2003) shows that when both spouses work regular full-time hours (39–45 hours a week), rather than long hours (more than 45 hours a week), respondents report higher life quality. This suggests a new typology, one that includes a more equal but at the same time "reasonable" division of paid work, what we call *dual moderate* or *bounded commitments* (see Table 11.2).

We also find, for wives, the value of a compensatory (*neotraditionalist*) arrangement, in that nonprofessionals married to husbands with profes-

Table 11.2   Dual-Earner, Middle-Class Couples' Work-Hour Strategies

Work-Hour Strategy	His Work Hours	Her Work Hours	%	N
High Commitments	45+	45+	21.2	170
Dual Moderates	39–45	39–45	13.0	104
Neotraditionalists	45+	<45	38.5	308
Crossover Commitments	<45	45+	10.7	86
Alternative Commitments	One partner works less than 39 hours, the other works no more than 45 hours		16.6	133

Source: Cornell Couples and Careers Study 1998–99. N = 801.

sional jobs tend to score highest on various life-quality measures. These arrangements may reflect lines of adaptation congruent with established social meanings and expectations regarding work and gender (the *neotraditionalists*). The *bounded* commitment strategy may also reflect current institutional realities, in that spouses who have "regular" (e.g., full-time) jobs but manage to limit the hours put in on those jobs may have the optimal arrangement in a world structured around "at least" full-time work.

Career development processes remain framed by the gendered breadwinner/homemaker template and by the rewards associated with it. For example, in the United States, couples willing to put in a combined total of 60 hours a week to earn a living would never choose to have both partners work 30 hours each. This is because the vast majority of part-time jobs lack the security, salary level, and future opportunities of full-time jobs, much less a whole array of benefits, including health insurance, pension plans, paid vacations, and sick leave. So, the couple can "choose" to have one spouse put in 40 hours a week, while the other puts in 20. But pragmatically, they may actually be better off, in terms of current earnings as well as their future income stream, to have one partner work 60 hours a week while the other remains out of the workforce. And again pragmatically, current earnings and their future income stream would probably be maximized if that long-hour worker were male, rather than female. Note that the decisions as to work hours, occupations, and even whether or not to enter the workforce are not individual decisions, but couple strategies, made in the light of existing institutional arrangements, reward systems, norms, and family needs. They are gendered decisions as well, with tremendous long-term implications for men and women and for gender inequality, more broadly.

WORK/LIFE COORDINATION AS A LIFE-COURSE PROCESS

Social scientists, like the broader culture in which they are embedded, have adopted the discourse of *balance, conflict,* and *strain* in studying the work and family interface (e.g., Duxbury, Higgins, and Lee 1994; Eckenrode and Gore 1990; Greenhaus and Beutell 1985; Higgins, Duxbury, and Irving 1992; Marks and MacDermid 1996; Moen 1989; Spain and Bianchi 1996). In doing so, they have retained an approach of theoretical and methodological individualism, developing hypotheses about and investigating the work/family stressors and well-being of individual workers (most frequently women). However, it is becoming increasingly evident that work/life strategies are typically family-level actions and are fluid, emergent processes (cf. Blossfeld and Drobnič 2001; Clarkberg and Merola 2003; Marks and MacDermid 1996; Moen 2003; Moen and Han 2001a, 2001b; Zhou and Moen 2001). To understand the reality of the contemporary work/family, or (as contemporary corporations define it) work/life, interface requires a focus on the dynamic interweave of diverse strands of the life course. In the case of dual-earner families, the focus should be on couple-level lines of adaptation and how they shift or, conversely, remain constant over the life course (Han and Moen 1999a, 1999b). "Balance" is not simply the adjudication of two competing roles (employee versus spouse/parent), but, for many contemporary couples, the three-way synchronization of "his" career, "her" career, and "their" family career. I believe that the metaphor of "balance" has outlived its usefulness, better replaced by a dynamic, life-course focus on work/life *synchronization* and *synergy* across the life course.

CAREER DEVELOPMENT AS A LIFE-COURSE PROCESS

Similarly, most stratification and occupational researchers have viewed career development as an individual process, with theoretical models of "antecedents" (in the form of markers of social location and the opportunity structure, family background, and individual ability) to explain patterns of occupational selection, mobility, achievement, earnings, and job shifts. These models represent theoretical individualism, but operationally are more variable-centered than person-centered (see also Coleman 1986). Person-centered models look at individuals or couples, and how continuity or change in their lives has certain consequences. By contrast, variable-centered models, such as multiple regression, focus on the impact of one *variable* on another (see Abbott 2001). By contrast, a life course framing of career development emphasizes its embeddedness in processes of continuity and change, social relations, situational exigencies, and historical/institutional realities (e.g., Han and Moen 1999a, 1999b; 2001;

Moen and Han 2001a, 2001b). Both the life course (Elder 1992, 1998; Heinz and Krüger 2001; Weymann and Heinz 1996) and ecology of human development (Bronfenbrenner 1979; Moen, Elder, and Lüscher 1995) paradigms underscore the changing social forces that shape the biographical contours and pacing of occupational career trajectories. While life-course models also typically pursue individualistic models of career paths, they are more person-centered than variable-centered. And life-course scholars remain attuned to the interrelatedness of experiences, as captured in the notion of linked lives (Elder 1998; Moen, Kim, and Hofmeister 2001). The study of women's career paths has also underscored the contingencies shaping women's experiences, and the value of a focus on linked careers (e.g., Han and Moen 1999a, 1999b; Heinz 1996a, 1996b; 1999; Krüger and Baldus 1999; Moen 1985; Moen and Han 2001a, 2001b).

CONCLUSIONS

Life-course scholars are well positioned to recast and broaden the study of both occupational career development and the work/life interface by focusing on linked strategies of adaptation (Moen and Wethington 1992). To do so requires recognition of (1) the value of using couples as the theoretical unit of inquiry, (2) possible life-stage variations in adaptive strategies and their effectiveness, and (3) the continuing salience of the outdated career and life-course regimes (consisting of prepackaged career lines and existing gender schema) in constricting strategic options. The contemporary organization of occupational careers is an example of "structural lag" (Moen 2003; Riley et al. 1994), where norms, policies, and practices fail to keep pace with the demographic realities and possibilities of a changing workforce. Couples' actions remain constrained by both structural arrangements (e.g., the absence of "good" part-time jobs) and by cognitions (e.g., about gender scripts) that may be outdated but continue to limit their set of possibilities. In light of such limited options, couples nevertheless make choices regarding each partner's occupational career progression as well as their own personal and family relationships. What is important to keep in mind is that these choices often serve to reconstruct and exacerbate gender inequality in a process of accumulation of advantage and disadvantage over the life course (Merton 1968; Moen 2001, 2003; O'Rand and Krecker 1990). Examining couples' conjoint occupational and family career development from a life-course vantage point is both theoretically and pragmatically compelling. It illustrates key policy challenges of our times: (1) recognition of the changing demography of the workforce and the corresponding mismatch between institutionalized career templates and contemporary reality; and (2) the need for and the opportunity to develop *innovate institutional arrangements,* alternative templates that expand the variety of occupational career lines to fit the new work force demography. What is required are social inventions of various forms of career "ladders" and "paths" that offer greater flexibility over the life course but that do not become more prescriptions for disadvantage.

ACKNOWLEDGMENTS

Research support for this chapter was provided by the Alfred P. Sloan Foundation (grants #96-6-9, 99-6-23) and the National Institute on Aging (NIA #2P50-AG11711-06).

REFERENCES

Abbott, Andrew. 2001. *Time Matters: On Theory and Method*. Chicago: University of Chicago Press.
Arthur, Michael B., Douglas T. Hall, and Barbara S. Lawrence (Eds.). 1989. *The Handbook of Career Theory*. Cambridge: Cambridge University Press.
Arthur, Michael B. and Denise M. Rousseau (Eds.). 1996. *The Boundaryless Career: A New Employment Principle for a New Organizational Era*. New York: Oxford University Press.
Bandura, Albert. 1982. "Self-efficacy Mechanism in Human Agency." *American Psychologist* 37:122–47.
Barley, Stephen R. 1989. "Careers, Identities, and Institutions: The Legacy of the Chicago School of Sociology." Pp. 41–65 in *Handbook of Career Theory*, edited by Michael B. Arthur, Douglas T. Hall, and Barbara S. Lawrence. New York: Cambridge University Press.
Barnett, Rosalind and Caryl Rivers. 1996. *She Works, He Works*. New York: Harper Collins.
Becker, Gary S. 1981. "Division of Labor in Households and Families." Pp. 30–53 in *A Treatise on the Family*, edited by G. S. Becker. Cambridge, MA: Harvard University Press.
Becker, Penny E. and Phyllis Moen. 1999. "Scaling Back: Dual-Career Couples' Work-family Strategies." *Journal of Marriage and the Family* 61:995–1007.
Bielby, William T. and Denise D. Bielby. 1992. "I Will Follow Him: Family Ties, Gender-Role Beliefs, and Reluctance to Relocate for a Better Job. *American Journal of Sociology* 97:1241–67.
Blair-Loy, Mary. 1999. "Career Patterns of Executive Women in Finance: An Optimal Matching Analysis." *American Journal of Sociology* 104:1346–97.
Blau, Francine D., Marianne A. Ferber, and Anne E. Winkler. 1998. *The Economics of Women, Men, and Work*. Upper Saddle River, NJ: Prentice Hall.
Blossfeld, Hans-Peter and Sonja Drobnič (Eds.). 2001. *Careers of Couples in Contemporary Societies: A Cross-National Comparison of the Transition from Male Breadwinner to Dual-Earner Families*. Oxford: Oxford University Press.
Blossfeld, Hans-Peter and Catherine Hakim. 1997. *Between Equalization and Mar-

ginalization: Women Working Part-Time in Europe and the United States of America. London: Oxford University Press.

Bolger, Niall, Anita DeLongis, Ronald C. Kessler, and Elaine Wethington. 1989. "The Contagion of Stress across Multiple Roles." *Journal of Marriage and the Family* 51:175–83.

Bourdieu, Pierre. 1984. *Distinction: A Social Critique of the Judgement of Taste*. Cambridge, MA: Harvard University Press.

Breiger, Ronald. 1995. "Social Structure and the Phenomenology of Attainment." *Annual Review of Sociology* 21:155–236.

Brines, Julie. 1994. "Economic Dependency, Gender, and the Division of Labor at Home." *American Journal of Sociology* 100:652–88.

Bronfenbrenner, Urie. 1979. *The Ecology of Human Development*. Cambridge, MA: Harvard University Press.

Buchmann, Marlis. 1989. *The Script of Life in Modern Society: Entry into Adulthood in a Changing World*. Chicago, IL: University of Chicago Press.

Christensen, Kathleen E. and Ralph E. Gomory. 1999. "Three Jobs, Two People." *Washington Post*, A21. June, 2.

Clarkberg, Marin. 1999. "The Price of Partnering: The Role of Economic Well-being in Young Adults' First Union Experiences." *Social Forces* 77:945–68.

Clarkberg, Marin and Stacey Merola. 2003. "Competing Clocks: Work and Leisure in Dual-Earner Couples." Chapter 3 in *It's About Time: Couples and Careers*, edited by Phyllis Moen. Ithaca, NY: Cornell University Press.

Clarkberg, Marin and Phyllis Moen. 1999. "The Time-Squeeze: Married Couples' Work-hour Patterns and Preferences." Pp. 15–23 in *Proceedings of the 51st Annual Meeting*, Vol. 1, edited by P. Voos. Madison, WI: Industrial Relations Research Association.

Clarkberg, Marin and Phyllis Moen. 2001. "Understanding the Time-Squeeze: Married Couples Preferred and Actual Work-Hour Strategies." *American Behavioral Scientist* 44:1115–36.

Coleman, James. 1986. *The Asymmetric Society*. Syracuse, NY: Syracuse University Press.

Coltrane, Scott and Masako Ishii-Kuntz. 1992. "Men's Housework: A Life-Course Perspective." *Journal of Marriage and the Family* 54:43–57.

Constantine, Larry L. 1986. *Practice of Theory in Family Therapy*. New York: Guilford.

Duxbury, Linda, Christopher Higgins, and Catherine Lee. 1994. "Work-Family Conflict: A Comparison by Gender, Family Type, and Perceived Control." *Journal of Family Issues* 15:449–66.

Eckenrode, John and Susan Gore. 1990. "Stress and Coping at the Boundary of Work and Family." Pp. 1–16 in *Stress Between Work and Family*, edited by John Eckenrode and Susan Gore. New York: Plenum.

Elder, Glen H., Jr. 1974. *Children of the Great Depression*. Chicago: University of Chicago Press.

Elder, Glen H., Jr. 1992. "The Life Course." Pp. 1120–30 in *The Encyclopedia of Sociology*, edited by Edgar F. Borgatta and Marie L. Borgatta. New York: Macmillan.

Elder, Glen H., Jr. 1995. "The Life-course Paradigm: Social Change and Individual Development." Pp. 101–39 in *Examining Lives in Context: Perspectives on the*

Ecology of Human Development, edited by Phyllis Moen, Glen H. Elder, Jr., and Karin Lüscher. Washington, DC: American Psychological Association.

Elder, Glen H., Jr. 1998. "The Life Course and Human Development." Pp. 939–91 in *Handbook of Child Psychology*, Vol. 1: *Theoretical Models of Human Development*, edited by William Damon. New York: John Wiley & Sons.

Elder, Glen H., Jr., Linda K. George, and Michael J. Shanahan. 1996. "Psychosocial Stress over the Life Course." Pp. 247–91 in *Psychosocial Stress: Perspectives on Structure, Theory, Life Course and Methods*, edited by Howard B. Kaplan. Orlando, FL: Academic Press.

England, Paula and George Farkes. 1986. *Households, Employment and Gender: A Social, Economic and Demographic View*. Hawthorne, NY: Aldine de Gruyter.

Feldberg, Rosalyn L. and Evelyn N. Glenn. 1979. "Male and Female: Job Versus Gender Models in the Sociology of Work." *Social Problems* 26:524–38.

Feldberg, Rosalyn L. and Evelyn N. Glenn. 1983. "Technology and Work Degradation: Effects of Office Automation on Women Clerical Workers." Pp. 59–78 in *Machina Ex Dea: Feminist Perspectives on Technology*, Chap. 4, edited by Joan Rothschild. New York: Pergamon.

Forest, Kay B., Phyllis Moen, and Donna Dempster-McClain. 1995. "Cohort Differences in the Transition to Motherhood: The Variable Effects of Education and Employment Before Marriage." *Sociological Quarterly* 36:315–36.

Giele, Janet Z. and Glen H. Elder, Jr. 1998. *Methods of Life-course Research: Qualitative and Quantitative Approaches*. Thousand Oaks, CA: Sage.

Greenhaus, Jeffrey H. and Nicholas J. Beutell. 1985. "Sources of Conflict between Work and Family Roles. *Academy of Management Review* 10:76–88.

Guillemard, Anne-Marie and Martin Rein. 1993. "Comparative Patterns of Retirement: Recent Trends in Developed Societies." *Annual Review of Sociology* 19: 469–503.

Hagestad, Gunhild O. and Bernice L. Neugarten. 1985. "Age and the Life Course." Pp. 35–61 in *Handbook of Aging and the Social Sciences*, 2nd edition, edited by Robert H. Binstock, Ethel Shanas, and Associates. New York: Van Nostrand Reinhold.

Hakim, Catherine. 1997. "Changing Forms of Employment: Organizations, Skills and Gender." *Urban Studies* 34:713–14.

Hall, Douglas T. (Ed.). 1996. *The Career Is Dead—Long Live the Career.*" San Francisco: Jossey-Bass.

Han, Shin-Kap and Phyllis Moen. 1999a. "Work and Family over Time: A Life-course Approach." *Annals of the American Academy of Political and Social Sciences* 562:98–110.

Han, Shin-Kap and Phyllis Moen. 1999b. "Clocking Out: Temporal Patterning of Retirement." *American Journal of Sociology* 105:191–236.

Han, Shin-Kap and Phyllis Moen. 2001. "Coupled Careers: Pathways through Work and Marriage in the United States." Pp. 201–31 in *Careers of Couples in Contemporary Societies: A Cross-National Comparison of the Transition from Male Breadwinner to Dual-Earner Families*, edited by Hans-Peter Blossfeld and Sonja Drobnič. Oxford: Oxford University Press.

Hays, Sharon. 1996. *The Cultural Contradictions of Motherhood*. New Haven, CT: Yale University Press.

Heinz, Walter R. (Ed.). 1991. *Theoretical Advances in Life-Course Research*. Weinheim, Germany: Deutscher Studien Verlag.

Heinz, Walter R. 1996a. "Transitions in Youth in Cross-Cultural Perspective: School-to-Work in Germany." Pp. 2–13 in *Youth in Transition to Adulthood: Research and Policy Implications*, edited by Burt Galaway and Joe Hudson. Toronto: Thompson.

Heinz, Walter R. 1996b. "Status Passages as Micro-Macro Linkages in Life-Course Research." Pp. 67–81 in *Society and Biography: Interrelationships between Social Structure, Institutions and the Life Course*, edited by Ansgar Weymann and Walter R. Heinz. Weinheim: Deutscher Studien Verlag.

Heinz, Walter R. (Ed.). 1999. *From Education to Work: Cross-National Perspectives*. New York: Cambridge University Press.

Heinz, Walter R. and Helga Krüger. 2001. "Life Course: Innovations and Challenges for Social Research." *Current Sociology* 49:29–45.

Hertz, Rosanna. 1986. *More Equal Than Others: Women and Men in Dual-Career Marriages*. Berkeley: University of California Press.

Higgins, Christopher A., Linda E. Duxbury, and Richard H. Irving. 1992. "Work-Family Conflict in the Dual Career Family." *Organizational Behavior and Human Decision Processes* 51:51–75.

Hiller, Dana V. and William W. Philliber. 1986. "The Division of Labor in Contemporary Marriage—Expectations, Perceptions, and Performance." *Social Problems* 33:191–201.

Hochschild, Arlie. 1989. *The Second Shift*. New York: Avon.

Hochschild, Arlie. 1997. *The Time Bind: When Work Becomes Home and Home Becomes Work*. New York: Metropolitan.

Hochschild, Arlie. 1999. "The Nanny Chain." *American Prospect* 11:32–36.

Hogan, Dennis. 1981. *Transitions and Social Change*. New York: Academic Press.

Jacobs, Jerry A. and Kathleen Gerson. 1998. "Who Are the Overworked Americans?" *Review of Social Economy* 56:442–59.

Kohli, Martin. 1986. "Social Organization and Subjective Construction of the Life Course." Pp. 271–92 in *Human Development and the Life Course: Multidisciplinary Perspectives*, edited by Aage B. Sörensen, Franz E. Weinert, and Lonnie R. Sherrod. Hillsdale, NJ: Lawrence Erlbaum.

Krüger, Helga. 1996. "Normative Interpretations of Biographical Processes." Pp. 129–46 in *Society and Biography: Interrelationships between Social Structure, Institutions and the Life Course*, edited by Ansgar Weymann and Walter R. Heinz. Weinheim: Deutscher Studien Verlag.

Krüger, Helga and Bernd Baldus. 1999. "Work, Gender, and the Life Course: Social Construction and Individual Experience." *Canadian Journal of Sociology* 24:27–56.

March, James G. and Johan P. Olsen. 1989. *Rediscovering Institutions*. New York: Free Press.

Marks, Stephen R. and Shelley M. MacDermid. 1996. "Multiple Roles and the Self: A Theory of Role Balance." *Journal of Marriage and the Family* 58:417–32.

Marshall, Victor W., Walter R. Heinz, Helga Krüger, and Anil Verma. 2001. *Restructuring Work and the Life Course*. Toronto: University of Toronto Press.

Merton, Robert K. 1968. *Social Theory and Social Structure*. New York: Free Press.

Meyer, John W. 1986. "The Institutionalization of the Life Course and Its Effects on the Self." Pp. 199–216 in *Human Development and the Life Course: Multidisciplinary Perspectives*, edited by Aage B. Sörensen, Franz E. Weinert, and Lonnie R. Sherrod. Hillsdale, NJ: Erlbaum.

Moen, Phyllis. 1985. "Continuities and Discontinuities in Women's Labor-Force Participation." Pp. 113–55 in *Life-Course Dynamics: 1960s to 1980s*, edited by Glen H. Elder, Jr. Ithaca, NY: Cornell University Press.

Moen, Phyllis. 1989. *Working Parents: Transformations in Gender Roles and Public Policies in Sweden*. Madison: University of Wisconsin Press.

Moen, Phyllis. 1992. *Women's Two Roles: A Contemporary Dilemma*. Westport, CT: Auburn House.

Moen, Phyllis. 1994. "Women, Work and Family: A Sociological Perspective on Changing Roles." Pp. 151–70 in *Age and Structural Lag: The Mismatch between People's Lives and Opportunities in Work, Family, and Leisure*, edited by Matilda W. Riley, Robert L. Kahn. and Anne Foner. New York: John Wiley & Sons.

Moen, Phyllis. 1998. "Recasting Careers: Changing Reference Groups, Risks, and Realities." *Generations* 22:40–45.

Moen, Phyllis. 2001. "The Career Quandary." *Population Reference Bureau Reports on America* 2(1):1–15.

Moen, Phyllis. 2003. *It's About Time: Couples and Careers*. Ithaca, NY: Cornell University Press.

Moen, Phyllis, Glen H. Elder, Jr., and Karin Lüscher (Eds.). 1995. *Examining Lives in Context: Perspectives on the Ecology of Human Development*. Washington, DC: American Psychological Association.

Moen, Phyllis and Kay B. Forest. 1990. "Working Parents, Workplace Supports, and Well-Being: The Swedish Experience." *Social Psychology Quarterly* 53:117–31.

Moen, Phyllis and Shin-Kap Han. 2001a. "Reframing Careers: Work, Family, and Gender." Pp. 424–45 in *Restructuring Work and the Life Course*, edited by Victor W. Marshall, Walter R. Heinz, Helga Krüger, and A. Verma. Toronto: University of Toronto Press.

Moen, Phyllis and Shin-Kap Han. 2001b. "Gendered Careers: A Life-Course Perspective." Pp. 42–57 in *Working Families: The Transformation of the American Home*, edited by R. Hertz and N. L. Marshall. Berkeley: University of California Press.

Moen, Phyllis, Jungmeen Kim, and Heather A. Hofmeister. 2001. "Couples' Work/Retirement Transitions, Gender, and Marital Quality." *Social Psychology Quarterly* 64:55–71.

Moen, Phyllis and Robert Orrange. 2002. "Careers and Lives: Socialization, Structural Lag, and Gendered Ambivalence." Pp. 231–60 in *Advances in Life-Course Research: New Frontiers in Socialization*, edited by R. A. Settersten, Jr. Stamford, CT: JAI.

Moen, Phyllis and Stephen Sweet. 2003. "Time Clocks: Work-Hour Strategies." Chapter 2 in *It's About Time: Couples' Career Strategies in Changing Community, Organizational, and Policy Contexts*, edited by Phyllis Moen. Ithaca, NY: Cornell University Press.

Moen, Phyllis, Stephen Sweet, and Bickley Townsend (with W. Wimonsate, L. B.

Kahn, V. Plassmann, and V. Banks). 2001. *How Family-Friendly Is Upstate New York?*. Ithaca, NY: Cornell University Press.

Moen, Phyllis and Elaine Wethington. 1992. "The Concept of Family Adaptive Strategies." *Annual Review of Sociology* 18:233–51.

Moen, Phyllis and Yan Yu. 2000. "Effective Work/Life Strategies: Working Couples, Work Conditions, Gender and Life Quality." *Social Problems* 47:291–326.

Mortimer, Jeylan T., Michael D. Finch, Seongryeol Ryu, Michael J. Shanahan, and Kathleen T. Call. 1996. "The Effects of Work Intensity on Adolescent Mental Health, Achievement, and Behavioral Adjustment: New Evidence from a Prospective Study." *Child Development* 67:1243–61.

O'Rand, Angela M. 1996. "Linking Social Structures to Personal Development." Pp. 67–81 in *Society and Biography: Interrelationships between Social Structure, Institutions and the Life Course,* edited by Ansgar Weymann and Walter R. Heinz. Weinheim: Deutscher Studien Verlag.

O'Rand, Angela M. and John C. Henretta. 1999. *Age and Inequality: Diverse Pathways Through Later Life.* Boulder, CO: Westview.

O'Rand, Angela M. and Margaret L. Krecker. 1990. "Concepts of the Life Cycle: Their History, Meanings and Uses in the Social Sciences." *Annual Review of Sociology* 16:241–62.

Orenstein, Peggy. 2000. *Flux : Women on Sex, Work, Kids, Love, and Life in a Half-Changed World.* New York: Doubleday.

Pavalko, Eliza K. and Brad Smith. 1999. "The Rhythm of Work: Health Effects on Women's Work Dynamics." *Social Forces* 77:1141–62.

Pittman, Joe F. and David Blanchard. 1996. "The Effects of Work History and Timing of Marriage on the Division of Household Labor: A Life-Course Perspective." *Journal of Marriage and the Family* 58:78–90.

Presser, Harriet B. 1994. "Employment Schedules Among Dual-earner Spouses and the Division of Household Labor by Gender." *American Sociological Review* 59:348–64.

Quick, Heather and Phyllis Moen. 2002. *Careers in Competition? An Analysis of Couples' Employment Trajectories.* Unpublished manuscript.

Repetti, Rena L. 1989. "Effects of Daily Workload on Subsequent Behavior During Marital Interaction: The Roles of Social Withdrawal and Spouse Support." *Journal of Personality and Social Psychology* 57:651–59.

Repetti, Rena L. and Jenifer Wood. 1997. "Effects of Daily Stress at Work on Mothers' Interactions with Preschoolers." *Journal of Family Psychology* 11:90–108.

Riley, Matilda W., Robert L. Kahn, and Anne Foner (Eds.). 1994. *Age and Structural Lag: The Mismatch between People's Lives and Opportunities in Work, Family, and Leisure.* New York: John Wiley & Sons.

Risman, Barbara J. 1998. *Gender Vertigo: American Families in Transition.* New Haven, CT: Yale University Press.

Rosenfeld, Rachel. 1992. "Job Mobility and Career Processes." *Annual Review of Sociology* 18:39–61.

Sampson, Robert J. and John H. Laub. 1993. *Crime in the Making: Pathways and Turning Points through Life.* Cambridge, MA: Harvard University Press.

Schor, Juliet and Douglas B. Holt. 2000. *The Consumer Society Reader*. New York: New Press.

Settersten, Richard A. and Karl Ulrich Mayer. 1997. "The Measurement of Age, Age Structuring, and the Life Course." *Annual Review of Sociology* 23:233–61.

Sewell, William H., Jr. 1992. "A Theory of Structure: Duality, Agency, and Trans-formations." *American Journal of Sociology* 98:1–29.

Shelton, Beth A. and Daphne John. 1996. "The Divisions of Household Labor." *Annual Review of Sociology* 22:299–322.

Spain, Daphne and Suzanne Bianchi. 1996. *Balancing Act*. New York: Russell Sage Foundation.

Spilerman, Seymour. 1977. "Careers, Labor-Market Structure, and Socioeconomic Attainment." *American Journal of Sociology* 83:551–93.

Swidler, Ann. 1986. "Culture in Action: Symbols and Strategies." *American Socio-logical Review* 51:273–86.

Tilly, Charles. 1999. "Durable Inequality." Pp. 15–33 in *A Nation Divided: Diversity, Inequality, and Community in American Society,* edited by Phyllis Moen, Donna Dempster-McClain, and H. A. Walker. Ithaca, NY: Cornell University Press.

Tolbert, Pamela S. and P. Monique Valcour. 2001. *Gender, Family, and Career in the Era of Boundarylessness: Determinants and Effects of Intra- and Interorganizational Mobility*. BLCC Working Paper #01-11, unpublished manuscript.

Turner, Ralph H. 1978. "The Role and the Person." *American Journal of Sociology* 84:1–23.

Weymann, Ansgar and Walter R. Heinz (Eds.). 1996. *Society and Biography*. Wein-heim: Deutscher Studien Verlag.

Wilensky, Harold L. 1961. "Orderly Careers and Social Participation: The Impact of Work History on Social Integration in the Middle Class." *American Sociological Review* 26:521–39.

Williams, Joan. 2000. *Unbending Gender: Why Family and Work Conflict and What to Do About It*. New York: Oxford University Press.

Zhou, Xueguang and Phyllis Moen. 2001. "Explaining Life Chances in China's Eco-nomic Transformation: A Life-Course Approach." *Social Science Research* 30:552–77.

Zhou, Xueguang, Nancy Tuma, and Phyllis Moen. 1995. "Social Stratification Dynamics under State Socialism: The Case of Urban China, 1949–1993." *Social Forces* 74:759–96.

Zhou, Xueguang, Nancy Tuma, and Phyllis Moen. 1997. "Institutional Change and Job-Shift Patterns in Urban China, 1949 to 1994." *American Sociological Review* 62(3):339–65.

|12|

Ties Between Lives

Dynamics of Employment Patterns of Spouses

Sonja Drobnič

LIFE-COURSE PERSPECTIVE AND LINKED LIVES

The inclusion of a chapter on life course and social structure in *Handbook of Modern Sociology* in the 1960s, a book that aimed to "summarize all of the major growing research areas of modern sociology" (Faris 1964), marks perhaps most clearly the beginning of a rapid intellectual endeavor through which the life-course perspective emerged in the following decades as an influential approach to studying human lives and their dynamics in time and place. Leonard Cain, the author of the chapter on life course in the *Handbook,* drew heavily on earlier writings on age status of individuals; however, his merit was that he positioned the concept of age status within the entire life course of individuals, and linked the life-course patterns to some major institutions, such as the family. According to his definition, "the 'life course' is used to refer primarily to those successive statuses individuals are called upon to occupy in various cultures and walks of life as a result of aging, and 'age status' refers to the system developed by a culture to give order and predictability to the course followed by individuals" (Cain 1964:278).

Since the 1960s, the life-course approach has developed into one of the most vibrant fields of social science inquiry, both in terms of conceptual and theoretical developments, and empirical research contributions (see Marshall and Mueller, Chapter 1 in this volume). Although there is no unified theory of the life course, life-course perspectives share many common principles. It is now generally accepted that conceptual issues in life-course research currently provide an accepted set of background assumptions that guide research on a number of substantive issues across the social sciences, as has been shown in a series of recent reviews of the field (e.g., Giele and Elder 1998; Hardy 1997; Heinz and Krüger 2001; Krüger 2001a; Marshall and Mueller this volume; Mayer 2000; Settersten 1999).

A systematic focus on age as a component of both individual lives and social structures has remained at a core of sociological perspectives on the life course (Elder 1975, 1985; Riley 1985, 1987; Riley, Johnson, and Foner 1972; Riley and Riley 1999; Settersten and Mayer 1997). In particular, the life-course approach has concentrated on those age-related transitions that are socially created, socially recognized, and shared (Hagestad and Neugarten 1985). Another important early achievement was the focus on the relationship between aging and social change or the intersection between the micro- and macrosociological levels. The meanings and uses of age, aging, and age-graded roles drew attention to the fact that time can be conceptualized along different dimensions, such as biographical or developmental life time, social time, family time, or historical time (Clausen 1972; Elder 1978; Elder and Caspi 1990; Hareven 1977; Kohli 1986).

Similar to life-span psychologists, life-course sociologists are interested in individual-level life outcomes. However, they put more emphasis on the environment and the role of social and historical contexts, recognizing that life courses evolve in a dynamic interplay between individuals and society. Individual lives are shaped by—and themselves shape—various levels of social structure, establishing reciprocal ties between changing structures and changing lives.

There has been a recognition that the life course is an element of social structure that is a product of individual action, organizational processes, and institutional and historical forces (Heinz 1991; Mayer and Tuma 1990), including state regulations (Mayer and Müller 1986; Mayer and Schoepflin 1989). This line of reasoning embedded life course in macrolevel sociological debates, raising questions on how structural conditions or institutions impact on individual lives or, vice versa, how life-course outcomes impact on structural and institutional change. An important impetus for this research tradition arose prominently with the spread of longitudinal studies and the analytic techniques that attempt to access the nature and temporal patterns of individual behavior while attending to the manner in which this behavior is embedded into organizational structures and institutional regulations. In particular, Ryder's (1965) proposal to use cohorts as a concept for studying the life course opened the field toward greater understanding of the interplay between social change and the life patterns of individuals at different life stages, or, in other words, the interplay between historical and biographical life time.

In Elder's (1974) pioneering study, *Children of the Great Depression*, and the response of other scholars to this work, the individual is brought into focus according to three different meanings of age: developmental, which refers to individuals in the aging process; social, which concerns the social timing and structure of lives; and historical, which places people in historical context through membership in specific birth cohorts. Since members of different cohorts encounter different segments of historical time as they proceed through their lives, each cohort is affected differently by historical change. Thus, the influence of historic events varies depending on the stage of life at which they are experienced.

The debate of the meaning and usefulness of the cohort model and the so-called age-cohort-period problem is still going on (Hardy and Waite 1997; Settersten 1999). Nevertheless, a careful operationalization of the age-cohort-period model is a powerful statistical tool for researchers (O'Brien 2000). Innumerable studies successfully applied the cohort approach to better understand the relationship between individual lives and social change (cf. Blossfeld 1986), particularly in time of rapid and radical social changes (Weymann, Sackmann, and Wingens 1999). Conceptually, cohort or period effects occur because macrolevel phenomena influence microlevel behavior. However, articulating the linkage across level of aggregation requires the conceptualization of mechanisms through which social structure affects individual behavior, and the acquisition of methodological tools to discriminate among competing explanations. Otherwise, the cohort becomes merely a methodological concept, not a theoretical one (Marshall 1984).

A conceptual framework that addresses the relationship between individual lives and social change, and simultaneously seeks to uncover some of the mechanisms through which these two levels are interconnected, is based on the principle of interdependent or linked lives, as first articulated by Elder. This approach has received much less attention among life-course scholars than the relationship between individual lives and institutional-level societal structures. The principle of interdependence, or of linked lives, is simply that individual lives are intimately connected to those of others, and that an individual's development is bound to, and shaped by, those ties (Settersten 1999:15). The concept has been proposed by Elder and Caspi (1990) as one of five principles to help us examine the link between social change and the life course. It locates all lives in relation to others who mediate the influence of social change. As Elder and Caspi put it, "All lives are lived interdependently, and this connectedness defines a medium through which historical change plays out its influence over time" (ibid.:221).

The recognition that an individual is embedded in social relations is implicitly taken into account already in the traditional sociological research, which is based on individuals as independent units of analysis.

A number of standard "variables" that we use in empirical research, such as gender, income, or occupational status, carry tacit information about the position of an individual and his/her relations with others within the social structure. However, an explicit consideration of concrete social ties is relatively rare. While we in principle recognize that lives are critically interwoven, we generally study lives as if they exist in isolation of others. It is therefore an important accomplishment of life-course research to have started addressing the issues of "linked lives" and the implications of interdependencies over time.

The interdependence of life histories is most salient when the life-course perspective is applied to the family unit. The life course of the family underscores the interdependent life histories of its members: The properties of the family as a whole are derived from the properties of the relationships between individuals in the family and not just from the characteristics of the individuals as separate persons (Elder and Caspi 1990). This conceptual framework suggests that instead of treating individuals as monad entities, we should consider individuals within the social matrix of relationships. The opportunities and constraints faced by an individual also reflect the progress of others in their life tasks, and social change has powerful consequences for the individual through the lives of related others.

Two aspects of interdependence are particularly relevant:

(1) For family members, ties between individuals can provide important resources and opportunities but also operate as burdens and constraints. Family members serve as sources of emotional and economic support during times of hardship, but they can also prevent individuals from exploiting options open to them in nonfamilial spheres. Within the ecology of human development perspective, for example, it has been shown that family adaptive strategies mediate the effects of the broader social environment on the positive, as well as the negative side. Internal family patterns and transitions may be harmful to children's development but also provide useful lessons in ways of coping with life's exigencies (Moen and Erickson 1995).

(2) Since events in the life of one individual have implications for the life of another, this interdependence creates the need to actively coordinate and synchronize lives as much as possible to avoid or reduce potential frictions. Therefore, some observed processes and individuals' trajectories may be difficult to comprehend if only individual characteristics are taken into account. They are rather the outcome of negotiation, coordination, and consideration of related others.

ILLUSTRATIVE EXAMPLES

The remainder of this chapter draws on research results from the Household Dynamics and Social Inequality project, conducted within the Life

Course Research Center at the University of Bremen in the period 1994–2001. Several studies in this project addressed the effects of household dynamics on individuals' employment patterns and occupational careers, taking the ties between family members and their characteristics into account. All these studies are longitudinal; they examine how life courses evolve over time and how the aspects of interdependence change in various stages of the life course of individuals. Empirical examples in this chapter are limited to former West Germany, where the patterns of investment in alternative family and market roles over the life course have been highly gendered. Former East Germany had a very different structure of the labor market and female employment (Schaeper and Falk in this volume; Trappe and Rosenfeld 1998), as well as disparate family formation and retirement patterns.

The following research questions will be addressed in this chapter:

- How does the *presence* of a spouse modify the effects of children on women's employment patterns?
- How do the *characteristics* of a spouse affect the employment behavior of married women?
- How do the *life-course patterns* of paid/unpaid labor in married couples affect the retirement decisions of married men?

Data are obtained from the German Socioeconomic Panel (GSOEP), a nationally representative longitudinal data set of persons, households, and families in the Federal Republic of Germany. The first data collection was carried out in 1984; there has been a further panel wave in every subsequent year. The panel provides information on household structure, individual characteristics of household members, family history, employment history from the age of fifteen on, work characteristics, income, health, and other dimensions relevant for the life-course research. The initial sample included almost six thousand households and over twelve thousand respondents—these were members of those households, at least sixteen years old, who filled out individual questionnaires. Since all adult members of a household have been interviewed, this gives us the opportunity to link the family members to each other and study how these relationships affect individual lives.

The method used in the studies is event-history analysis. The dependent variable is transition rate between various labor-market states, such as a move from full-time employment to homemaking, or a transition into retirement. The hazard rate is estimated using the piecewise constant exponential model (Blossfeld and Rohwer 1995; Rohwer and Pötter 1998). With this flexible hazard rate specification, no unjustified restriction is imposed on the data; instead, we allow data to tell how the hazard behaves as a function of time. Independent variables can be time-constant or time-varying. Time-varying covariates whose values are not fixed at the beginning of the spell but can change within the duration of an episode are included in the analysis through the episode-splitting method.

Example 1: Variable Effects of Children on Women's Employment Patterns

Women's employment is a widely studied phenomenon. Researchers are particularly interested in the causes and effects of women's work, and in determinants of the considerable differences between countries in this respect (Blossfeld and Hakim 1997; Gornick, Meyers, and Ross 1998). In spite of a dramatic increase in female labor-force participation, women, in general, continue to assume the primary responsibility for childcare and other household tasks, and combining employment and family responsibilities remains an obstacle for the achievement of women's equality in the labor market. Therefore, to better understand the unfolding of women's employment careers over their lifetime, it is imperative to take their household and family context into account. In other words, the family dynamics of interdependent lives has a profound influence on trajectories and transitions experienced by individual women in various life domains, and specifically on their employment careers.

In the study reported in detail in Drobnič, Blossfeld, and Rohwer (1999), we examined the dynamic relationship between the family life cycle and women's employment patterns over the life course, comparing American and (West) German women. Using the data on employment histories, "employment patterns" were operationalized as moves over time between the following labor-market states: full-time employment, part-time employment, and nonemployment, which consisted of various inactivity statuses, such as schooling, unemployment, or homemaking. We made a distinction between full-time and part-time employment because household work and the presence of young children require extensive input of time that is particularly difficult to combine with full-time employment. Part-time work may offer the flexibility required to meet family obligations and may allow women to maintain ties to the labor market. Information on 4,537 women from the waves 1984–1993 has been used.

While controlling for women's individual characteristics, birth cohorts, and historical periods, we aimed to assess the effects of children of various ages and the effect of marital partner on the likelihood of women's moves between the labor-market states. Marriage and childbearing refer to the emergence of interdependent lives. When constructing the data set, we "followed" individual women over their family life course—assessing if and when they married, when their children were born, and how they grew older. We divided the childrearing history into the following stages:

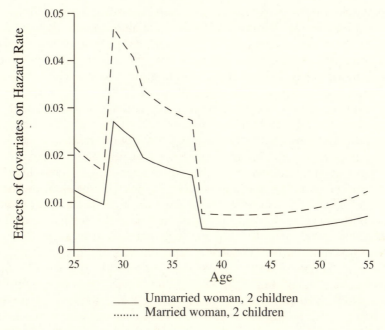

Figure 12.1 Transition from full-time employment to nonemployment over the life span 25–55 years, women with two children.

the presence of preschool children (age 0–6), school children (age 7–17), and grown-up children (age 18 and over), in order to distinguish changing demands of children on their mother. With more than one child, a higher priority was given to the youngest child. Also, the number of children was included as a separate variable to take into account the greater financial needs of families with several children. Both the number of children and the dummies describing the age of the youngest child were time-varying covariates. Also, marital status was included in a time-varying form, entailing the following states: married without children, married with at least one child. The reference category was not married. We distinguished two types of marriages to assess the effects of marriage itself and to be able to distinguish the effects of children for married and unmarried mothers.

A detailed description of the study and the estimates of hazard models are given in Drobnič et al. (1999). Instead of presenting the estimates, I propose here to refer to some selected results, using graphical tools. Figure 12.1 presents a plot of an estimated hazard rate of moving from full-time employment to nonemployment over the life span 25–55 years. The curves are computed by taking into account the estimated statistically significant coefficients for age, marriage, and childrearing. The graph shows a simulated example of two women with identical characteristics who gave birth to their first child at the age of twenty-nine, and the second child at the age of thirty-two. The ages and the number of children change over the life course accordingly. The only difference between the women is that one was married at the age of twenty-five and remained married during the observation window, while the other one was not married.

The graphic presentation in this chapter is an alternative means of displaying results of model estimates. It is necessarily incomplete and schematic; nevertheless, the simulated curves vividly reveal the estimated effects of covariates. The risk of moving from full-time employment to nonemployment, as showed by the plotted hazard rates in Figure 12.1, increases strikingly with the birth of the first child and remains high until the second child reaches school age. A partial drop in the simulated hazard rate at the time of birth of the second child is due to a negative effect of the number of children on the likelihood of leaving full-time employment. Thus, women with more children are less likely to leave employment, under the condition that they have been employed full-time in the first place.

Another notable finding is that the hazard rate differs for married and unmarried women. As indicated by the dashed line, the likelihood of exiting full-time employment is intensified for married mothers. Since the effects are multiplicative, the combination of children and marital partner is a particularly powerful factor that drives women out of the labor market.

When transition from nonemployment into full-time employment is examined, strong effects of children are apparent again. The likelihood of entering full-time employment drops decisively when women have children of preschool age (Figure 12.2). This drop is particularly deep for unmarried women who otherwise—particularly at younger ages—exhibit a high risk of entering full-time employment, compared to married women.

To emphasize again, these simulations are fairly crude: no interaction effects are considered, the operationalization of children's demands on their mother's time and other resources is imprecise, the dynamics over the life course is simplified. Nevertheless, these visual examples convincingly show that childrearing responsibilities strongly guide women's occupational decisions, and their behavior is modified by the presence of a husband. We get insight into the individuals' employment dynamics over the life course, and how this is mediated not through the individuals' own traits and resources but through interdependence with others—in this case children and marital partners.

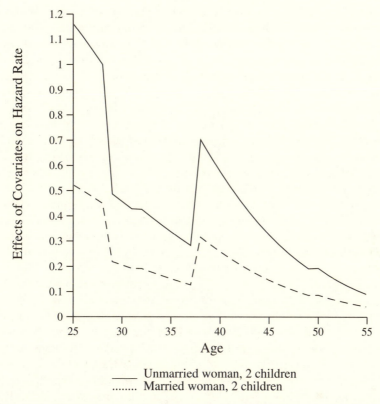

Figure 12.2 Transition from Nonemployment to Full-Time Employment Over the Life Span 25–55 Years, Women with Two Children.

Example 2: The Impact of Spouse's Resources on Women's Work

The second example focuses on married couples and examines how spouses in (West) Germany coordinate their employment behavior over the life course. This approach is based on a symmetric perspective, trying to examine the interdependencies of husbands' and wives' transitions between full-time or part-time paid work and unpaid household work. We examined the extent and nature of these interdependencies, starting at the time of entry into marriage, and varying across the family life cycle as well as between social classes. We used data from the German Socio-Economic Panel for the period 1984–1991. The sample consisted of 1289 couples for whom all required information was available. Event-history analysis was employed in order to consider the development of husbands' and wives' careers over the life course and across a broad range of marriage cohorts. This long-term longitudinal approach allowed married couples' employment careers to be studied in the context of a changing system of social stratification. Three specific questions were addressed in the study. (1) To what extent are the transitions between (full-time and part-time) paid market work and unpaid housework gendered within marital unions in West Germany? (2) To what degree do spouses marry assortatively and how does this affect their employment relationships over the family cycle? (3) Do class-specific differences in the division of labor between husbands and wives become more or less important across marriage cohorts? The results of this study and corresponding analyses for several other countries are reported in Blossfeld and Drobnič (2001).

To summarize briefly, in terms of occupational scores and earnings potentials of first jobs, husbands and wives show strong homogamous tendencies, which was an expected outcome of our analysis. However, a relatively large proportion of spouses also exhibit differences in their career resources, and these differences span in both directions. Not only are cases where men have considerably higher earnings potentials than their wives relatively frequent, but so are cases where women surpass their husbands in levels of career resources, particularly in younger marriage cohorts. The economic theory of the family predicts the division of labor between a husband and a wife on the basis of the comparative advantage and does not per se assign the housework to wives. Economic theory argues that the partner with greater comparative advantage in the market (that is, higher wage rate) will specialize in paid work and the other partner will specialize in housework in order to maximize their shared unitary utility. This division of labor maximizes a joint utility function of the couple due to the greater resulting efficiency in the division of labor. Due to high homogamy and the symmetry of the differences in earnings potentials of husbands and wives, one would reasonably expect that in some couples husbands with lower earnings capacity would specialize in household production or work part-time. However, the empirical examination shows that the employment trajectories of couples in West Germany are extraordinarily gender-specific. As a consequence, the transition between paid work and homemaking could only be studied for wives, and no parallel analysis for men was feasible.

I will therefore present some selected results for wives only. To comply with the previous illustrative example, let us simulate transition rates from full-time employment into the status of homemaker for two women who are both married, have two children, come from the same social class of origin but differ in their educational levels and occupational prestige scores—one of them has an occupational score of a secretary and the other one the highest occupational score of a physician. Using the estimated

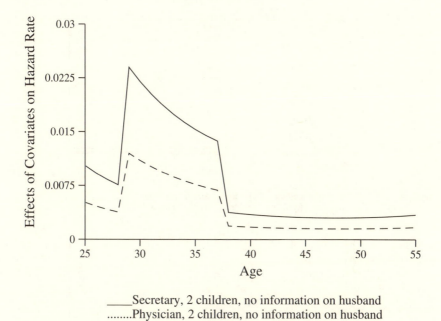

_____Secretary, 2 children, no information on husband
........Physician, 2 children, no information on husband

Figure 12.3 Transition from Full-Time Employment to Nonemployment Over the Life Span 25–55 Years, Women with Differing Educational Levels and Occupational Prestige Scores.

coefficients for age, children, education, and occupational score, the plotted curves again indicate that children have a decisive impact on the likelihood of exiting employment (Figure 12.3). In addition, this analysis shows that the impact varies in line with women's occupational resources. Fewer occupational resources promote the likelihood of leaving the job; a secretary in our simulated example exhibits a considerably higher exit rate than a female physician.

However, when the information on husband's education and occupation is included in the analysis, it becomes obvious how important his characteristics are for the employment behavior of the wife. The higher the husband's education, the more likely women are to leave their employment. This effect is additionally strengthened by a good occupational position of the husband. Overall, husband's resources have an impeding effect on wife's labor-force participation.

Again, I simulate various situations to illustrate how the effects of husbands modify the transition rate of wives from full-time employment to homemaking. In the upper part of Figure 12.4, information on husband's

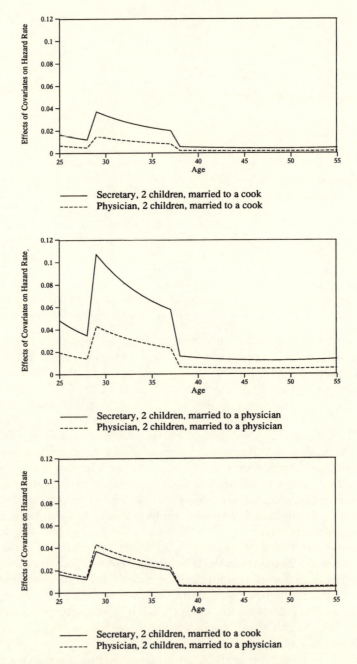

Figure 12.4   Effect of Husbands on Transition to Homemaker.

schooling and job position in our example cases is included. A secretary and a female physician, married at the age of twenty-five and having two children, are now both married to a husband with eleven years of education and a rather low occupational score of 43.1, which is a score assigned to a cook (Wegener 1985). Neither woman is very likely to interrupt her work and the difference in the hazard rate between them becomes rather small.

The situation would have been very different had both women been married to a physician, as shown in the middle part of Figure 12.4. Now the rate for both women increases somewhat already at the beginning of marriage and escalates—particularly for the secretary—at the time of birth of the first child. This persuasively illustrates the impact of the husband's position on his wife's employment behavior. Particularly when the husband has a much higher occupational position than his wife—that is when the differences in resources that the couple brings into the marriage are large—there is a strong increase in her likelihood to become a housewife. In such households, the traditional family pattern with strict division of market work for husband and domestic work for wife is most commonly found. Also, the impact of a preschool child strongly depends on the husband's job position. If the husband has a higher social position, a traditional role model is fostered and there is a high tendency to interrupt employment when there are small children in the family.

Finally, a more realistic situation with strong marriage homogamy is simulated in the lower graph. This time, the secretary is married to a cook, and the female doctor to another physician. For the first time we observe a situation where the hazard rate for the two women gets reversed. Now the exit rate is somewhat higher for the higher skilled woman, which indicates that at a certain point the husband's resources simply override a woman's own career assets. Even if the female physician has a much higher income potential than a secretary, she will be more likely to interrupt employment when she is married to a husband with a high social status. Hence, by omitting the effects of the husband and focusing on the wife's individual resources only, one would make a wrong prediction with regard to the employment behavior of these women.

This example first shows that interdependencies within the family are highly gendered, and illustrates the processes that generate and shape the breadwinner family model. Gender-neutral theories, such as the economic theory of the family, cannot explain individuals' trajectories over the life course in the employment sphere on gender-neutral grounds. Second, a cross-national comparison of the effects of partners' characteristics on women's employment over the life course (see country-specific contributions in Blossfeld and Drobnič 2001) demonstrates that these effects are not universal. Although all countries included in the project exhibit gendered life-course patterns and gender-specific interdependencies, the specific impact of the husband varies in terms of strength and direction, and clearly reflects welfare regime patterns. In countries with a typical social democratic welfare state regime, for example Sweden, or in (former) state socialist countries, the effects tend to go in the opposite direction: in most of these countries, there is a positive association between husbands' occupational resources and wives' employment participation. Thus, there is an additional—indirect, less visible, and often not acknowledged—impact of state regulations and welfare systems on individual life courses through the intersecting lives.

Example 3: Spouses' Division of Labor and Retirement Timing

To avoid the impression that "interdependencies" are in effect solely "dependencies" of female lives on other family members, let me briefly summarize the study of retirement timing in a household context, using longitudinal data on employment and family careers. Men's work lives have traditionally been viewed as independent of the family domain. Few studies have found effects of family transitions and family-related experiences on men's career transitions, and those who did seem to be concentrated on later stages of men's working life (Carr and Sheridan 2001; O'Rand and Farkas 2002; Szinovacz, Ekerdt, and Vinick 1992).

Also the study reported here refers to the time of final exit from the labor force. Retirement was operationalized as a self-reported status, and transition into retirement was examined for unmarried and married men. Since in (West) Germany patterns of investment into alternative family and market roles over the life course are highly gendered, married men were further divided into a subsample of men whose wives were not employed at the age of fifty, and "working spouses," where both partners were employed at age fifty. In this way we roughly distinguished between dual-earner partnerships in later life, which is a rather atypical arrangement in older cohorts, and those that portrayed a traditional division of paid/unpaid labor over the life course.

Data were drawn from the German Socioeconomic Panel Study 1984–1996. An event history analysis was conducted using a piecewise-constant hazard model with time-varying covariates, separately for unmarried men ($n = 193$), married men with nonemployed wives ($n = 995$), and men in working couples ($n = 545$). A dynamic model of retirement took into account the linkages between the life-course stages, interrelations among various life domains, and the interdependencies of life histories of family and household members. The determinants of retirement decisions considered in the analyses were early life-course employment patterns, employment characteristics in later life, health situation, and household circumstances, including income level. Detailed results are presented in Drobnič (2002, 2003).

The findings indicate that while there are many common characteristics, there are also systematic variations among subsamples. In terms of descriptive statistics, unmarried men, on the one hand, differ in several aspects from married men: they have lower education, lower occupational scores, lower income, and are less often homeowners than married men. They tend to work in smaller firms, and seem to have fewer health problems. Also, the proportion of guest workers is higher among unmarried than married men. The subsamples of married men, on the other hand, are remarkably similar in most individual characteristics and also in their average retirement age. However, in spite of similarities in the timing of retirement, there are discernible differences in factors that drive the retirement process. For older men in "traditional" couples, household income and wealth play an important role. Husbands respond strongly to financial incentives and the share of their contribution to the household income. A long-term responsibility for the economic well-being of the household seems to have a critical impact on their retirement timing. Being a primary or sole wage earner makes their contribution to the household income more crucial. The higher their share in household income and the larger the household, the less likely they are to withdraw from the labor force. However, household size and household income are not significant determinants of retirement behavior for husbands in dual-worker couples. This suggests that a working wife and her contribution to the household's economic well-being in older age lessens the constraints faced by her spouse and enables him to make a retirement decision more autonomously.

DISCUSSION AND IMPLICATIONS

I have argued in this chapter that in spite of impressive advances in life-course research, much remains to be learned about interdependence of lives and how ties between individuals modify the courses of lives and individuals' experiences over time. Several important themes emerged from our research that have relevance for conceptual and analytical issues concerning interdependence in life-course research.

First, empirical evidence not only reveals a disparate structure of men's and women's life courses that continue to unfold in different directions, but also a highly gendered nature of interdependencies. Therefore, theories that adhere to the view that the relations underlying the division of labor in the household are fundamentally gender-neutral are not able to explain individual trajectories and employment patterns over life time. The neoclassical economic model of the family, for example, assumes that the family behaves as if it were trying to allocate the time of its members to satisfy a common set of "family" preferences or a joint utility function. Under the gender-neutral assumptions of this model, the comparative advantage of one partner over the other drives the decisions to allocate time to market or household production, and the spouse-specific sources of nonearned income exert the same effects on family allocative behavior. However, our research indicates that these processes do not unfold on gender-neutral grounds. Ties between spouses or ties between parents and children are highly gender-specific in their form and consequences. Future research should focus on the variety of these forms and consequences. Next, although linkages among women's work and family roles have been amply documented, researchers should explore whether a conceptually more refined analysis might not reveal also that men's work lives are affected by the demands of family life and the ties to related others.

Second, we must not only document the effects of interdependencies better but also try to understand them better. As hypothesized in the introduction, ties between individuals can be facilitating or constraining in their repercussions. Do women who leave employment because of child-rearing feel restrained in their career aspirations and long-term employment plans or do they accept it as a welcome, normatively supported opportunity to concentrate on homemaking and family care? Our research reveals that in Germany, wives of better-educated husbands with higher-status occupations and higher income potentials are significantly more likely to exit and remain out of the labor market, net of women's own occupational resources, than other women. Are women with high-income husbands more under pressure to give up their occupational aspirations and retreat to domesticity in the absence of financial strains, or are they—because of an adequate family income—better able to afford to settle down to full-time mothering and home managing? We do not know much about the personal implications of life transitions and consequences of interdependencies, and how individuals themselves perceive their situation.

Likewise, we do not know much about how the decisions about life transitions are made and how they are negotiated between the partners or other involved individuals. In examining these themes, efforts should be made to tap the variability that most likely governs the nature, meaning, and consequences of interdependence over time. As Gerson (1985) reminds us, women are not a homogeneous group. They are individuals with differing resources, situated in variable social contexts. They vary in their orientations, capacities, and abilities, as well as preferences for domesticity or employment careers. These orientations and preferences are strongly influenced by social change and can shift dramatically across birth cohorts and within one's own course of life; however, a change in orientations is not always adequately measured by changing behaviors (Krüger 2001b).

Therefore, to repeat the plea, both research on observed life-course dynamics as well as the meanings of these dynamics for the individuals is needed to adequately understand life courses and daily experiences in lives as they are actually lived.

Finally, cross-national research demonstrates that theories that try to explain the decision-making processes concerning the division of labor within couples as independent of institutional constellations and cultural traditions within which these decisions are made can only to a certain degree explain the actual outcomes. They might fit the specific historical periods or class-specific relationships but start losing explanatory power in another historical time or in another country context (Drobnič and Blossfeld 2001). It is reasonable to assume that couples in diverse circumstances attempt to negotiate their actions in order to coordinate the family and work sphere. It is difficult to understand the differences in outcomes if only individual and couple characteristics are taken into account. Instead, life courses and the links between lives have to be studied in their embeddedness into organizational structures and institutional regulations. Often, as Krüger (2001b:413) argues, the modern life-course regime counts on couples, not on individuals. Not only are lives regulated and structured by institutions and the state with its policies, but so are the interdependencies between and among lives.

REFERENCES

Blossfeld, Hans-Peter. 1986. "Career Opportunities in the Federal Republic of Germany: A Dynamic Approach to the Study of Life-Course, Cohort, and Period Effects." *European Sociological Review* 23:208–25.

Blossfeld, Hans-Peter and Sonja Drobnič (Eds.). 2001. *Careers of Couples in Contemporary Societies: From Male Breadwinner to Dual-Earner Families*. Oxford: Oxford University Press.

Blossfeld, Hans-Peter and Catherine Hakim (Eds.). 1997. *Between Equalization and Marginalization: Women Working Part-Time in Europe and the United States of America*. Oxford: Oxford University Press.

Blossfeld, Hans-Peter and Götz Rohwer. 1995. *Techniques of Event History Modeling: New Approaches to Causal Analysis*. Mahwah, NJ: Lawrence Erlbaum.

Cain, Leonard D., Jr. 1964. "Life Course and Social Structure." Pp. 272–309 in *Handbook of Modern Sociology*, edited by R. E. L. Faris. Chicago: Rand McNally.

Carr, Deborah and Jennifer Sheridan. 2001. "Family Turning-Points and Career Transitions at Midlife." Pp. 201–27 in *Restructuring Work and the Life Course*, edited by V. W. Marshall, W. R. Heinz, H. Krüger, and A. Verma. Toronto: University of Toronto Press.

Clausen, John A. 1972. "The Life Course of Individuals." Pp. 457–514 in *Aging and Society*, Vol. 3, *A Sociology of Age Stratification*, edited by M. White Riley, M. Johnson, and A. Foner. New York: Russell Sage Foundation.

Drobnič, Sonja. 2002. "Retirement Timing in Germany: The Impact of Household Characteristics." *International Journal of Sociology* 32(3):75–102.

Drobnič, Sonja. 2003. "Men's Transition to Retirement: Does the Wife Matter?" *Schmollers Jahrbuch—Applied Social Science Studies* 123(1):177–87.

Drobnič, Sonja and Hans-Peter Blossfeld. 2001. "Careers of Couples and Trends in Inequality." Pp. 371–86 in *Careers of Couples in Contemporary Societies: From Male Breadwinner to Dual-Earner Families*, edited by H.-P. Blossfeld and S. Drobnič. Oxford: Oxford University Press.

Drobnič, Sonja, Hans-Peter Blossfeld, and Götz Rohwer. 1999. "Dynamics of Women's Employment Patterns over the Family Life Course: A Comparison of the United States and Germany." *Journal of Marriage and the Family* 61(1):133–46.

Elder, Glen H., Jr. 1974. *Children of the Great Depression*. Chicago: University of Chicago Press.

Elder, Glen H., Jr. 1975. "Age Differentiation and the Life Course." *Annual Review of Sociology* 1:165–90.

Elder, Glen H., Jr. 1978. "Family History and the Life Course." Pp. 17–64 in *Transitions. The Family and the Life Course in Historical Perspective*, edited by T. K. Hareven. New York: Academic Press.

Elder, Glen H., Jr. 1985. "Perspectives on the Life Course." Pp. 23–49 in *Life-Course Dynamics. Trajectories and Transitions, 1968–1980*, edited by G. H. Elder, Jr. Ithaca, NY: Cornell University Press.

Elder, Glen H., Jr., and Avshalom Caspi. 1990. "Studying Lives in a Changing Society: Sociological and Personological Explorations." Pp. 201–47 in *Studying Persons and Lives*, edited by A. I. Rabin et al. New York, NY: Springer.

Faris, Robert E. L. 1964. "Preface." Pp. V–VI in *Handbook of Modern Sociology*, edited by R. E. L. Faris. Chicago: Rand McNally.

Gerson, Kathleen. 1985. *Hard Choices. How Women Decide about Work, Career, and Motherhood*. Berkeley: University of California Press.

Giele, Janet Z. and Glen H. Elder, Jr. (Eds.). 1998. *Methods of Life-Course Research. Qualitative and Quantitative Approaches*. Thousand Oaks, CA: Sage.

Gornick, Janet C, Marcia K. Meyers, and Katherin E. Ross. 1998. "Public Policies and the Employment of Mothers: A Cross-National Study." *Social Science Quarterly* 79(1):35–54.

Hagestad, Gunhild O. and Bernice L. Neugarten. 1985. "Age and the Life Course." Pp. 35–61 in *Handbook of Aging and the Social Sciences*, 2nd ed., edited by R. H. Binstock and E. Shanas. New York: van Nostrand Reinhold.

Hardy, Melissa A. (Ed.). 1997. *Studying Age and Social Change: Conceptual and Methodological Issues*. Thousand Oaks, CA: Sage.

Hardy, Melissa A. and Linda Waite. 1997. "Doing Time: Reconciling Biography with History in the Study of Social Change." Pp. 1–21 in *Studying Age and Social Change: Conceptual and Methodological Issues*, edited by M. A. Hardy. Thousand Oaks, CA: Sage.

Hareven, Tamara K. 1977. "Family Time and Historical Time." *Daedalus* 106 (Spring):57–70.

Heinz, Walter R. (Ed.). 1991. *The Life Course and Social Change: Comparative Perspectives*. Weinheim: Deutscher Studien Verlag.

Heinz, Walter R. and Helga Krüger. 2001. "Life Course: Innovations and Challenges for Social Research." *Current Sociology* 49(2):29–45.

Kohli, Martin. 1986. "The World We Forgot: A Historical Review of the Life Course." Pp. 271–303 in *Later Life. The Social Psychology of Aging,* edited by V. W. Marshall. Beverly Hills, CA: Sage.

Krüger, Helga. 2001a. "Geschlecht, Territorien, Institutionen. Beitrag zu einer Soziologie der Lebenslauf-Relationalität." Pp. 257–99 in *Individualisierung und Verflechtung. Geschlecht und Generation im Lebenslaufregime,* edited by C. Born and H. Krüger. München: Juventa.

Krüger, Helga. 2001b. "Social Change in Two Generations: Employment Patterns and Their Costs for Family Life." Pp. 401–23 in *Restructuring Work and the Life Course,* edited by V. W. Marshall, W. R. Heinz, H. Krüger, and A. Verma. Toronto: University of Toronto Press.

Marshall, Victor W. 1984. "Tendencies in Generational Research: From the Generation to the Cohort and Back to the Generation." Pp. 207–18 in *Intergenerational Relationships,* edited by V. Garms-Homolova, E. M. Hoerning, and D. Schaeffer. Lewiston, NY: Hogrefe.

Mayer, Karl Ulrich. 2000. "Promises Fulfilled? A Review of 20 Years of Life-Course Research." *European Journal of Sociology (Archives Européennes de Sociologie)* 41(2):259–82.

Mayer, Karl Ulrich and Nancy Brandon Tuma. 1990. "Life-Course Research and Event History Analysis: An Overview." Pp. 3–20 in *Event History Analysis in Life-Course Research,* edited by K. U. Mayer and N. Brandon Tuma. Madison: University of Wisconsin Press.

Mayer, Karl Ulrich and Walter Müller. 1986. "The State and the Structure of the Life Course." Pp. 217–45 in *Human Development and the Life Course: Multidisciplinary Perspectives,* edited by A. B. Sørensen, F. E. Weinert, and L. R. Sherrod. Hillsdale, NJ: Lawrence Erlbaum.

Mayer, Karl Ulrich and Urs Schoepflin. 1989. "The State and The Life Course." *Annual Review of Sociology* 15:187–209.

Moen, Phyllis and Ann Erickson. 1995. "Linked Lives: A Transgenerational Approach to Resilience." Pp. 169–210 in *Examining Lives in Context. Perspectives on the Ecology of Human Development,* edited by P. Moen, G. H. Elder, Jr., and K. Lüscher. Washington, DC: American Psychological Association.

O'Brien, Robert M. 2000. "Age Period Cohort Characteristic Models." *Social Science Research* 29:123–39.

O'Rand, Angela M. and Janice I. Farkas. 2002. "Couples' Retirement Timing in the United States in the 1990s. The Impact of Market and Family Role Demands on Joint Work Exits." *International Journal of Sociology* 32(3):11–29.

Riley, Matilda White. 1985. "Age Strata in Social Systems." Pp. 369–411 in *Handbook of Aging and the Social Sciences,* 2nd ed., edited by R. H. Binstock and E. Shanas. New York: van Nostrand Reinhold.

Riley, Matilda White. 1987. "On the Significance of Age in Sociology." *American Sociological Review* 52:1–14.

Riley, Matilda White, Marilyn Johnson, and Anne Foner. 1972. *Aging and Society.* Vol. 3, *A Sociology of Age Stratification.* New York: Russell Sage Foundation.

Riley, Matilda White and John W. Riley, Jr. 1999 "Sociological Research on Age: Legacy and Challenge." *Ageing and Society* 19:123–32.

Rohwer, Götz and Ulrich Pötter. 1998. *TDA User's Manual*. Bochum: Ruhr-Universität Bochum.

Ryder, Norman B. 1965. "The Cohort as a Concept in the Study of Social Change." *American Sociological Review* 30:843–61.

Settersten, Richard A., Jr. 1999. *Lives in Time and Place. The Problems and Promises of Developmental Science*. Amityville, NY: Baywood.

Settersten, Richard A., Jr., and Karl Ulrich Mayer. 1997. "The Measurement of Age, Age Structuring, and the Life Course." *Annual Review of Sociology* 23:233–61.

Szinovacz, Maximiliane, David J. Ekerdt, and Barbara H. Vinick (Eds.). 1992. *Families and Retirement*. Newbury Park, CA: Sage.

Trappe, Heike and Rachel A. Rosenfeld. 1998. "A Comparison of Job-Shifting Patterns in the Former East Germany and the Former West Germany." *European Sociological Review* 14(4):343–68.

Wegener, Bernd. 1985. "Gibt es Sozialprestige?" *Zeitschrift für Soziologie* 14(3): 209–35.

Weymann, Ansgar, Reinhold Sackmann, and Matthias Wingens. 1999. "Social Change and the Life Course in East Germany: A Cohort Approach to Inequalities." *International Journal of Sociology and Social Policy* 19(9-11):85–108.

|13|

Changes in Family Roles and Arrangements Between Generations

An Indicator for the Modernization of Gender Relations?

Claudia Born

INTRODUCTION

Changed gender roles are an expression of the individualization process which has been unfolding in Western societies over the last fifty years. This chapter explores whether the modernization tendencies postulated by the individualization thesis can indeed be observed, i.e., whether the ways in which men and women plan and shape their lives are converging. Such tendencies would be an indication of a reduction in existing gender-specific social inequality. In addressing this question I will outline women's and men's beliefs (and behavior) concerning family roles over three generations and assess their development toward gender equality.

I argue and empirically support the proposition that changes in family representation and roles across cohorts clearly indicate a socially desired and strived for process of increasing equalization, yet at the same time an increasing asymmetry between the sexes (Born and Krüger 2001; Koppetsch and Burkart 1999). The latter finding contradicts the widespread assumption that such asymmetry had been overcome (Oechsle and Geissler 1998).

GENDER AND LIFE AREAS AS DIMENSIONS FOR CONVERGENCE

In sociological debates in which the category gender plays a role, convergence trends are discussed from different perspectives and adduced to support contradictory conclusions. One camp considers the category gender to have become increasingly irrelevant. This position is most prominently but not exclusively represented by Beck and Beck-Gernsheim (1994). They argue that the most important demands made on individuals are associated with the labor market—precisely the domain in which, due to women's increased integration, they are becoming equal to men. Though there are slight differences among scholars' assessments of the degree to which women have already succeeded in approximating their life courses to those of men's—Beck-Gernsheim (1983) speaks of women's "late" or "catch-up" individualization (*"nachgeholte Individualisierung"*), while Bertram and Borrmann-Müller (1988) observe a female "modernization lag"—they all agree that the labor market plays the dominant role in structuring the life course (cf. Weymann 1998; Mayer 1998). The employment system is thus regarded as the most relevant locus of convergence processes and women are considered to be the agents of these processes (Kohli 1994).

Indeed, German women's education, achievement, motivation, and expectation of qualified employment are becoming ever more similar to those of men. Furthermore, the increasing rate of women's labor-market participation signifies a changed reality in gender roles and gender relations. Since the labor market is the area in which ideas of gender equalization and role redefinition began, it seems logical to focus on this societal system to look for increasing convergence in how men and women arrange their lives. Some scholars (e.g., Gottschall 2000) rightly argue, however, that such a labor-market-centered view fails to take into consideration the demands of caregiving in the family sphere. Given that family labor is performed mostly by women, they—subordinated to both societal subsystems—are subject to the predicament of "double-socialization" (Becker-Schmidt 1987). Women's continuous obligation to perform reproductive work and the resulting structure of the demands they face—often contradictory to and conflicting with those of the labor market—thus necessitate inclusion of the family in research on gender-role equalization, not its exclusion as in market-focused studies.

Findings from research on the family conducted within the context of gender relationships show overall that the image of the family and the conceptions related to its development have changed both for women and men in the direction of convergence. But upon closer examination, this image proves to be inconsistent and partially contradictory with respect to both men and women: On the one hand there is the image of the new, involved father ("committed fatherhood": Fthenakis 1999) as opposed to fathers whose central concern is to defend the employment sphere against demands from the family sphere (Liebold 2001). Similarly diverse, if not contradictory, findings have been ascertained for women: On the one hand their interests and attitude are described as "expecting an egalitarian part-nership and a fair division of labor" (Sommerkorn 1995:271), yet Hopf and Hartwig (2001:195) come to the conclusion on the basis of their investiga-tion that "women . . . [are] far from transcending traditional role demands and pursuing unconventional life designs." They use the term "readiness to be submissive" to characterize the young women "who would never dream of asking their partners to take over the housework and childcare." Further indications of complementarity—not convergence—in gender relations are scholars' ascertainment of women being dominant in carry-ing out family tasks (*"Fürsorgedominanz":* Böhnisch 1997) and of men being forgetful of everyday things (*"Alltagsvergessenheit":* Honegger 1991). Yet this "contradictory diversity" (Lüscher 2001) notwithstanding, family role conceptions have clearly changed over the course of the last four decades.

Analyzing processes of change and convergence in the life courses of men and women in the United States, Kathleen Gerson (1993) perceives a modernization gap on behalf of men. While women are structurally inte-grated into the labor market and their life courses in this respect approxi-mate those of men, men evince a modernization gap concerning their integration into the family. This gap in behavior and attitudes is particu-larly striking when compared to those of women of the same generation. Cause for optimism concerning the aspired synchronization of men's and women's life courses can be found, however, when different male genera-tions are compared. Though men are actually situated in a "No Man's Land" (Gerson 1993), Gerson (2001) sees signs of a "gender revolution." When Krüger and Levy (2000:388) concede that "it is no longer bipolarity and role segregation that dominate in family life but a balancing act within a diverse continuum of grades of complementarity," then the main change is named. From an intergenerational perspective, though, the question concerning the direction of these changes—whether they lead to conver-gence—remains open. We also find opposing assessments of which life sphere—the labor market or the family—is the dominant locus of gender equalization processes, as well as of which gender is the agent in the process of closing the modernization gap.

As indicated in the title, this chapter focuses on the family sphere. But what is the justification for this exclusive emphasis on family roles? Are we not making the same demarcation error as those who study the labor mar-ket in isolation (see critically Moen and Han 2001)? And, in view of the "dissolving post-familial family diversity" (Beck 1993:154), has not "the family" been exhausted as a field of study, or at least lost its relevance?

Both questions can clearly be answered negatively. First, the family is more than just the place where the division of family chores between the genders can be observed. The family phase, which is located in the middle of the adult life course, occurs in "tandem" (see Krüger, Chapter 2 in this volume) with paid employment. The interlacing of these two life spheres thus has to be arranged both by each individual involved (the mother and the father)[1] and jointly in a process of negotiation between partners. Although the family is not the only place where two individuals of different gender interrelate, it can be conceived of as the place where the social-structural arrangements of gender and institutional relations intersect (cf. Born and Krüger 2001; Bird 2001; Gottschall and Bird 2003). Second, in spite of the diversification of family forms and the increased options for individuals in arranging their life courses, the high personal relevance of the family—understood here as entering or holding a position in a two-parent family—has not changed in (at least) the last fifty years (cf. as summaries Busch, Nauck, and Nave-Herz 1999; Liebold 2001; Lüscher 2001). Lauterbach (1999) finds that in Germany more than 80 percent of persons age thirty to forty are married and live in families with children. Nave-Herz (1994) talks accordingly of "the diversity of family forms within narrow confines" (*"Pluralität in Grenzen"*). In our own studies discussed below, there are no indications of a decline in the importance of the family in the life courses of the research participants, and this holds for both men and women in all three generations/cohorts investigated.

DATA AND METHODS

The above contention of the high and persistent relevance of the family for individual life courses stems from the following analysis, based on several waves of two longitudinal studies (A and B), conducted at the Special Research Centre "Status Passages and Risks in the Life Course" at Bremen University.[2] The results of both studies were analyzed with respect to changes in life-course patterns and biographical interpretations concerning work and family from an intergenerational perspective. Relevant here is the fact that these studies cover three "family formation generations" and explore the interface between family and employment. As the same methods were used in both studies, their findings are compatible and constitute an empirically grounded contribution to the question of whether convergence trends exist in the ways men and women plan and shape their (family) lives.

Though both studies' research designs combined quantitative and qualitative methods,[3] my analysis will refer primarily to the material gathered qualitatively. It stems from semistructured interviews ("problem-centered" interviews: Witzel 2000)—conducted with men and women in all three cohorts. The texts were interpreted by means of a theme-centered analysis. This approach begins by identifying themes (either predetermined or emerging during the interviews) and proceeds by systematically exploring similarities and differences in the research participants' statements in the context of their sociodemographic and familial/working characteristics.

Study A, conducted between 1988 and 1999, was a prospective panel that investigated the transition from vocational training to employment of young adults in two economically contrasting German regions. A sample (n = 2000) of young skilled blue- and white-collar workers (with an average age of 20.7 in 1998) were surveyed in four quantitative panel waves between 1989 and 1997/1998 in order to record their early work and family careers. Qualitative semistructured interviews were conducted with a theoretically significant subsample. At the center of this longitudinal study lay the transition from vocational training to employment, with a focus on its biographical shaping and objective course. One topic in the qualitative material was participants' orientations and actions in the context of family formation and (planned) family arrangements from the perspective of gender. At the time of their final interview, the participants were in their late twenties. As in Study B, gender issues were systematically taken into account.

Study B, conducted between 1988 and 1996, retrospectively investigated changing life-course patterns in Germany over the past fifty years. Central issues were gender, the labor market, the family, and their interrelations. The study consists of three substudies with different participants: The first was conducted with women at the transition to retirement. In their sixties when under study, they belonged to the birth cohort of 1930, were trained for skilled jobs directly after World War II, then got married and became mothers in the early 1950s. The subsequent research phase focused on their husbands. In terms of their age and work career/labor-market position they were in the same biographical transitions as their wives. These research participants are members of the "postwar generation" (see Freier and Kuhn 1984). The third and final phase of this study investigated their adult children (sons and daughters). Born in the 1950s, their formative years were in the late 1960s, and they started to form a family in the early 1970s. The early 1970s in Germany were a period in which fundamental social change and destandardization of living arrangements occurred, e.g., the unprecedented expansion of part-time work, the first radical decline in birth rates, and a sharp increase in cohabitation, divorce rates, and one-parent families (see Born and Krüger 2002). Accordingly, the research participants in this third phase are members of the cohorts currently held responsible for the "detraditionalization of family bounds" (Kaufmann 1993:107), and had mostly established their own adult lives when interviewed. They were not only asked how they were dealing or planning to deal with family work (in combination/relation to employment) but also how their lifestyle was related to the life courses of their parents. In each of these studies (women/husbands/adult children), on the basis of a quantitative survey of life-course events and turning points a theoretically based qualitative sample was chosen. This allowed for forming subgroups and systematically relating differences in interpretation patterns to the participants' gender, specific life-course pattern, intrafamilial tradition, etc. In sum, for two successive generations, Study B examined both the linking of lives and convergence tendencies between male and female life-course patterns from the perspective of gender (see Krüger 1996; Lorenz-Meyer 1999). Indeed, with reference to the B-Study cohorts analyzed here, it seems appropriate to use the term "generation." Kohli und Szydlik (2000) have bemoaned the inflationary usage—also among sociologists—of this term. To avoid this pitfall, they recommend employing the concept only in its narrowest sense and according to strict definitional criteria. Despite their parsimonious use of the concept, Kohli and Szydlik ascribe to Study B's cohorts the status of societal generations. Further, they see them "as an example of linkages between familial and cultural generations" (ibid.:16). The members of the most recent cohorts analyzed here (the research participants of Study A), however, do not meet these criteria of a common generational fate, neither in the political, economic or cultural dimension (see the diverse contributions in Kohli and Szydlik 2000).

Viewed together, the data from Studies A and B can be used to track a historical process (see Figure 13.1 and Table 13.1). Most of the respondents, at least at the start of their employment history, had attained an equivalent level of qualification and were thus at least similar with respect to their sociostructural position and sociocultural milieu (on the significance of milieu for gender relationships in relation to the division of labor in the family/household, see Koppetsch and Burkart 1999).

Since the focus of this chapter is on individual family roles and arrangements, findings of the theme-centered analyses will be presented in terms of how familial gender roles have changed across generations, i.e., whether a degendering or synchronization process has occurred. The analysis focuses on the social practices of family life in two (family-connected) generations (B data), or, for the youngest cohort (A data), how they envisage these. While the first two generations had their family formation phase in the 1950s and 1970s, respectively, the third were still involved in the process of family formation when interviewed in the 1990s. The window of observation covers the historical period referred to as "social modernity," characterized by individualization (Beck, Giddens, and Lash 1994).

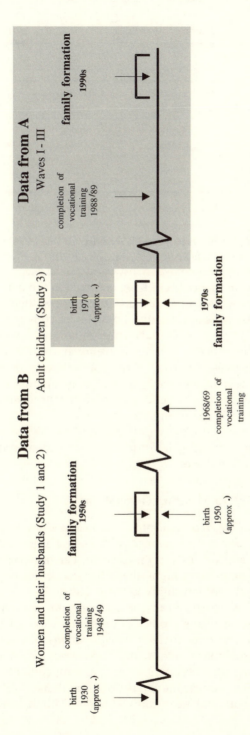

Figure 13.1 Chronology of Events in the Intergenerational Succession Resulting from the Pooling of the A and B Data.

Table 13.1   Empirical Data

	Wave I (male and female)	Wave II (male and female)	Wave III (male and female)
A: Quantitative sample	n = 2230	n = 1304	n = 1040
Qualitative sample	n = 198	n = 113	n = 98
	Study 1 (women)	Study 2 (husbands)	Study 3 (adult children)
B: Quantitative sample	n = 220	n = 74	n = 149
Qualitative sample	n = 52	n = 37	n = 46

FROM MEN'S MODERNIZATION DEFICIT TO WOMEN'S MODERNIZATION RETREAT?

Our findings confirm that changes have occurred in the family roles realized or envisaged by women and men. If we follow their development across generations, we can discern tendencies of convergence between men and women. These processes of change in family roles do not consistently approach the level of similarity, however. In contrast to the aspired synchronization between the roles of men and women, once more there are indications of tendencies toward a greater segregation across generations. From the perspective of gender, these desynchronization processes are strongly related to female family roles.

To support this contention, I will first chronologically depict different generations' notions and practice of family roles and subsequently compare these across generations.

Gender and Family Roles within Generations

The members of *the oldest generation,* who formed their families in the 1950s, can be considered the reference and baseline group for modernization processes of family roles. For this postwar generation—and here our findings corroborate those of numerous other studies—separate domains of male and female responsibility were a culturally and normatively anchored reality. The female adult normal biography prescribed a role of nonemployed housewife and mother. For men it was continuous employment that, due to men's unrestricted participation in and availability to the labor market, secured the family's material existence. For members of this generation, marriage and children were a "natural certainty" realized in nearly all cases. For women the family was the dominant life area, and they carried the sole and near complete responsibility for it, without contradiction, their whole lives through. Complementing the female family role was the husbands' adoption of the breadwinner role, which, our studies show, they pursued just as naturally throughout their work lives. Everyday domestic work and participation in child or parental care were not part of their family role. And even in their 1990s, when interviewed, they still clung to the gender-specific traditional family model. Thus when questioned, a husband—and within the postwar generation there is little variation from this position—responded: "Even today I'd tell ya that a woman is a housewife . . . that's the way it is, isn't it? If she's married, then she stays at home" (Born and Krüger 2002:128).

Their wives see things completely differently: A large majority of them fulfilled their desire to participate in the labor market. In interviews these women presented a positive view of their paid employment, even though it was normatively hardly accepted and in most cases resisted by their husbands. They did play down its subjective importance, however.[4] At the level of evaluative generalizations, they attributed greater importance to the family and family duties. As a result, their behavior is complementary to that of their husbands, even though these women set modernization processes in motion by the expansion of their role to include paid employment. Due to the culturally expected and actually existing gendered division of labor, whose distinguishing feature is women's economic and social dependency on men, in the generation that formed their families in the early 1950s the question of gender equality was not posed. As interviewees put it, "We just didn't think about things like that" (for a summary discussion see Born, Krüger, and Lorenz-Meyer 1996).

This changed drastically for *the generation who started families in the 1970s*. Although the women in the oldest generation of our study did not even contemplate equality for themselves, it was an issue for their sons and daughters. As one woman said (and sought to achieve in her children's upbringing), "There should be at least some equality." And though they lived their family lives in a very traditional way, they valued the "three-phase-model" (identified by Myrdal and Klein in the late 1950s, suggesting a homemaker period for mothers between the phases of employment) very positively, and recommended it to their daughters.

Set in motion by an improved economic situation (Germany's period of postwar prosperity known as the "economic miracle") and by the debate on the expansion of education and equality of opportunity, different, more expansive ideals emerged for both men and women. These manifested themselves in the perception and configuration of men's family role. German sociologists speak of an epochal change in men's understanding of their roles. As a result, men, relative to the previous generation, overcame their modernization deficit. The right to independence as an element of adulthood now became normatively acceptable for women, too, as a goal they demanded and achieved. Since employment is an important precondition for personal autonomy, in this generation gainful employment became an integral part of the female adult life context.

Most members of this generation—and hence most of our research participants—formed their family during the 1970s and also married and had children. By the age of thirty-five, 74 percent of our sample have experienced marriage, 60 percent are (still) married, 20 percent are (still) single, and 59 percent have children. But both these events—marriage and parenthood—as well as family formation, have lost their taken-for-granted character, for both men and women. The recognition of the time squeeze and availability dilemma associated with the combination of paid employment and childcare in the family produces changes in the division of labor that require negotiation processes between the partners. Men no longer see a woman's role as exclusively restricted to the family. The attitude shared by nearly all men in this (middle) generation was clearly expressed in the following remark by one of our male interview partners: "For me, there's no reason why she shouldn't [i.e., why his wife shouldn't work, C.B.] and many reasons why she should: the child bla bla, the family budget, her retirement pension, gaining skills, not falling behind" (Born and Krüger 2002:128). And they do not consider their function in the family to be exclusively that of the breadwinner. In connection with starting his own family (in the 1970s), one male interview partner observed: "The question: child . . . or children is now slowly becoming concrete, from the age aspect. And I would lean toward saying we'll have a child. And then we'll have to figure out who does what [referring to the familial division of labor between partners, C.B.]." Although in light of our analyses it would be an exaggeration to say, as Bullinger (1988) does, that the new father role is a reaction to the new power of women and came about solely as a result of their pressure, men's participation in family work has become more of a matter of course as a response to women's expectations and claims for equality in a partnership and a fairer division of labor.

The result, however, is a nearly unchanged arrangement of gender-specific domains. As (predominantly part-time) employed mothers, women are responsible for family tasks, while men remain primarily breadwinners. Both men and women consensually justify this arrangement as the rational consequence of the demands of the institutions involved. Thus the above-cited father continues: "And . . . we have already spoken about my partner staying at home for a while [after the birth of the child, C.B.], also simply for income reasons. For a nursery-school teacher, supporting a family with one or more children—that's just not, or hardly, possible" (Born and Krüger 2002:133). Since institutional frameworks—especially the gender-segmented labor market, which produces inequality of opportunity—force parents to a gender-specific division of labor between family and work, members of the 1970 family formation generation fear the reproduction of hierarchical gender relationships due to unequal access to money. Negatively construing relations of inequality in their partnerships, individuals within families consciously seek to overcome such potential inequality by modernizing their relationship with their partner. The "private" everyday experienced relationship is explicitly stressed as egalitarian. Regardless of the actual division of labor, autonomy is stressed as being essential for both partners and finds its visible expression in the carrying out of separate activities (see Born et al. 1996).

A comparison of the cohorts reveals clear processes of convergence that are now being driven by both gender groups. Modernization processes among men relative to the previous generation, which had been ascertained above all by Gerson (1993), are hereby confirmed also for German society. The major change in attitudes between the generations of the fathers and sons and the rather minor changes in the relation of work and family between the generations of mothers and daughters is expressed with particular clarity in the following statements by two sisters. One of them recounts: "Actually my mother always worked and really enjoyed working—just like me later. I have always worked too, always [despite having two children, C.B.]." And the other sister, living in the same situation, observes: "Just that working [referring to her mother's employment, C.B.] back then wasn't necessarily normal to my father; for my husband it's pretty normal that I work" (Born and Krüger 2002:129).

In *the 1990 family formation cohort*, it is harder to find clear-cut evidence of a continuation or further development of these processes of convergence and modernization. Instead, individuals' notions of family roles reveal an increasing divergence between the genders. And this comes mostly from the women. Compared to the men, they more frequently refer positively to the classical pattern of gender-specific role division. They develop future plans for their own families that are in line with the traditional model and with the corresponding complementary traditional role for their husbands, who themselves often do not share these notions in such an explicit manner. It is certainly possible to recognize modernization processes in the men's ideas about the configuration of their family and work roles. In comparison with the 1970 generation, these new male roles have been considerably extended. It is not only that some of the male respondents emphasize their desire and intention to take on their share of childcare, but they also consciously concentrate their career plans on the time prior to starting a family. When they have children, they argue, they will need time to be active fathers, but this should not occur at the expense of their function as the family breadwinner. This recognition of the reconciliation of work and family as a conflict area in their own lives, and the (admittedly modest) search for individual solutions, could be interpreted as a further modernization of their understanding of family roles, possibly even as the beginning of a dual orientation that until now was characteristic only of women's lives.

A further sign of rapprochement could be that some young men would like, at least for a limited time, to swap roles and take a period of parental leave. In intergenerational comparison, this development is new, remembering of course that this concerns the formulation of ideas and expectations not yet practiced: Indeed, Bird (2001) found that from the introduction of parental leave (*Erziehungsurlaub*) in 1986 until its extension to three years in 2001, the share of fathers in the 1990 cohort claiming it never exceeded 2 percent. The men would probably encounter resistance from their female partners if they attempted to take parental leave because these young women, although they take their male partners' wish seriously, nearly universally seek to avert it. Instead, they hold onto their monopoly on childcare and maternal role fulfillment. When asked about their future family plans these young women frequently anticipate an employment break of uncertain duration. They consider their own gainful employment, and specifically a return to the labor market after a period as a homemaker, as a potential resource that can be flexibly marshaled, but for which they do not make concrete plans. Kühn (2002) found that this behavior does not strictly correlate with specific types of working careers. We do find occupationally specific female life courses even in the youngest cohort, however, such that the ones with the worst working conditions in terms of income and occupational advancement start to become homemakers earlier than the ones whose learned occupations offer better conditions.[5] In intergenerational comparison, it would seem that a shift has taken place in women's notions of the phase of active motherhood. This is no longer viewed as a time of dual orientation toward work and the family, but as a time in which the family dominates.

Changes in Family Roles in an Intergenerational Perspective

In spite of young women's conspicuous family orientation and its legitimization by recourse to the "normality" of this gendered life-course pattern, as opposed to the structural constraints adduced by the 1970 generation, this is not a renaissance of the 1950s model. The differences between the family formation generations of 1990 and 1950 are too great, although the possible consequences may be similar. Unlike the 1950 generation, for whom starting a family with gendered role participation was regarded as natural for both men and women, for the 1990 family formation cohort nothing is societally "preprogrammed" (as members of the elder cohort express their situation). Marriage and parenthood have changed in this period from an unalterable certainty to a mere option.

Accordingly, members of the youngest cohort are compelled to engage in negotiation processes regarding the shaping of their own family life. Not only are marriage and parenthood no longer a matter of course, but scheduling, time management, and work sharing have to be planned and discussed. This behavior, which we initially observed between partners of the 1970 generation, has now become normal and pervasive. Both this development and men's notions of their family role show that, culturally, nothing can be taken for granted. Yet in our sample, even in stable partnerships, processes of communication and reconciliation with regard to these issues take place astonishingly late, and have often not yet taken place by the age of twenty-eight to thirty, when subjects were interviewed for the third time. In the youngest cohort we encounter couples who, despite having bought a house together, had not talked about forming a family, and do not even know whether their partner wants to have children (see Witzel and Kühn 2001). There are certainly several reasons for this behavior. First, it appears to be part of a conflict avoidance strategy and the expression of ambivalence and frequently articulated uncertainty regarding future plans (see Kühn 2002). It can also, especially for women, be read as an expression of a "new" autonomy or realized individualization. Those young women who did make their decision to become mothers do not seem to be prepared to compromise their goal of a "traditionally oriented" family role, and are unshakably certain of its achievement. And it is in the self-confident articulation of family notions, even if these run counter to their partner's interests, that we find the greatest difference relative to the 1950 family formation generation. Among men, too, if one compares the 1990 with the 1950 family formation cohorts in terms of their family notions and family roles, the differences could not be greater: While it was nearly impossible for the elder male generation even to participate in any kind of domestic labor or child care, in the 1990s a number of young men aver with some credibility that they would like to devote themselves exclusively to homemaking—at least for a limited period of time.

In addition to the aforementioned similarities, major differences between the 1990 and 1970 cohorts can also be observed. In the 1970 generation, women wanted to participate in paid employment and for this reason expected and successfully demanded that their husbands assume more responsibility for family work. Our analyses show that these women's objective was to come closer to the egalitarian and equitable partnership to which they aspired. A family life characterized by a fair division of labor between equal partners was a central concern of the 1970 generation and viewed as an expression of equality between men and women.

In the youngest generation this is no longer an issue for women (nor for men for that matter). In accordance with the findings in another recent study, we ascertain in our sample too "how little the idea of equality is present in the accounts of the young women" (Hopf and Hartwig 2001:10). Contrary to Hopf's findings, however, there is no evidence in our interviews that the lack of thought given to issues of equality or dependency in the configuration of family roles or gender relations can be interpreted as a sign of women's "readiness to be submissive," as Hopf and Hartwig (ibid.:195) conclude from their research. On the contrary, we suggest that this lack of reflection takes place against the background of the assumption of equality. Equality is not only demanded as a matter of course, but is also viewed as a given and considered to exist, and therefore does not need to be continuously claimed and secured in an egalitarian division of labor or continuous material independence. Even if definitive statements on this topic cannot be found in our interviews, it appears that the self-direction expressed by these women with respect to their life plans is proof of their independence and protection from possible social or financial dependency—something that was of great concern to the 1970 generation. An interesting question is: How can this apparent "backlash" among young women be explained, and how can this be reconciled with processes of convergence between the genders?

GENDER AND FAMILY ROLES: EXTENT AND LIMITS OF THE SYNCHRONIZATION PROCESSES

The pattern described above for the 1990 cohort—a modern (full-time working) father actively integrated in family work and a traditional mother clinging to her right as homemaker and child carer—is, of course, not the only one we found. The family notions held by both the young men and women are more diverse, reflecting indeed the increased individualization experienced over the last quarter of the twentieth century (see Kühn 2002). Against the background of the discussion of processes of convergence and modernization in gender relations and arrangements, however, the female group upon whom I have focused is certainly not a minority that could be disregarded, all the more since these findings are also found in other empirical studies on Germany. Young women are convinced that they live in an egalitarian society. They do not pay much attention to gender differences. And intergenerational comparison indeed provides evidence of a development from the "existence of a culture of inequality" to an "existence of a culture of equality" (Müller 1998) and therefore attests—at the cultural level—to growing gender symmetry. When Müller nevertheless insightfully characterizes the belief in equality on behalf of the young women as the "permanent anticipation of equity," it is because gender-specific discrimination and structural social inequality have not disappeared altogether, even if not constantly and immediately experienced in women's everyday lives. The regulation of parental leave is an example. Theoretically both parents can take it. But as the benefit associated with it is a fixed amount and unrelated to the previous earnings of the person taking it, it is (nearly) always the mother who claims it, for the organizational structure of the labor market perpetuates gender-specific discrimination with regard to income levels. Nevertheless, the regulatory framework of parental leave forces parents to choose their family arrangement individually. This decision is made jointly by the members of the (egalitarian) couple. More generally: The loss of normative models prescribing how to live one's (gender-specific) life compels couples to negotiate. As this is done in an egalitarian manner, young females do not subjectively experience gender inequality. Accordingly, they underestimate its relevance to their own situation and overestimate the significance of individual decision. They have a very individualistic perception of their life courses and are certain that their lives and lifestyles are mainly the result of their individual decisions. This self-ascription of responsibility is both a result and an expression of individualization processes. The realization of individualization with its parameters of self-direction and personal responsibility—a process described by Hettlage (2000) as one in which the individuals perceive themselves as the center of action and decision-making—has the paradoxical consequence that young women are more strongly steered into gender-typical life-course tracks and abstain from setting degendering processes in motion. Meanwhile men, "individualized" and also sincerely taking part in the negotiation and decision-making processes concerning (future) family arrangements with their female partners, experience and contribute to an opposite dilemma: As long as they maintain (or are forced to maintain) their breadwinner function by being fully integrated in the labor market, an increase and not a further decrease of gender asymmetry is likely to occur. There is reason to assume that what Bourdieu (see Burkart 1994:16) held to be a general finding of his work on the reproduction of social inequality is especially true for young women: "The freedom of the individual is mostly only appearance, sustained by the western ideology of individualism."

NOTES

1. Scientific as well as political debate and public discussion resulting from the difficult questions of how to plan, organize, and live one's life are summarized as the problem of reconciling work and the family. But this is discussed above all for women as mothers (see Born et al. 1996; Bird 2001).

2. Study A was conducted under the direction of Walter R. Heinz; Study B was conducted under the direction of Helga Krüger and Claudia Born.

3. For a discussion of the research design see Schaeper, Kühn, and Witzel 2001 (Study A) and Krüger 2001 (Study B). The empirical data are described in Figure 13.1.

4. The large number of working women in this generation (as well as their desire and realization of vocational training during the immediate postwar period) proves that women of this generation already had an occupational orientation. It is this female generation that initiated the social change. But as these women did it individually (although by many simultaneously) it remained hidden to our popular understanding of that generation and for a long time to sociological analysis as well (see Krüger 1996).

5. Kühn is working with the empirical data gathered in Study A (the youngest cohort), which are analyzed in his doctoral thesis "Biographiegestaltung junger Frauen und Männer—Familiengründung als Planungsproblem."

REFERENCES

Beck, Ulrich. 1993. *Die Erfindung des Politischen*. Frankfurt a.M.: Suhrkamp.
Beck, Ulrich and Elisabeth Beck-Gernsheim. 1994. "Individualisierung in modernen Gesellschaften—Perspektiven und Kontroversen einer subjektorientierten Soziologie." Pp. 10–39 in *Riskante Freiheiten. Individualisierung in modernen Gesellschaften*, edited by U. Beck and E. Beck-Gernsheim. Frankfurt a.M.: Suhrkamp.
Beck, Ulrich, Anthony Giddens, and Scott Lash. 1994. *Reflexive Modernisation. Politics, Tradition and Aesthetics in the Modern Social Order*. Cambridge: Polity.
Beck-Gernsheim, Elisabeth. 1983. "Vom 'Dasein für andere' zum Anspruch auf ein Stück 'eigenes Leben.' Individualisierungsprozesse im weiblichen Lebenszusammenhang." *Soziale Welt* 34:308–40.
Becker-Schmidt, Regina. 1987. "Die doppelte Vergesellschaftung—die doppelte Unterdrückung." Pp. 10–25 in *Die andere Hälfte der Gesellschaft*, edited by L. Unterkircher and I. Wagner. Wien: OGB-Verlag.
Bertram, Hans and Renate Borrmann-Müller. 1988. "Von der Hausfrau zur Berufsfrau? Der Einfluss struktureller Wandlungen des Frauseins auf familiales Zusammenleben." Pp. 251–72 in *Frauensituation. Veränderungen in den letzten zwanzig Jahren*, edited by U. Gerhardt und Y. Schütze. Frankfurt a.M.: Suhrkamp.
Bird, Katherine. 2001. "The Institutional Shaping of Female Life Courses: How Maternity-Leave Regulations Affect Female Employment Participation." Paper presented to the International Symposium "Institutions, Interrelations, Sequences: The Bremen Life-Course Approach." University of Bremen, 26–28 September.
Böhnisch, Lothar. 1997. "Über die alten und neuen Väter." Pp. 155–66 in *Familien. Eine interdisziplinäre Einführung*, edited by L. Böhnisch and K. Lenz. Weinheim/Munich: Juventa.
Born, Claudia and Helga Krüger (Eds.). 2001. *Individualisierung und Verflechtung. Geschlecht und Generation im deutschen Lebenslaufregime*. Weinheim/Munich: Juventa.

Born, Claudia and Helga Krüger. 2002. "Vaterschaft und Väter im Kontext sozialen Wandels. Über die Notwendigkeit der Differenzierung zwischen strukturellen Gegebenheiten und kulturellen Wünschen." Pp. 117–43 in *Männer als Väter. Sozialwissenschaftliche Theorie und Empirie,* edited by H. Walter. Gießen: Psychosozial-Verlag.

Born, Claudia, Helga Krüger, and Dagmar Lorenz-Meyer. 1996. *Der unentdeckte Wandel. Annäherung an das Verhältnis von Struktur und Norm im weiblichen Lebenslauf.* Berlin: Edition Sigma.

Bullinger, Hermann. 1988. *Wenn Männer Vater werden. Schwangerschaft, Geburt und die Zeit danach im Erleben von Männern. Überlegungen—Informationen— Erfahrungen.* Reinbek: Rowohlt.

Burkart, Günter. 1994. *Die Entscheidung zur Elternschaft. Eine empirische Kritik von Individualisierungs- und Rational-Choice-Theorien.* Stuttgart: Enke.

Busch, F. W., Bernhard Nauck, and Rosemarie Nave-Herz (Eds.). 1999. *Aktuelle Forschungsfelder der Familienwissenschaft,* Vol. 1, *Familie und Gesellschaft.* Würzburg: Ergon-Verlag.

Freier, Anna-Elisabeth and Annette Kuhn (Eds.). 1984. *Das Schicksal Deutschlands liegt in der Hand seiner Frauen: Frauen in der deutschen Nachkriegsgeschichte.* Vol. 5, *Frauen in der Geschichte.* Düsseldorf: Schwann.

Fthenakis, E. Wassilios. 1999. *Engagierte Vaterschaft: Die sanfte Revolution in der Familie.* Opladen: Leske and Budrich.

Gerson, Kathleen. 1993. *No Man's Land. Men's Changing Commitments to Family and Work.* New York: Basic Books.

Gerson, Kathleen. 2001. "Children of the Gender Revolution: Some Theoretical Questions and Preliminary Notes from the Field." Pp. 446–61 in *Restructuring Work and the Life Course,* edited by V. W. Marshall, W. R. Heinz, H. Krüger, and A. Verma. Toronto: University of Toronto Press.

Gottschall, Karin. 2000. *Soziale Ungleichheit und Geschlecht. Kontinuitäten und Brüche, Sackgassen und Erkenntnispotential im deutschen soziologischen Diskurs.* Opladen: Leske and Budrich.

Gottschall, Karin and Katherine Bird. 2003. "Family-Leave Policies and Labor-Market Segregation in Germany—Reinvention or Reform of the Male Breadwinner?" *Review of Policy Research* (forthcoming).

Hettlage, Robert. 2000. "Individualisierung, Pluralisierung, Postfamiliarisierung. Dramatische oder dramatisierte Umbrüche im Modernisierungsprozess der Familie?" *Zeitschrift für Familienforschung* 12:72–97.

Honegger, Claudia. 1991. *Die Ordnung der Geschlechter: die Wissenschaften von Menschen und das Weib 1750–1850.* Frankfurt a.M.: Campus.

Hopf, Christel and Myriam Hartwig (Eds.). 2001. *Liebe und Abhängigkeit. Partnerschaftsbeziehungen junger Frauen.* Weinheim: Juventa.

Kaufmann, Franz-Xaver. 1993. "Generationenbeziehungen und Generationenverhältnisse im Wohlfahrtsstaat." Pp. 95–108 in *Generationenbeziehungen in "postmodernen" Gesellschaften. Konstanzer Beiträge zur sozialwissenschaftlichen Forschung,* Band 7. Konstanz: Universitätsverlag.

Kohli, Martin. 1994. "Institutionalisierung und Individualisierung der Erwerbsbiographie." Pp. 219–44 in *Riskante Freiheiten. Individualisierung in modernen Gesellschaften,* edited by U. Beck and E. Beck-Gernsheim. Frankfurt a.M.: Suhrkamp.

Kohli, Martin and Marc Szydlik (Eds.). 2000. *Generationen in Familie und Gesellschaft*. Opladen: Leske and Budrich.

Koppetsch, Cornelia and Günter Burkart. 1999. *Die Illusion der Emanzipation: Zur Wirksamkeit latenter Geschlechtsnormen im Milieuvergleich*. Konstanz: Universitätsverlag.

Krüger, Helga. 1996. "Normative Interpretations of Biographical Processes." Pp. 129–46 in *Society and Biography. Interrelationships Between Social Structure, Institutions and the Life Course*, edited by A. Weymann and W. R. Heinz. Weinheim: Deutscher Studien Verlag.

Krüger, Helga. 2001. "Social Change in Two Generations. Employment Patterns and Their Costs for Family Life." Pp. 401–23 in *Restructuring Work and the Life Course*, edited by V. W. Marshall, W. R. Heinz, H. Krüger, and A. Verma. Toronto: University of Toronto Press.

Krüger, Helga and René Levy. 2000. "Masterstatus, Familie und Geschlecht. Vergessene Verknüpfungslogiken zwischen Institutionen des Lebenslaufs." *Berliner Journal für Soziologie* 3:379–401.

Kühn, Thomas. 2002. *Biographiegestaltung junger Frauen und Männer. Familiengründung als Planungsproblem*. Ph.D. thesis. University of Bremen.

Lauterbach, Wolfgang. 1999. "Familie und private Lebensformen, oder: Geht der Gesellschaft die Familie aus?" Pp. 239–54 in *Deutschland im Wandel. Sozialstrukturelle Analysen. Ein Sonderband der Zeitschrift Gegenwartskunde*, edited by W. Glatzer and I. Ostner. Opladen: Leske and Budrich.

Liebold, Renate. 2001. *"Meine Frau managt das ganze Leben zuhause . . ." Partnerschaft und Familie aus der Sicht männlicher Führungskräfte*. Wiesbaden: Westdeutscher Verlag.

Lorenz-Meyer, Dagmar. 1999. *The Gendered Politics of Generational Contracts. Changing Discourses and Practices of Intergenerational Commitments in West Germany*. Thesis submitted for the degree of Doctor of Philosophy, London.

Lüscher, Kurt. 2001. *Widersprüchliche Vielfalt. Neue Perspektiven zum juristischen und soziologischen Verständnis von Ehe und Familie*. Arbeitspapier Nr. 37. Universität Konstanz, Fachbereich Geschichte und Soziologie, Forschungsbereich "Gesellschaft und Familie."

Mayer, Karl Ulrich. 1998. "German Survivors of World War II. The Impact on the Life Course of the Collective Experience of Birth Cohorts." Pp. 229–46 in *Social Structures and Human Lives*, Vol. 1, *Social Change and the Life Course*, edited by B. J. Huber and B. B. Hess. Newbury Park, CA: Sage.

Moen, Phyllis and Han Shin-Kap. 2001. "Reframing Careers: Work, Family, and Gender." Pp. 424–45 in *Restructuring Work and the Life Course*, edited by V. W. Marshall, W. R. Heinz, H. Krüger, and A. Verma. Toronto: University of Toronto Press.

Müller, Ursula. 1998. "Asymmetrische Geschlechterkultur in Organisationen und Frauenförderung als Prozess—mit Beispielen aus Betrieben und der Universität." *Zeitschrift für Personalforschung* 2:123–42.

Nave-Herz, Rosemarie. 1994. *Familie heute—Wandel der Familienstrukturen und Folgen für die Erziehung*. Darmstadt: Wissenschaftliche Buchgesellschaft.

Oechsle, Mechthild and Birgit Geissler (Eds.). 1998. *Die ungleiche Gleichheit. Junge Frauen und der Wandel im Geschlechterverhältnis*. Opladen: Leske and Budrich.

Schaeper, Hildegard, Thomas Kühn, and Andreas Witzel. 2001. "The Transition from Vocational Training to Employment in Germany: Does Region Matter?" Pp. 61–83 in *Restructuring Work and the Life Course*, edited by V. M. Marshall, W. R. Heinz, H. Krüger, and A. Verma. Toronto: University of Toronto Press.

Sommerkorn, Ingrid. 1995. "Das Geschlechterverhältnis als Bildungsaufgabe der Schule: Die doppelte Lebensorientierung—ein notwendiges Thema im Unterricht." Pp. 259–77 in *Familie im Brennpunkt von Wissenschaft und Forschung*, edited by B. Nauck and C. Onnen-Isemann. Neuwied: Luchterhand.

Weymann, Ansgar. 1998. *Sozialer Wandel. Theorien zur Dynamik der modernen Gesellschaft*. Weinheim/Munich: Juventa.

Witzel, Andreas. 2000. "The Problem-Centered Interview." *Forum Qualitative Social Research* (on-line) 1(1). http://qualitative-research.net/fqs/vol1no1/1-00art-19.htm.

Witzel, Andreas and Thomas Kühn. 2001. "Biographiemanagement und Planungschaos. Arbeitsmarktplatzierung und Familiengründung bei jungen Erwachsenen." Pp. 55–82 in *Individualisierung und Verflechtung. Geschlecht und Generation im deutschen Lebenslaufregime*, edited by C. Born and H. Krüger. Weinheim/Munich: Juventa.

Index